BARAKAMON

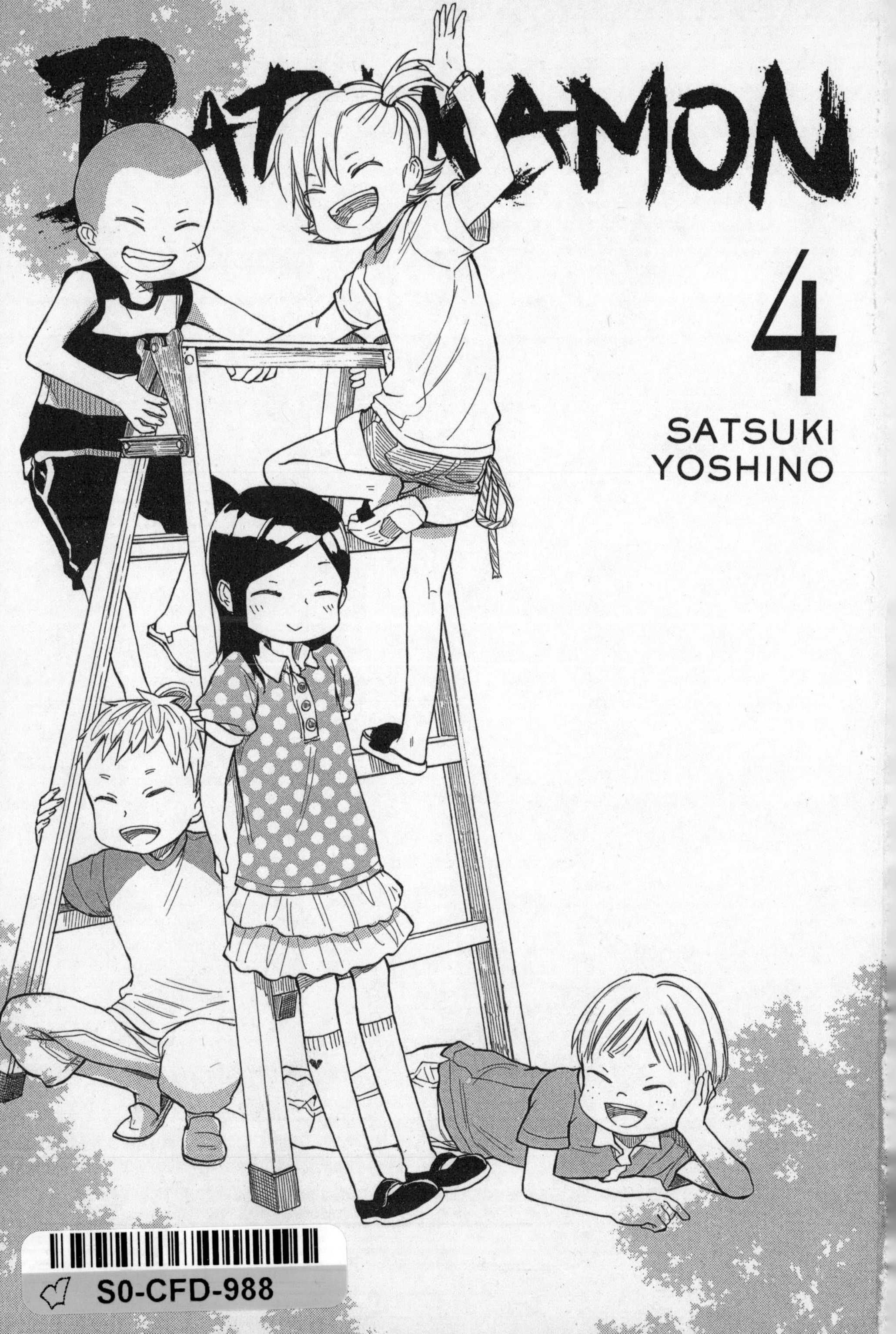

4

SATSUKI
YOSHINO

Contents

ACT.27
MISENBAN
(Translation: Minding the Store)

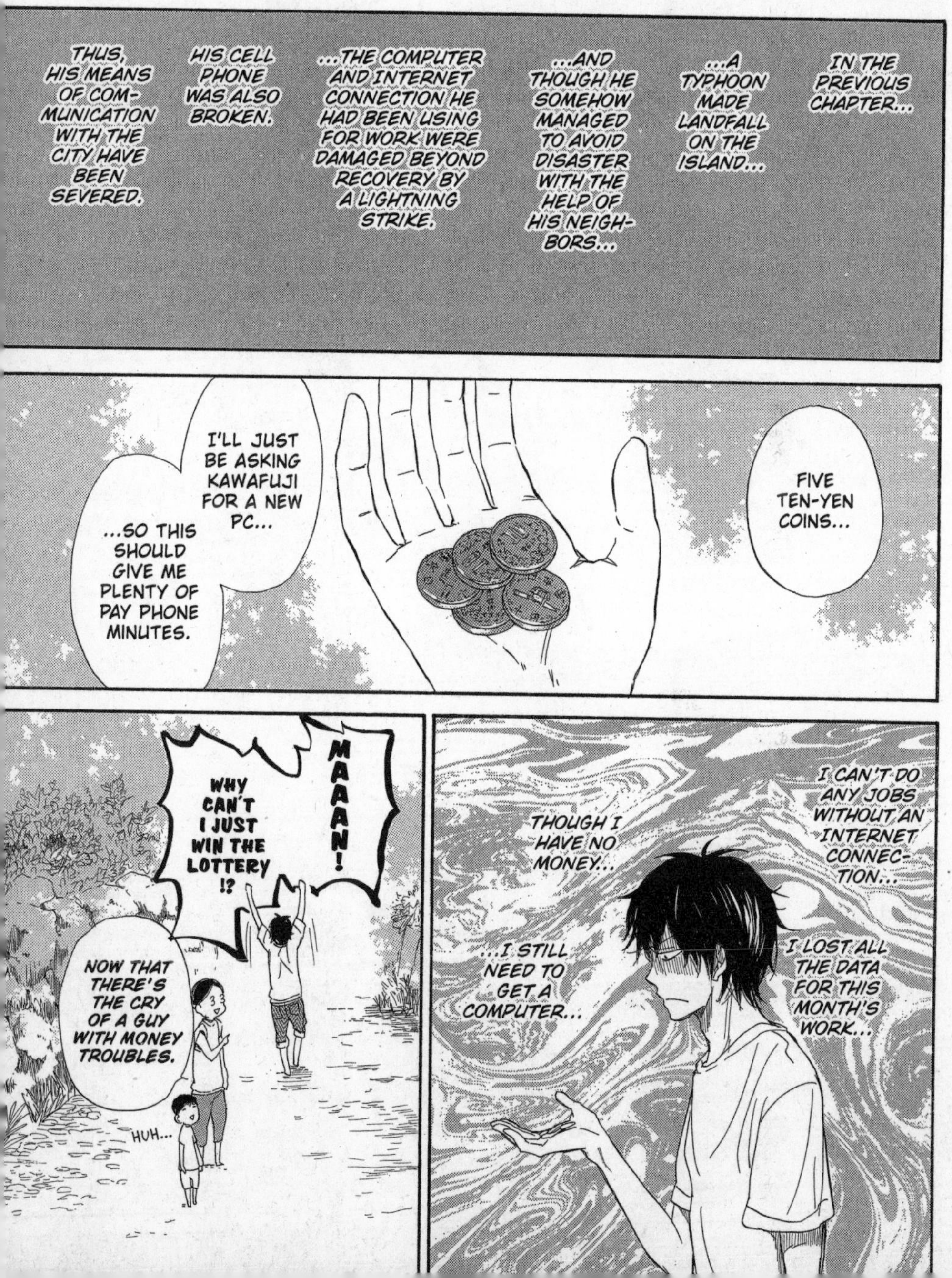
IN THE PREVIOUS CHAPTER...
...A TYPHOON MADE LANDFALL ON THE ISLAND...
...AND THOUGH HE SOMEHOW MANAGED TO AVOID DISASTER WITH THE HELP OF HIS NEIGHBORS...
...THE COMPUTER AND INTERNET CONNECTION HE HAD BEEN USING FOR WORK WERE DAMAGED BEYOND RECOVERY BY A LIGHTNING STRIKE.
HIS CELL PHONE WAS ALSO BROKEN.
THUS, HIS MEANS OF COMMUNICATION WITH THE CITY HAVE BEEN SEVERED.
FIVE TEN-YEN COINS...
I'LL JUST BE ASKING KAWAFUJI FOR A NEW PC...
...SO THIS SHOULD GIVE ME PLENTY OF PAY PHONE MINUTES.
I CAN'T DO ANY JOBS WITHOUT AN INTERNET CONNECTION...
THOUGH I HAVE NO MONEY...
I LOST ALL THE DATA FOR THIS MONTH'S WORK...
...I STILL NEED TO GET A COMPUTER...
MAAAAN!
WHY CAN'T I JUST WIN THE LOTTERY!?
NOW THAT THERE'S THE CRY OF A GUY WITH MONEY TROUBLES.
HUH...

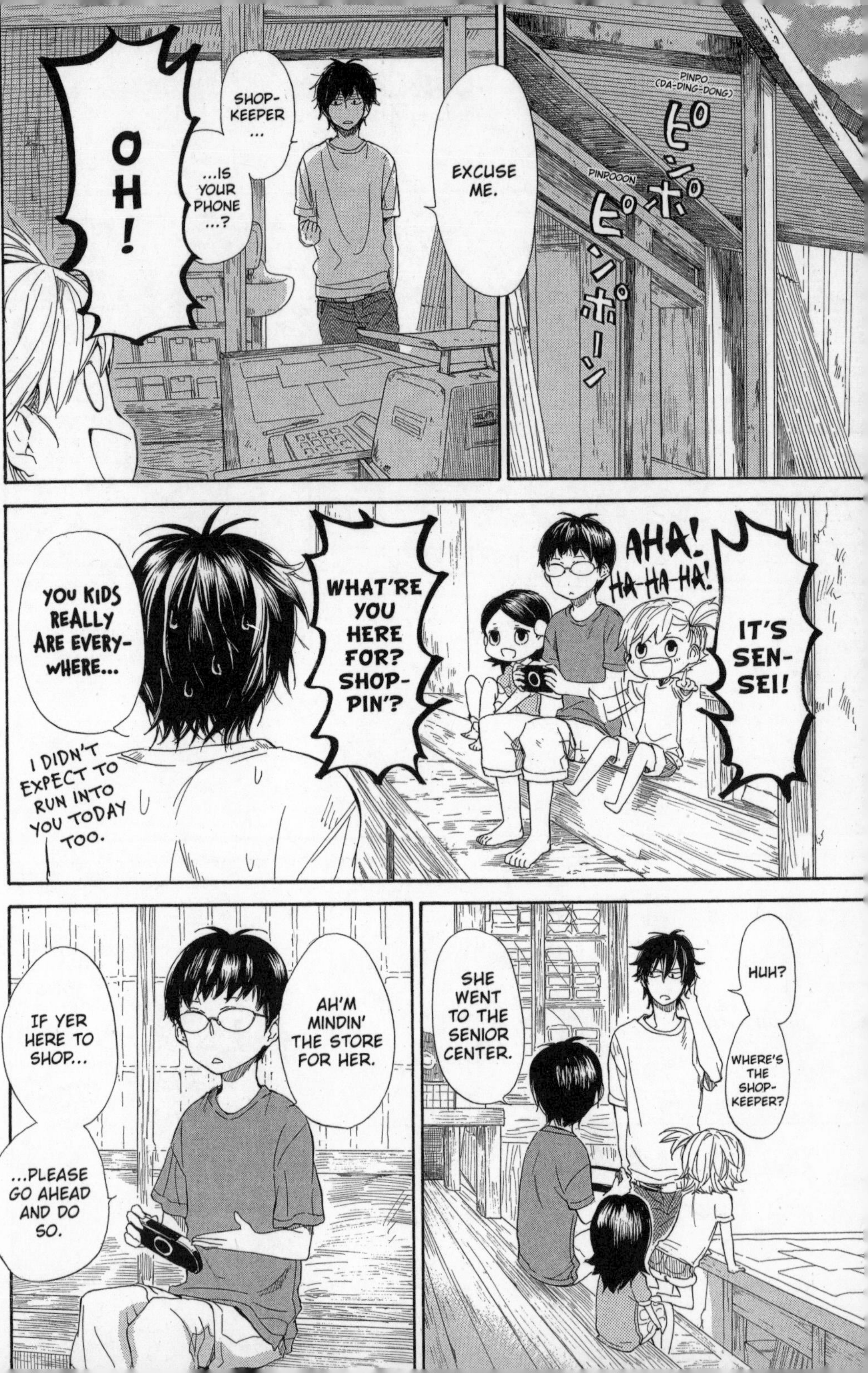
PINPO (DA-DING-DONG)
ピンポ
PINPOOON
ピンポーン
EXCUSE ME.
SHOP-KEEPER ...
...IS YOUR PHONE ...?
OH!
IT'S SEN-SEI!
AHA! HA-HA-HA!
WHAT'RE YOU HERE FOR? SHOP-PIN'?
YOU KIDS REALLY ARE EVERY-WHERE...
I DIDN'T EXPECT TO RUN INTO YOU TODAY TOO.
HUH?
WHERE'S THE SHOP-KEEPER?
SHE WENT TO THE SENIOR CENTER.
AH'M MINDIN' THE STORE FOR HER.
IF YER HERE TO SHOP...
...PLEASE GO AHEAD AND DO SO.

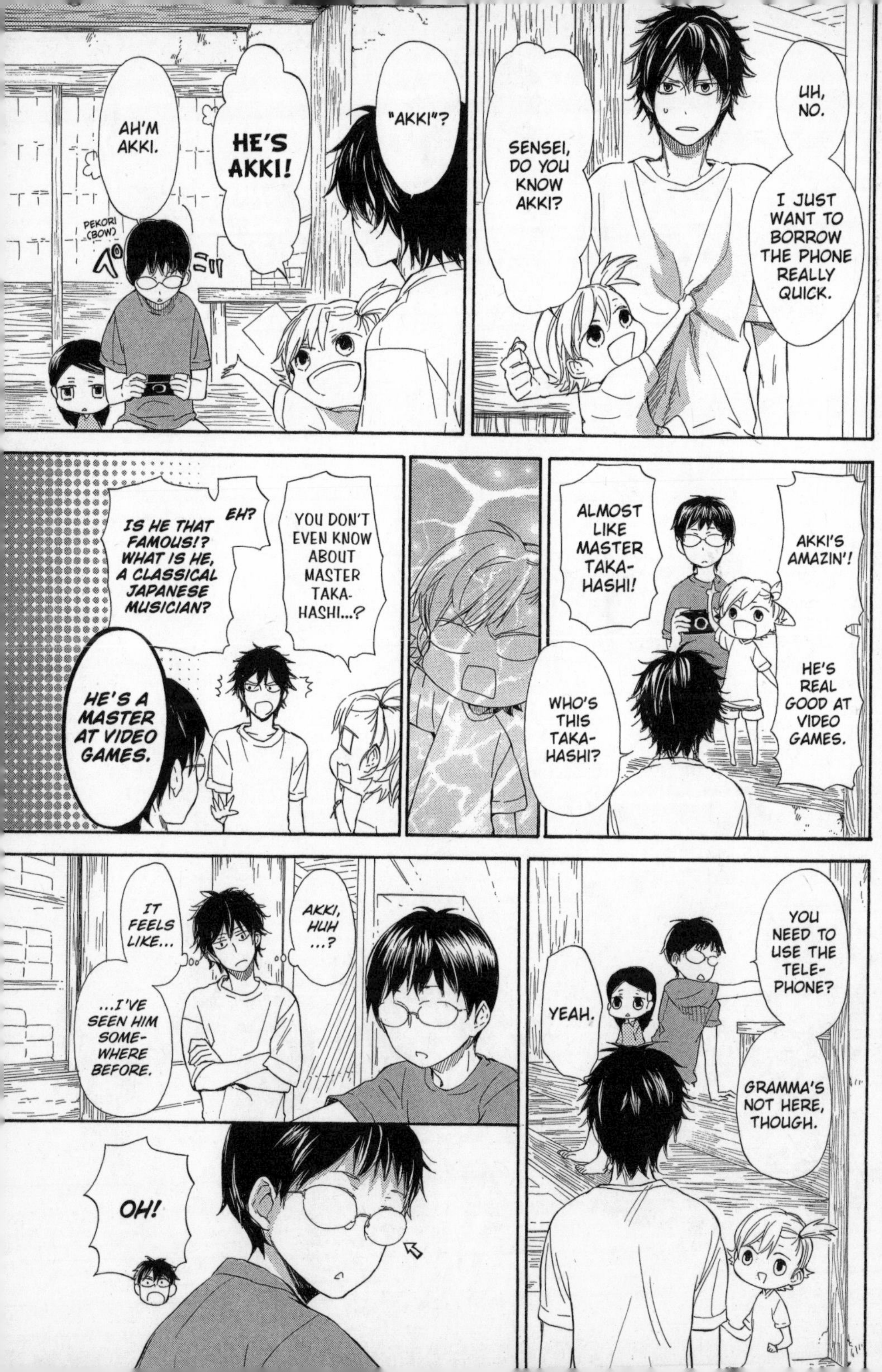
SENSEI, DO YOU KNOW AKKI?
UH, NO.
I JUST WANT TO BORROW THE PHONE REALLY QUICK.
"AKKI"?
HE'S AKKI!
PEKORI (BOW)
AH'M AKKI.
AKKI'S AMAZIN'!
ALMOST LIKE MASTER TAKA-HASHI!
HE'S REAL GOOD AT VIDEO GAMES.
WHO'S THIS TAKA-HASHI?
YOU DON'T EVEN KNOW ABOUT MASTER TAKA-HASHI...?
EH?
IS HE THAT FAMOUS!? WHAT IS HE, A CLASSICAL JAPANESE MUSICIAN?
HE'S A MASTER AT VIDEO GAMES.
YOU NEED TO USE THE TELE-PHONE?
YEAH.
GRAMMA'S NOT HERE, THOUGH.
AKKI, HUH ...?
IT FEELS LIKE...
...I'VE SEEN HIM SOME-WHERE BEFORE.
OH!

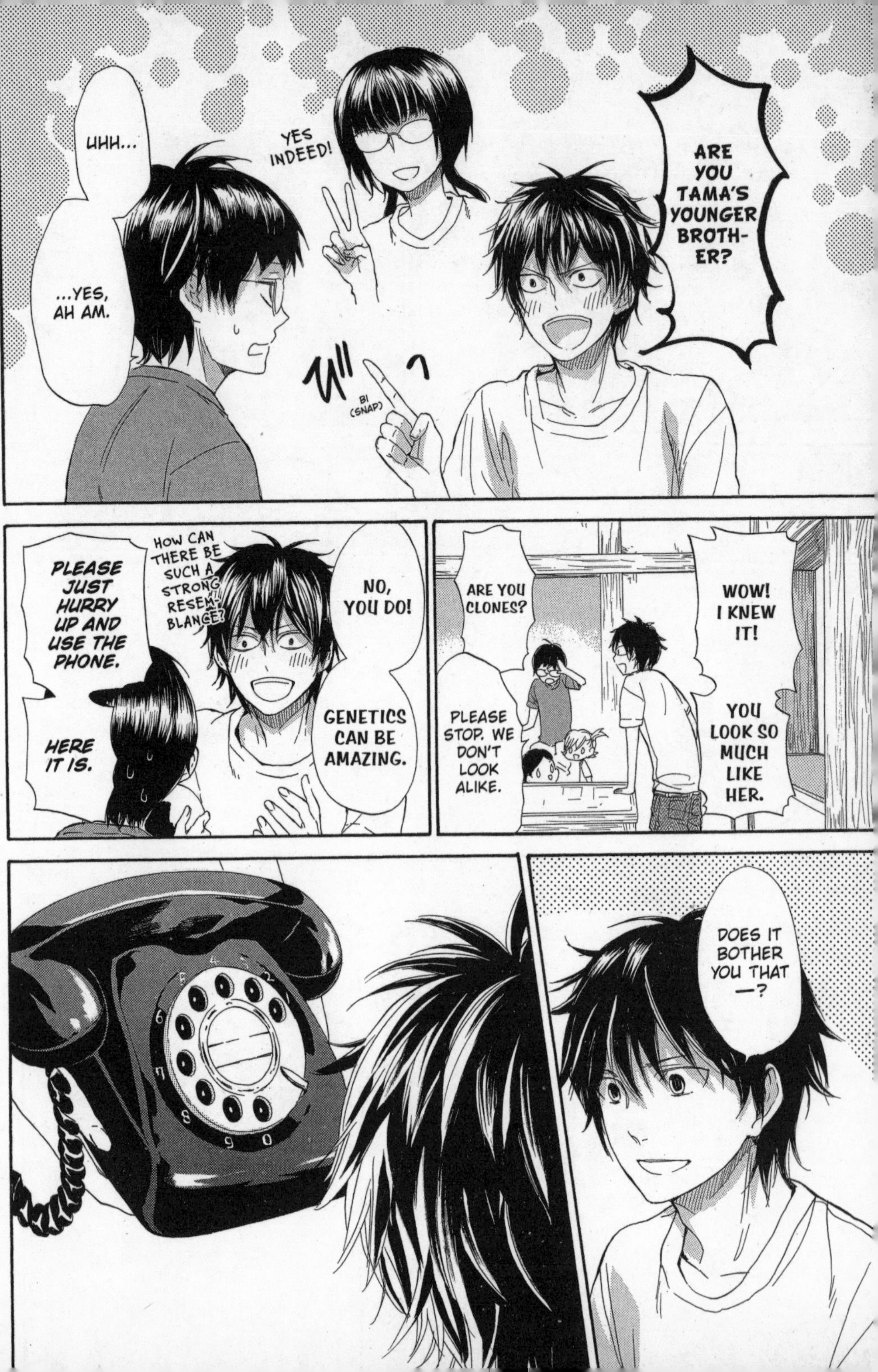
ARE YOU TAMA'S YOUNGER BROTH-ER?
YES INDEED!
UHH...
BI (SNAP)
...YES, AH AM.
WOW! I KNEW IT!
YOU LOOK SO MUCH LIKE HER.
ARE YOU CLONES?
PLEASE STOP. WE DON'T LOOK ALIKE.
NO, YOU DO!
HOW CAN THERE BE SUCH A STRONG RESEM-BLANCE?
GENETICS CAN BE AMAZING.
PLEASE JUST HURRY UP AND USE THE PHONE.
HERE IT IS.
DOES IT BOTHER YOU THAT —?

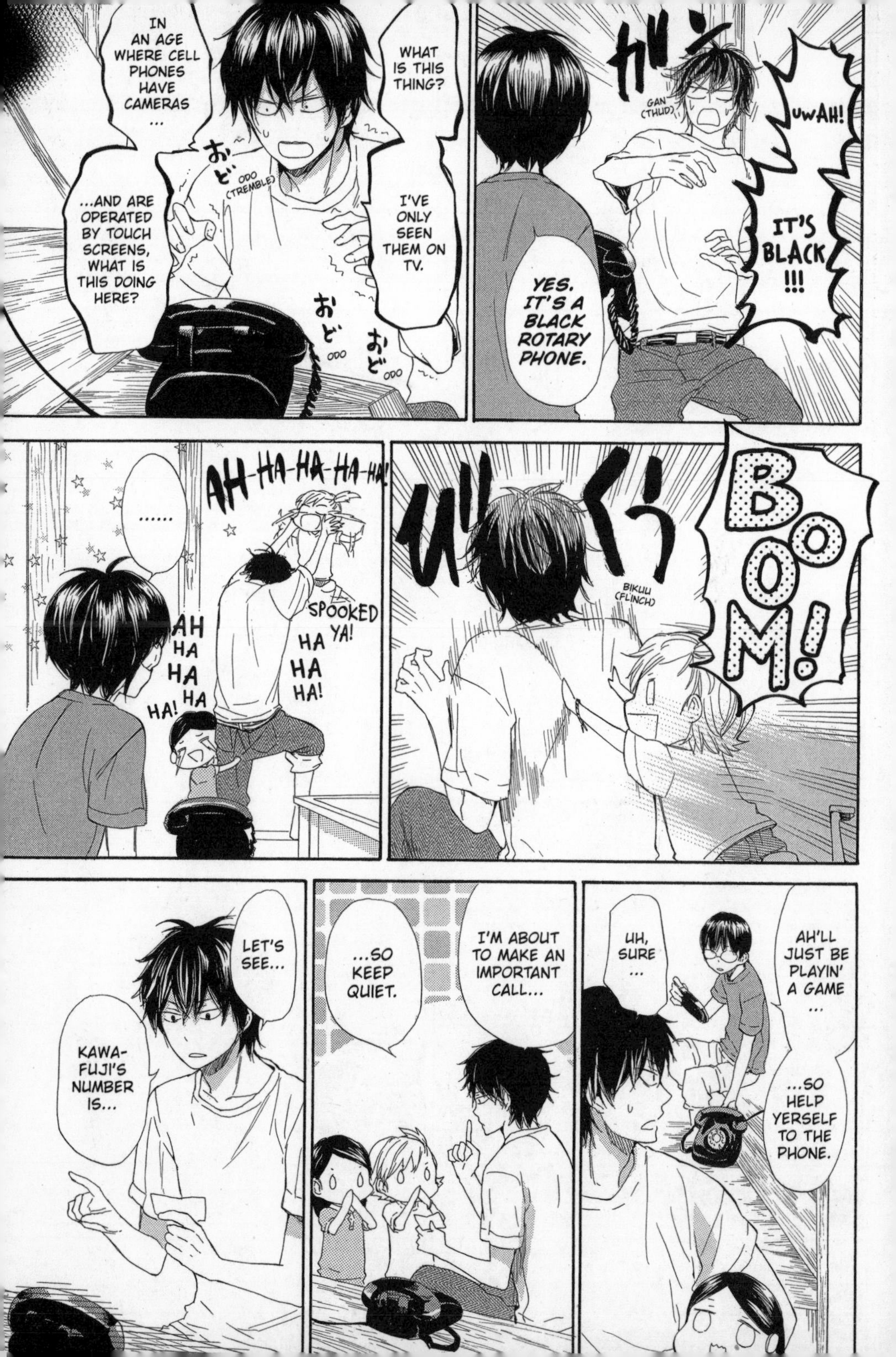
ガン
GAN (THUD)
UWAH!
IT'S BLACK!!!
YES. IT'S A BLACK ROTARY PHONE.
WHAT IS THIS THING?
IN AN AGE WHERE CELL PHONES HAVE CAMERAS ...
おど
ODO (TREMBLE)
I'VE ONLY SEEN THEM ON TV.
...AND ARE OPERATED BY TOUCH SCREENS, WHAT IS THIS DOING HERE?
おど ODO
おど ODO
BOOM!
BIKUU (FLINCH)
AH-HA-HA-HA-HA!
SPOOKED YA!
HA HA HA HA!
......
AH HA HA HA HA!
AH'LL JUST BE PLAYIN' A GAME ...
UH, SURE ...
...SO HELP YOURSELF TO THE PHONE.
I'M ABOUT TO MAKE AN IMPORTANT CALL...
...SO KEEP QUIET.
LET'S SEE...
KAWA-FUJI'S NUMBER IS...

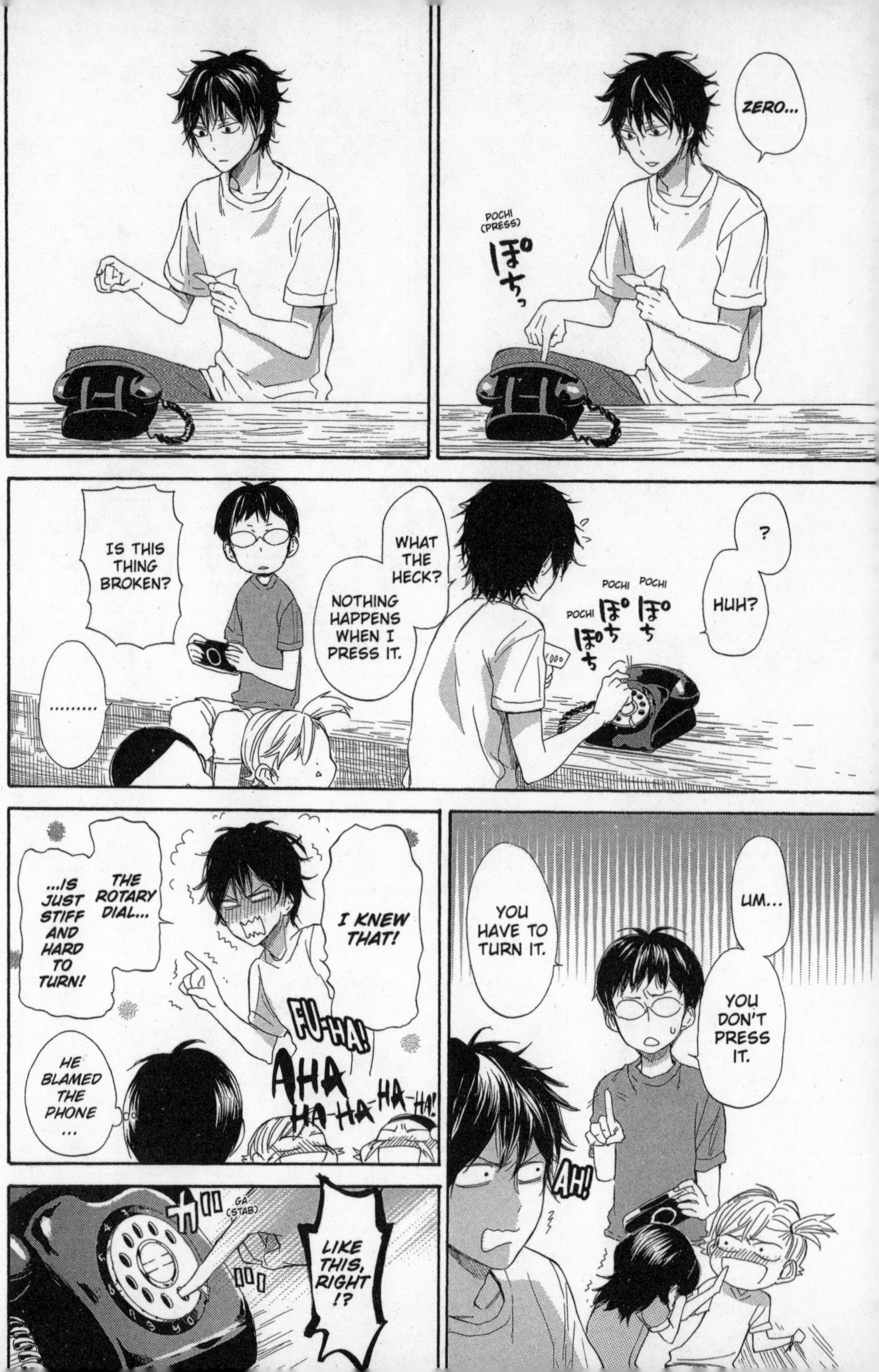

ZERO...
POCHI (PRESS)
ぽちっ
?
HUH?
POCHI POCHI POCHI
ぽち ぽち ぽち
WHAT THE HECK?
NOTHING HAPPENS WHEN I PRESS IT.
IS THIS THING BROKEN?
....
UM...
YOU HAVE TO TURN IT.
YOU DON'T PRESS IT.
AH!
I KNEW THAT!
THE ROTARY DIAL...
...IS JUST STIFF AND HARD TO TURN!
FU-HA!
AHA HA-HA-HA-HA!
HE BLAMED THE PHONE...
LIKE THIS, RIGHT!?
GA (STAB)

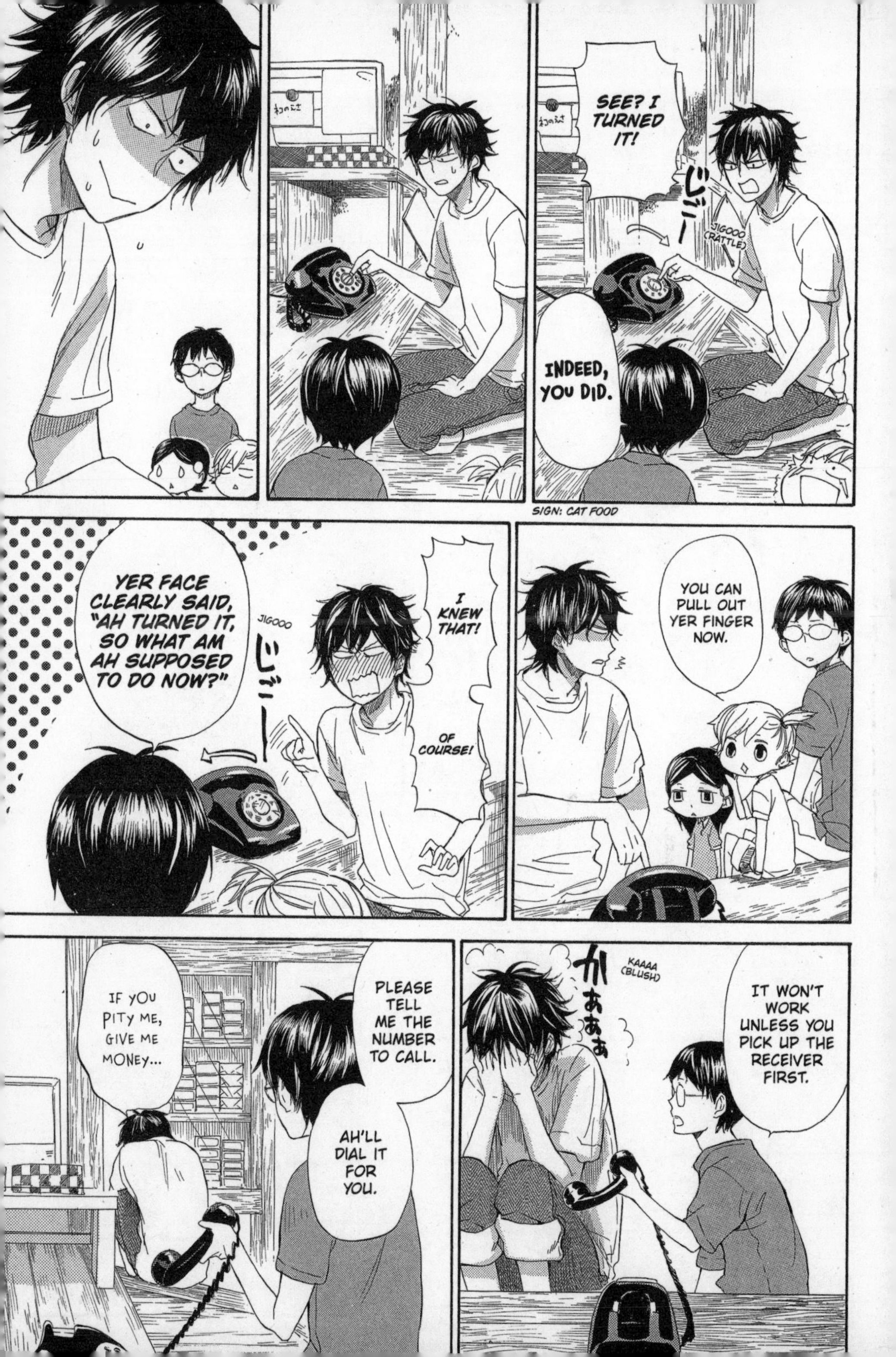
SEE? I TURNED IT!
じごー
JIGOOO (RATTLE)
INDEED, YOU DID.
SIGN: CAT FOOD
YOU CAN PULL OUT YER FINGER NOW.
I KNEW THAT!
OF COURSE!
JIGOOO
じごー
YER FACE CLEARLY SAID, "AH TURNED IT, SO WHAT AM AH SUPPOSED TO DO NOW?"
かあああ
KAAAA (BLUSH)
IT WON'T WORK UNLESS YOU PICK UP THE RECEIVER FIRST.
PLEASE TELL ME THE NUMBER TO CALL.
AH'LL DIAL IT FOR YOU.
IF YOU PITY ME, GIVE ME MONEY...

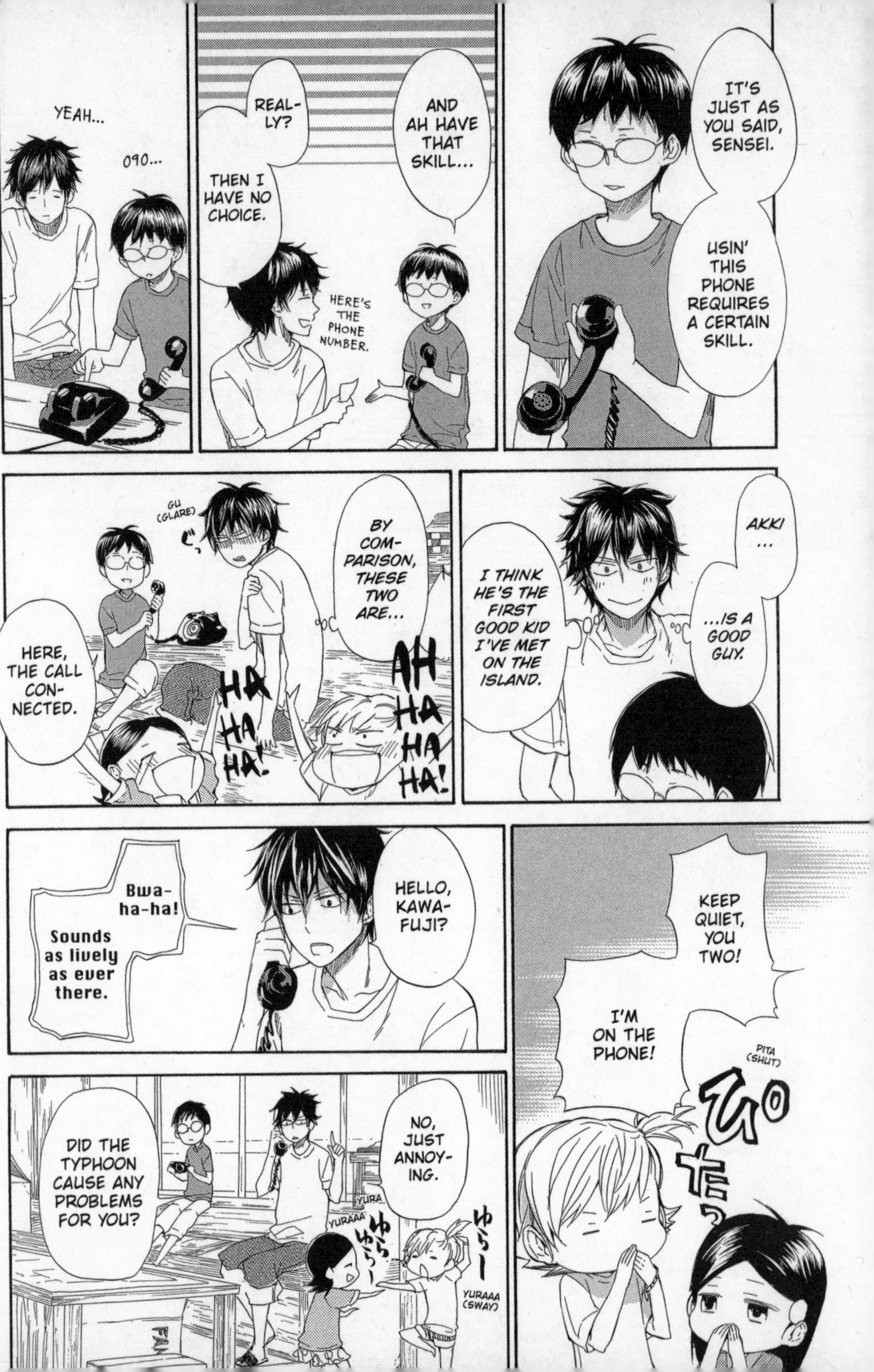

IT'S JUST AS YOU SAID, SENSEI.
USIN' THIS PHONE REQUIRES A CERTAIN SKILL.
AND AH HAVE THAT SKILL...
REAL-LY?
THEN I HAVE NO CHOICE.
HERE'S THE PHONE NUMBER.
YEAH...
090...
AKKI...
...IS A GOOD GUY.
I THINK HE'S THE FIRST GOOD KID I'VE MET ON THE ISLAND.
BY COM-PARISON, THESE TWO ARE...
AH HA HA HA HA!
GU (GLARE)
HA HA HA HA!
HERE, THE CALL CON-NECTED.
KEEP QUIET, YOU TWO!
I'M ON THE PHONE!
PITA (SHUT)
HELLO, KAWA-FUJI?
Bwa-ha-ha!
Sounds as lively as ever there.
NO, JUST ANNOY-ING.
YURA
YURAAA
YURAAA (SWAY)
DID THE TYPHOON CAUSE ANY PROBLEMS FOR YOU?

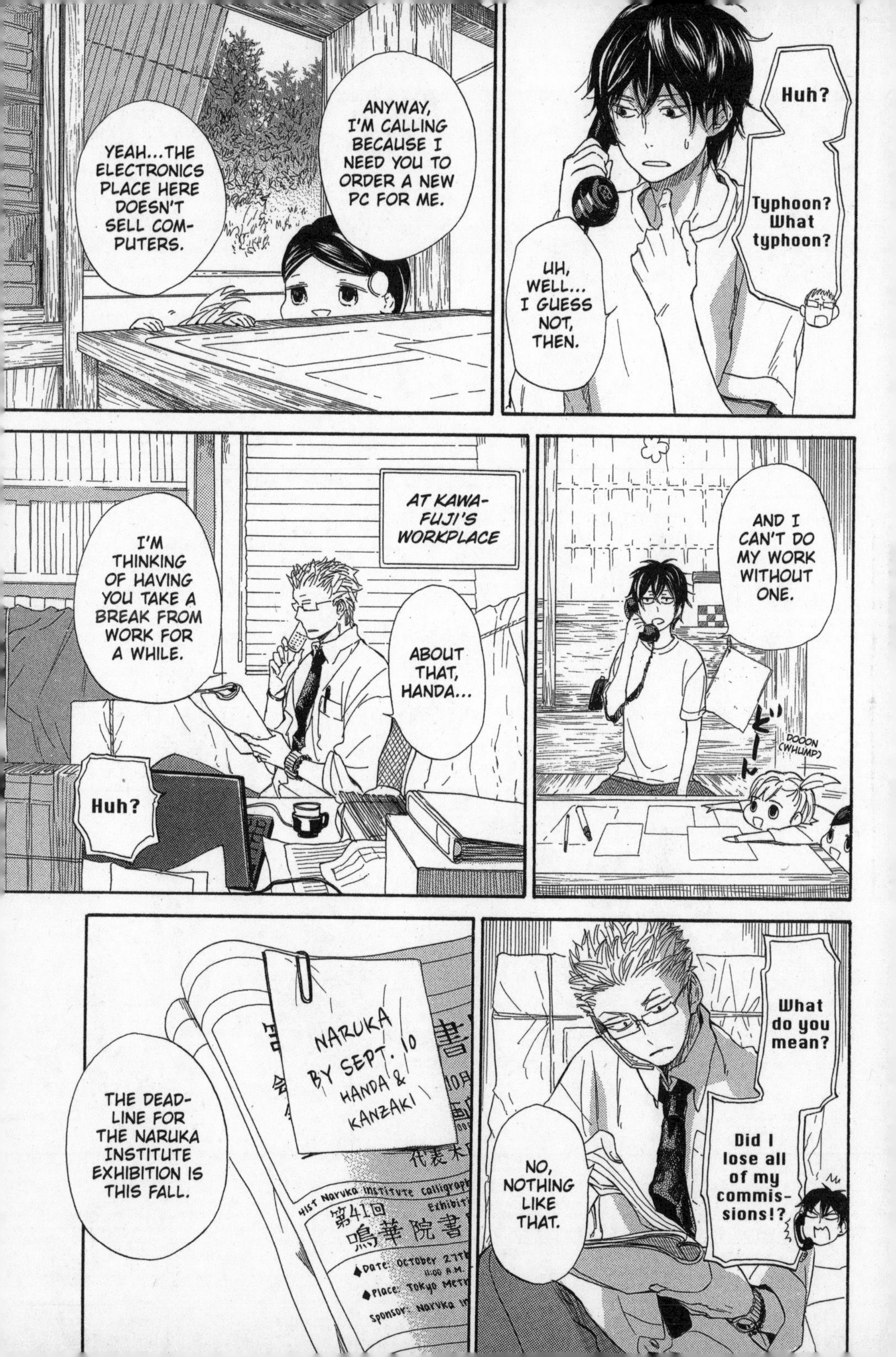
Huh?
Typhoon? What typhoon?
UH, WELL... I GUESS NOT, THEN.
ANYWAY, I'M CALLING BECAUSE I NEED YOU TO ORDER A NEW PC FOR ME.
YEAH...THE ELECTRONICS PLACE HERE DOESN'T SELL COMPUTERS.
AND I CAN'T DO MY WORK WITHOUT ONE.
DOOON (WHUMP)
AT KAWAFUJI'S WORKPLACE
ABOUT THAT, HANDA...
I'M THINKING OF HAVING YOU TAKE A BREAK FROM WORK FOR A WHILE.
Huh?
What do you mean?
Did I lose all of my commissions!?
NO, NOTHING LIKE THAT.
NARUKA BY SEPT. 10 HANDA & KANZAKI
THE DEADLINE FOR THE NARUKA INSTITUTE EXHIBITION IS THIS FALL.
第41回
Date: October 27th
11:00 A.M.

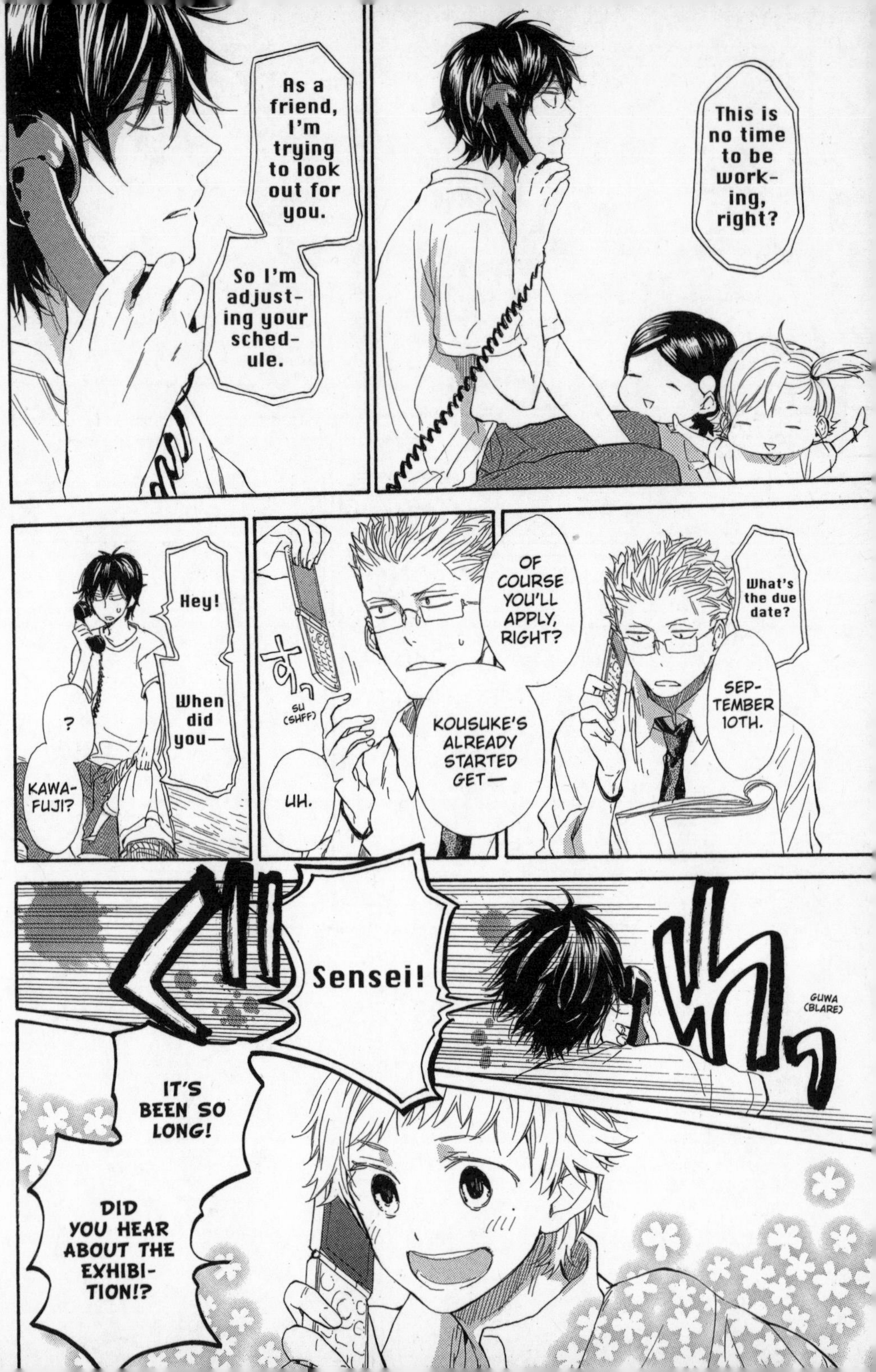
This is no time to be working, right?
As a friend, I'm trying to look out for you.
So I'm adjusting your schedule.
What's the due date?
SEPTEMBER 10TH.
OF COURSE YOU'LL APPLY, RIGHT?
KOUSUKE'S ALREADY STARTED GET—
SU (SHFF)
UH.
Hey!
When did you—
?
KAWAFUJI?
Sensei!
GUWA (BLARE)
IT'S BEEN SO LONG!
DID YOU HEAR ABOUT THE EXHIBITION!?

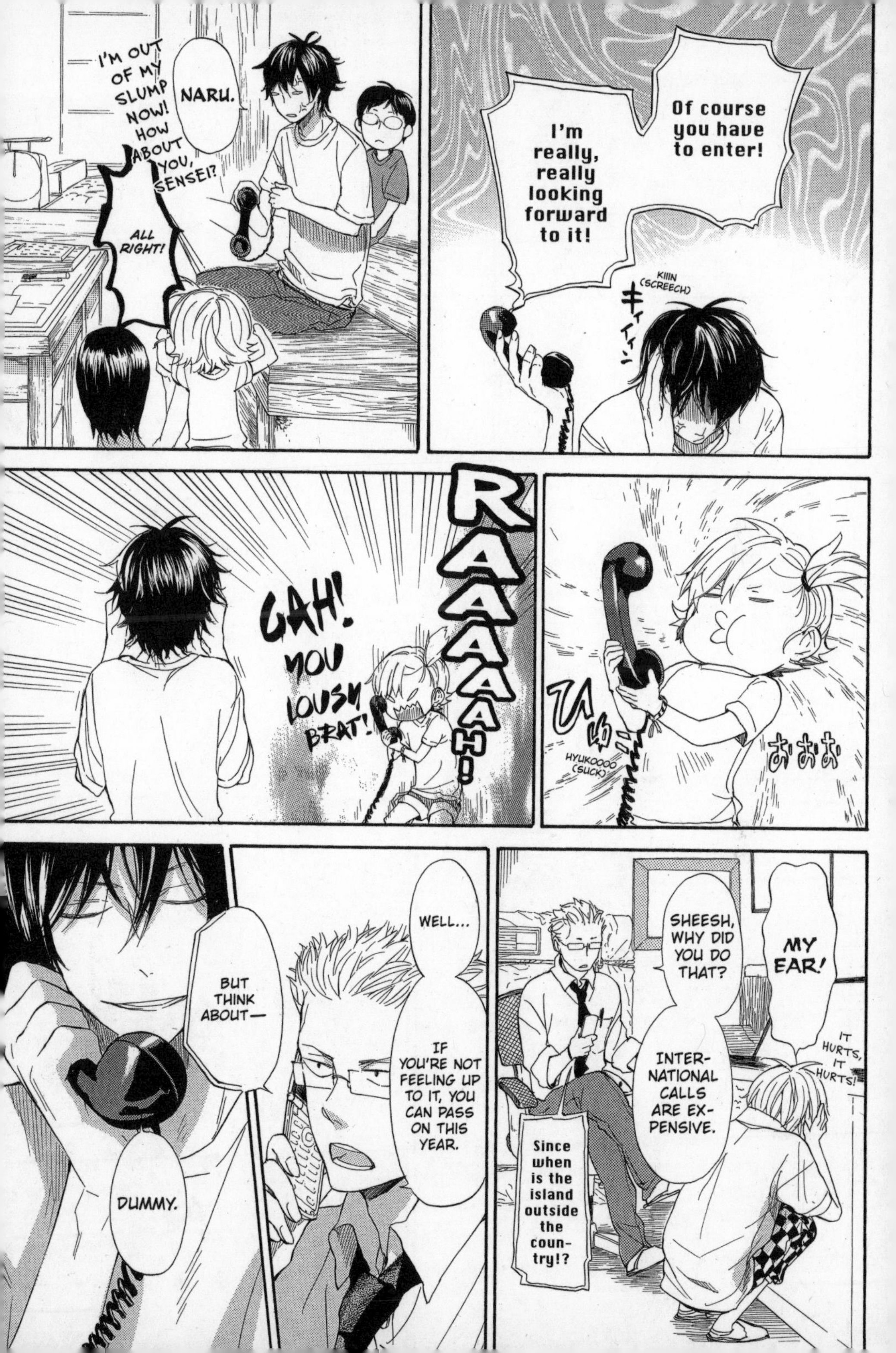
Of course you have to enter!
I'm really, really looking forward to it!
KIIIN (SCREECH)
NARU.
I'M OUT OF MY SLUMP NOW! HOW ABOUT YOU, SENSEI!?
ALL RIGHT!
ひゅ〜
HYUKOOOO (SUCK)
おおお
RAAAAAH!
GAH! YOU LOUSY BRAT!
MY EAR!
SHEESH, WHY DID YOU DO THAT?
IT HURTS, IT HURTS!
INTER-NATIONAL CALLS ARE EX-PENSIVE.
Since when is the island outside the country!?
WELL...
IF YOU'RE NOT FEELING UP TO IT, YOU CAN PASS ON THIS YEAR.
BUT THINK ABOUT—
DUMMY.

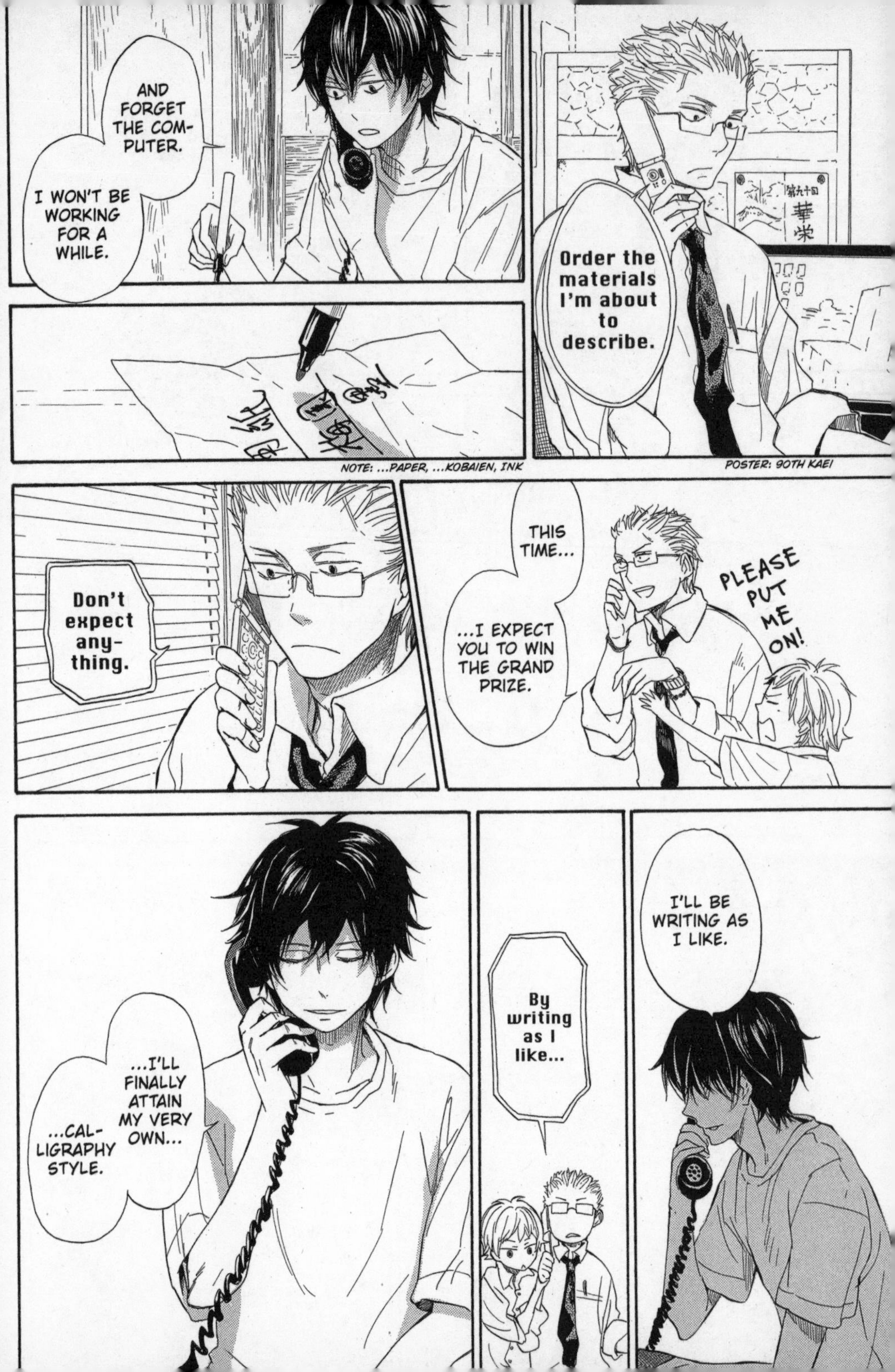
Order the materials I'm about to describe.
AND FORGET THE COM-PUTER.
I WON'T BE WORKING FOR A WHILE.
NOTE: ...PAPER, ...KOBAIEN, INK
POSTER: 90TH KAEI
THIS TIME...
...I EXPECT YOU TO WIN THE GRAND PRIZE.
PLEASE PUT ME ON!
Don't expect any-thing.
I'LL BE WRITING AS I LIKE.
By writing as I like...
...I'LL FINALLY ATTAIN MY VERY OWN...
...CAL-LIGRAPHY STYLE.

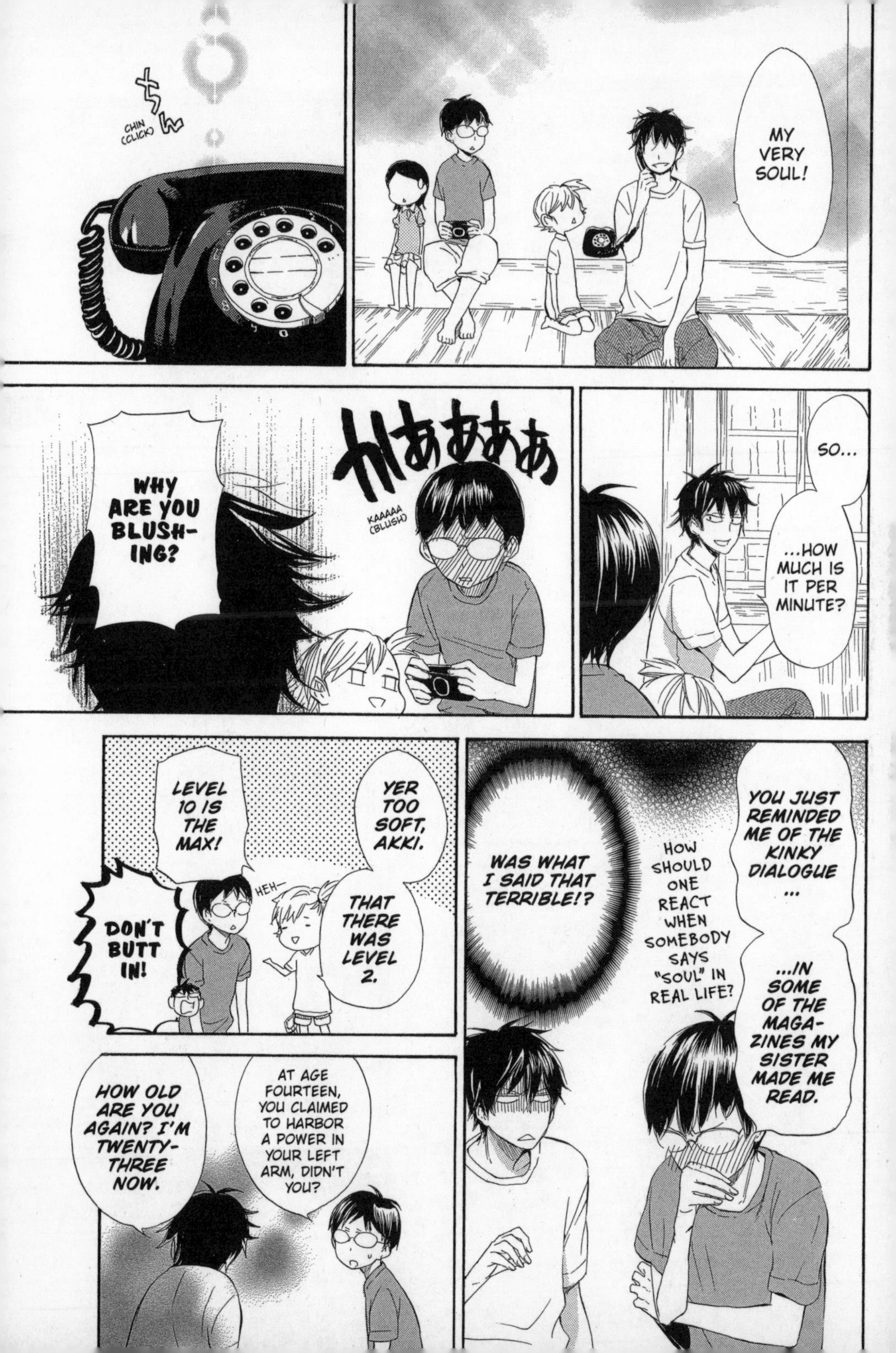

MY VERY SOUL!
ちん
CHIN (CLICK)
SO...
...HOW MUCH IS IT PER MINUTE?
かあああぁ
KAAAAA (BLUSH)
WHY ARE YOU BLUSH-ING?
YOU JUST REMINDED ME OF THE KINKY DIALOGUE...
...IN SOME OF THE MAGA-ZINES MY SISTER MADE ME READ.
HOW SHOULD ONE REACT WHEN SOMEBODY SAYS "SOUL" IN REAL LIFE?
WAS WHAT I SAID THAT TERRIBLE!?
YER TOO SOFT, AKKI.
THAT THERE WAS LEVEL 2.
LEVEL 10 IS THE MAX!
HEH—
DON'T BUTT IN!
AT AGE FOURTEEN, YOU CLAIMED TO HARBOR A POWER IN YOUR LEFT ARM, DIDN'T YOU?
HOW OLD ARE YOU AGAIN? I'M TWENTY-THREE NOW.

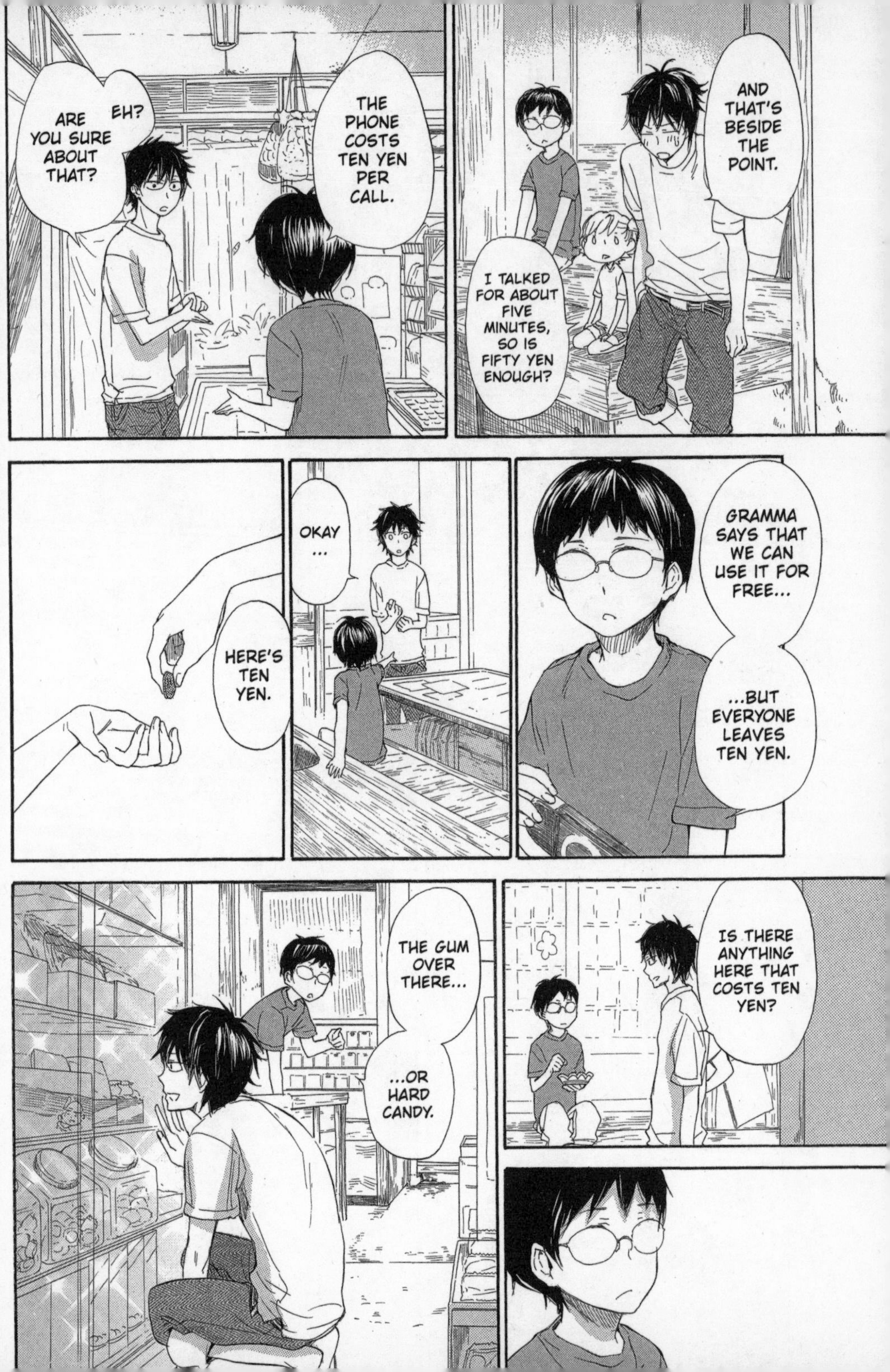
AND THAT'S BESIDE THE POINT.
I TALKED FOR ABOUT FIVE MINUTES, SO IS FIFTY YEN ENOUGH?
THE PHONE COSTS TEN YEN PER CALL.
EH?
ARE YOU SURE ABOUT THAT?
GRAMMA SAYS THAT WE CAN USE IT FOR FREE...
...BUT EVERYONE LEAVES TEN YEN.
OKAY ...
HERE'S TEN YEN.
IS THERE ANYTHING HERE THAT COSTS TEN YEN?
THE GUM OVER THERE...
...OR HARD CANDY.

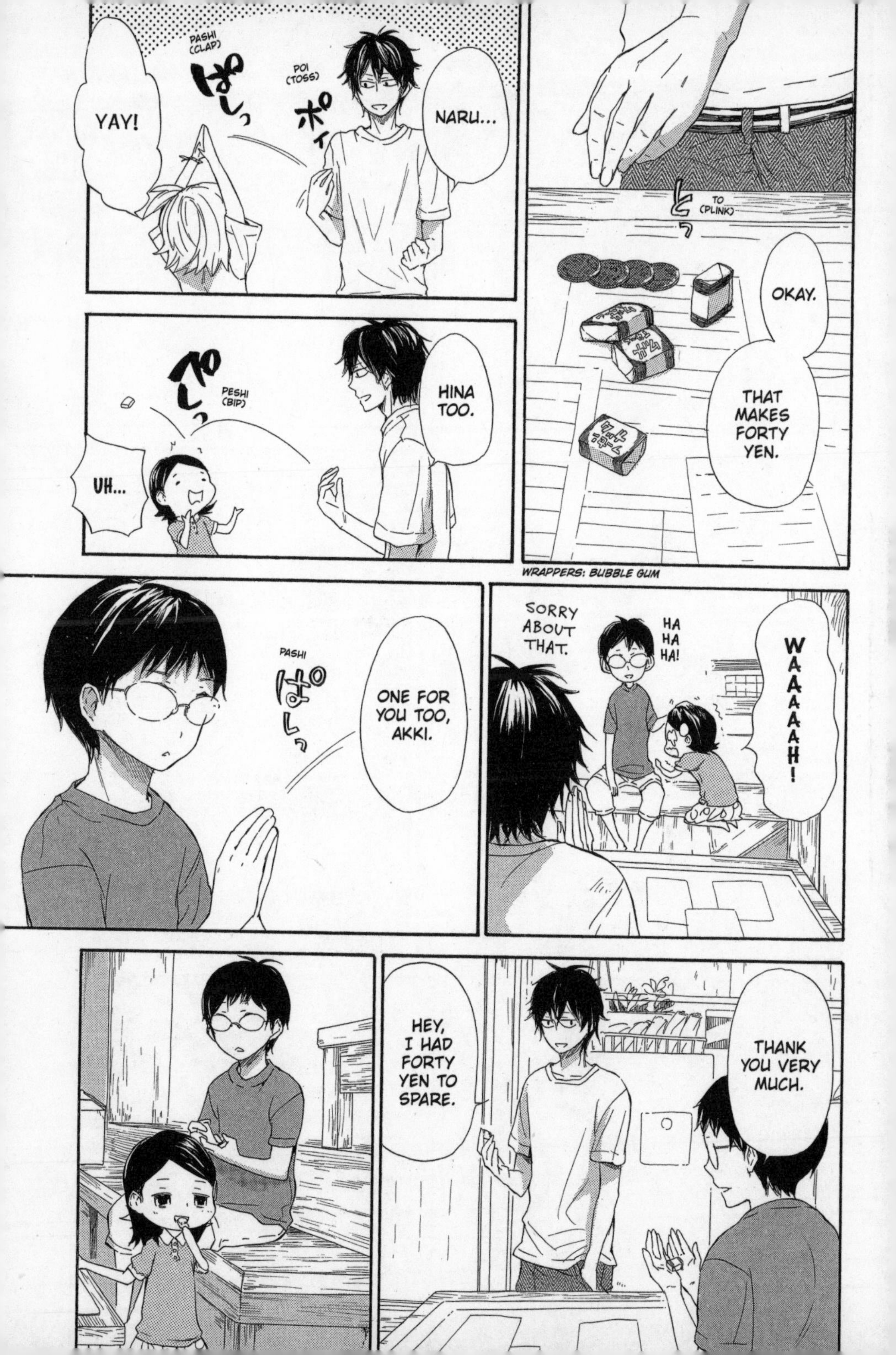
TO (PLINK)
OKAY.
THAT MAKES FORTY YEN.
WRAPPERS: BUBBLE GUM
NARU...
POI (TOSS)
PASHI (CLAP)
YAY!
HINA TOO.
PESHI (BIP)
UH...
WAAAAAAH!
HA HA HA!
SORRY ABOUT THAT.
ONE FOR YOU TOO, AKKI.
PASHI
THANK YOU VERY MUCH.
HEY, I HAD FORTY YEN TO SPARE.

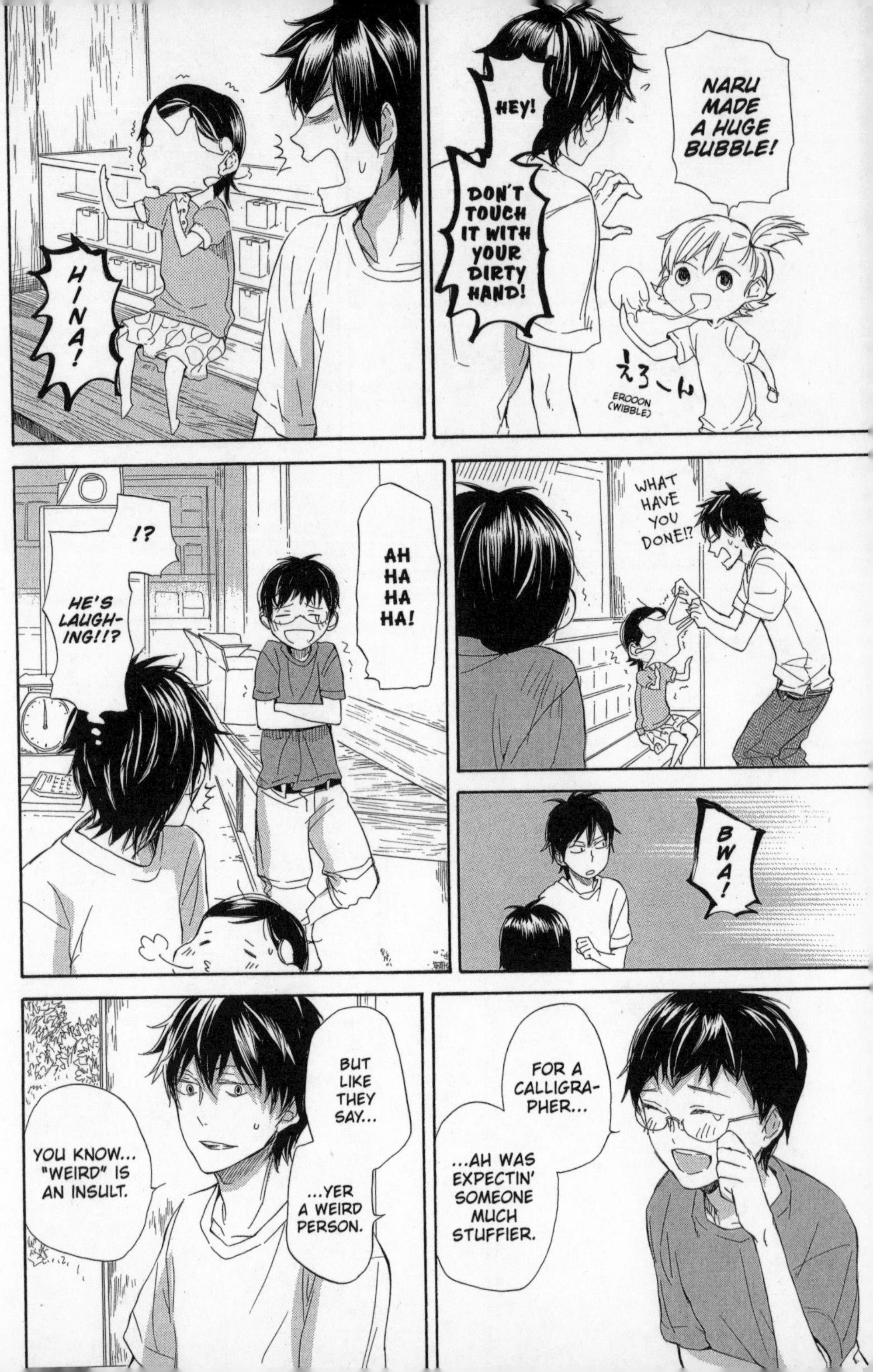
NARU MADE A HUGE BUBBLE!
HEY!
DON'T TOUCH IT WITH YOUR DIRTY HAND!
えろ〜ん
EROOON (WIBBLE)
HINA!
WHAT HAVE YOU DONE!?
BWA!
AH HA HA HA HA!
!?
HE'S LAUGH-ING!!?
FOR A CALLIGRA-PHER...
...AH WAS EXPECTIN' SOMEONE MUCH STUFFIER.
BUT LIKE THEY SAY...
...YER A WEIRD PERSON.
YOU KNOW... "WEIRD" IS AN INSULT.

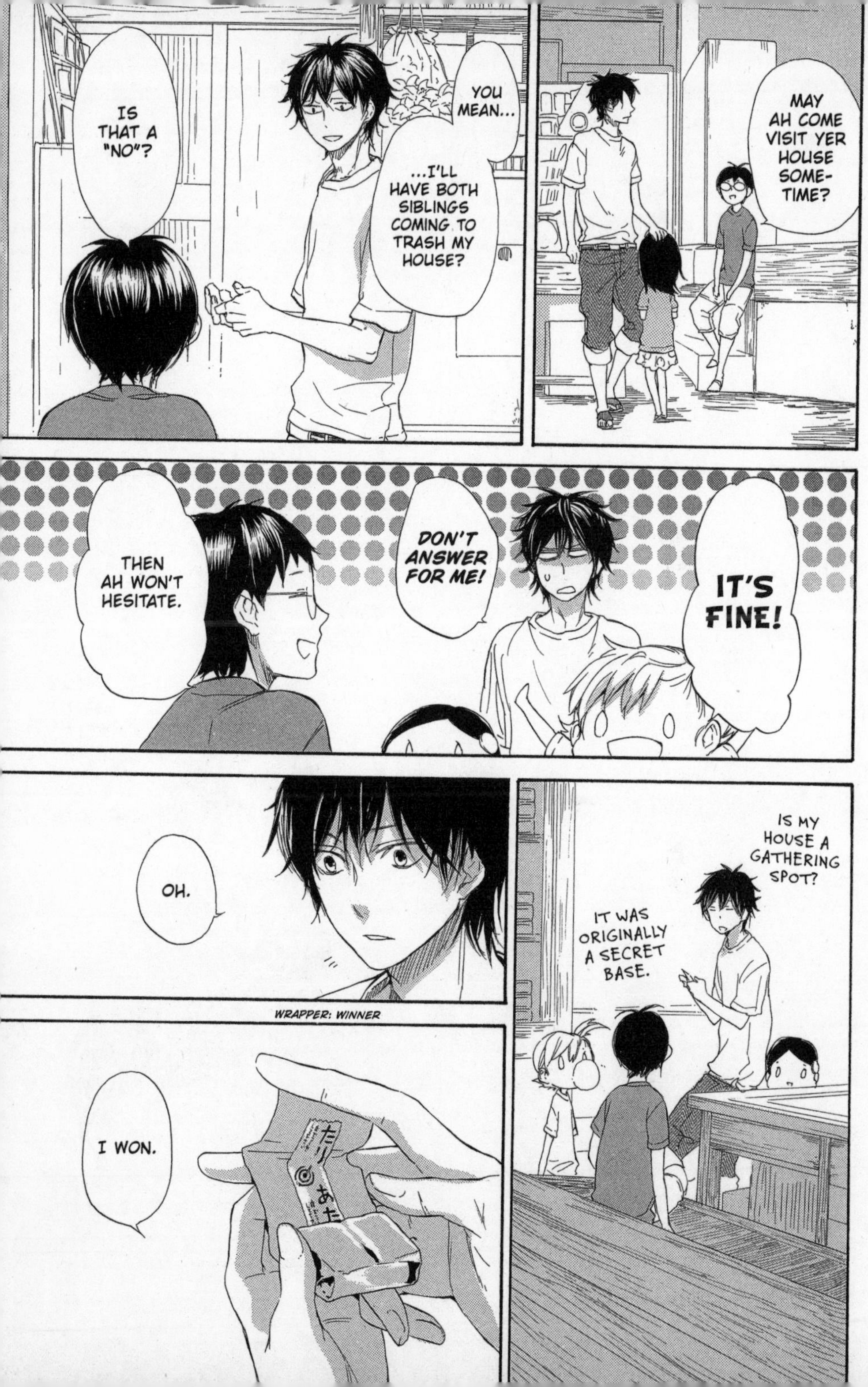
MAY AH COME VISIT YER HOUSE SOME-TIME?
YOU MEAN...
...I'LL HAVE BOTH SIBLINGS COMING TO TRASH MY HOUSE?
IS THAT A "NO"?
IT'S FINE!
DON'T ANSWER FOR ME!
THEN AH WON'T HESITATE.
IS MY HOUSE A GATHERING SPOT?
IT WAS ORIGINALLY A SECRET BASE.
OH.
WRAPPER: WINNER
I WON.

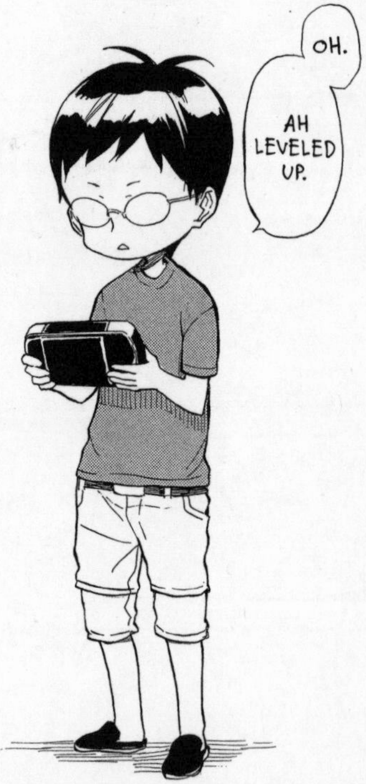
OH.
AH LEVELED UP.

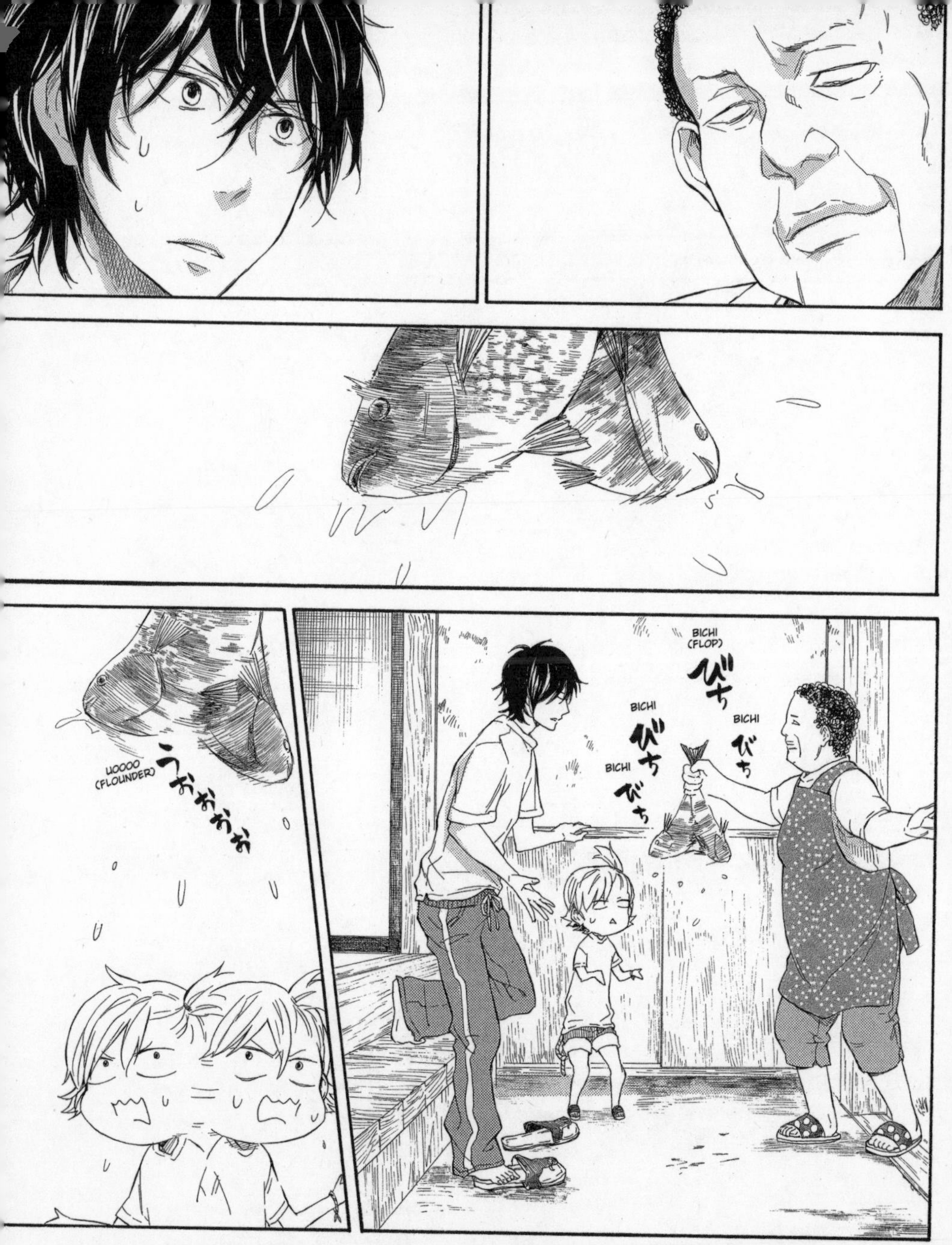
BICHI (FLOP)
びち
BICHI
びち
BICHI
びち
BICHI
びち
UOOOO (FLOUNDER)
うおおおお

ACT.28
KURE-IWO
(Translation: Large-scale Blackfish)

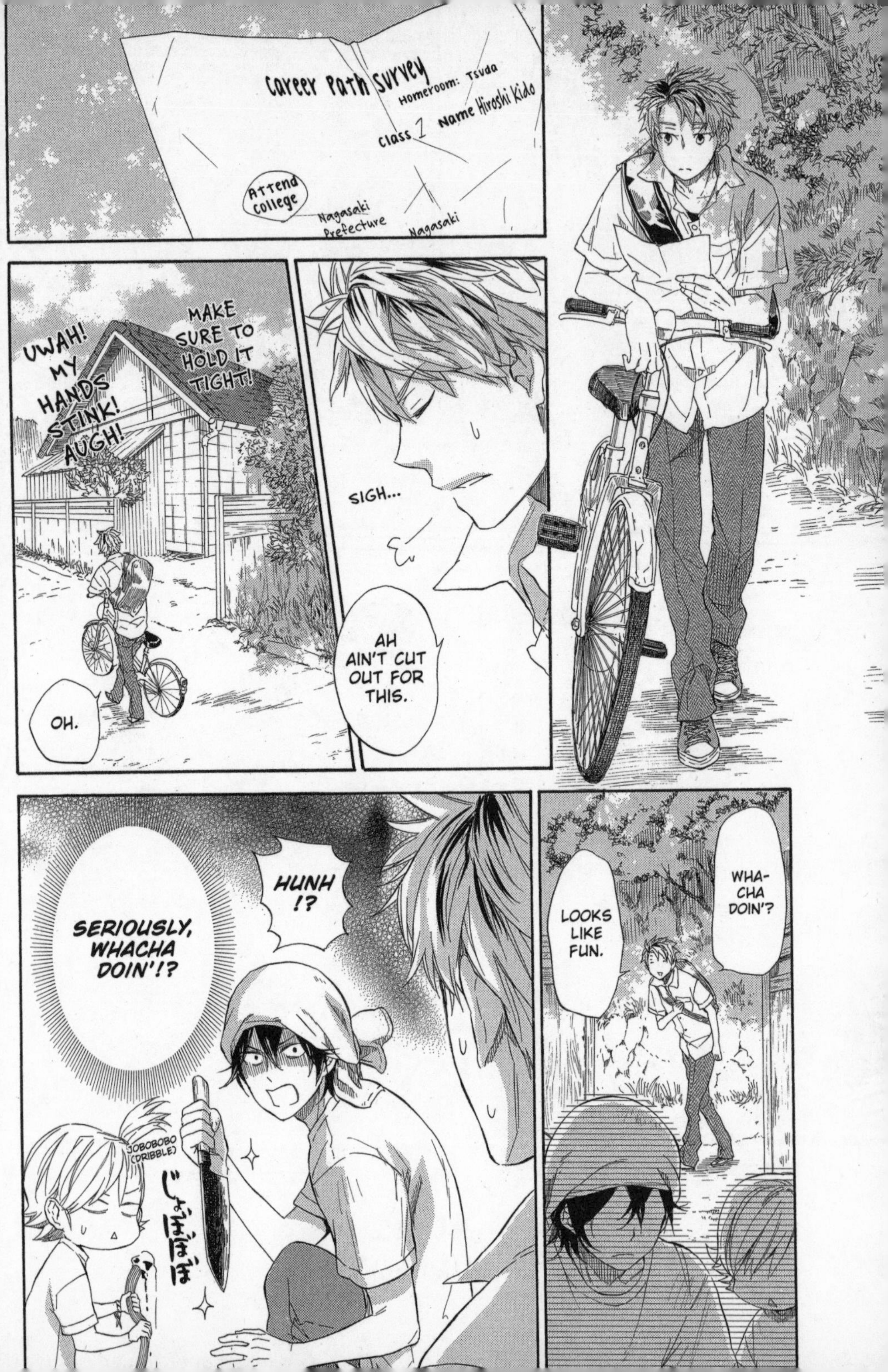
Career Path Survey
Homeroom: Tsuda
Class 1 Name Hiroshi Kido
Attend College
Nagasaki Prefecture
Nagasaki
SIGH...
AH AIN'T CUT OUT FOR THIS.
MAKE SURE TO HOLD IT TIGHT!
UWAH! MY HANDS STINK! AUGH!
OH.
WHA-CHA DOIN'?
LOOKS LIKE FUN.
HUNH !?
SERIOUSLY, WHACHA DOIN'!?
JOBOBOBO (DRIBBLE)
じょぼぼぼ

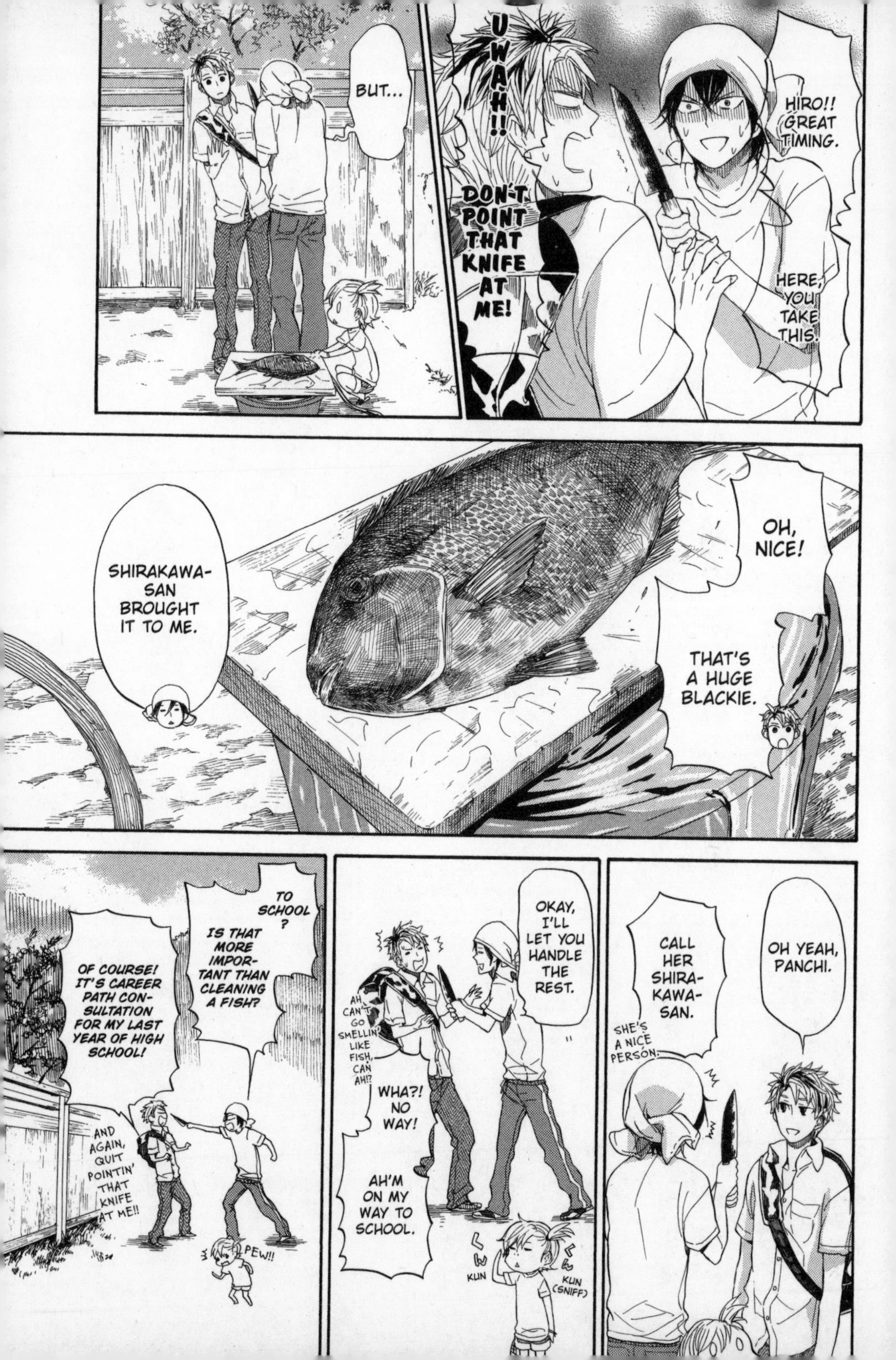
HIRO!! GREAT TIMING.
UWAH!!
HERE, YOU TAKE THIS.
DON'T POINT THAT KNIFE AT ME!
BUT...
OH, NICE!
THAT'S A HUGE BLACKIE.
SHIRAKAWA-SAN BROUGHT IT TO ME.
OH YEAH, PANCHI.
CALL HER SHIRAKAWA-SAN.
SHE'S A NICE PERSON.
OKAY, I'LL LET YOU HANDLE THE REST.
WHA?! NO WAY!
AH CAN'T GO SMELLIN' LIKE FISH, CAN AH!?
AH'M ON MY WAY TO SCHOOL.
KUN
KUN (SNIFF)
TO SCHOOL?
IS THAT MORE IMPORTANT THAN CLEANING A FISH?
OF COURSE! IT'S CAREER PATH CONSULTATION FOR MY LAST YEAR OF HIGH SCHOOL!
AND AGAIN, QUIT POINTIN' THAT KNIFE AT ME!!
PEW!!

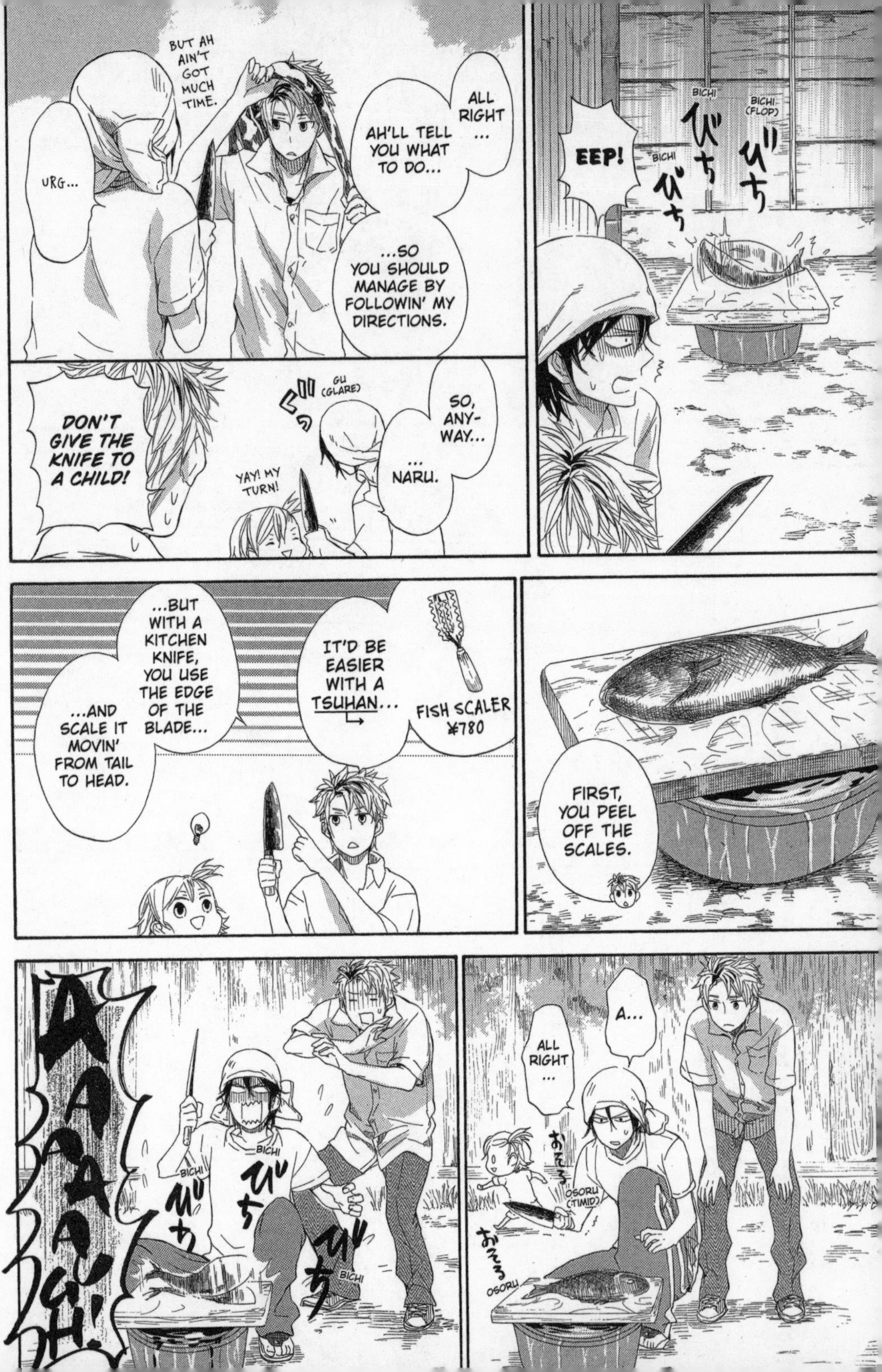
EEP!
BICHI
BICHI (FLOP)
BICHI
びち
びち
びち
BUT AH AIN'T GOT MUCH TIME.
URG...
ALL RIGHT ...
AH'LL TELL YOU WHAT TO DO...
...SO YOU SHOULD MANAGE BY FOLLOWIN' MY DIRECTIONS.
SO, ANYWAY...
... NARU.
GU (GLARE)
YAY! MY TURN!
DON'T GIVE THE KNIFE TO A CHILD!
FIRST, YOU PEEL OFF THE SCALES.
IT'D BE EASIER WITH A TSUHAN...
FISH SCALER ¥780
...BUT WITH A KITCHEN KNIFE, YOU USE THE EDGE OF THE BLADE...
...AND SCALE IT MOVIN' FROM TAIL TO HEAD.
A...
ALL RIGHT ...
OSORU (TIMID)
OSORU
BICHI
BICHI
BICHI
AAAAAGH!!

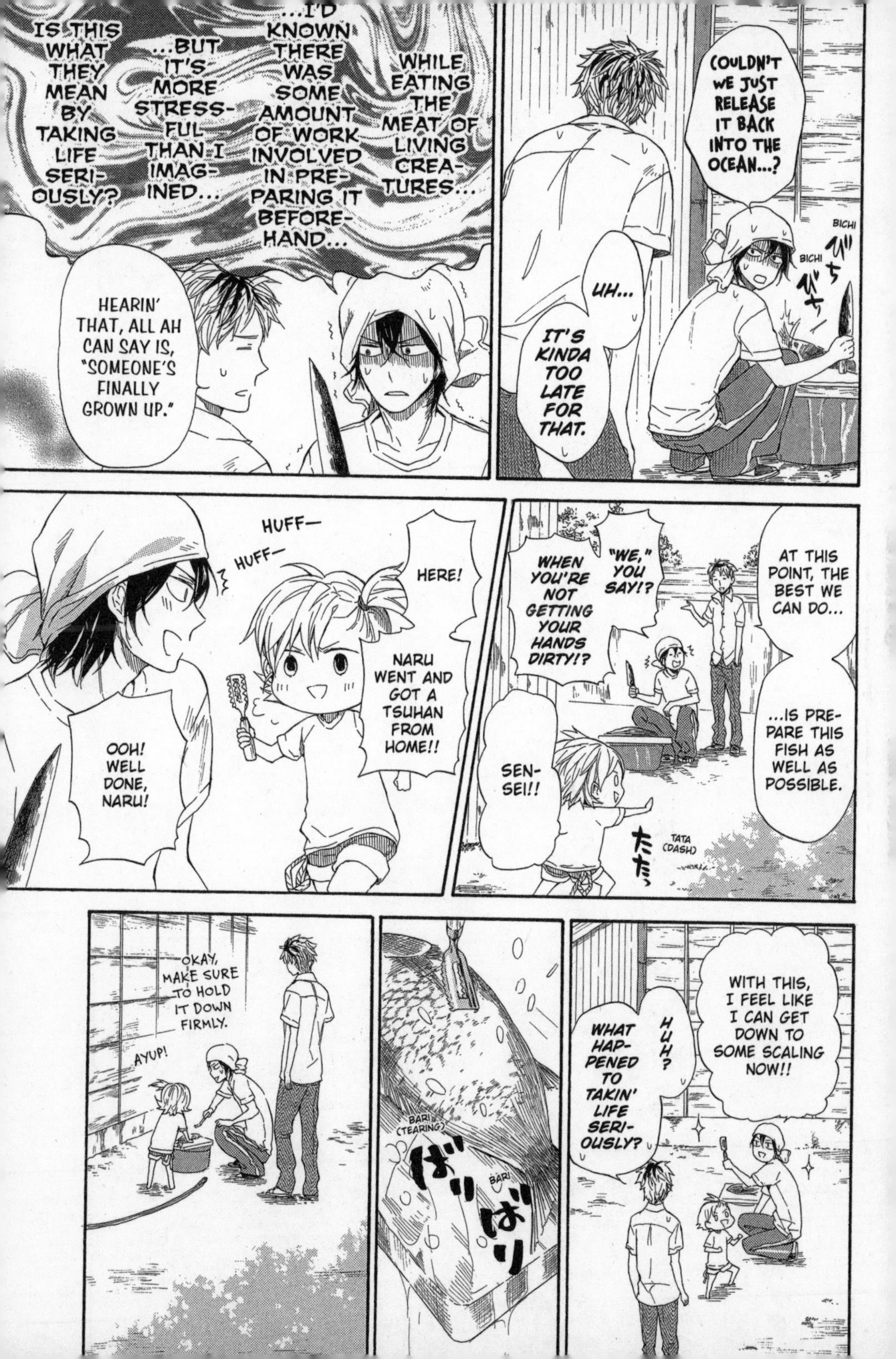
COULDN'T WE JUST RELEASE IT BACK INTO THE OCEAN...?
BICHI
BICHI
UH...
IT'S KINDA TOO LATE FOR THAT.
WHILE EATING THE MEAT OF LIVING CREATURES...
...I'D KNOWN THERE WAS SOME AMOUNT OF WORK INVOLVED IN PREPARING IT BEFOREHAND...
...BUT IT'S MORE STRESSFUL THAN I IMAGINED...
IS THIS WHAT THEY MEAN BY TAKING LIFE SERIOUSLY?
HEARIN' THAT, ALL AH CAN SAY IS, "SOMEONE'S FINALLY GROWN UP."
AT THIS POINT, THE BEST WE CAN DO...
...IS PREPARE THIS FISH AS WELL AS POSSIBLE.
"WE," YOU SAY!?
WHEN YOU'RE NOT GETTING YOUR HANDS DIRTY!?
SENSEI!!
TATA (DASH)
HERE!
NARU WENT AND GOT A TSUHAN FROM HOME!!
HUFF—
HUFF—
OOH! WELL DONE, NARU!
WITH THIS, I FEEL LIKE I CAN GET DOWN TO SOME SCALING NOW!!
HUH?
WHAT HAPPENED TO TAKIN' LIFE SERIOUSLY?
BARI (TEARING)
BARI
OKAY, MAKE SURE TO HOLD IT DOWN FIRMLY.
AYUP!

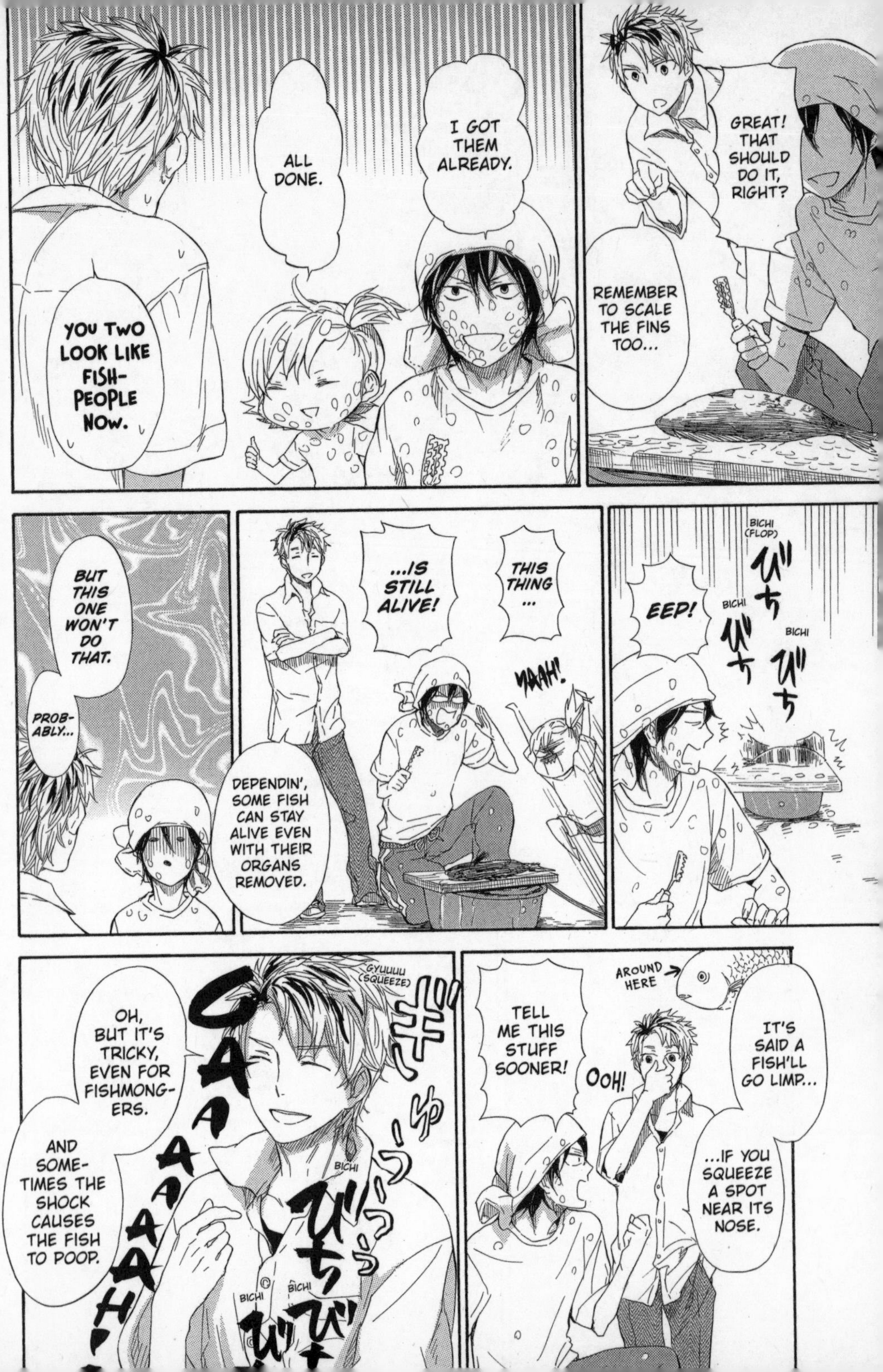
GREAT! THAT SHOULD DO IT, RIGHT?
REMEMBER TO SCALE THE FINS TOO...
I GOT THEM ALREADY.
ALL DONE.
YOU TWO LOOK LIKE FISH-PEOPLE NOW.
BICHI (FLOP)
びち
EEP!
BICHI
びち
BICHI
びち
THIS THING...
...IS STILL ALIVE!
NAAH!
DEPENDIN', SOME FISH CAN STAY ALIVE EVEN WITH THEIR ORGANS REMOVED.
BUT THIS ONE WON'T DO THAT.
PROB-ABLY...
AROUND HERE
IT'S SAID A FISH'LL GO LIMP...
TELL ME THIS STUFF SOONER!
OOH!
...IF YOU SQUEEZE A SPOT NEAR ITS NOSE.
GYUUUU (SQUEEZE)
ぎゅううっ
GAAAAAAH!
OH, BUT IT'S TRICKY, EVEN FOR FISHMONGERS.
AND SOME-TIMES THE SHOCK CAUSES THE FISH TO POOP.
BICHI
びちっ
BICHI BICHI
びちびち

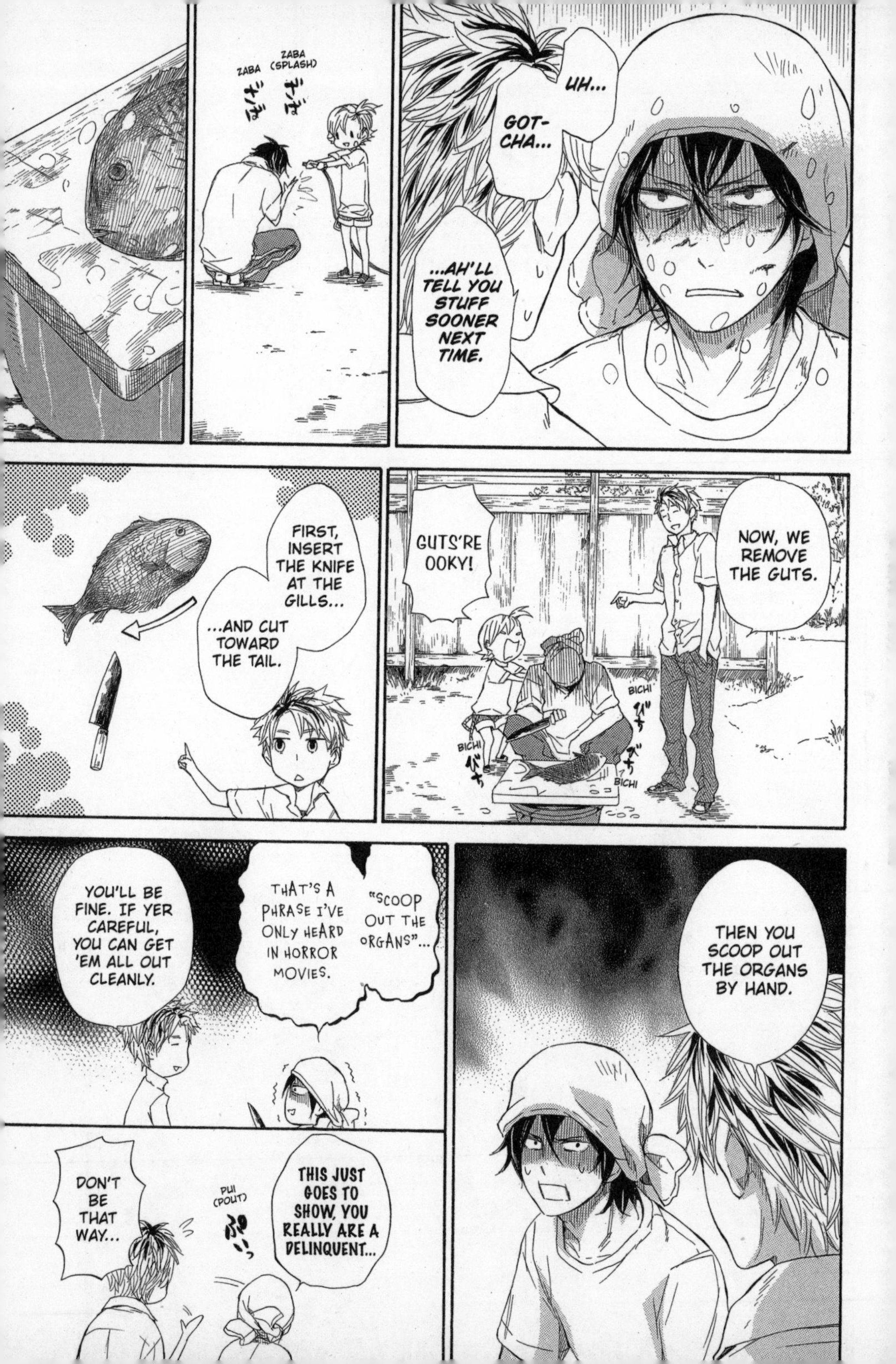
UH...
GOT-CHA...
...AH'LL TELL YOU STUFF SOONER NEXT TIME.
ZABA (SPLASH)
ざば
ZABA
ざば
NOW, WE REMOVE THE GUTS.
GUTS'RE OOKY!
BICHI
びち
BICHI
びち
BICHI
びち
FIRST, INSERT THE KNIFE AT THE GILLS...
...AND CUT TOWARD THE TAIL.
THEN YOU SCOOP OUT THE ORGANS BY HAND.
"SCOOP OUT THE ORGANS"...
THAT'S A PHRASE I'VE ONLY HEARD IN HORROR MOVIES.
YOU'LL BE FINE. IF YER CAREFUL, YOU CAN GET 'EM ALL OUT CLEANLY.
THIS JUST GOES TO SHOW, YOU REALLY ARE A DELINQUENT...
PUI (POUT)
ぷいっ
DON'T BE THAT WAY...

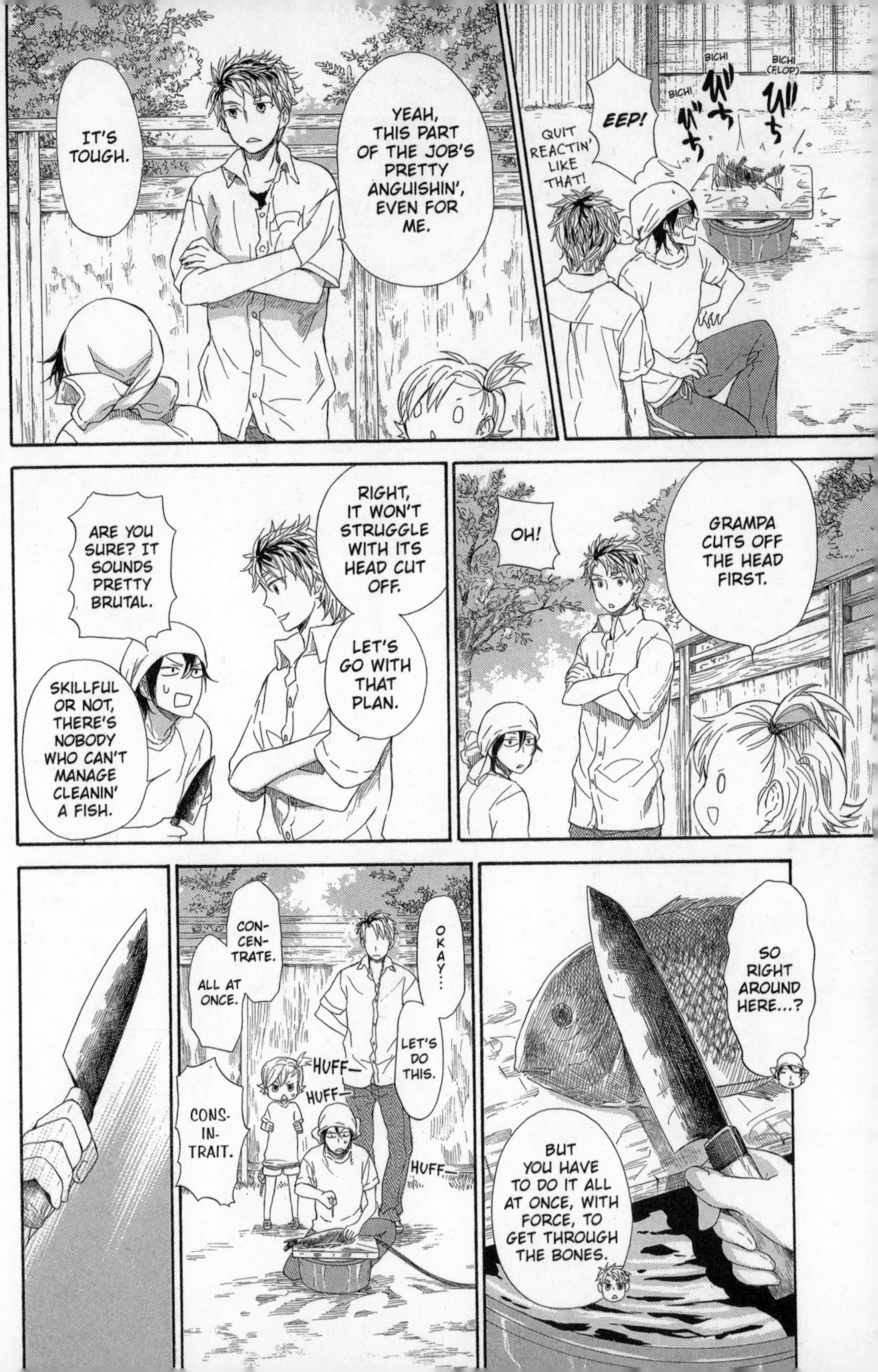
BICHI
BICHI (FLOP)
BICHI
EEP!
QUIT REACTIN' LIKE THAT!
YEAH, THIS PART OF THE JOB'S PRETTY ANGUISHIN', EVEN FOR ME.
IT'S TOUGH.
GRAMPA CUTS OFF THE HEAD FIRST.
OH!
RIGHT, IT WON'T STRUGGLE WITH ITS HEAD CUT OFF.
LET'S GO WITH THAT PLAN.
ARE YOU SURE? IT SOUNDS PRETTY BRUTAL.
SKILLFUL OR NOT, THERE'S NOBODY WHO CAN'T MANAGE CLEANIN' A FISH.
SO RIGHT AROUND HERE...?
BUT YOU HAVE TO DO IT ALL AT ONCE, WITH FORCE, TO GET THROUGH THE BONES.
OKAY...
CON-CEN-TRATE.
ALL AT ONCE.
LET'S DO THIS.
HUFF—
HUFF—
CONS-IN-TRAIT.
HUFF—

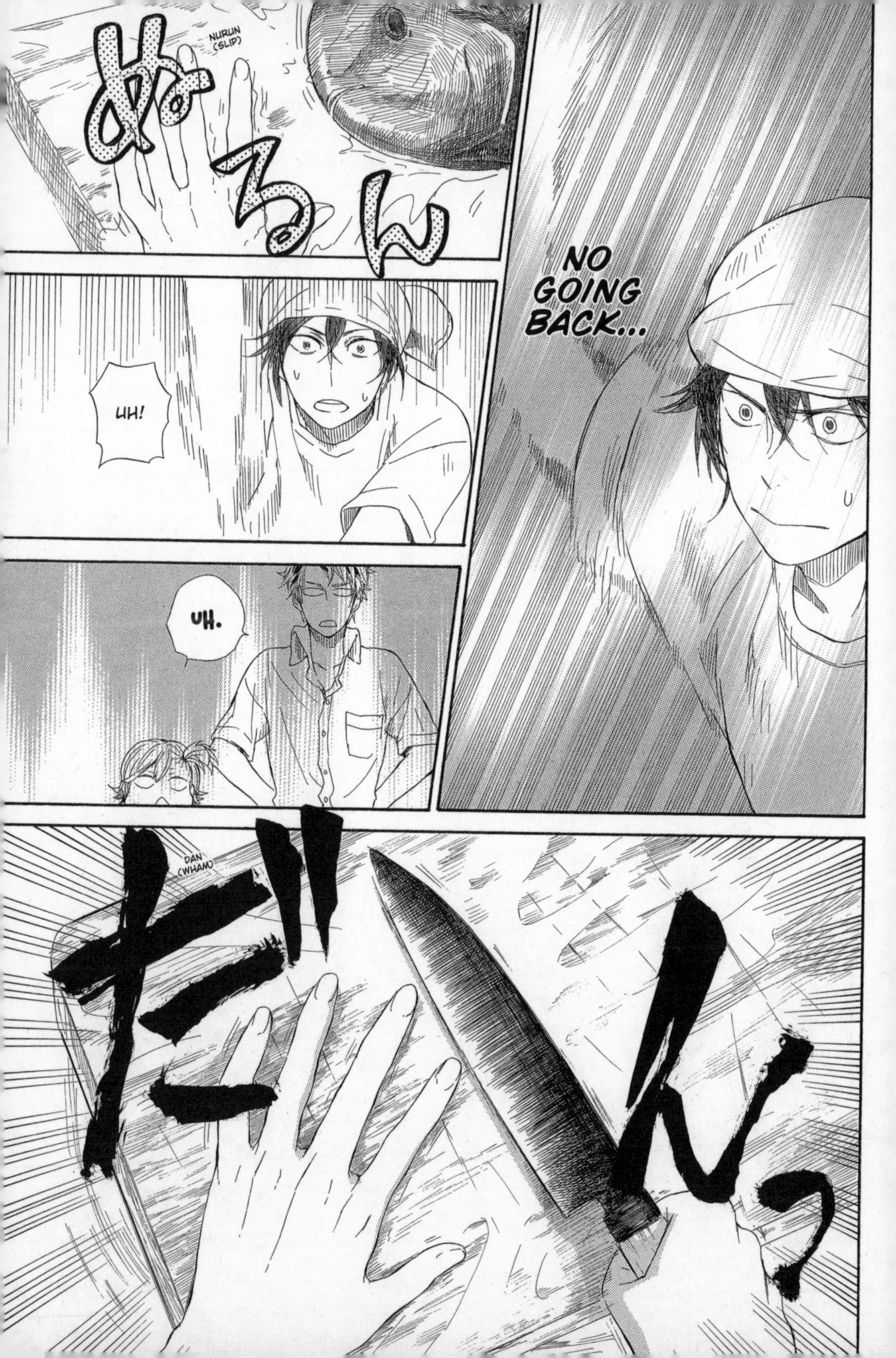

NO GOING BACK...
NURUN (SLIP)
UH!
UH.
DAN (WHAM)

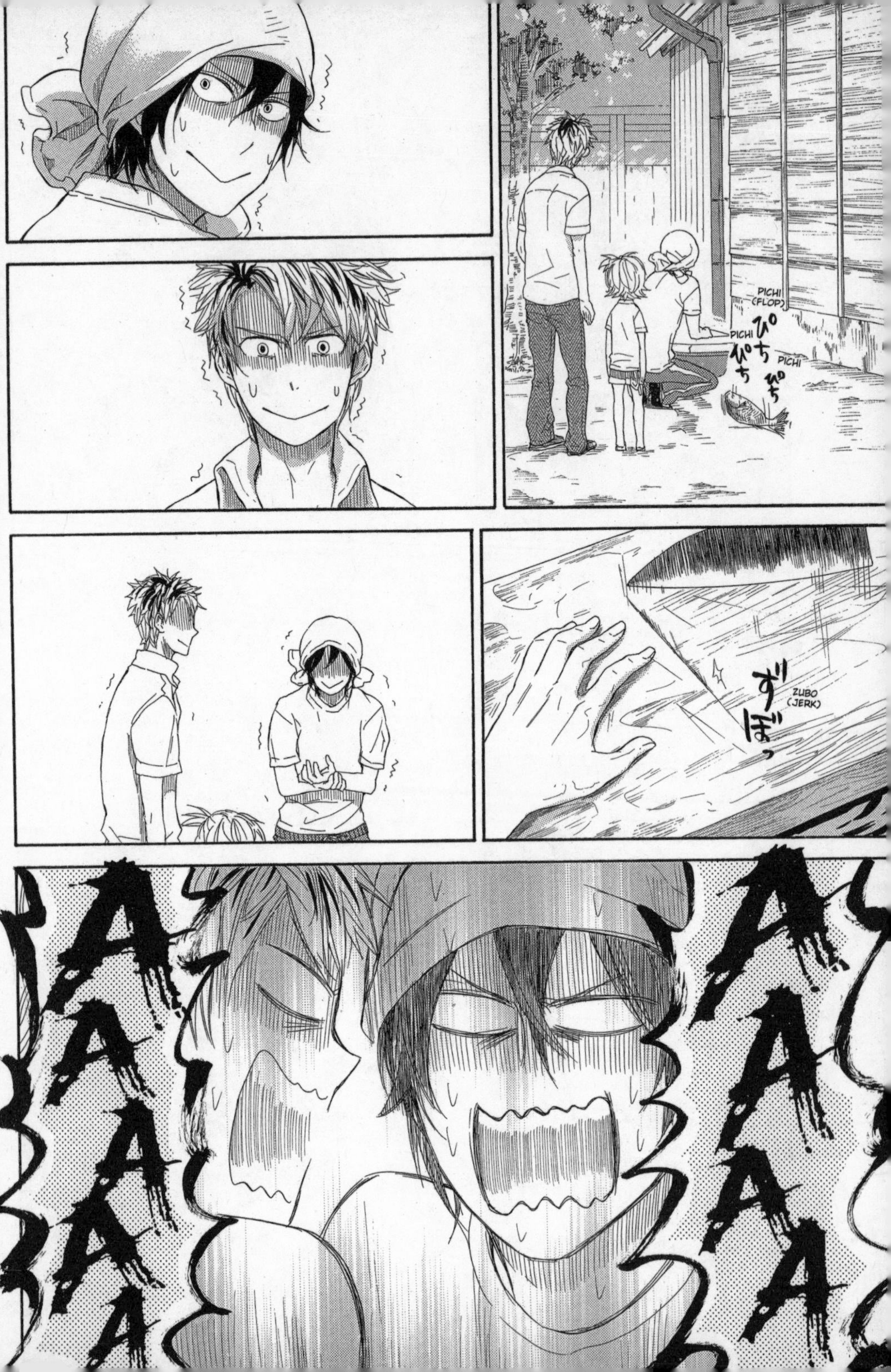

PICHI (FLOP)
ぴち
PICHI
ぴち
PICHI
ぴち
ずぼっ
ZUBO (JERK)
AAAAAA
AAAAA

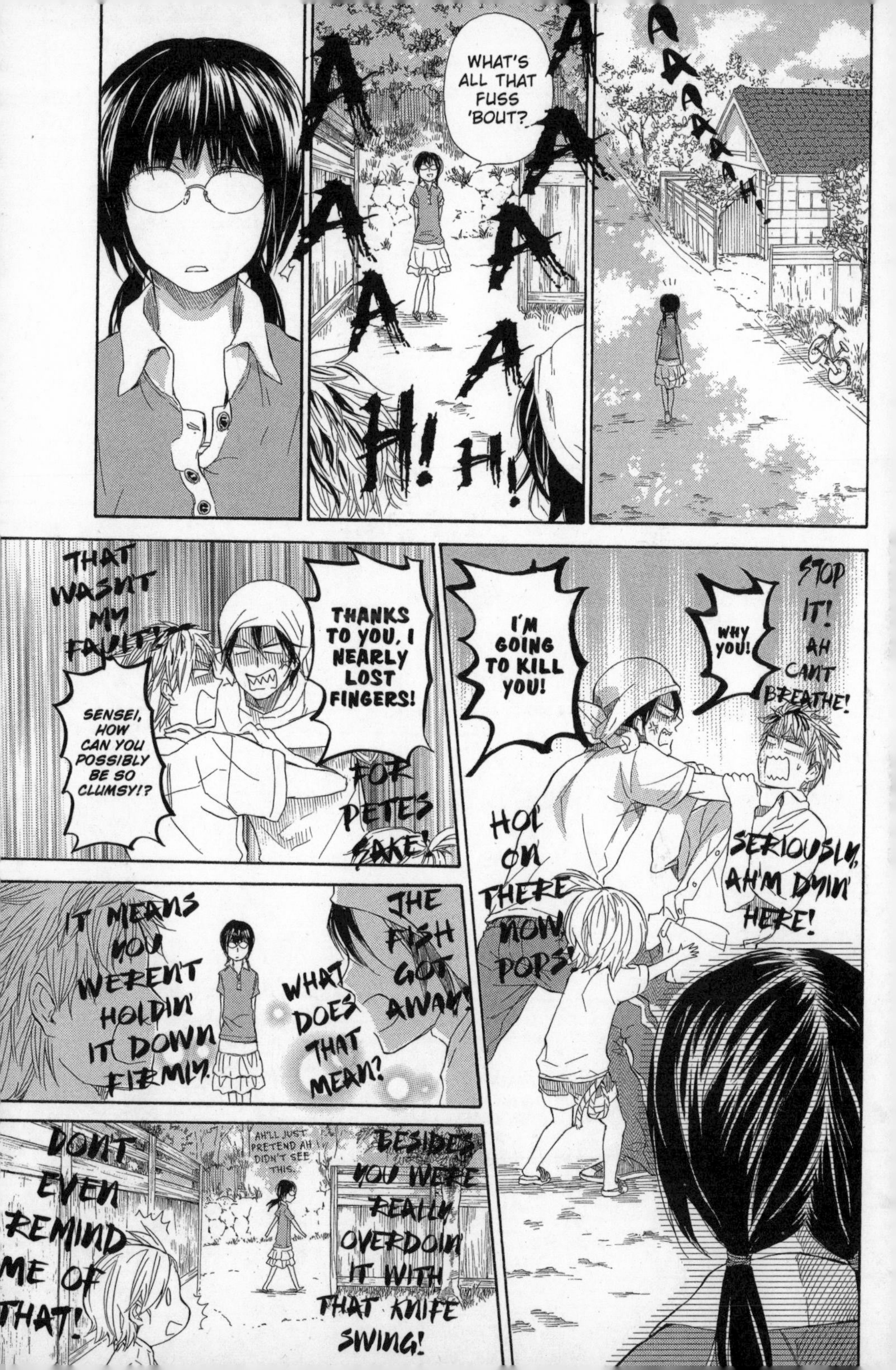
AAAAAAH!
WHAT'S ALL THAT FUSS 'BOUT?
AAAAH!
AAAH!
I'M GOING TO KILL YOU!
WHY YOU!
STOP IT! AH CANT BREATHE!
HOL' ON THERE NOW, POPS!
SERIOUSLY, AH'M DYIN' HERE!
THANKS TO YOU, I NEARLY LOST FINGERS!
THAT WASNT MY FAULT!
SENSEI, HOW CAN YOU POSSIBLY BE SO CLUMSY!?
FOR PETES SAKE!
THE FISH GOT AWAY!
WHAT DOES THAT MEAN?
IT MEANS YOU WERENT HOLDIN' IT DOWN FIRMLY.
BESIDES YOU WERE REALLY OVERDOIN IT WITH THAT KNIFE SWING!
AH'LL JUST PRETEND AH DIDN'T SEE THIS.
DONT EVEN REMIND ME OF THAT!

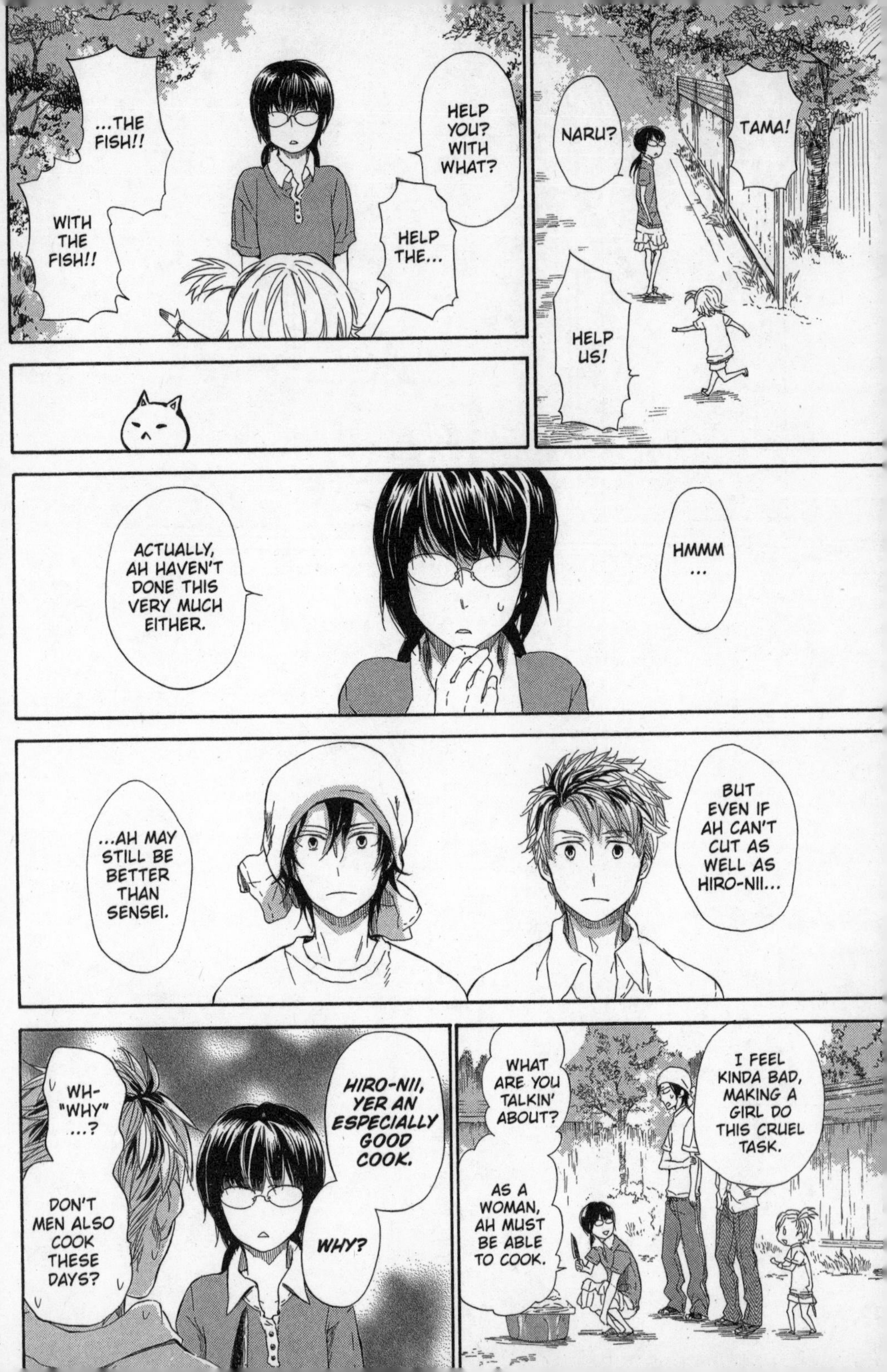
TAMA!
NARU?
HELP US!
HELP YOU? WITH WHAT?
HELP THE...
...THE FISH!!
WITH THE FISH!!
HMMM ...
ACTUALLY, AH HAVEN'T DONE THIS VERY MUCH EITHER.
BUT EVEN IF AH CAN'T CUT AS WELL AS HIRO-NII...
...AH MAY STILL BE BETTER THAN SENSEI.
I FEEL KINDA BAD, MAKING A GIRL DO THIS CRUEL TASK.
WHAT ARE YOU TALKIN' ABOUT?
AS A WOMAN, AH MUST BE ABLE TO COOK.
HIRO-NII, YER AN ESPECIALLY GOOD COOK.
WHY?
WH- "WHY" ...?
DON'T MEN ALSO COOK THESE DAYS?

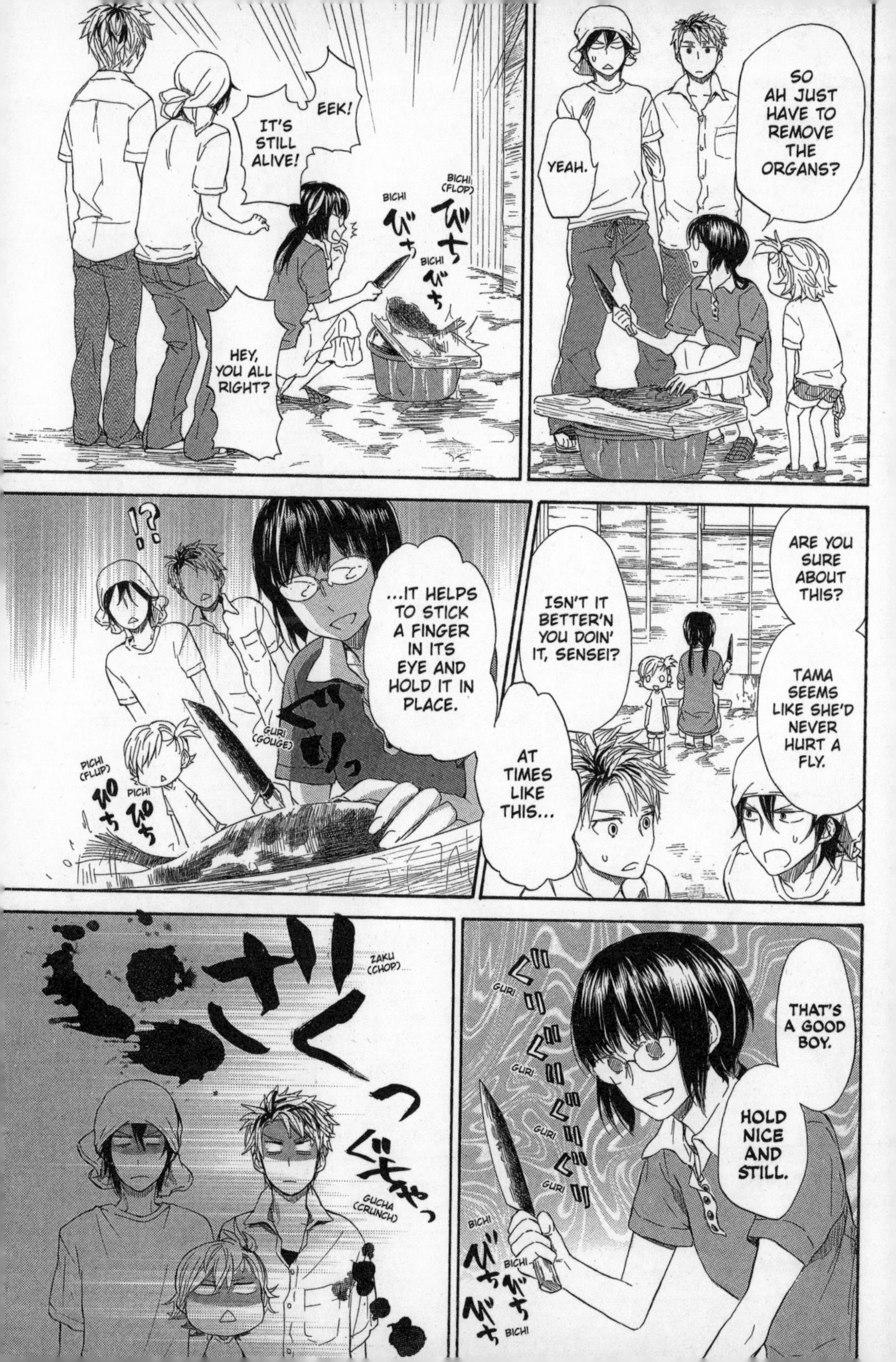
SO AH JUST HAVE TO REMOVE THE ORGANS?
YEAH.
EEK!
IT'S STILL ALIVE!
BICHI (FLOP)
BICHI
BICHI
HEY, YOU ALL RIGHT?
ARE YOU SURE ABOUT THIS?
TAMA SEEMS LIKE SHE'D NEVER HURT A FLY.
ISN'T IT BETTER'N YOU DOIN' IT, SENSEI?
AT TIMES LIKE THIS...
...IT HELPS TO STICK A FINGER IN ITS EYE AND HOLD IT IN PLACE.
GURI (GOUGE)
PICHI (FLUP)
PICHI
THAT'S A GOOD BOY.
HOLD NICE AND STILL.
GURI
GURI
GURI
GURI
BICHI
BICHI
BICHI
ZAKU (CHOP)
GUCHA (CRUNCH)

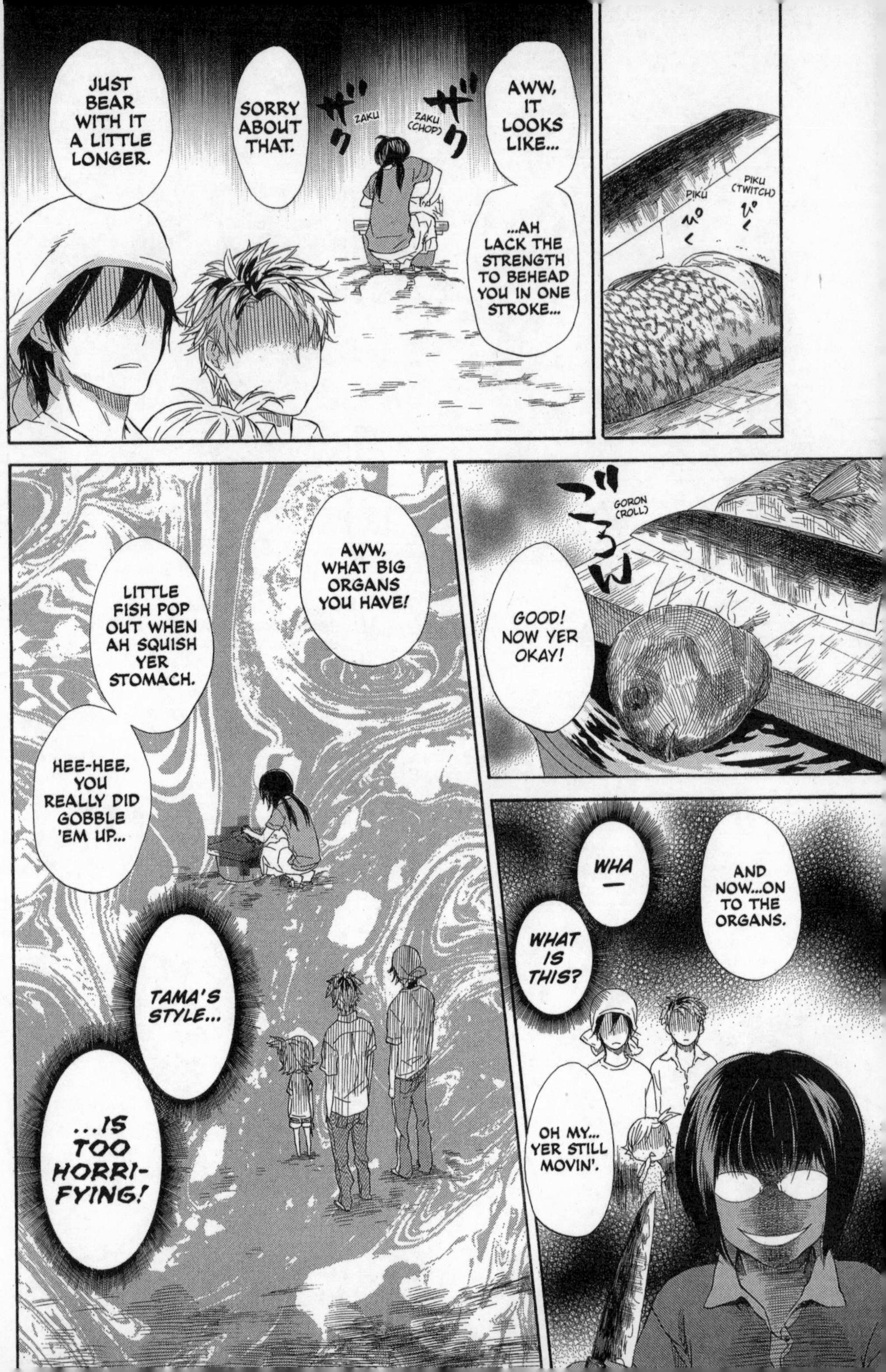
PIKU (TWITCH)
PIKU
AWW, IT LOOKS LIKE...
...AH LACK THE STRENGTH TO BEHEAD YOU IN ONE STROKE...
ZAKU (CHOP)
ZAKU
SORRY ABOUT THAT.
JUST BEAR WITH IT A LITTLE LONGER.
GORON (ROLL)
GOOD! NOW YER OKAY!
AND NOW...ON TO THE ORGANS.
WHA—
WHAT IS THIS?
OH MY... YER STILL MOVIN'.
AWW, WHAT BIG ORGANS YOU HAVE!
LITTLE FISH POP OUT WHEN AH SQUISH YER STOMACH.
HEE-HEE, YOU REALLY DID GOBBLE 'EM UP...
TAMA'S STYLE...
...IS TOO HORRI-FYING!

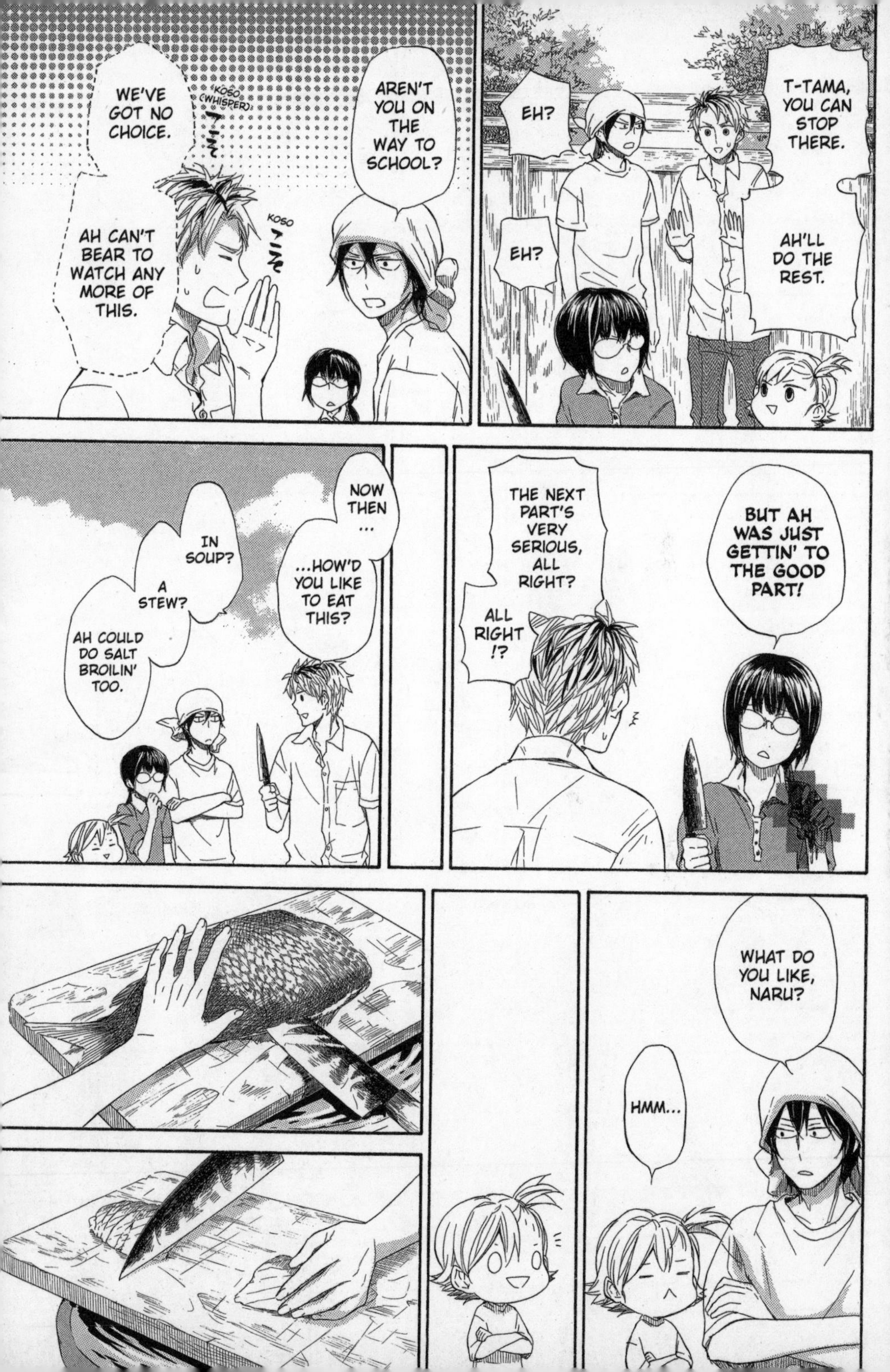
T-TAMA, YOU CAN STOP THERE.
EH?
AH'LL DO THE REST.
EH?
AREN'T YOU ON THE WAY TO SCHOOL?
KOSO (WHISPER)
WE'VE GOT NO CHOICE.
KOSO
AH CAN'T BEAR TO WATCH ANY MORE OF THIS.
BUT AH WAS JUST GETTIN' TO THE GOOD PART!
THE NEXT PART'S VERY SERIOUS, ALL RIGHT?
ALL RIGHT!?
NOW THEN ...
...HOW'D YOU LIKE TO EAT THIS?
IN SOUP?
A STEW?
AH COULD DO SALT BROILIN' TOO.
WHAT DO YOU LIKE, NARU?
HMM...

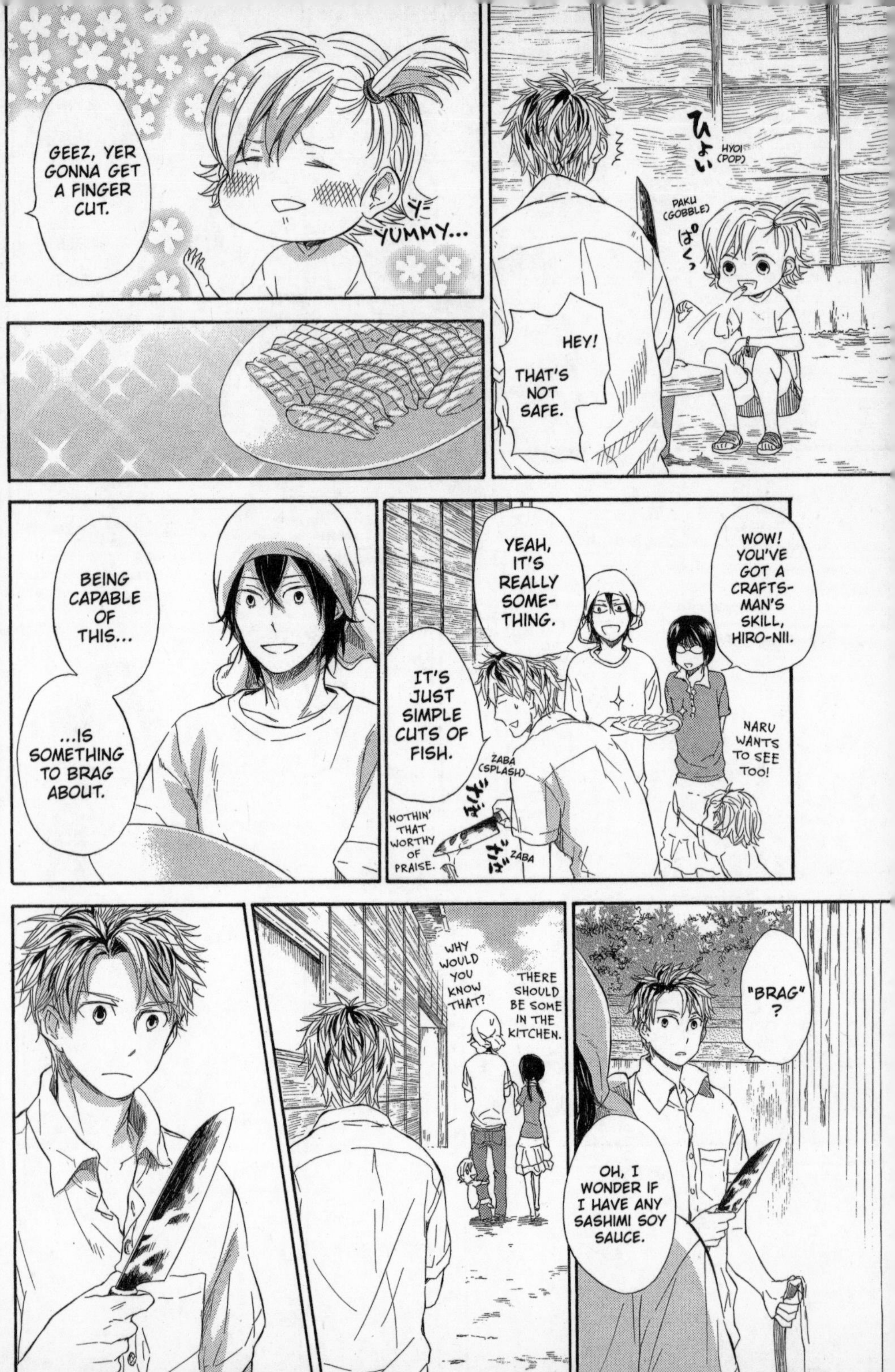
ひょい
HYOI (POP)
ぱくっ
PAKU (GOBBLE)
HEY! THAT'S NOT SAFE.
Y- YUMMY...
GEEZ, YER GONNA GET A FINGER CUT.
WOW! YOU'VE GOT A CRAFTS-MAN'S SKILL, HIRO-NII.
YEAH, IT'S REALLY SOME-THING.
NARU WANTS TO SEE TOO!
IT'S JUST SIMPLE CUTS OF FISH.
ZABA (SPLASH)
ざば
ZABA
ざば
NOTHIN' THAT WORTHY OF PRAISE.
BEING CAPABLE OF THIS...
...IS SOMETHING TO BRAG ABOUT.
"BRAG"?
OH, I WONDER IF I HAVE ANY SASHIMI SOY SAUCE.
THERE SHOULD BE SOME IN THE KITCHEN.
WHY WOULD YOU KNOW THAT?

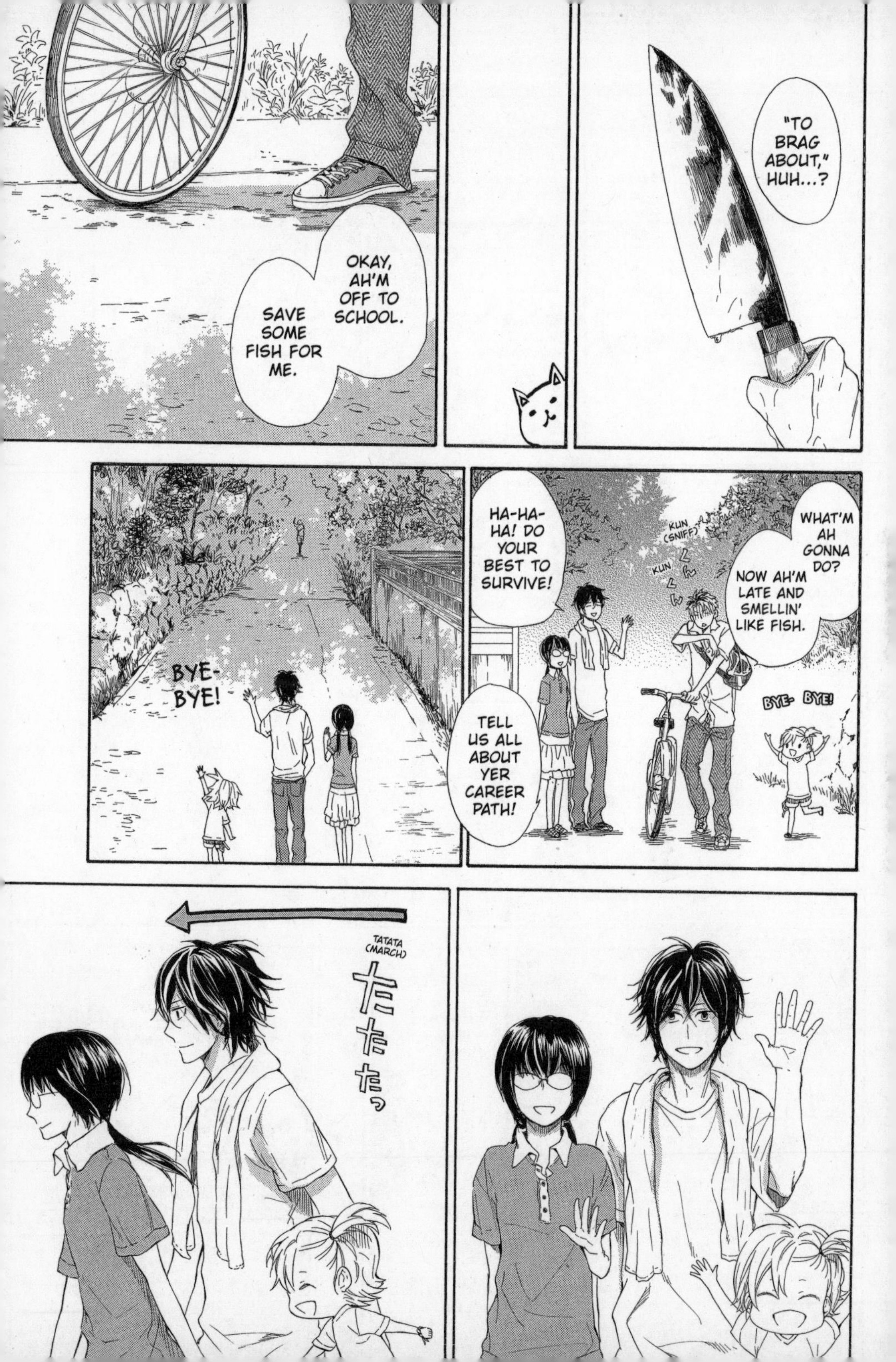
"TO BRAG ABOUT," HUH...?
OKAY, AH'M OFF TO SCHOOL.
SAVE SOME FISH FOR ME.
WHAT'M AH GONNA DO?
NOW AH'M LATE AND SMELLIN' LIKE FISH.
KUN (SNIFF)
KUN
HA-HA-HA! DO YOUR BEST TO SURVIVE!
BYE- BYE!
TELL US ALL ABOUT YER CAREER PATH!
BYE-BYE!
TATATA (MARCH)
たたたっ

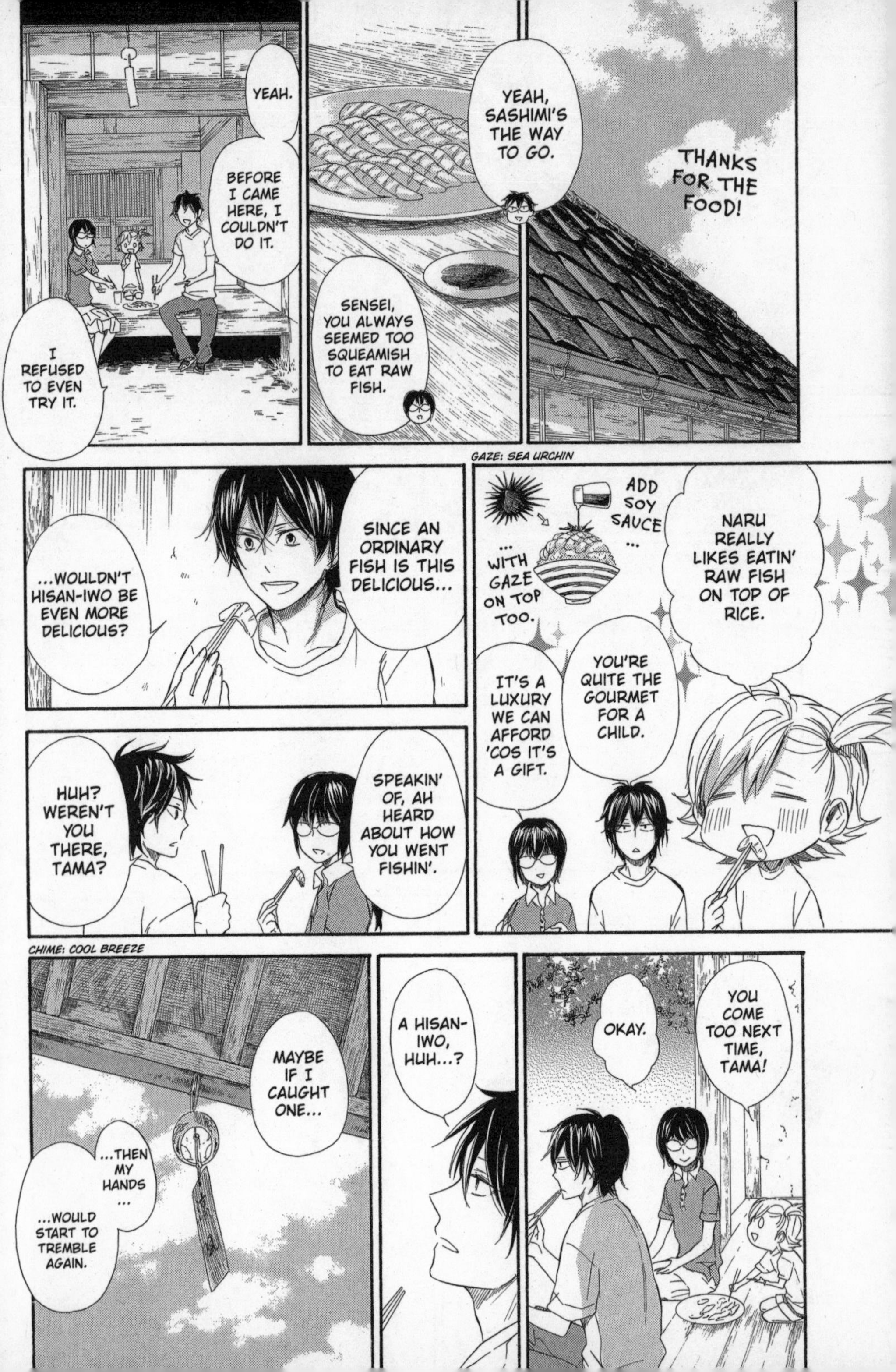
THANKS FOR THE FOOD!
YEAH, SASHIMI'S THE WAY TO GO.
SENSEI, YOU ALWAYS SEEMED TOO SQUEAMISH TO EAT RAW FISH.
YEAH.
BEFORE I CAME HERE, I COULDN'T DO IT.
I REFUSED TO EVEN TRY IT.
GAZE: SEA URCHIN
NARU REALLY LIKES EATIN' RAW FISH ON TOP OF RICE.
ADD SOY SAUCE ...
... WITH GAZE ON TOP TOO.
YOU'RE QUITE THE GOURMET FOR A CHILD.
IT'S A LUXURY WE CAN AFFORD 'COS IT'S A GIFT.
SINCE AN ORDINARY FISH IS THIS DELICIOUS...
...WOULDN'T HISAN-IWO BE EVEN MORE DELICIOUS?
SPEAKIN' OF, AH HEARD ABOUT HOW YOU WENT FISHIN'.
HUH? WEREN'T YOU THERE, TAMA?
CHIME: COOL BREEZE
YOU COME TOO NEXT TIME, TAMA!
OKAY.
A HISAN-IWO, HUH...?
MAYBE IF I CAUGHT ONE...
...THEN MY HANDS ...
...WOULD START TO TREMBLE AGAIN.

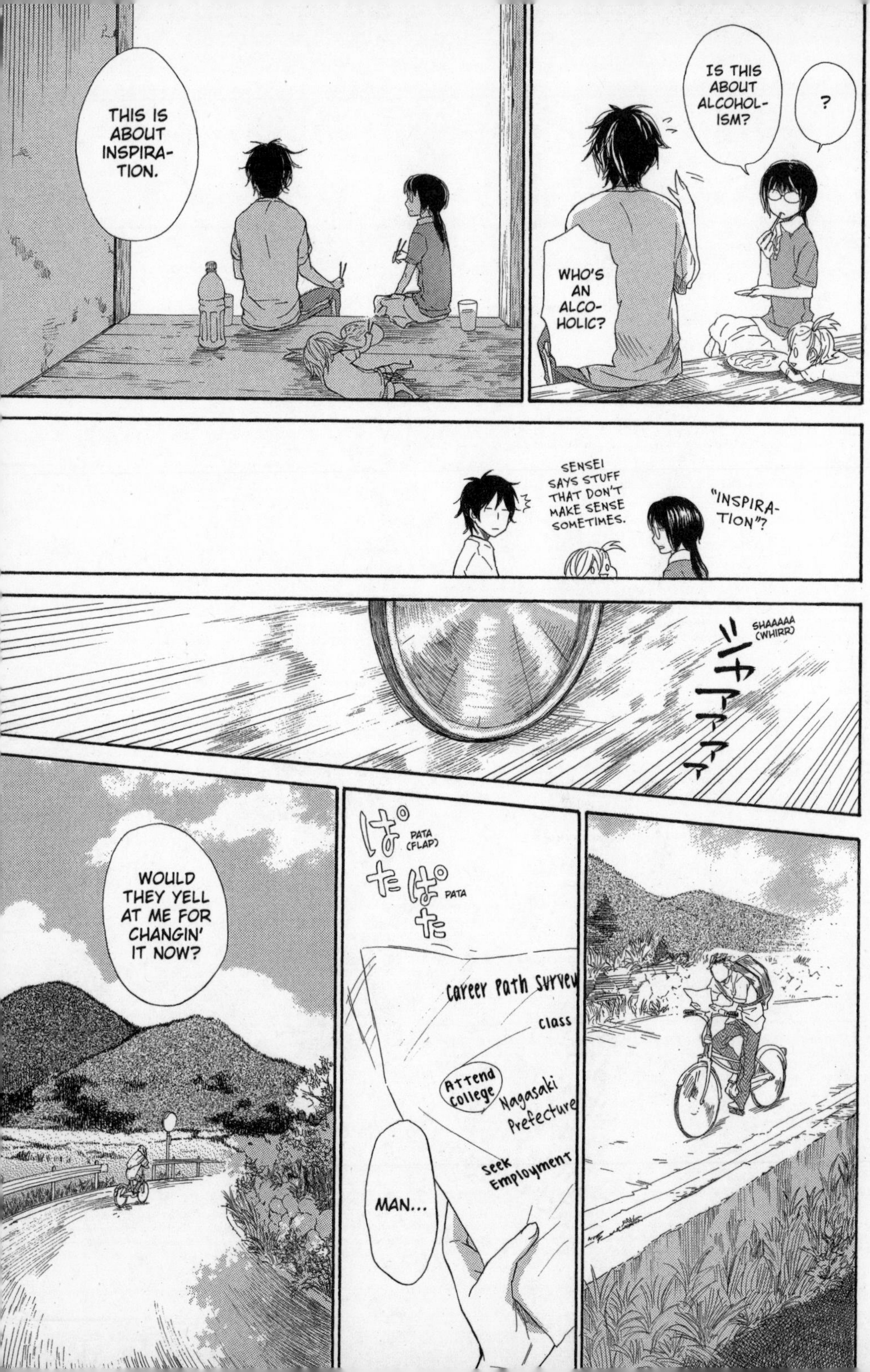
?
IS THIS ABOUT ALCOHOL-ISM?
WHO'S AN ALCO-HOLIC?
THIS IS ABOUT INSPIRA-TION.
"INSPIRA-TION"?
SENSEI SAYS STUFF THAT DON'T MAKE SENSE SOMETIMES.
シャアアアア
SHAAAAA (WHIRR)
ぱたぱた
PATA (FLAP) PATA
Career Path Survey
Class
Attend college
Nagasaki Prefecture
Seek Employment
MAN...
WOULD THEY YELL AT ME FOR CHANGIN' IT NOW?

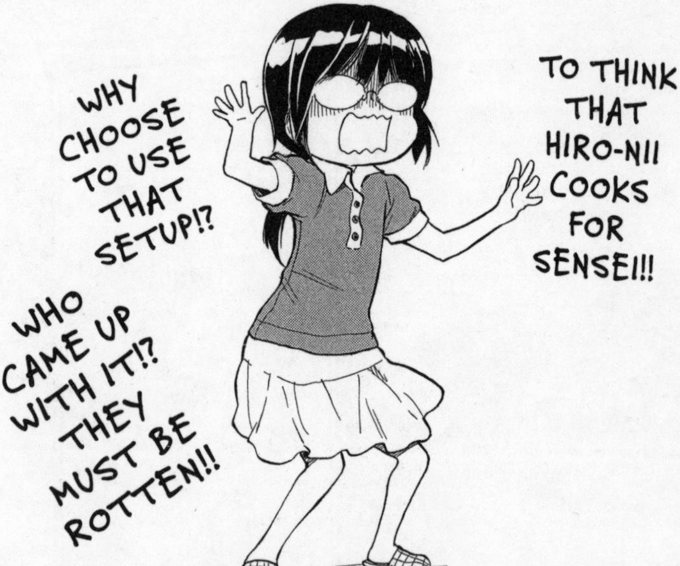
TO THINK THAT HIRO-NII COOKS FOR SENSEI!!
WHY CHOOSE TO USE THAT SETUP!?
WHO CAME UP WITH IT!? THEY MUST BE ROTTEN!!

ACT.29 ENBA

(Translation: Dragonfly)

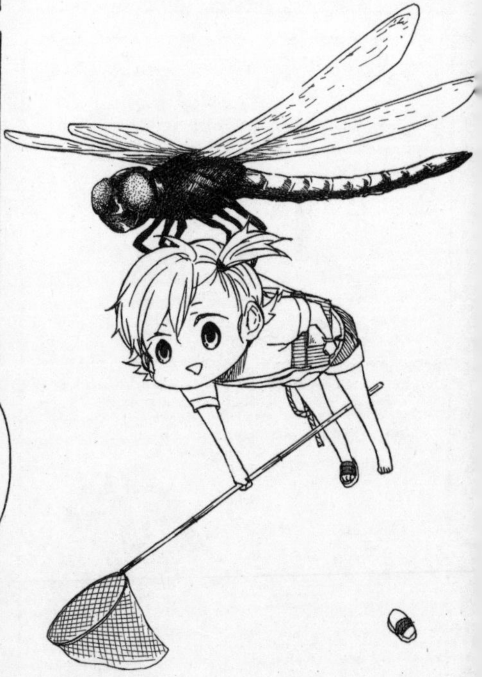

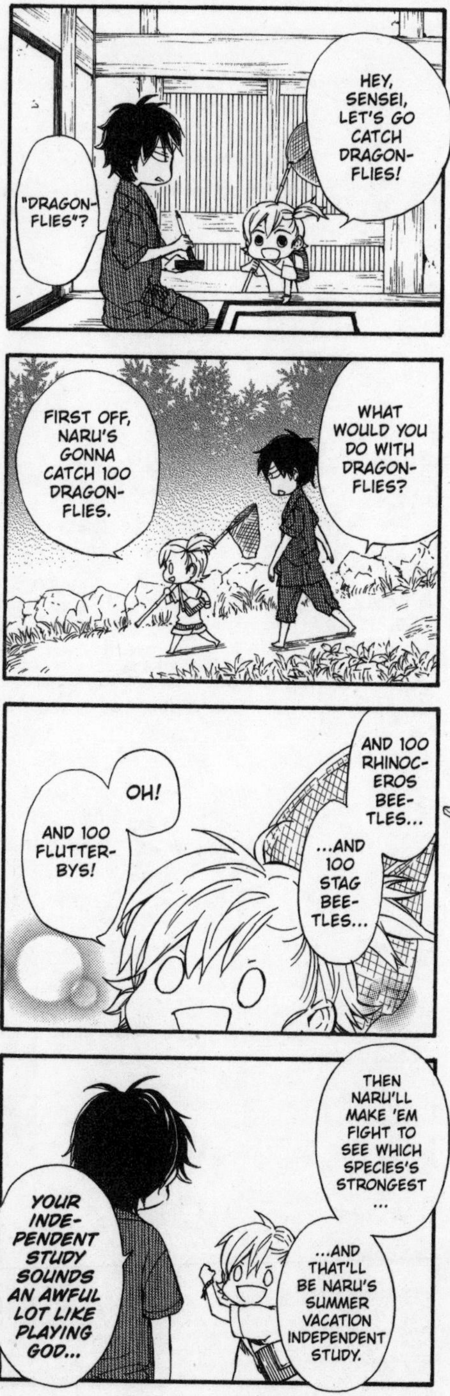

HEY, SENSEI, LET'S GO CATCH DRAGON-FLIES!
"DRAGON-FLIES"?
WHAT WOULD YOU DO WITH DRAGON-FLIES?
FIRST OFF, NARU'S GONNA CATCH 100 DRAGON-FLIES.
AND 100 RHINOC-EROS BEE-TLES...
...AND 100 STAG BEE-TLES...
OH!
AND 100 FLUTTER-BYS!
THEN NARU'LL MAKE 'EM FIGHT TO SEE WHICH SPECIES'S STRONGEST ...
...AND THAT'LL BE NARU'S SUMMER VACATION INDEPENDENT STUDY.
YOUR INDE-PENDENT STUDY SOUNDS AN AWFUL LOT LIKE PLAYING GOD...

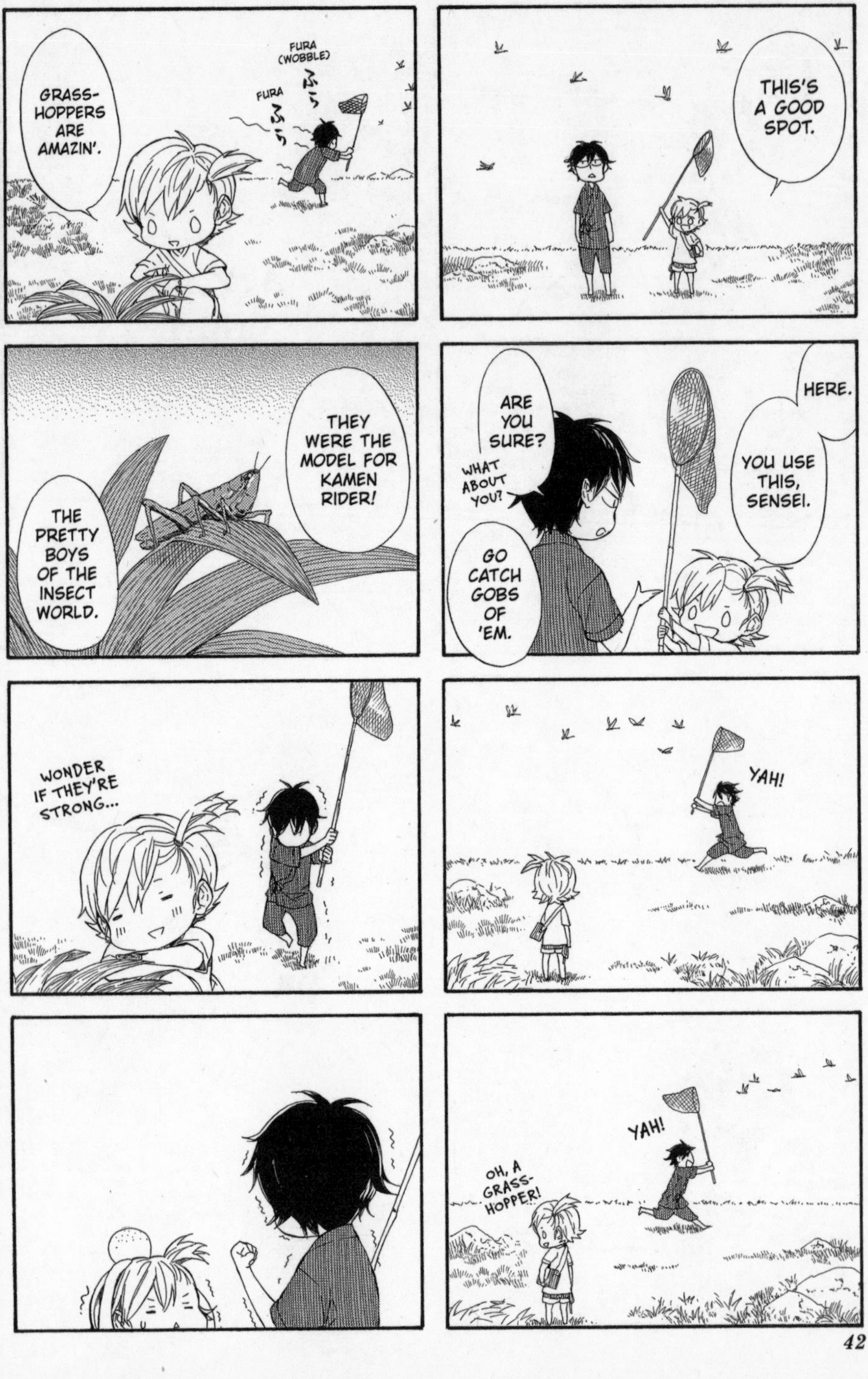
THIS'S A GOOD SPOT.
FURA (WOBBLE) ふら
FURA ふら
GRASS-HOPPERS ARE AMAZIN'.
HERE.
YOU USE THIS, SENSEI.
ARE YOU SURE?
WHAT ABOUT YOU?
GO CATCH GOBS OF 'EM.
THEY WERE THE MODEL FOR KAMEN RIDER!
THE PRETTY BOYS OF THE INSECT WORLD.
YAH!
WONDER IF THEY'RE STRONG...
YAH!
OH, A GRASS-HOPPER!

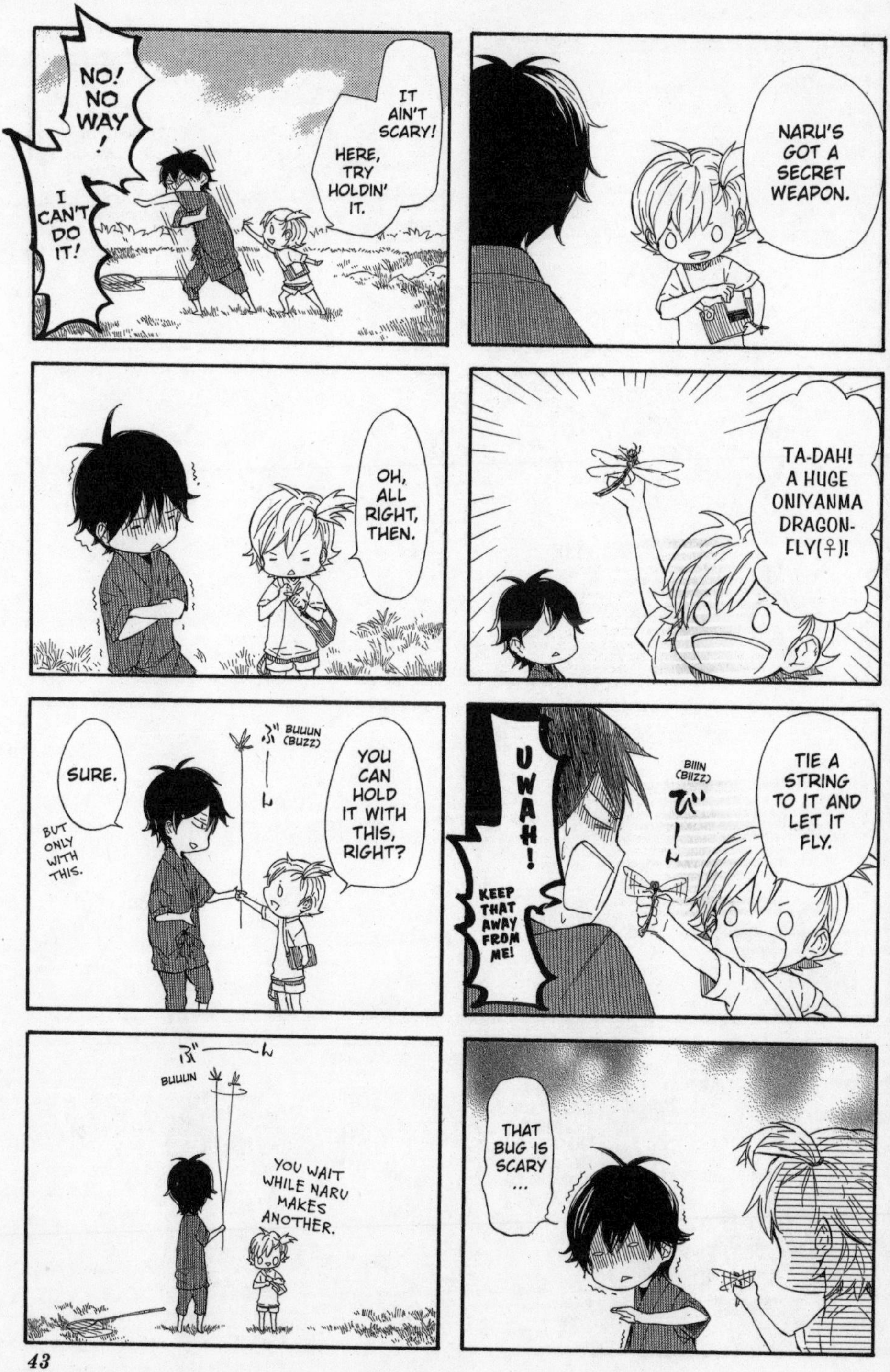
NARU'S GOT A SECRET WEAPON.
IT AIN'T SCARY!
HERE, TRY HOLDIN' IT.
NO! NO WAY!
I CAN'T DO IT!
TA-DAH! A HUGE ONIYANMA DRAGON-FLY(♀)!
OH, ALL RIGHT, THEN.
TIE A STRING TO IT AND LET IT FLY.
BIIN (BIIZZ)
びーん
UWAH!
KEEP THAT AWAY FROM ME!
YOU CAN HOLD IT WITH THIS, RIGHT?
BUUUN (BUZZ)
ぶーん
SURE.
BUT ONLY WITH THIS.
THAT BUG IS SCARY ...
ぶーん
BUUUN
YOU WAIT WHILE NARU MAKES ANOTHER.

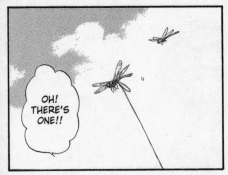

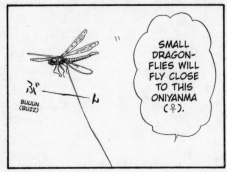

SMALL DRAGONFLIES WILL FLY CLOSE TO THIS ONIYANMA (♀).
ぶーーん
BUUUN (BUZZ)
OH! THERE'S ONE!!
ENBA HOHH!
BUUUN
ぶーーん
ENBA HOHH!
GUIIIN (TUG)
TAKE THAT!
PECHI (PLOP)
OOH!
ENBA HOHH!
NUUUB (ZZUB)
ENBA HOHH!
GURUUUN (SWING)
GOT ONE!
AMAZING! TO THINK YOU CAN CATCH THEM THAT EASILY.
WHAT'S "ENBA HO"?
ENBA HOHH!
EVEN IN THE INSECT WORLD, NONE CAN RESIST A WOMAN'S CHARMS.
YOU'RE ONLY SEVEN. DON'T SAY THAT.

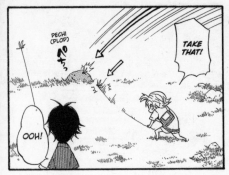

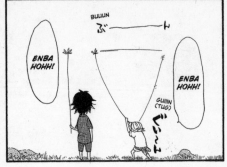

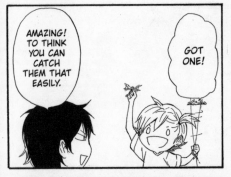

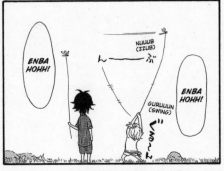

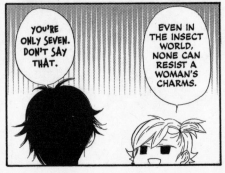

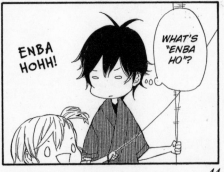

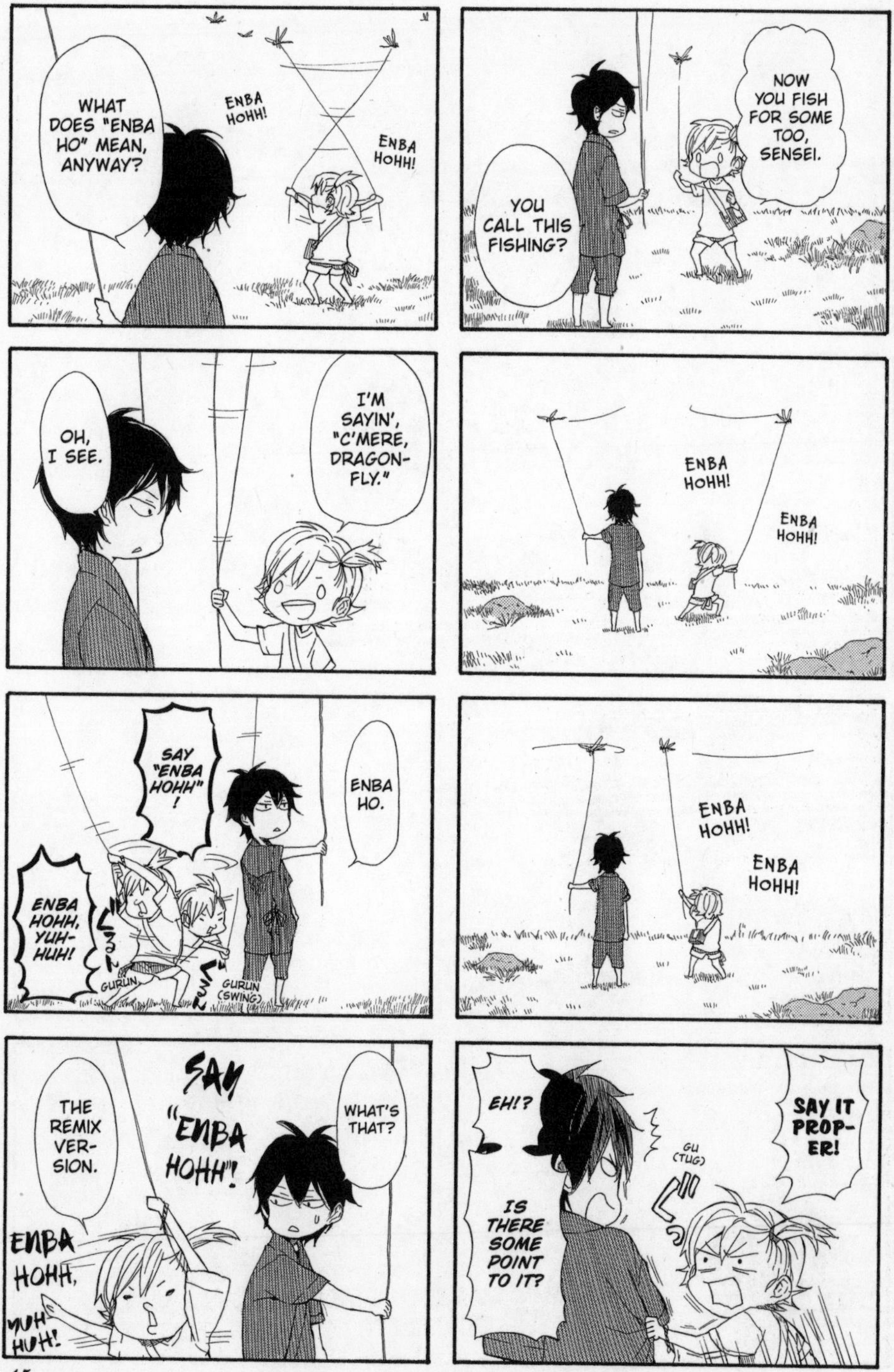
NOW YOU FISH FOR SOME TOO, SENSEI.
YOU CALL THIS FISHING?
ENBA HOHH!
ENBA HOHH!
WHAT DOES "ENBA HO" MEAN, ANYWAY?
ENBA HOHH!
ENBA HOHH!
I'M SAYIN', "C'MERE, DRAGON-FLY."
OH, I SEE.
ENBA HOHH!
ENBA HOHH!
ENBA HO.
SAY "ENBA HOHH"!
ENBA HOHH, YUH-HUH!
GURUN (SWING)
GURUN
SAY IT PROP-ER!
GU (TUG)
EH!?
IS THERE SOME POINT TO IT?
WHAT'S THAT?
SAY "ENBA HOHH"!
THE REMIX VER-SION.
ENBA HOHH, YUH HUH!

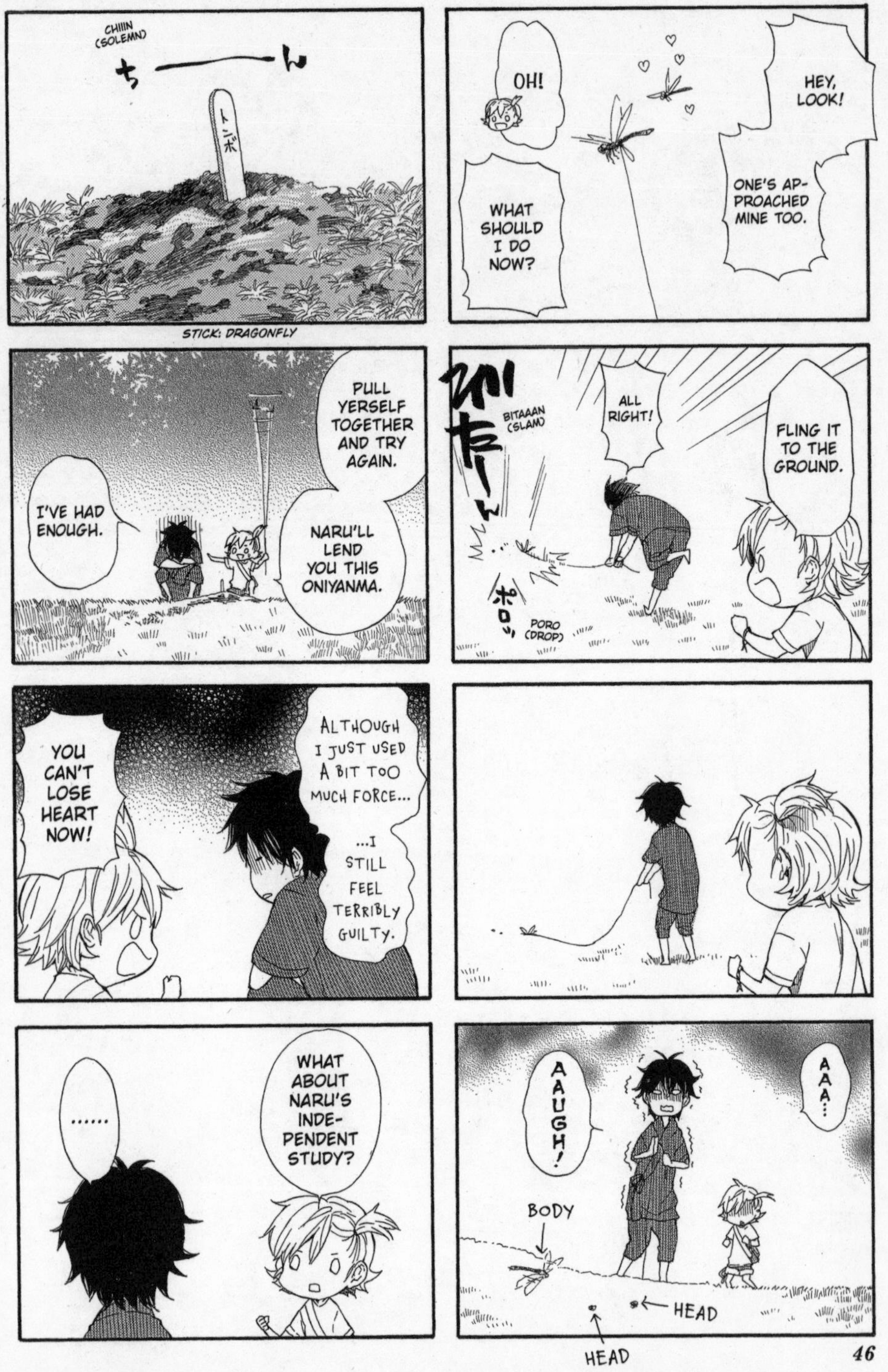
HEY, LOOK!
ONE'S AP-PROACHED MINE TOO.
OH!
WHAT SHOULD I DO NOW?
CHIIIN (SOLEMN)
ち——ん
トンボ
STICK: DRAGONFLY
FLING IT TO THE GROUND.
ALL RIGHT!
BITAAAN (SLAM)
PORO (DROP)
PULL YERSELF TOGETHER AND TRY AGAIN.
NARU'LL LEND YOU THIS ONIYANMA.
I'VE HAD ENOUGH.
ALTHOUGH I JUST USED A BIT TOO MUCH FORCE...
...I STILL FEEL TERRIBLY GUILTY.
YOU CAN'T LOSE HEART NOW!
AAA...
AAUGH!
BODY
HEAD
HEAD
WHAT ABOUT NARU'S INDE-PENDENT STUDY?
......

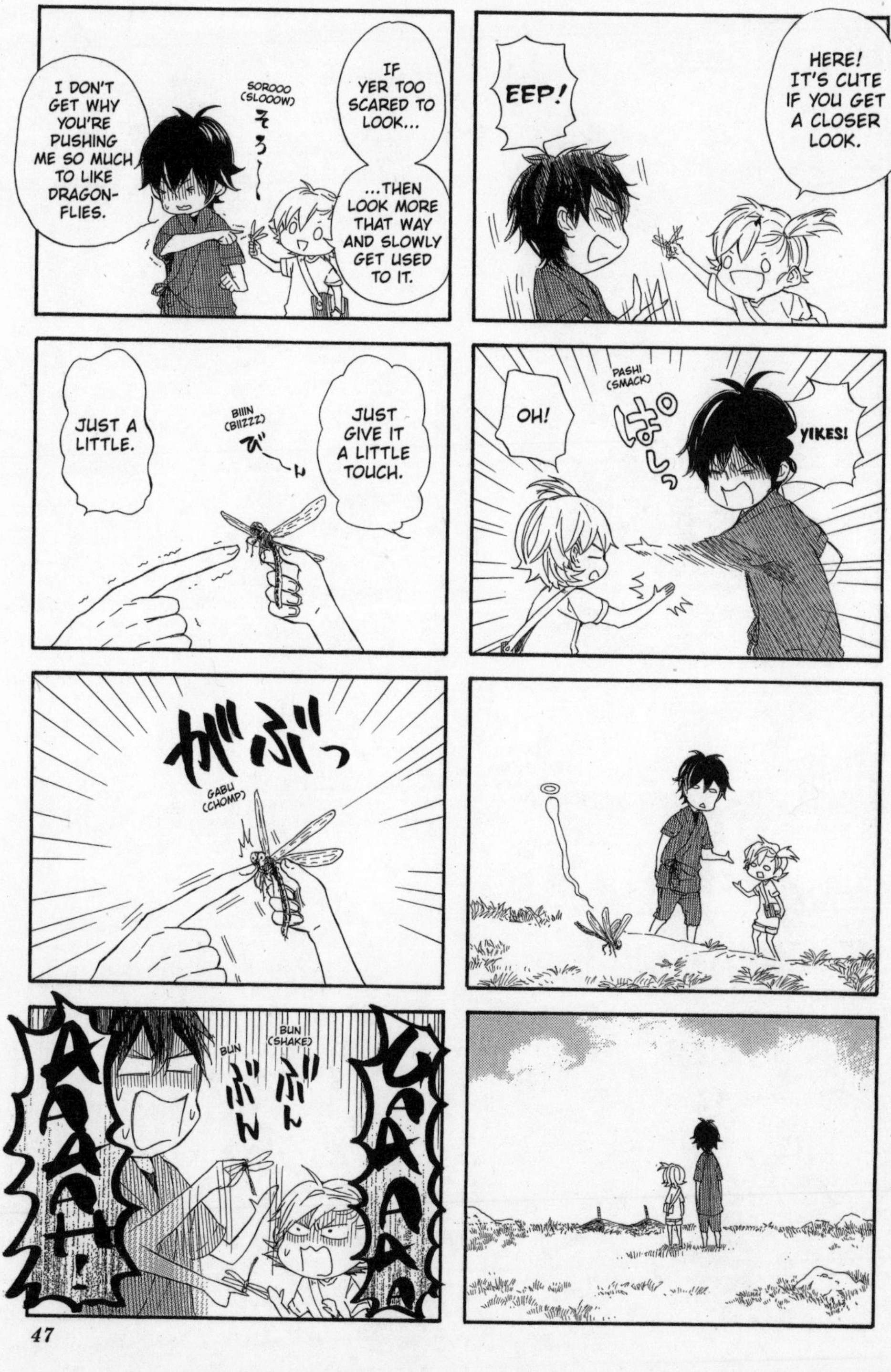
HERE! IT'S CUTE IF YOU GET A CLOSER LOOK.
EEP!
IF YER TOO SCARED TO LOOK...
...THEN LOOK MORE THAT WAY AND SLOWLY GET USED TO IT.
SOROOO (SLOOOW)
そろ〜
I DON'T GET WHY YOU'RE PUSHING ME SO MUCH TO LIKE DRAGON-FLIES.
YIKES!
PASHI (SMACK)
ぱしっ
OH!
JUST GIVE IT A LITTLE TOUCH.
BIIN (BIIZZZ)
び〜ん
JUST A LITTLE.
がぶっ
GABU (CHOMP)
UAAAA!
BUN (SHAKE)
ぶん
BUN
ぶん
AAAAH!

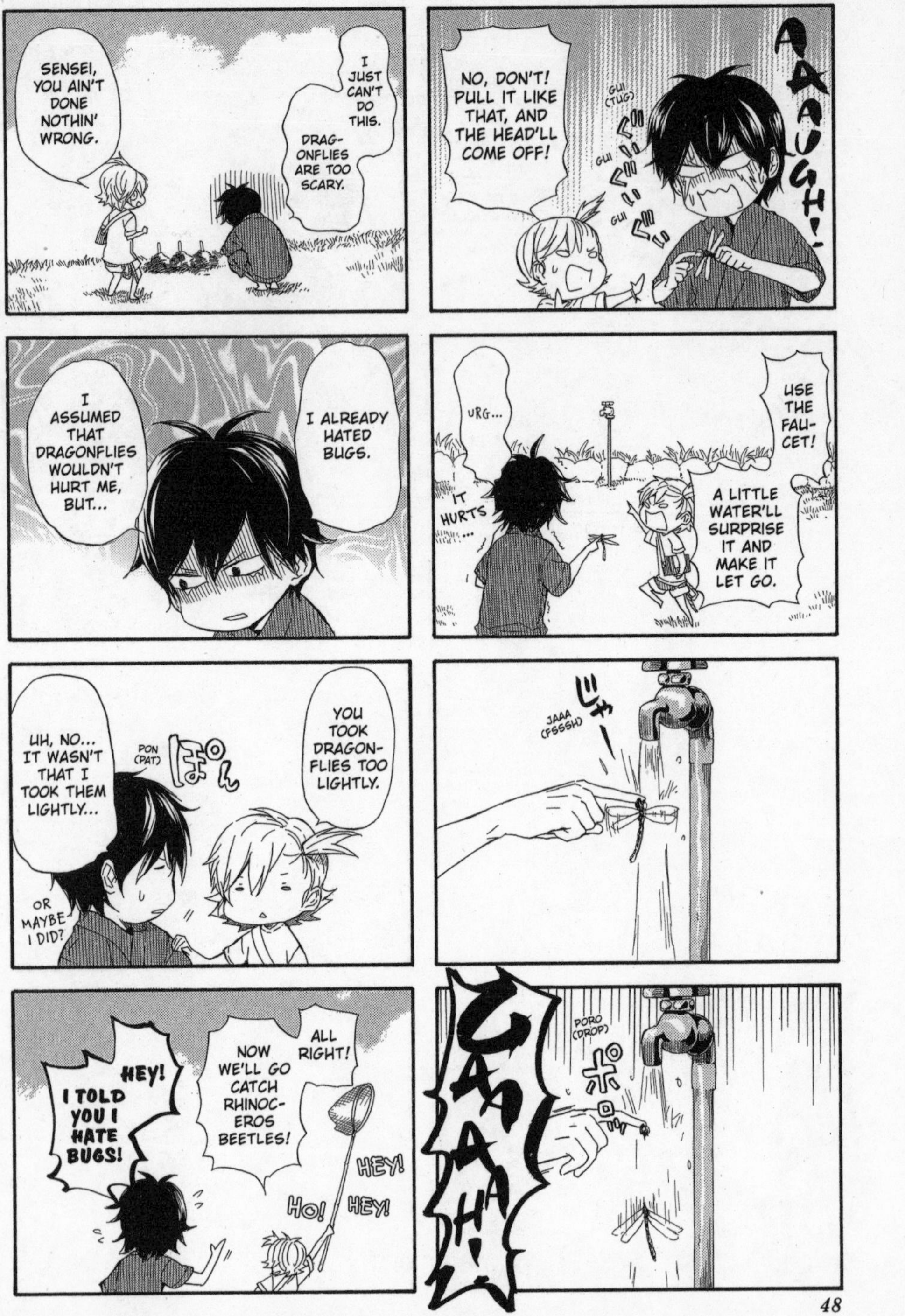
AAAUGH!
NO, DON'T! PULL IT LIKE THAT, AND THE HEAD'LL COME OFF!
GUI (TUG)
GUI
GUI
I JUST CAN'T DO THIS.
DRAGONFLIES ARE TOO SCARY.
SENSEI, YOU AIN'T DONE NOTHIN' WRONG.
USE THE FAUCET!
A LITTLE WATER'LL SURPRISE IT AND MAKE IT LET GO.
URG...
I IT HURTS...
I ALREADY HATED BUGS.
I ASSUMED THAT DRAGONFLIES WOULDN'T HURT ME, BUT...
JAAA (FSSSH)
YOU TOOK DRAGONFLIES TOO LIGHTLY.
PON (PAT)
UH, NO... IT WASN'T THAT I TOOK THEM LIGHTLY...
OR MAYBE I DID?
PORO (DROP)
AAAH!
ALL RIGHT!
NOW WE'LL GO CATCH RHINOCEROS BEETLES!
HEY!
HEY!
HO!
HEY! I TOLD YOU I HATE BUGS!

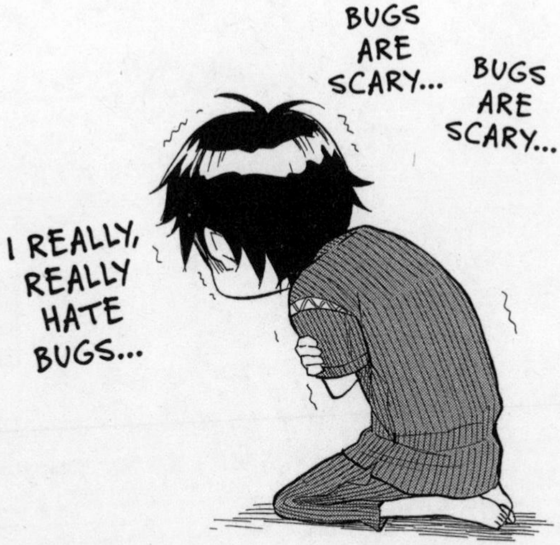
BUGS ARE SCARY...
BUGS ARE SCARY...
I REALLY, REALLY HATE BUGS...

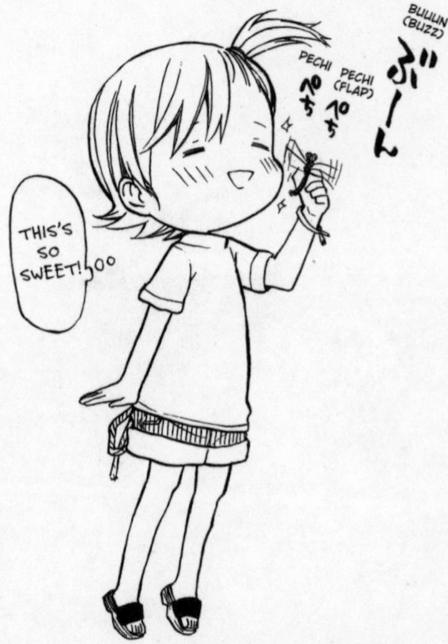
BUUUN (BUZZ)
ぶーん
PECHI PECHI (FLAP)
ぺちぺち
THIS'S SO SWEET!

ACT.30
KAGYA...?
(Translation: The Key Is...?)

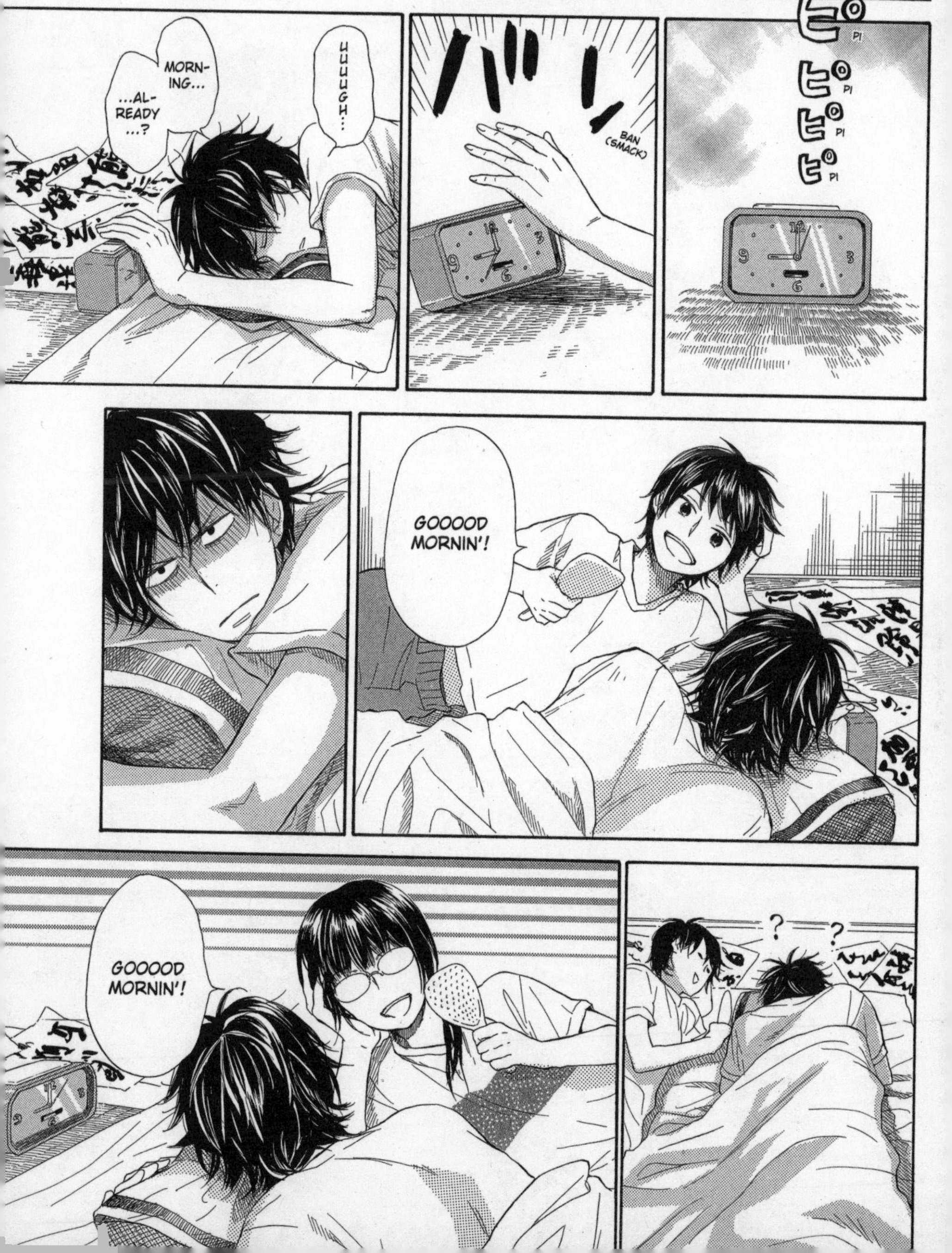
PI (BEEP)
PI
PI
PI
PI
PI
BAN (SMACK)
UUUUGH...
MORNING... ...ALREADY...?
GOOOOD MORNIN'!
? ?
GOOOOD MORNIN'!

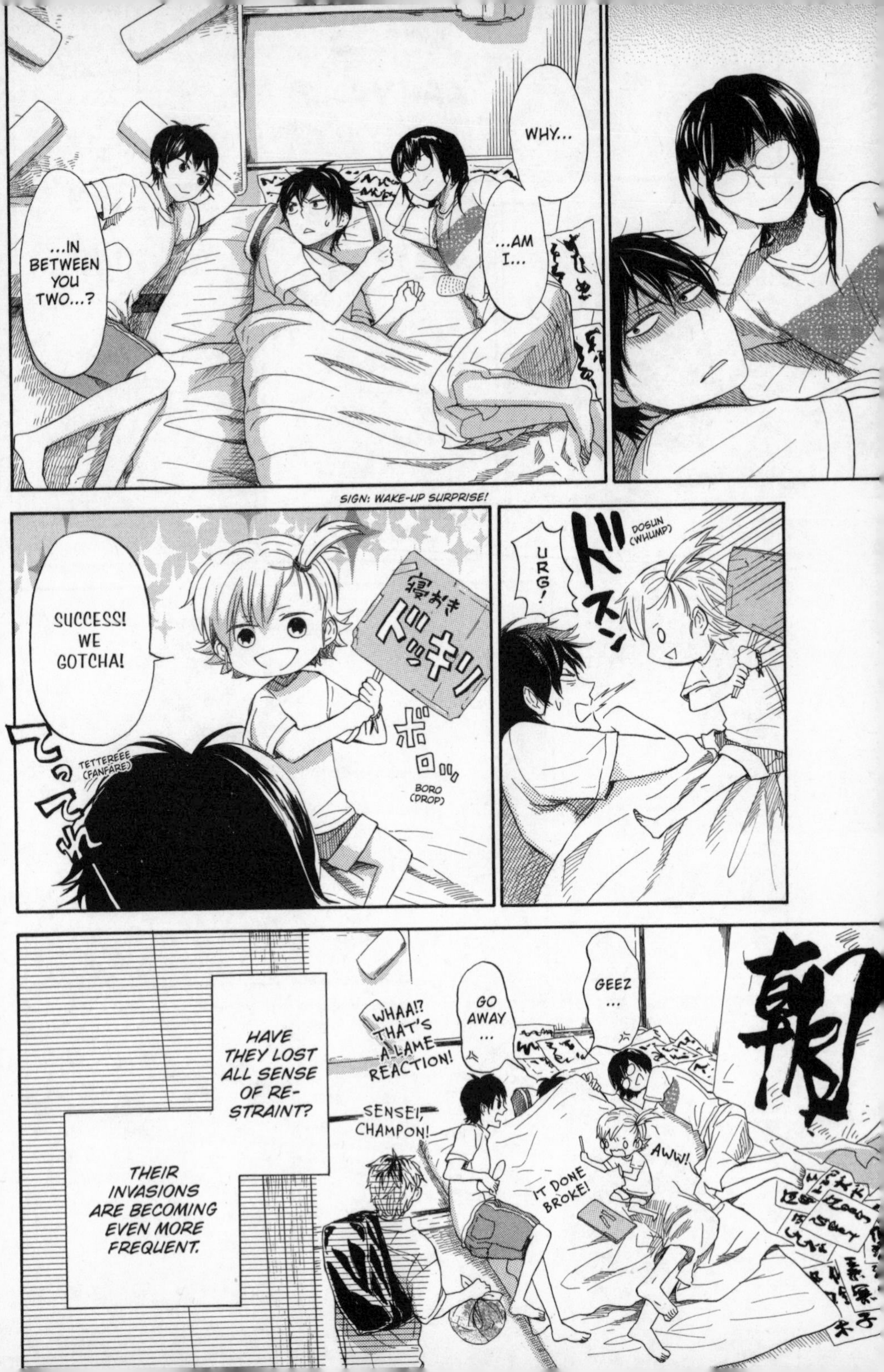
WHY...
...AM I...
...IN BETWEEN YOU TWO...?
SIGN: WAKE-UP SURPRISE!
ドスン
DOSUN (WHUMP)
URG!
寝おき ドッキリ
SUCCESS! WE GOTCHA!
TETTEREEE (FANFARE)
ボロッ
BORO (DROP)
GEEZ...
GO AWAY...
WHAA!? THAT'S A LAME REACTION!
HAVE THEY LOST ALL SENSE OF RE-STRAINT?
SENSEI, CHAMPON!
AWW!
IT DONE BROKE!
THEIR INVASIONS ARE BECOMING EVEN MORE FREQUENT.

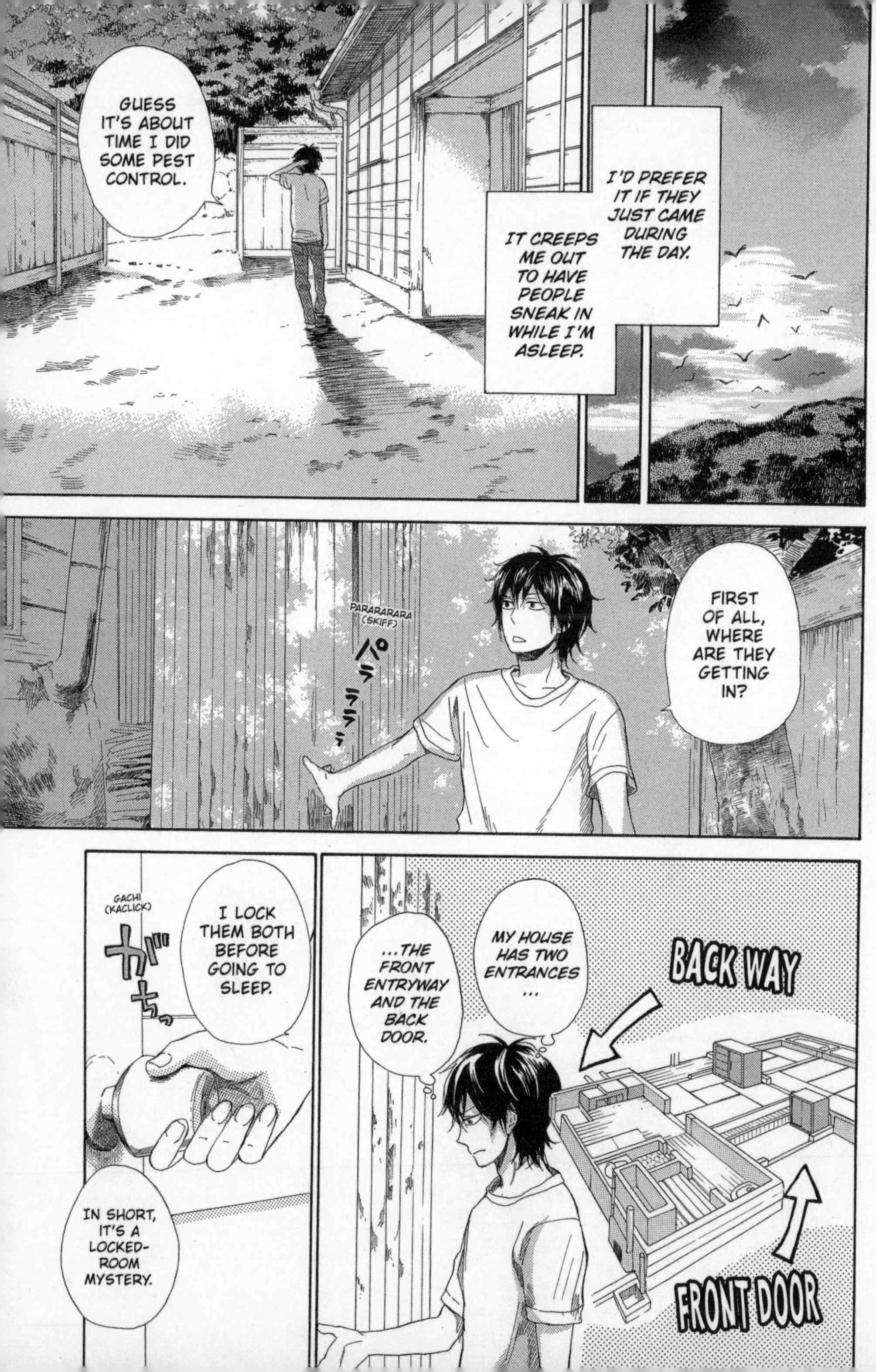
I'D PREFER IT IF THEY JUST CAME DURING THE DAY.
IT CREEPS ME OUT TO HAVE PEOPLE SNEAK IN WHILE I'M ASLEEP.
GUESS IT'S ABOUT TIME I DID SOME PEST CONTROL.
FIRST OF ALL, WHERE ARE THEY GETTING IN?
PARARARARA (SKIFF)
パラララ
BACK WAY
MY HOUSE HAS TWO ENTRANCES...
...THE FRONT ENTRYWAY AND THE BACK DOOR.
FRONT DOOR
I LOCK THEM BOTH BEFORE GOING TO SLEEP.
GACHI (KACLICK)
がちゃ
IN SHORT, IT'S A LOCKED-ROOM MYSTERY.

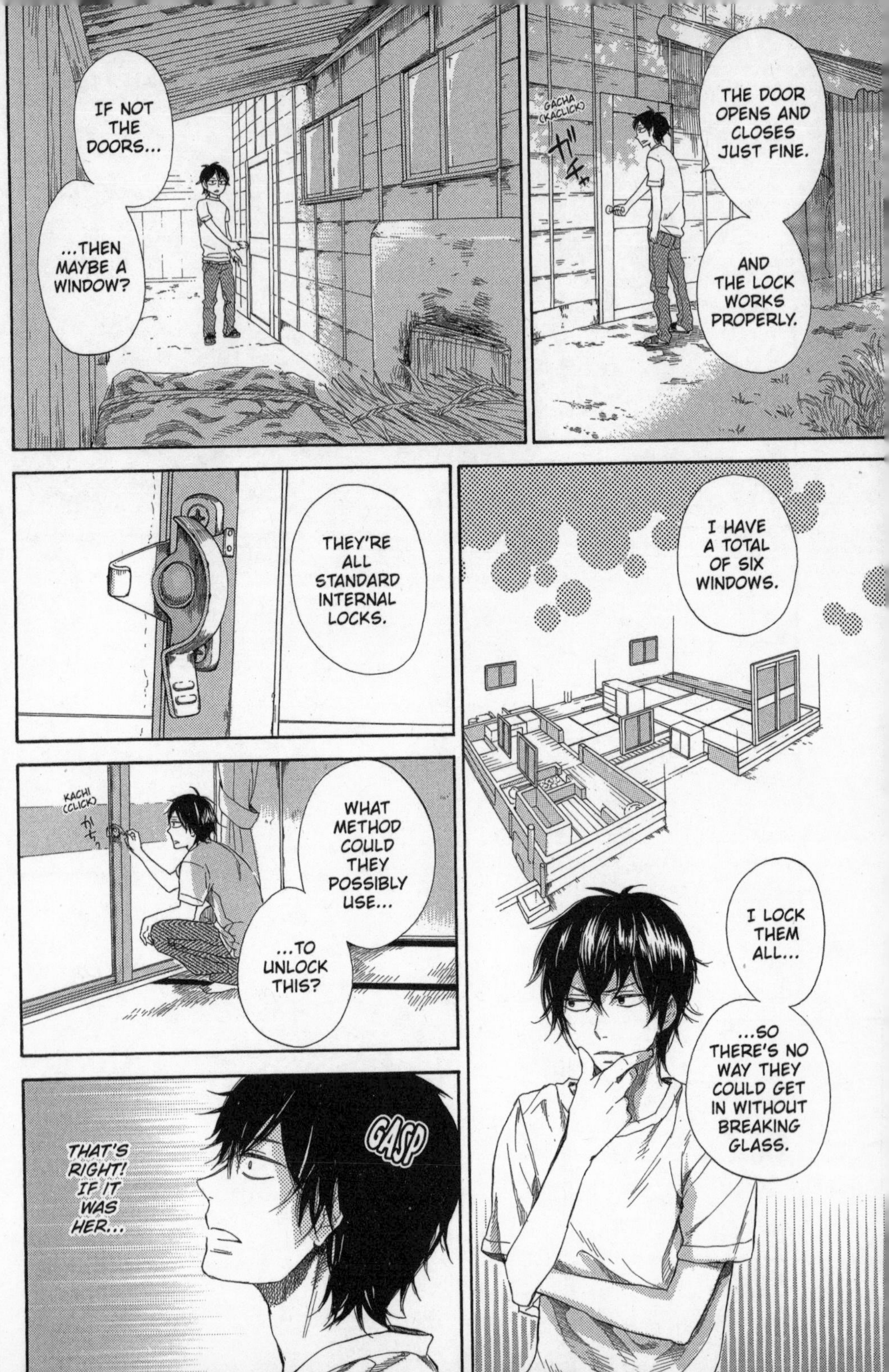
GACHA (KACLICK)
ガチャ
THE DOOR OPENS AND CLOSES JUST FINE.
AND THE LOCK WORKS PROPERLY.
IF NOT THE DOORS...
...THEN MAYBE A WINDOW?
I HAVE A TOTAL OF SIX WINDOWS.
THEY'RE ALL STANDARD INTERNAL LOCKS.
KACHI (CLICK)
カチッ
WHAT METHOD COULD THEY POSSIBLY USE...
...TO UNLOCK THIS?
I LOCK THEM ALL...
...SO THERE'S NO WAY THEY COULD GET IN WITHOUT BREAKING GLASS.
GASP
THAT'S RIGHT! IF IT WAS HER...

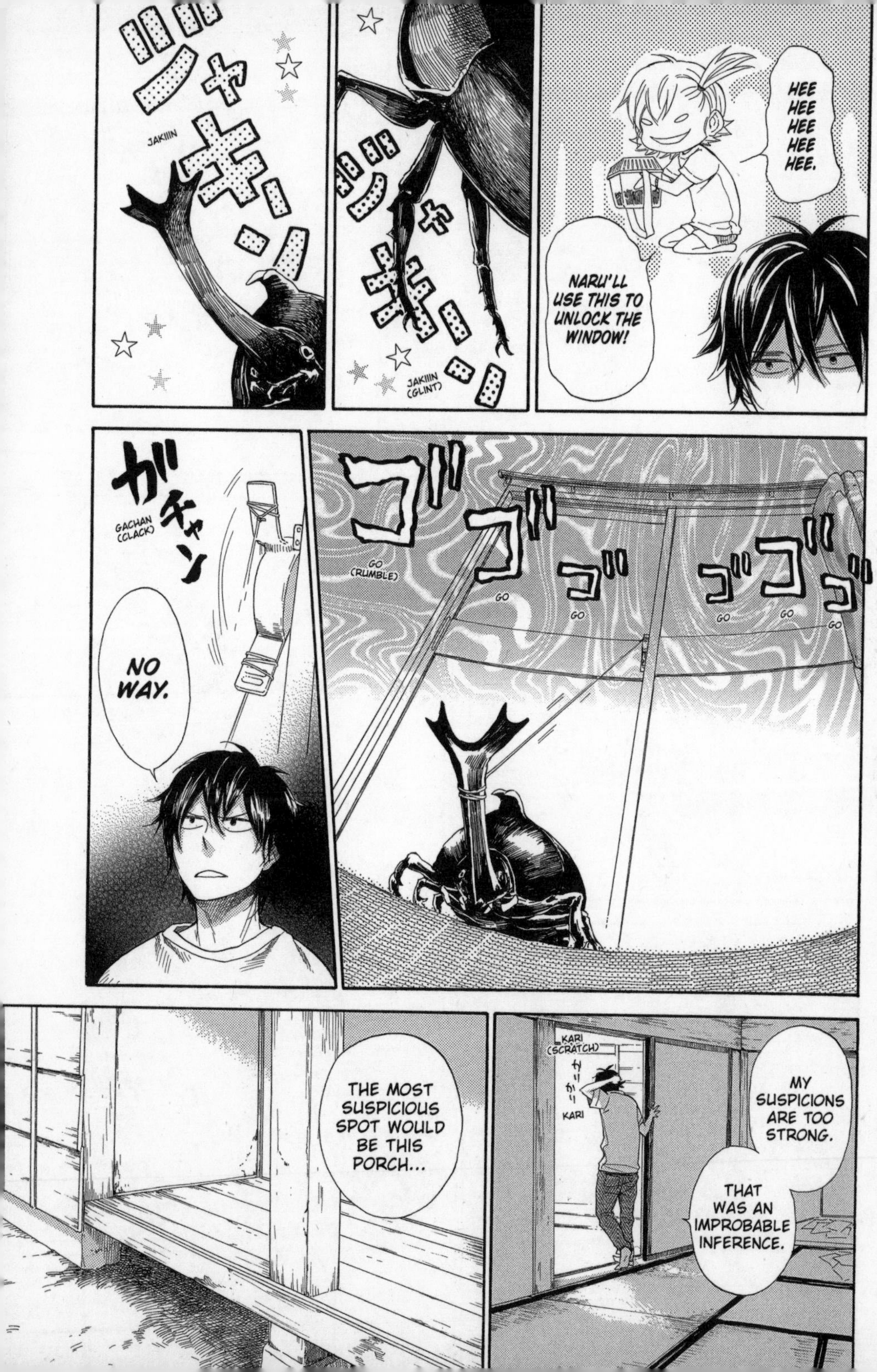
HEE HEE HEE HEE HEE.
NARU'LL USE THIS TO UNLOCK THE WINDOW!
ジャキーン
JAKIIIN (GLINT)
ジャキーン
JAKIIIN
ゴゴゴゴゴゴ
GO (RUMBLE)
GO
GO
GO
GO
GO
ガチャン
GACHAN (CLACK)
NO WAY.
KARI (SCRATCH)
かりかり
KARI
MY SUSPICIONS ARE TOO STRONG.
THAT WAS AN IMPROBABLE INFERENCE.
THE MOST SUSPICIOUS SPOT WOULD BE THIS PORCH...

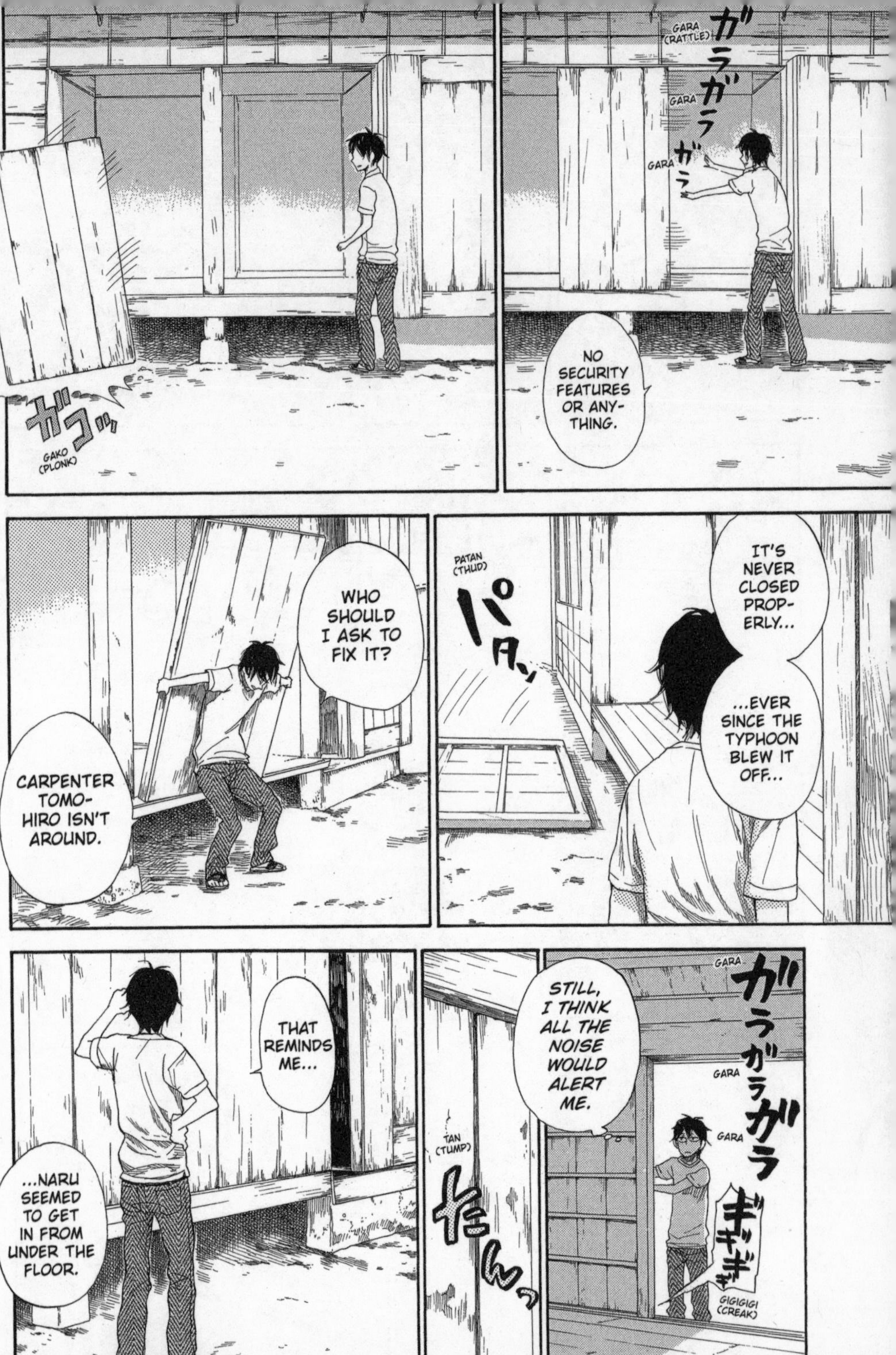
ガラ GARA (RATTLE)
ガラ GARA
ガラ GARA
NO SECURITY FEATURES OR ANYTHING.
ガコッ GAKO (PLONK)
IT'S NEVER CLOSED PROPERLY...
...EVER SINCE THE TYPHOON BLEW IT OFF...
パタッ PATAN (THUD)
WHO SHOULD I ASK TO FIX IT?
CARPENTER TOMOHIRO ISN'T AROUND.
ガラ GARA
ガラ GARA
ガラ GARA
STILL, I THINK ALL THE NOISE WOULD ALERT ME.
ギギギ GIGIGIGI (CREAK)
たんっ TAN (TUMP)
THAT REMINDS ME...
...NARU SEEMED TO GET IN FROM UNDER THE FLOOR.

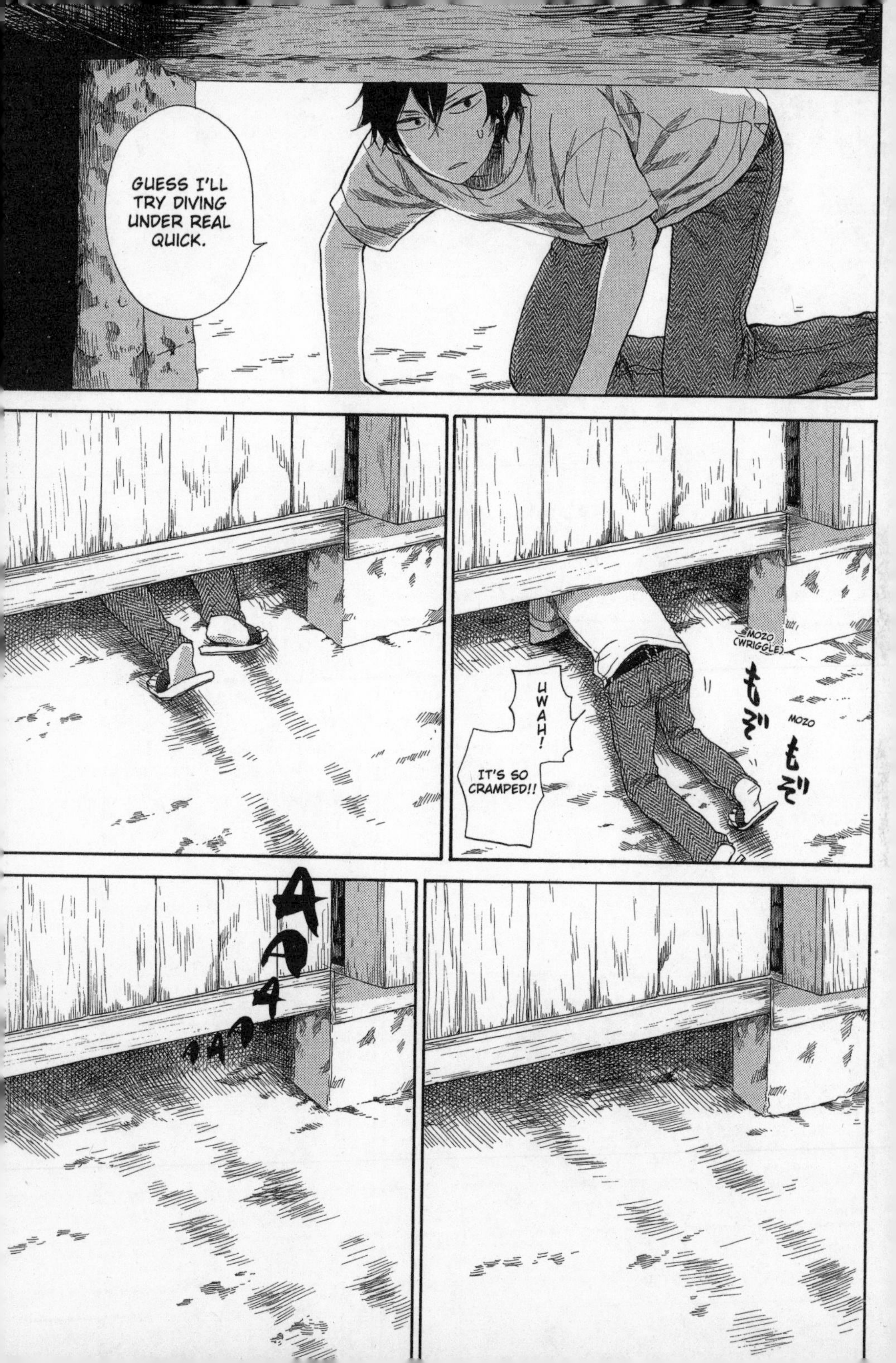
GUESS I'LL TRY DIVING UNDER REAL QUICK.
MOZO (WRIGGLE)
もぞ
MOZO
もぞ
UWAH!
IT'S SO CRAMPED!!

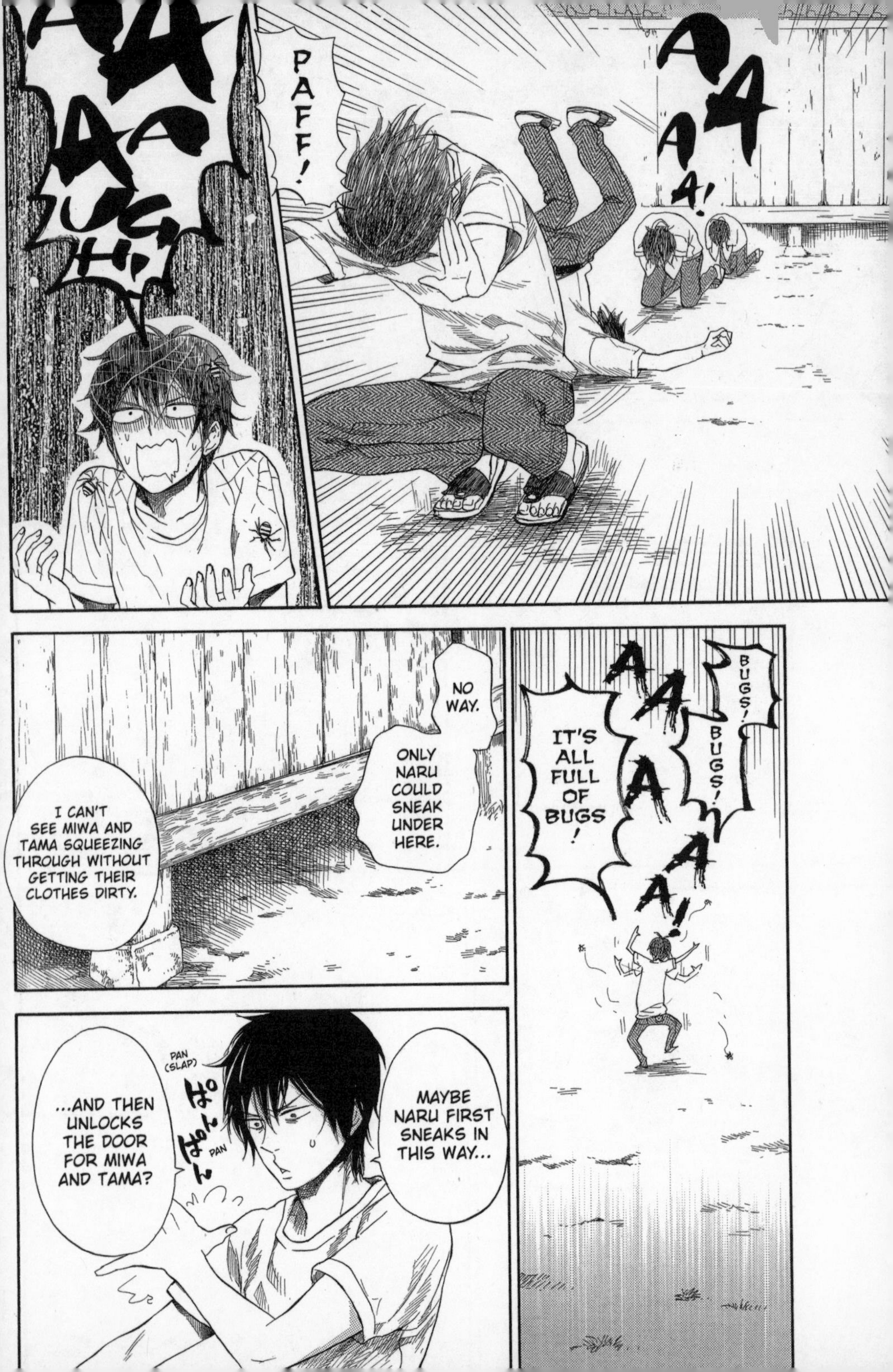
AAAA!
PAFF!
AAAAUGHH!
BUGS! BUGS!
AAAAA!
IT'S ALL FULL OF BUGS!
NO WAY.
ONLY NARU COULD SNEAK UNDER HERE.
I CAN'T SEE MIWA AND TAMA SQUEEZING THROUGH WITHOUT GETTING THEIR CLOTHES DIRTY.
MAYBE NARU FIRST SNEAKS IN THIS WAY...
PAN (SLAP)
ぱんぱん
PAN
...AND THEN UNLOCKS THE DOOR FOR MIWA AND TAMA?

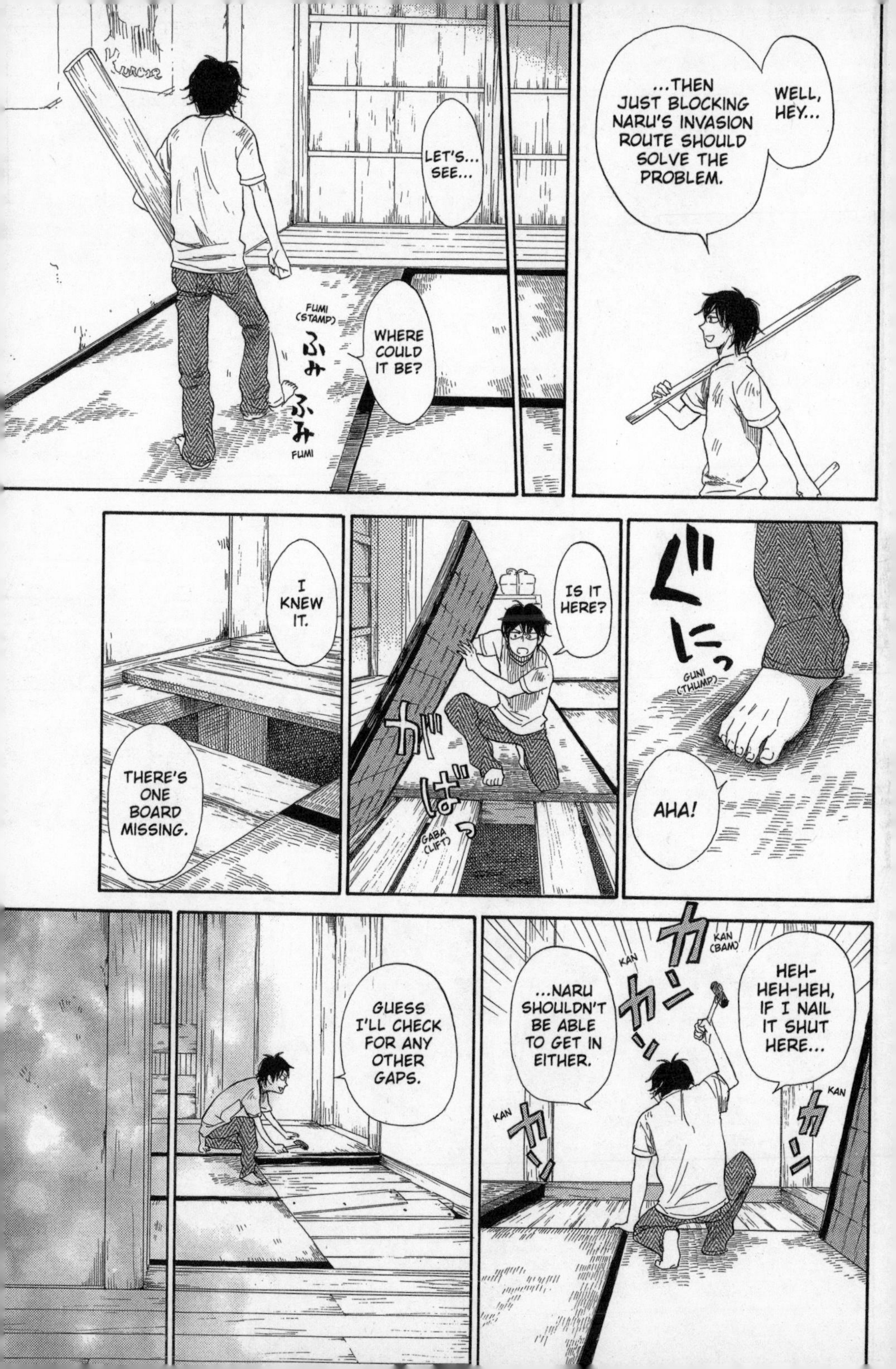
WELL, HEY...
...THEN JUST BLOCKING NARU'S INVASION ROUTE SHOULD SOLVE THE PROBLEM.
LET'S... SEE...
WHERE COULD IT BE?
FUMI (STAMP)
ふみ
ふみ
FUMI
ぐにっ
GUNI (THUMP)
AHA!
IS IT HERE?
がばっ
GABA (LIFT)
I KNEW IT.
THERE'S ONE BOARD MISSING.
カン
KAN (BAM)
HEH-HEH-HEH, IF I NAIL IT SHUT HERE...
KAN
カン
...NARU SHOULDN'T BE ABLE TO GET IN EITHER.
KAN
カン
KAN
カン
GUESS I'LL CHECK FOR ANY OTHER GAPS.

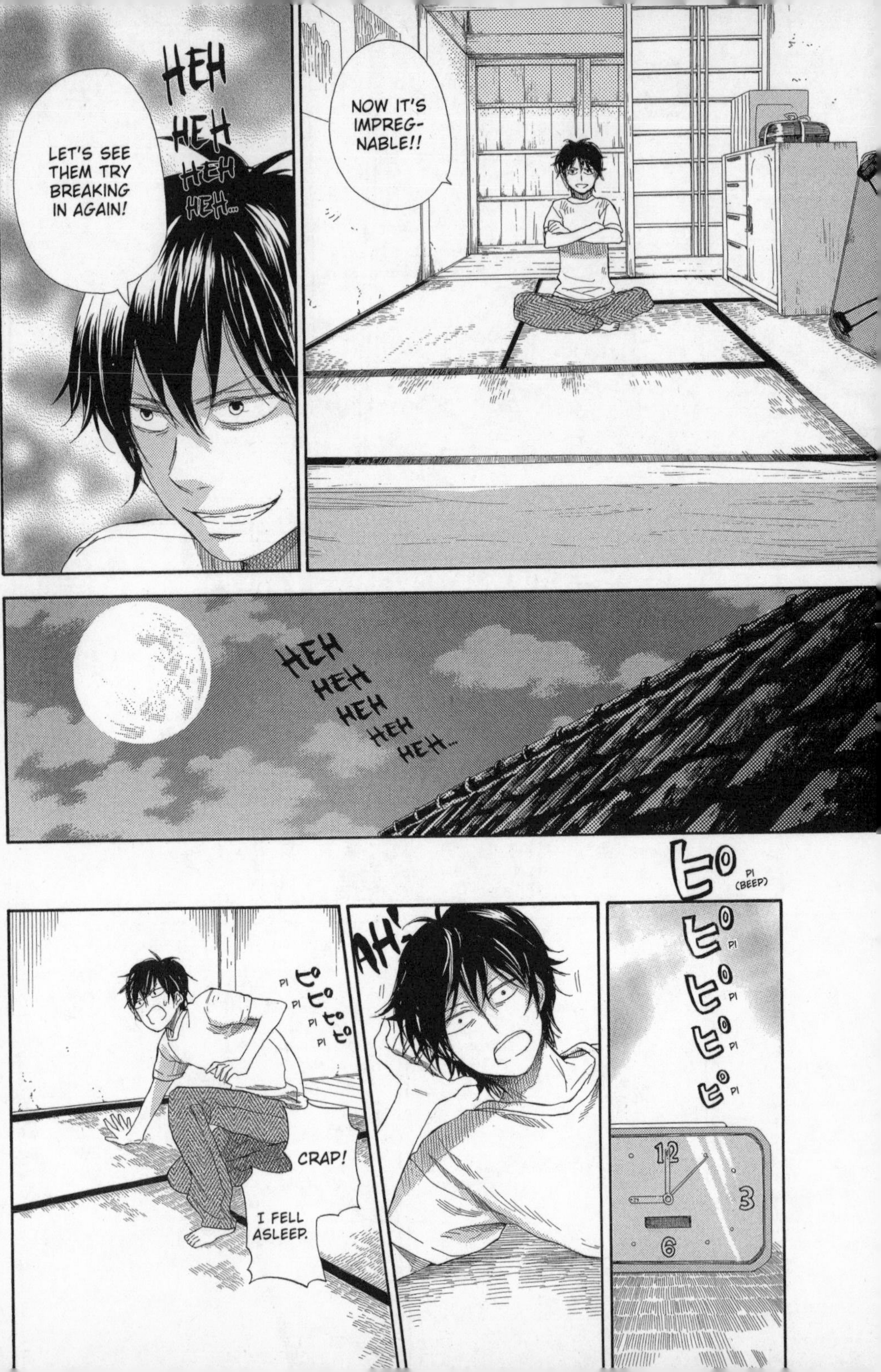
NOW IT'S IMPREGNABLE!!
HEH HEH HEH HEH...
LET'S SEE THEM TRY BREAKING IN AGAIN!
HEH HEH HEH HEH HEH...
ピ PI (BEEP)
ピ PI
ピ PI
ピ PI
ピ PI
AH!
ピピピピ PI PI PI PI
CRAP!
I FELL ASLEEP.

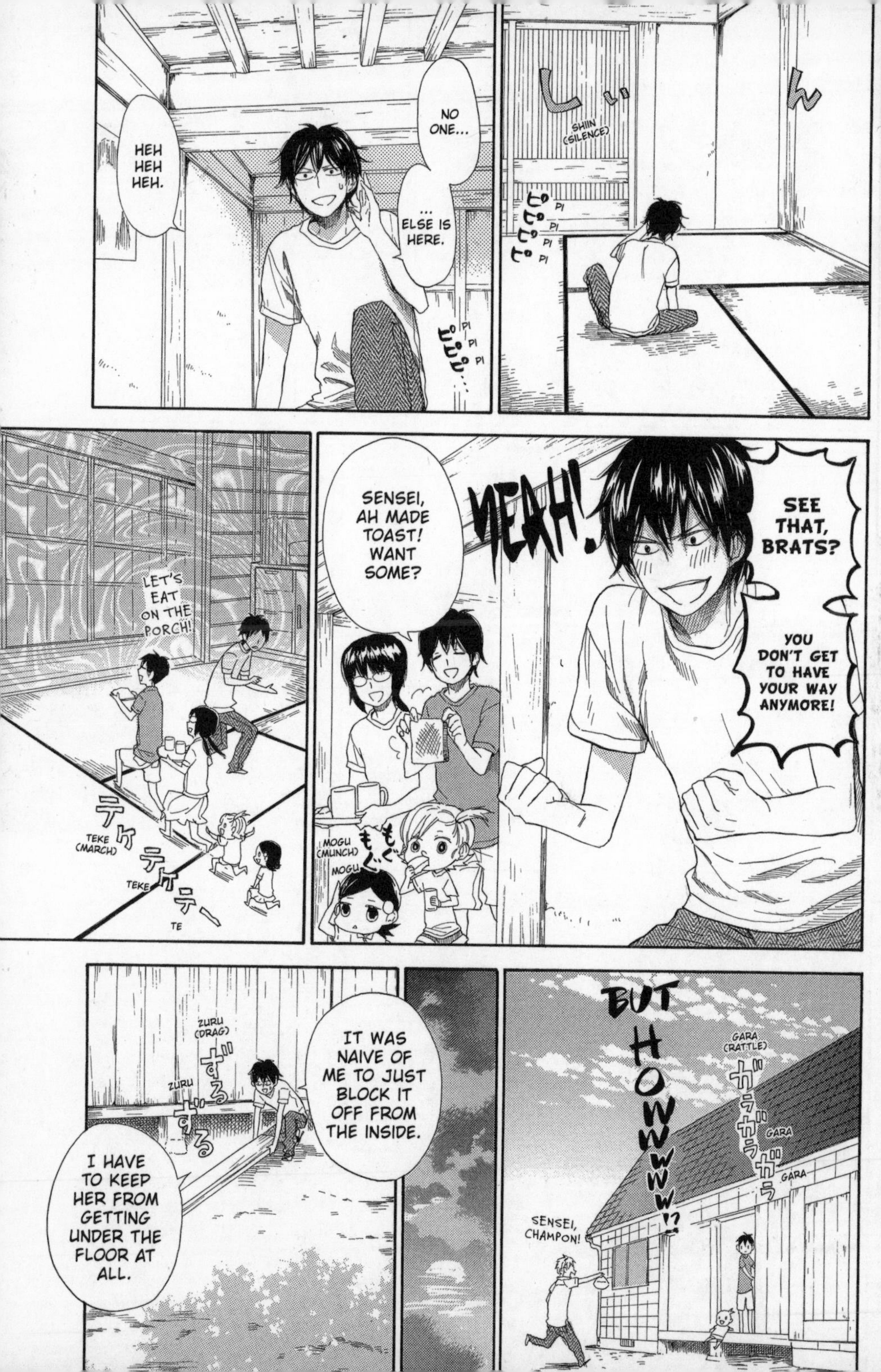
しいん
SHIIN (SILENCE)
ピピピピ
PI PI PI PI
NO ONE...
...ELSE IS HERE.
HEH HEH HEH.
ピピピ…
PI PI PI
SEE THAT, BRATS?
YOU DON'T GET TO HAVE YOUR WAY ANYMORE!
YEAH!
SENSEI, AH MADE TOAST! WANT SOME?
もぐもぐ
MOGU (MUNCH) MOGU
LET'S EAT ON THE PORCH!
テケテケテ～
TEKE (MARCH) TEKE TE
BUT HOWWWWW!?
ガラガラガラ
GARA (RATTLE) GARA GARA
SENSEI, CHAMPON!
IT WAS NAIVE OF ME TO JUST BLOCK IT OFF FROM THE INSIDE.
I HAVE TO KEEP HER FROM GETTING UNDER THE FLOOR AT ALL.
ずるずる
ZURU (DRAG) ZURU

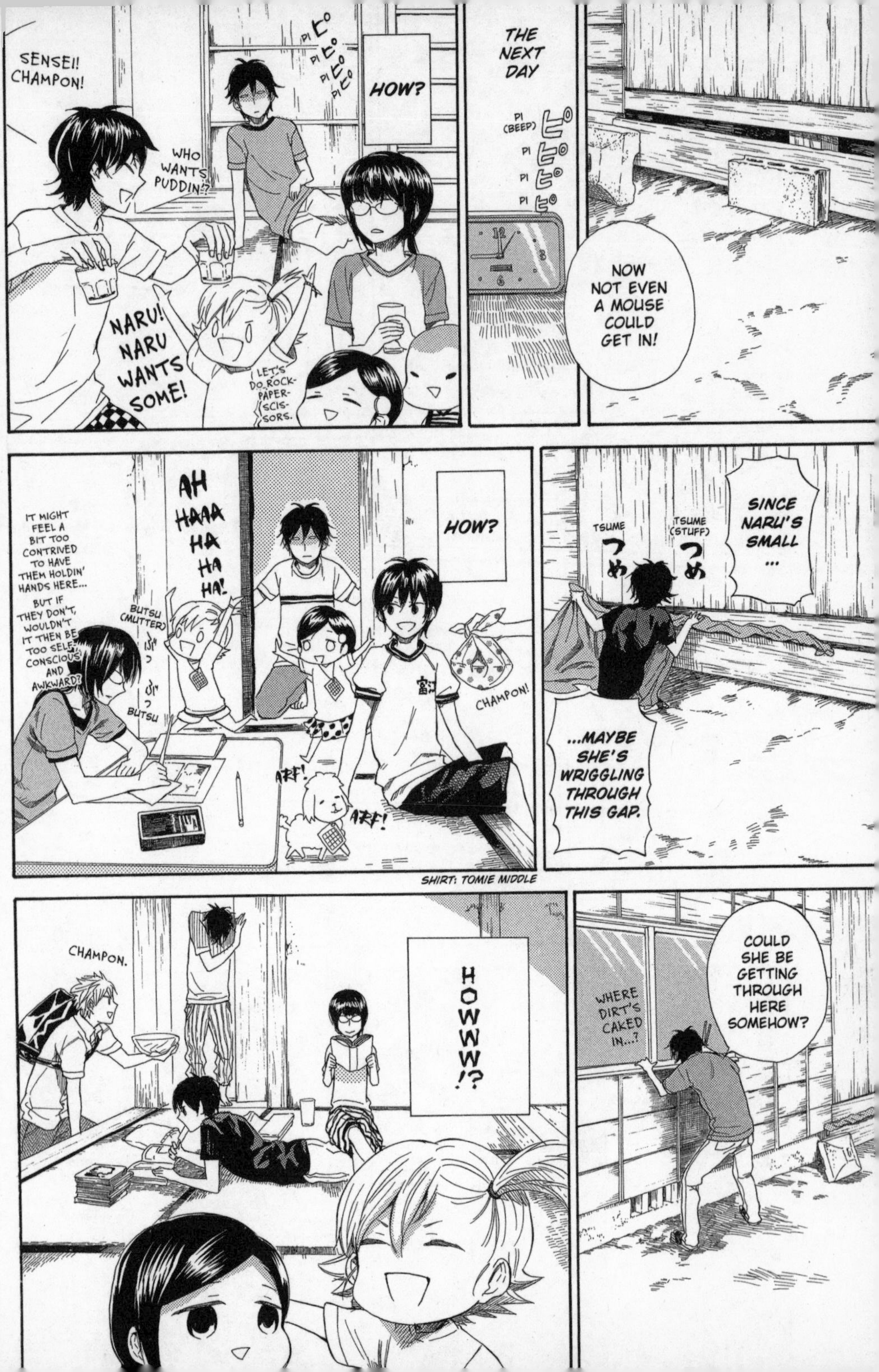
NOW NOT EVEN A MOUSE COULD GET IN!
THE NEXT DAY
PI (BEEP) PI PI PI
ピピピピ
HOW?
PI PI PI PI
WHO WANTS PUDDIN'?
SENSEI! CHAMPON!
LET'S DO ROCK-PAPER-SCISSORS.
NARU! NARU WANTS SOME!
SINCE NARU'S SMALL...
TSUME (STUFF) TSUME
つめつめ
...MAYBE SHE'S WRIGGLING THROUGH THIS GAP.
HOW?
CHAMPON!
AH HAAA HA HA HA!
BUTSU (MUTTER) BUTSU
IT MIGHT FEEL A BIT TOO CONTRIVED TO HAVE THEM HOLDIN' HANDS HERE... BUT IF THEY DON'T, WOULDN'T IT THEN BE TOO SELF-CONSCIOUS AND AWKWARD?
ARF! ARF!
SHIRT: TOMIE MIDDLE
COULD SHE BE GETTING THROUGH HERE SOMEHOW?
WHERE DIRT'S CAKED IN...?
HOWWW!?
CHAMPON.

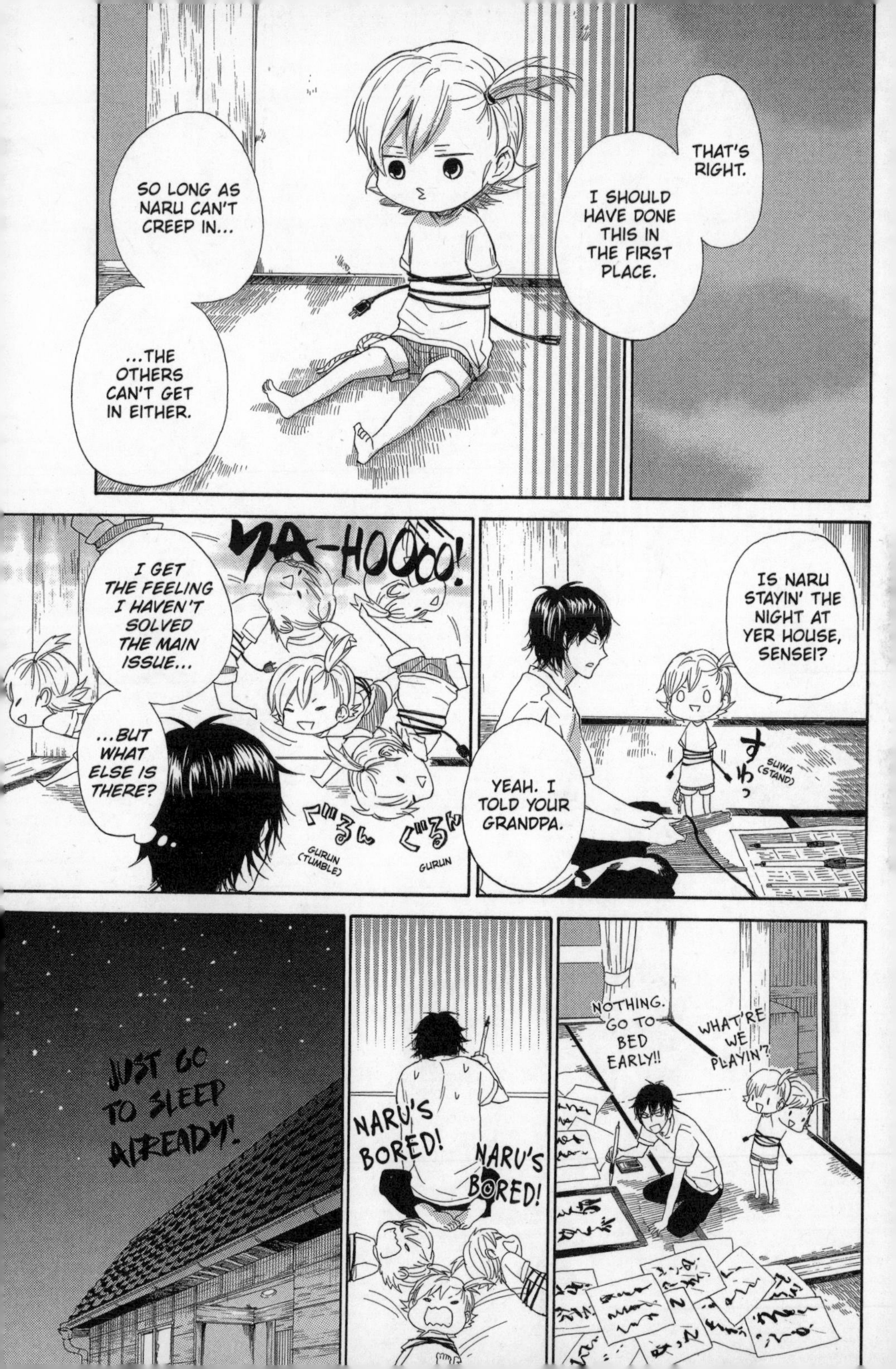
THAT'S RIGHT.
I SHOULD HAVE DONE THIS IN THE FIRST PLACE.
SO LONG AS NARU CAN'T CREEP IN...
...THE OTHERS CAN'T GET IN EITHER.
IS NARU STAYIN' THE NIGHT AT YER HOUSE, SENSEI?
すわっ
SUWA (STAND)
YEAH. I TOLD YOUR GRANDPA.
YA-HOOOO!
I GET THE FEELING I HAVEN'T SOLVED THE MAIN ISSUE...
...BUT WHAT ELSE IS THERE?
ぐるん ぐるん
GURUN (TUMBLE)
GURUN
WHAT'RE WE PLAYIN'?
NOTHING. GO TO BED EARLY!!
NARU'S BORED!
NARU'S BORED!
JUST GO TO SLEEP ALREADY!

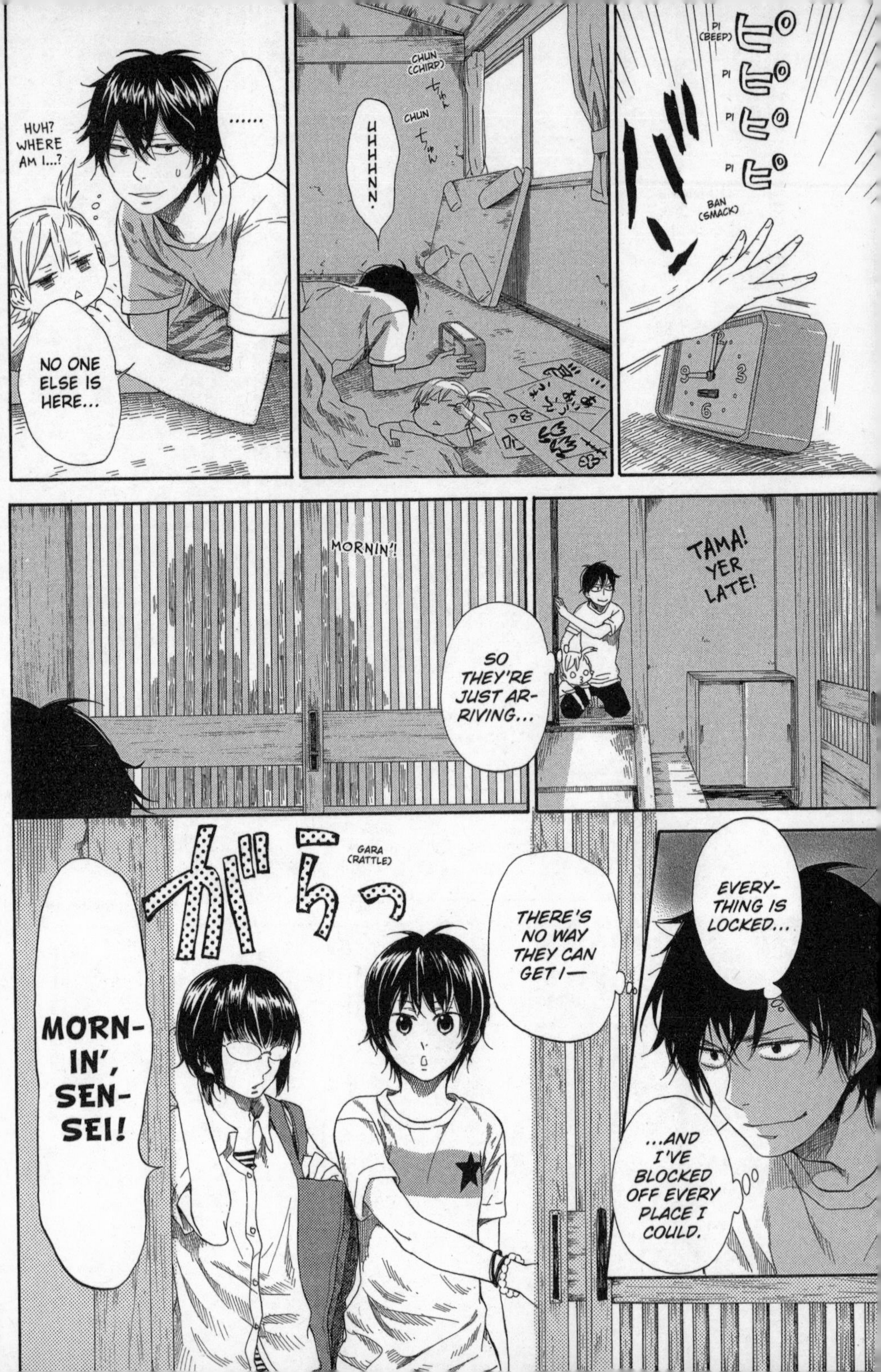
PI (BEEP) ピ
PI ピ
PI ピ
PI ピ
BAN (SMACK) バン
CHUN (CHIRP) ちゅん
CHUN ちゅん
UHHHHNN.
......
HUH? WHERE AM I...?
NO ONE ELSE IS HERE...
TAMA! YER LATE!
SO THEY'RE JUST AR-RIVING...
MORNIN'!
EVERY-THING IS LOCKED...
...AND I'VE BLOCKED OFF EVERY PLACE I COULD.
THERE'S NO WAY THEY CAN GET I—
GARA (RATTLE) がらっ
MORN-IN', SEN-SEI!

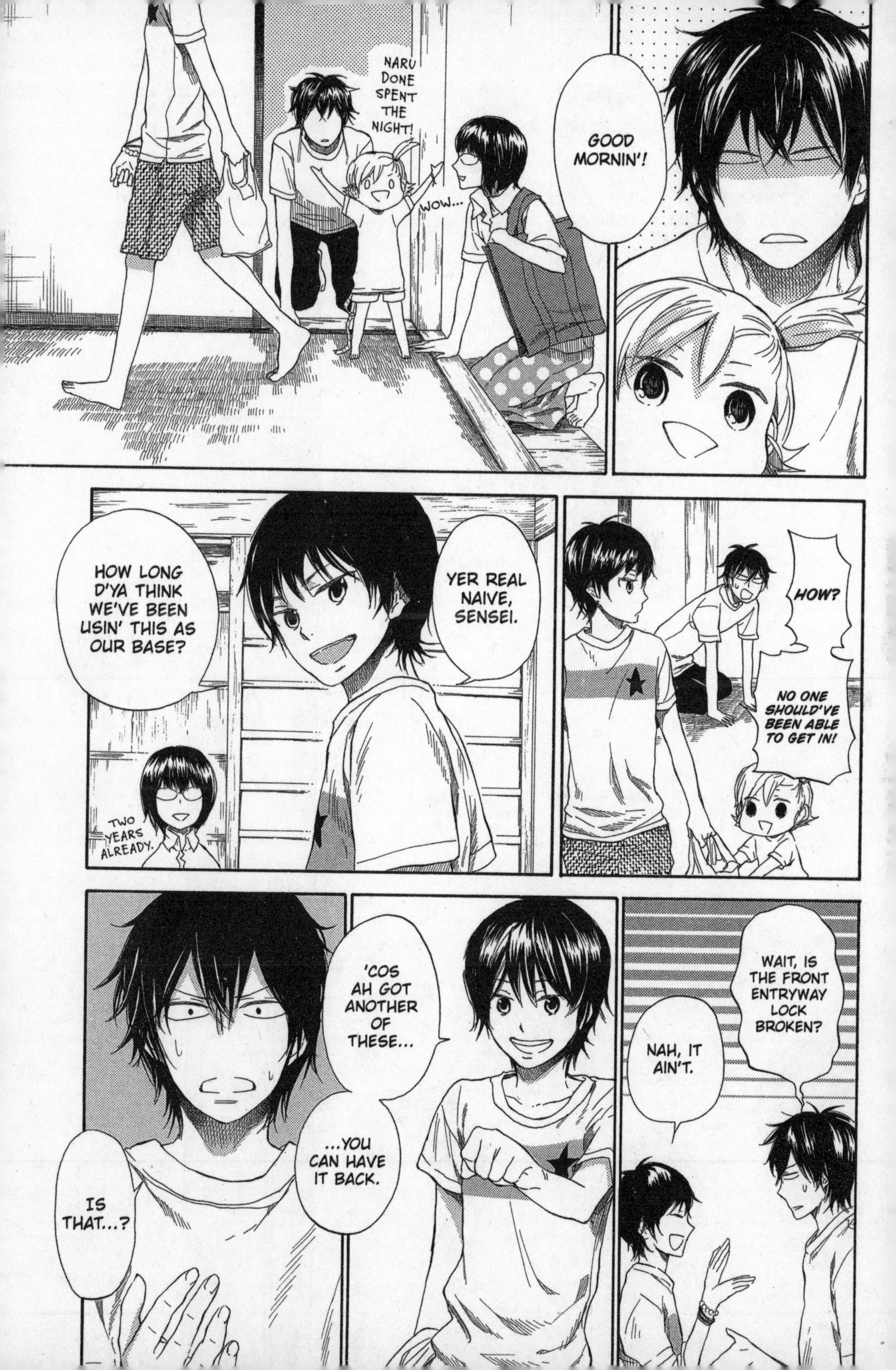
GOOD MORNIN'!
NARU DONE SPENT THE NIGHT!
WOW...
HOW?
NO ONE SHOULD'VE BEEN ABLE TO GET IN!
YER REAL NAIVE, SENSEI.
HOW LONG D'YA THINK WE'VE BEEN USIN' THIS AS OUR BASE?
TWO YEARS ALREADY.
WAIT, IS THE FRONT ENTRYWAY LOCK BROKEN?
NAH, IT AIN'T.
'COS AH GOT ANOTHER OF THESE...
...YOU CAN HAVE IT BACK.
IS THAT...?

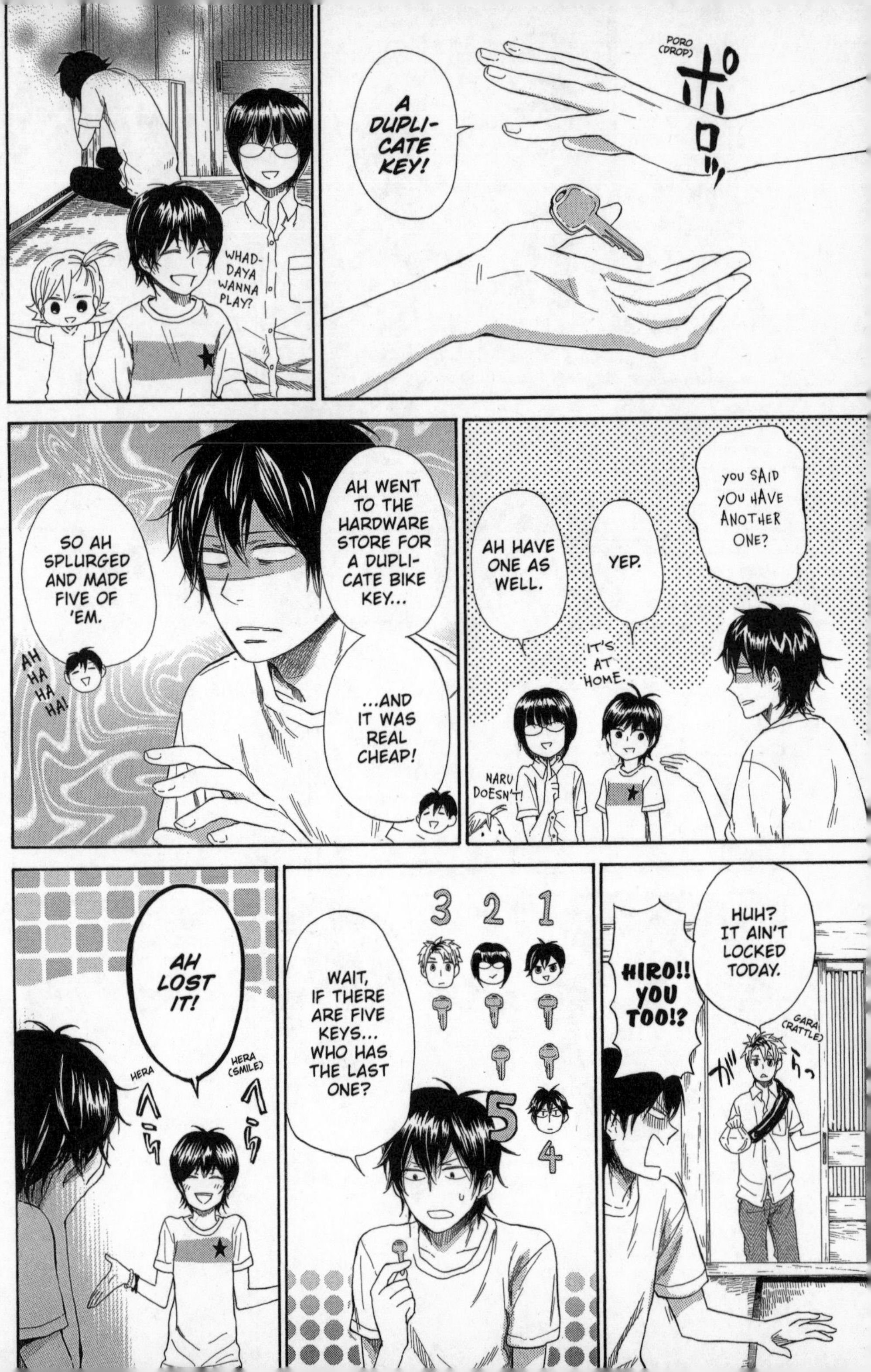
POR0 (DROP)
ポロッ
A DUPLI-CATE KEY!
WHAD-DAYA WANNA PLAY?
YOU SAID YOU HAVE ANOTHER ONE?
YEP.
IT'S AT HOME.
AH HAVE ONE AS WELL.
NARU DOESN'T!
AH WENT TO THE HARDWARE STORE FOR A DUPLI-CATE BIKE KEY...
...AND IT WAS REAL CHEAP!
SO AH SPLURGED AND MADE FIVE OF 'EM.
AH HA HA HA!
HUH? IT AIN'T LOCKED TODAY.
GARA (RATTLE)
ガラッ
HIRO!! YOU TOO!?
3
2
1
WAIT, IF THERE ARE FIVE KEYS... WHO HAS THE LAST ONE?
5
4
AH LOST IT!
HERA (SMILE)
へら
HERA
へら

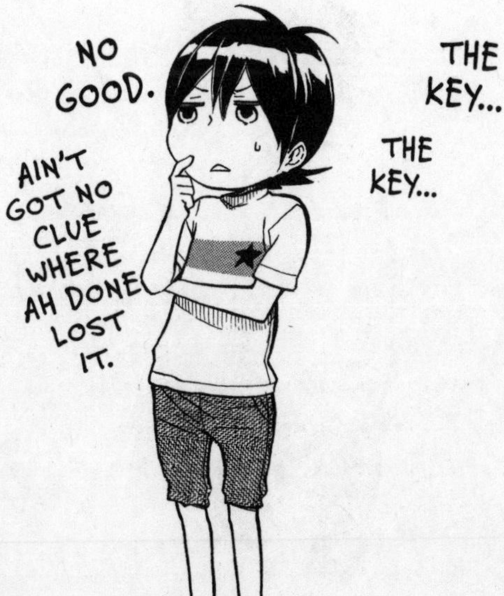
THE KEY...
THE KEY...
NO GOOD.
AIN'T GOT NO CLUE WHERE AH DONE LOST IT.

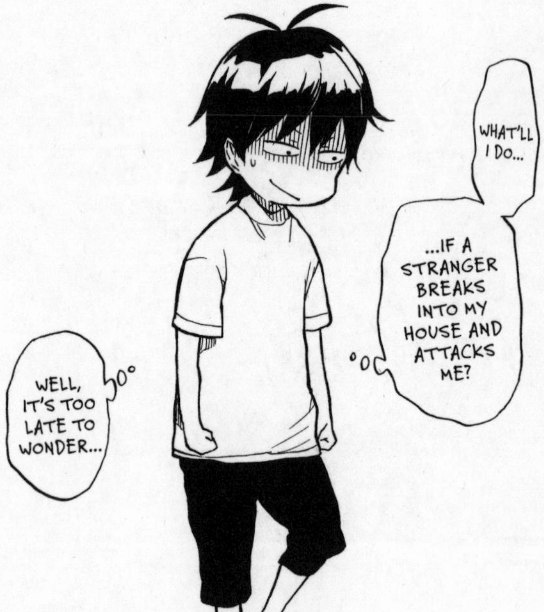
WHAT'LL I DO...
...IF A STRANGER BREAKS INTO MY HOUSE AND ATTACKS ME?
WELL, IT'S TOO LATE TO WONDER...

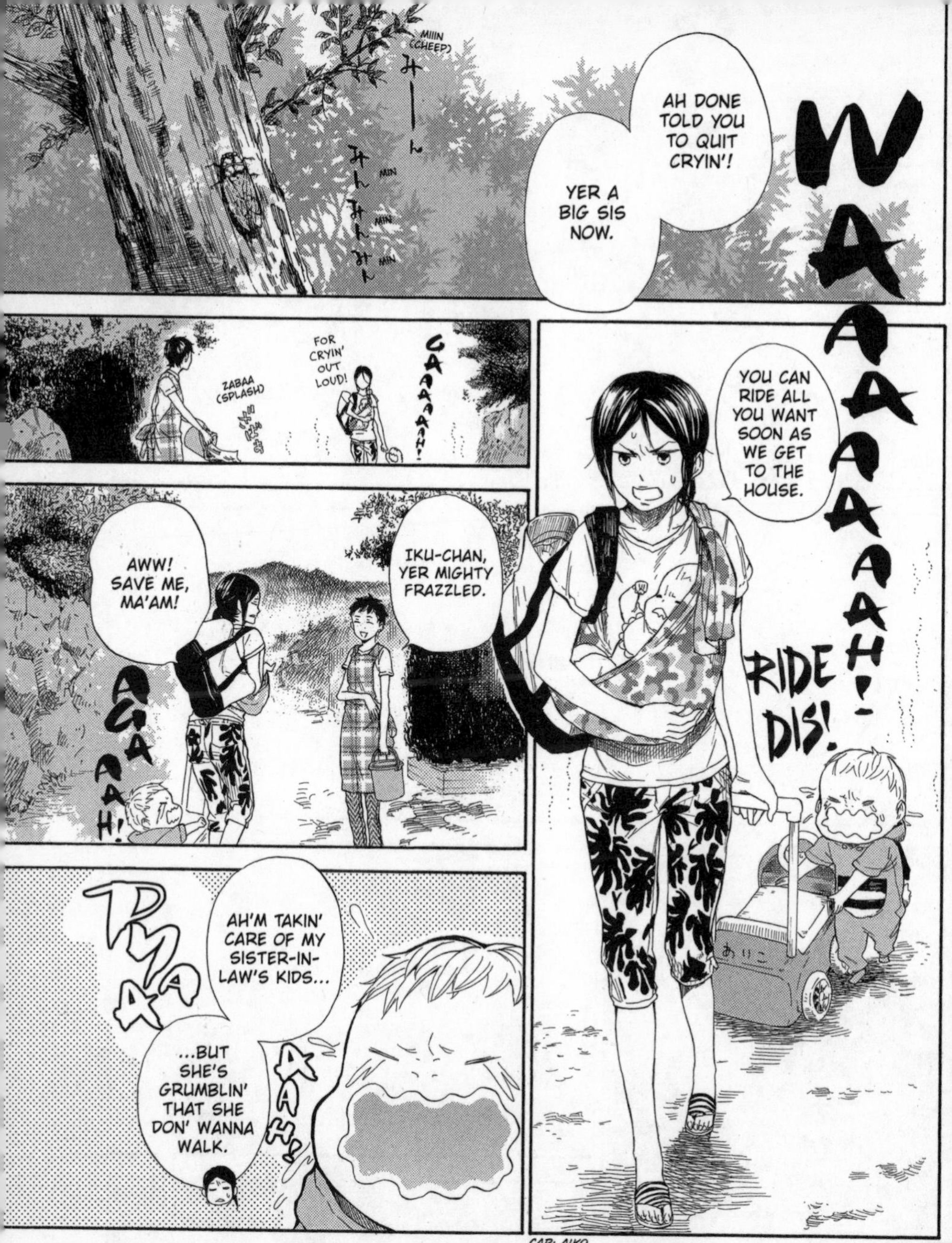
AH DONE TOLD YOU TO QUIT CRYIN'!
YER A BIG SIS NOW.
WAAAAAAAAH!
MIIN (CHEEP)
MIN
MIN
MIN
YOU CAN RIDE ALL YOU WANT SOON AS WE GET TO THE HOUSE.
RIDE DIS!
GAAAAAAH!
FOR CRYIN' OUT LOUD!
ZABAA (SPLASH)
IKU-CHAN, YER MIGHTY FRAZZLED.
AWW! SAVE ME, MA'AM!
AGAAAAH!
AH'M TAKIN' CARE OF MY SISTER-IN-LAW'S KIDS...
...BUT SHE'S GRUMBLIN' THAT SHE DON' WANNA WALK.
MAAA
AAH!

CAR: AIKO

ACT.31 TOHOUSHINOTA

(Translation: Got Lost)

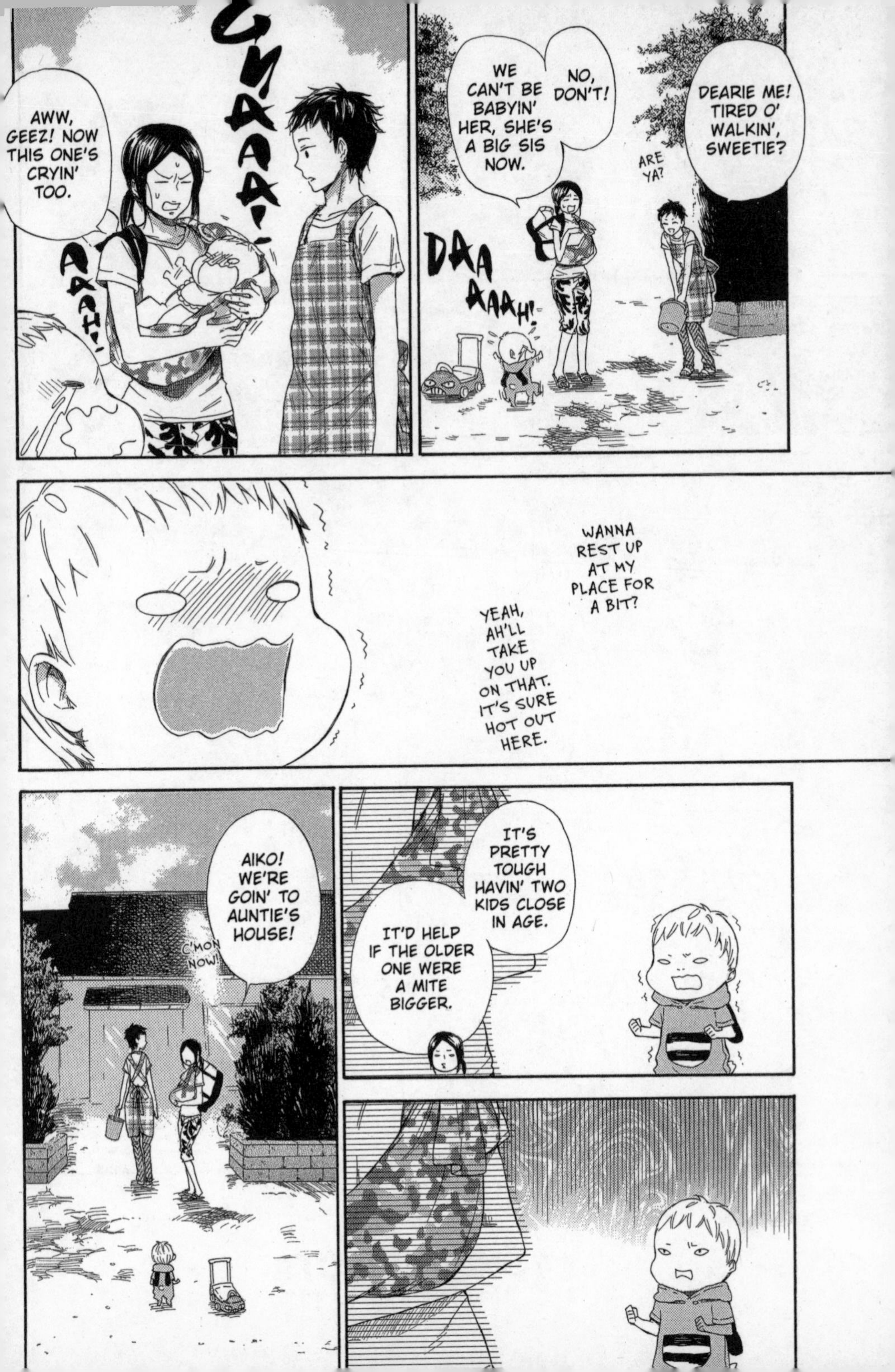
DEARIE ME! TIRED O' WALKIN', SWEETIE?
ARE YA?
NO, DON'T!
WE CAN'T BE BABYIN' HER, SHE'S A BIG SIS NOW.
DAAAAAH!
GNAAA!
AWW, GEEZ! NOW THIS ONE'S CRYIN' TOO.
AAAH!
WANNA REST UP AT MY PLACE FOR A BIT?
YEAH, AH'LL TAKE YOU UP ON THAT. IT'S SURE HOT OUT HERE.
IT'S PRETTY TOUGH HAVIN' TWO KIDS CLOSE IN AGE.
IT'D HELP IF THE OLDER ONE WERE A MITE BIGGER.
AIKO! WE'RE GOIN' TO AUNTIE'S HOUSE!
C'MON NOW!

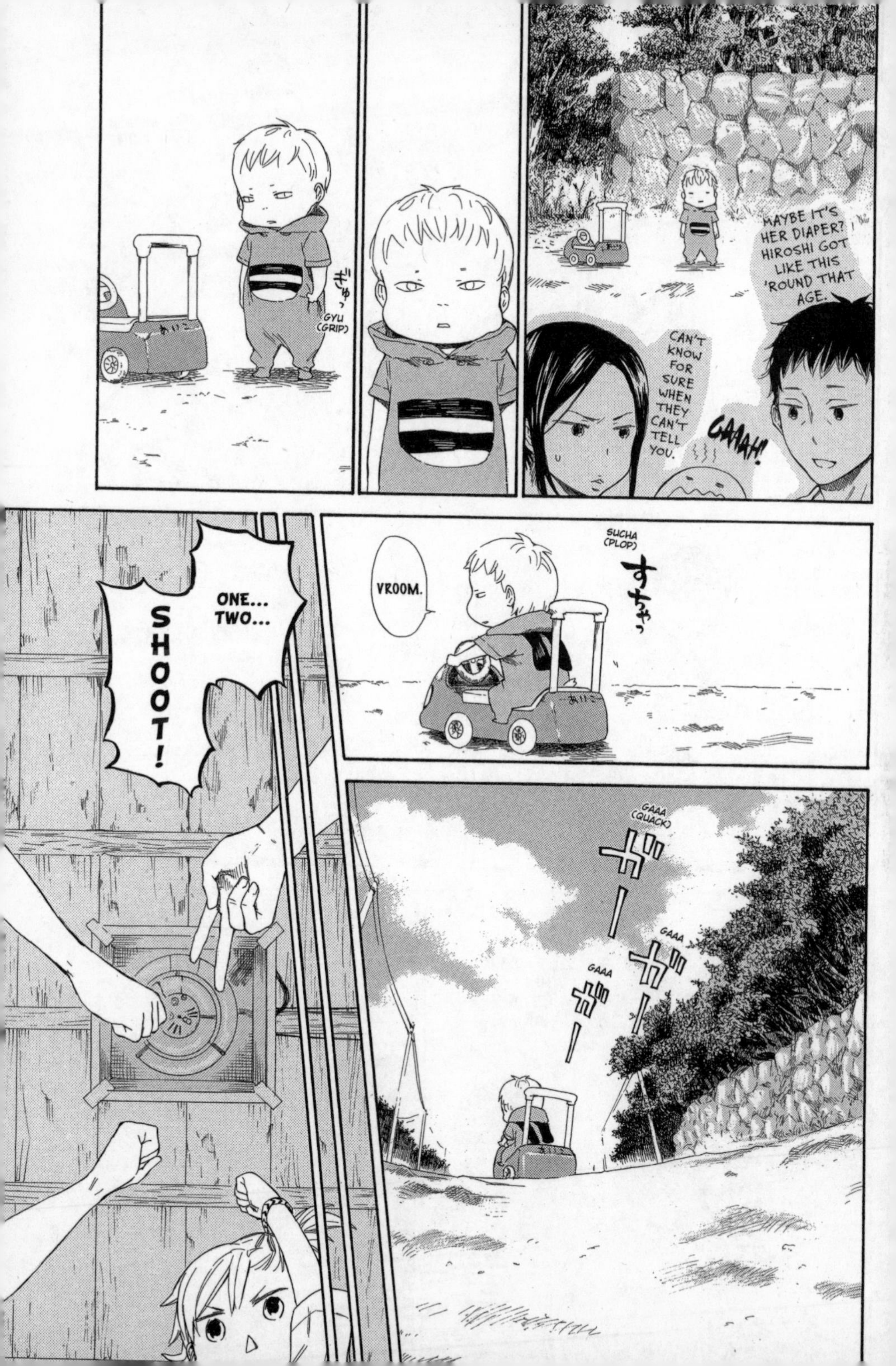
MAYBE IT'S HER DIAPER? HIROSHI GOT LIKE THIS 'ROUND THAT AGE.
CAN'T KNOW FOR SURE WHEN THEY CAN'T TELL YOU.
GAAAH!
ぎゅっ
GYU (GRIP)
VROOM.
すちゃっ
SUCHA (PLOP)
ガーガーガー
GAAA (QUACK)
GAAA
GAAA
ONE... TWO...
SHOOT!

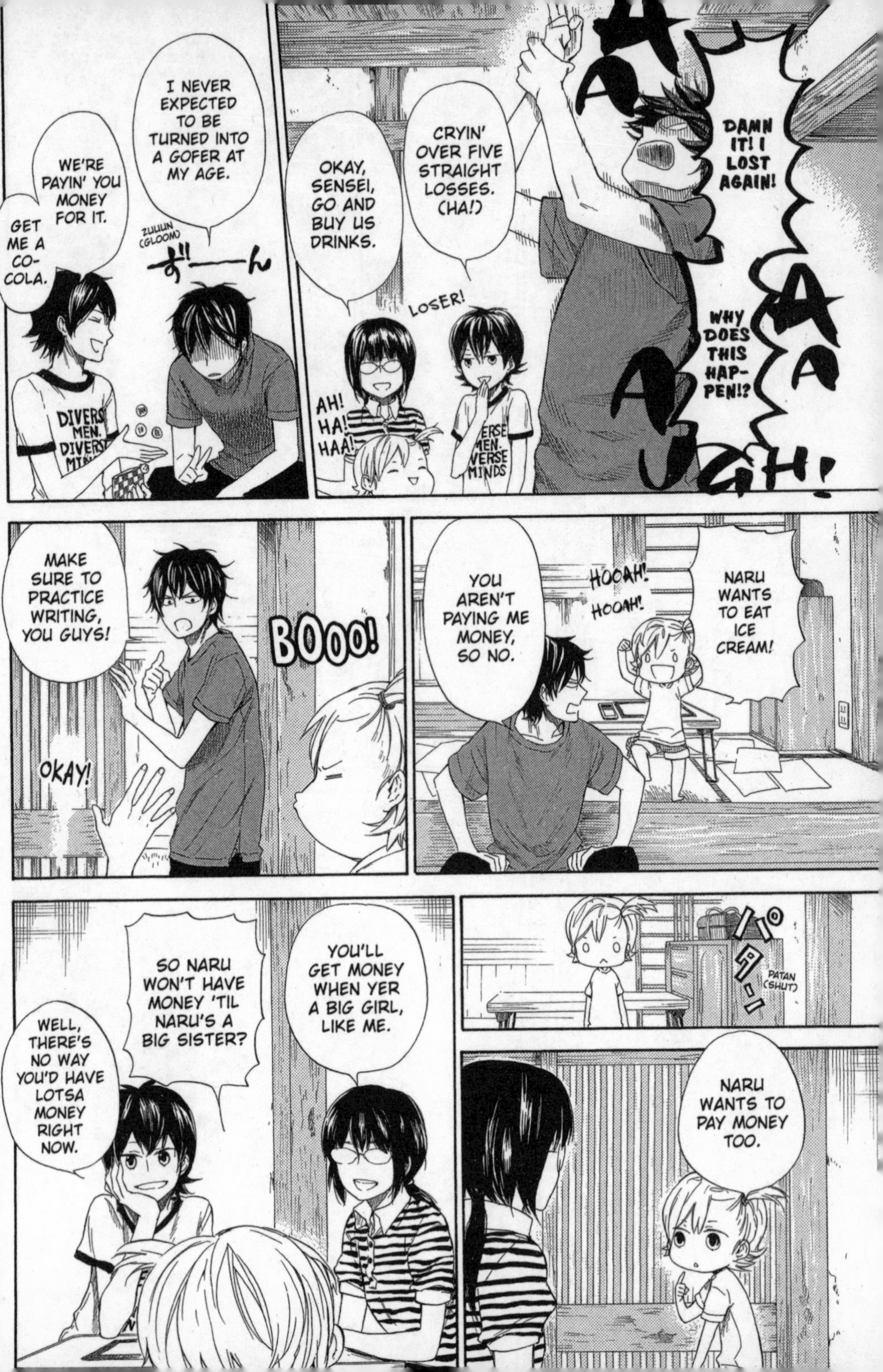
AAAAAAAGH!
DAMN IT! I LOST AGAIN!
WHY DOES THIS HAP-PEN!?
CRYIN' OVER FIVE STRAIGHT LOSSES. (HA!)
OKAY, SENSEI, GO AND BUY US DRINKS.
LOSER!
AH! HA! HAA!
I NEVER EXPECTED TO BE TURNED INTO A GOFER AT MY AGE.
ZUUUN (GLOOM)
ず——ん
WE'RE PAYIN' YOU MONEY FOR IT.
GET ME A CO-COLA.
NARU WANTS TO EAT ICE CREAM!
HOOAH!
HOOAH!
YOU AREN'T PAYING ME MONEY, SO NO.
BOOO!
MAKE SURE TO PRACTICE WRITING, YOU GUYS!
OKAY!
パタ—ン
PATAN (SHUT)
NARU WANTS TO PAY MONEY TOO.
YOU'LL GET MONEY WHEN YER A BIG GIRL, LIKE ME.
SO NARU WON'T HAVE MONEY 'TIL NARU'S A BIG SISTER?
WELL, THERE'S NO WAY YOU'D HAVE LOTSA MONEY RIGHT NOW.

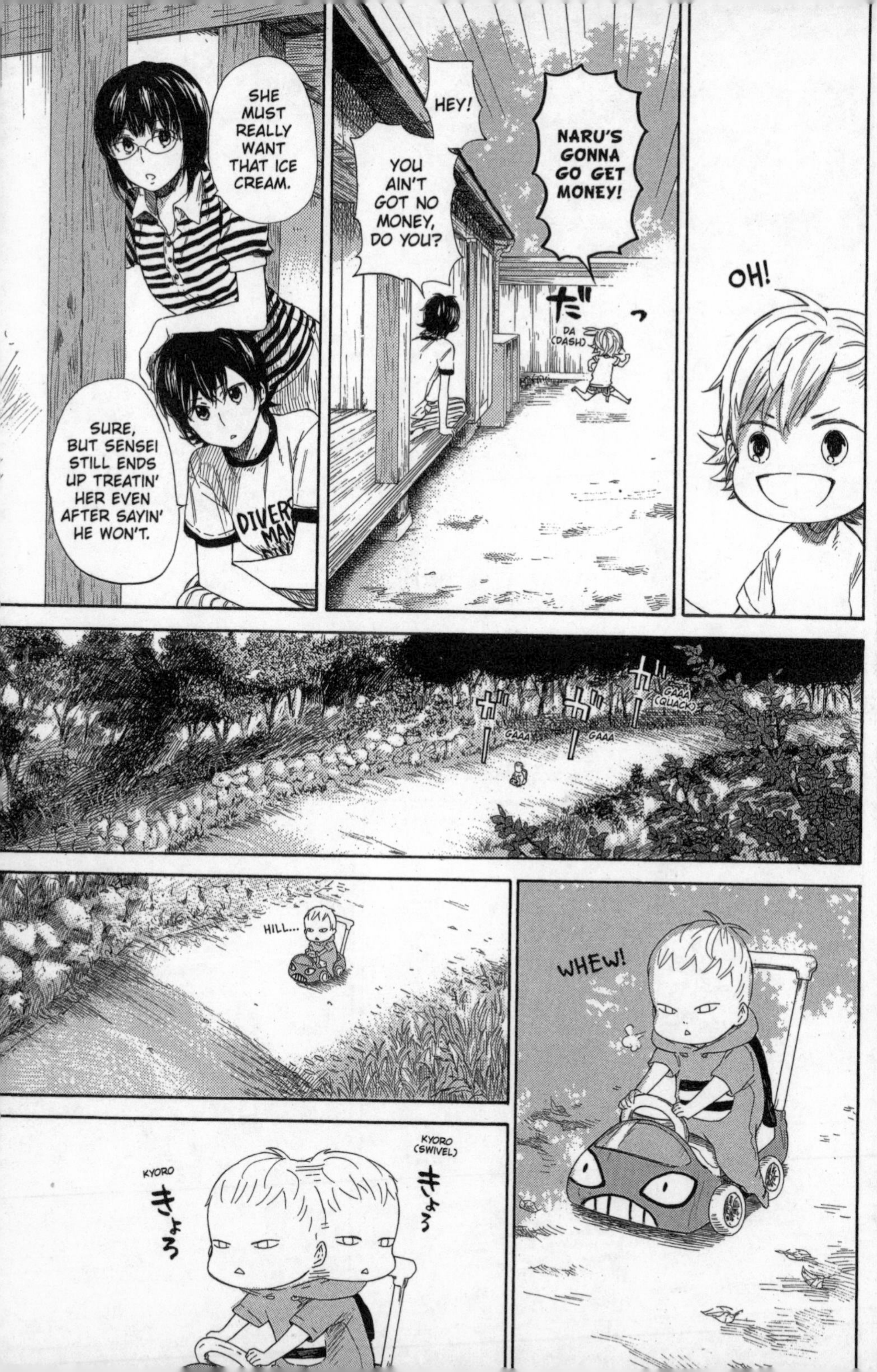

OH!
NARU'S GONNA GO GET MONEY!
HEY!
YOU AIN'T GOT NO MONEY, DO YOU?
だっ
DA (DASH)
SHE MUST REALLY WANT THAT ICE CREAM.
SURE, BUT SENSEI STILL ENDS UP TREATIN' HER EVEN AFTER SAYIN' HE WON'T.
ガー
GAAA (QUACK)
ガー
GAAA
ガー
GAAA
WHEW!
HILL...
きょろ
KYORO (SWIVEL)
きょろ
KYORO

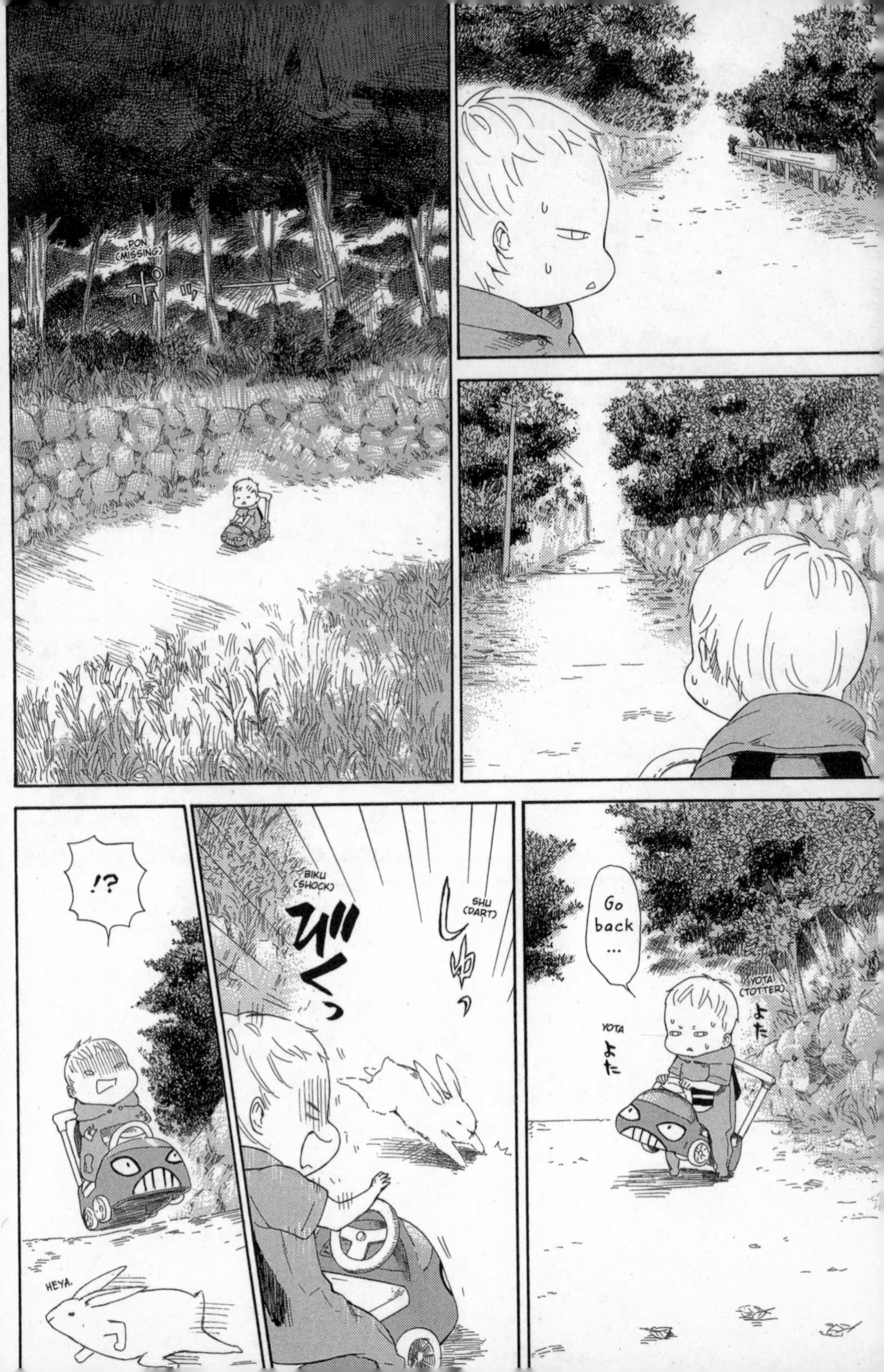
PON (MISSING)
Go back ...
YOTA (TOTTER)
よた
YOTA
よた
BIKU (SHOCK)
びくっ
SHU (DART)
しゅっ
!?
HEYA.

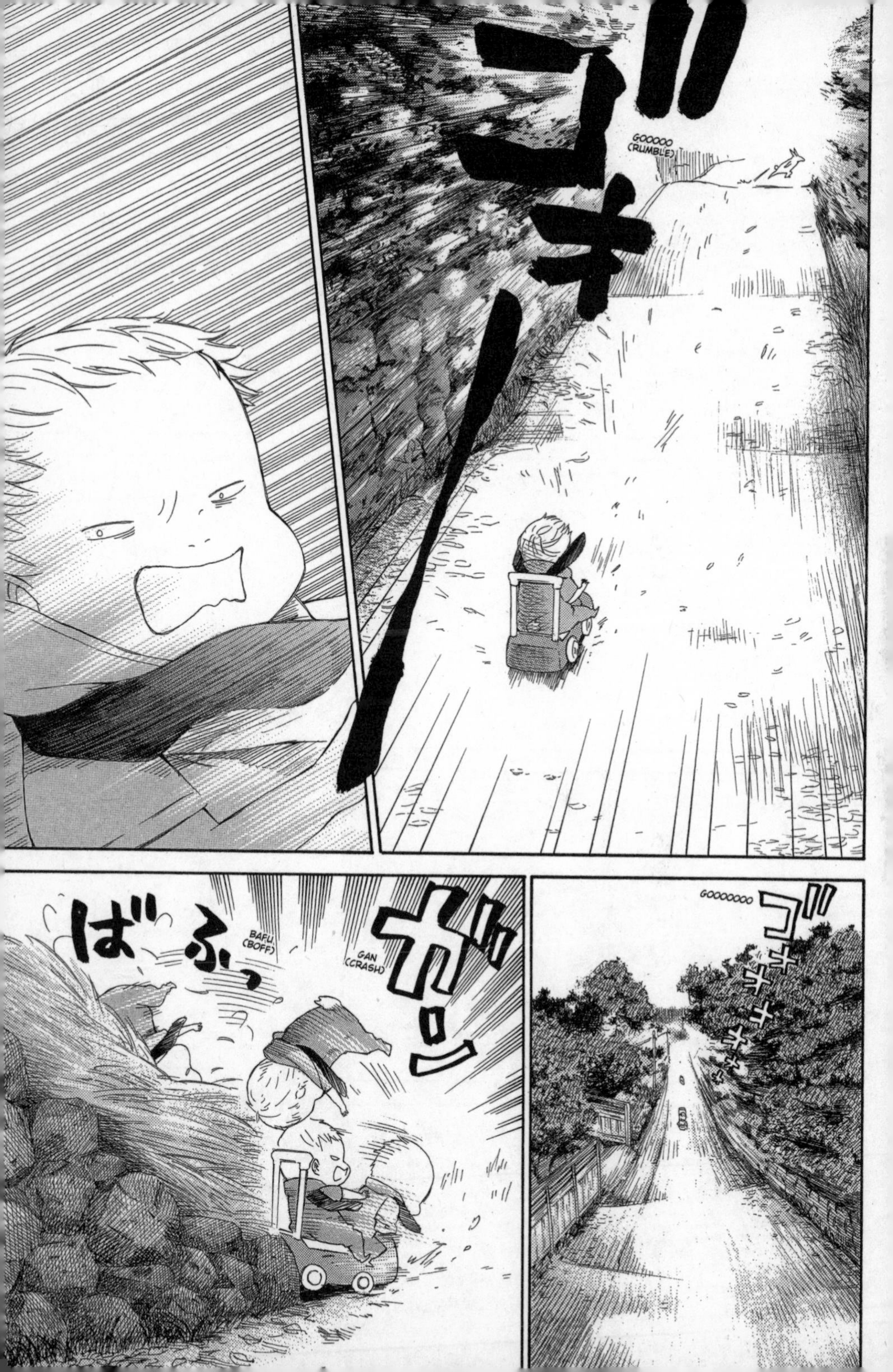
ゴオー
GOOOOO (RUMBLE)
ゴオオオオォ
GOOOOOOO
ガン
GAN (CRASH)
ばふっ
BAFU (BOFF)

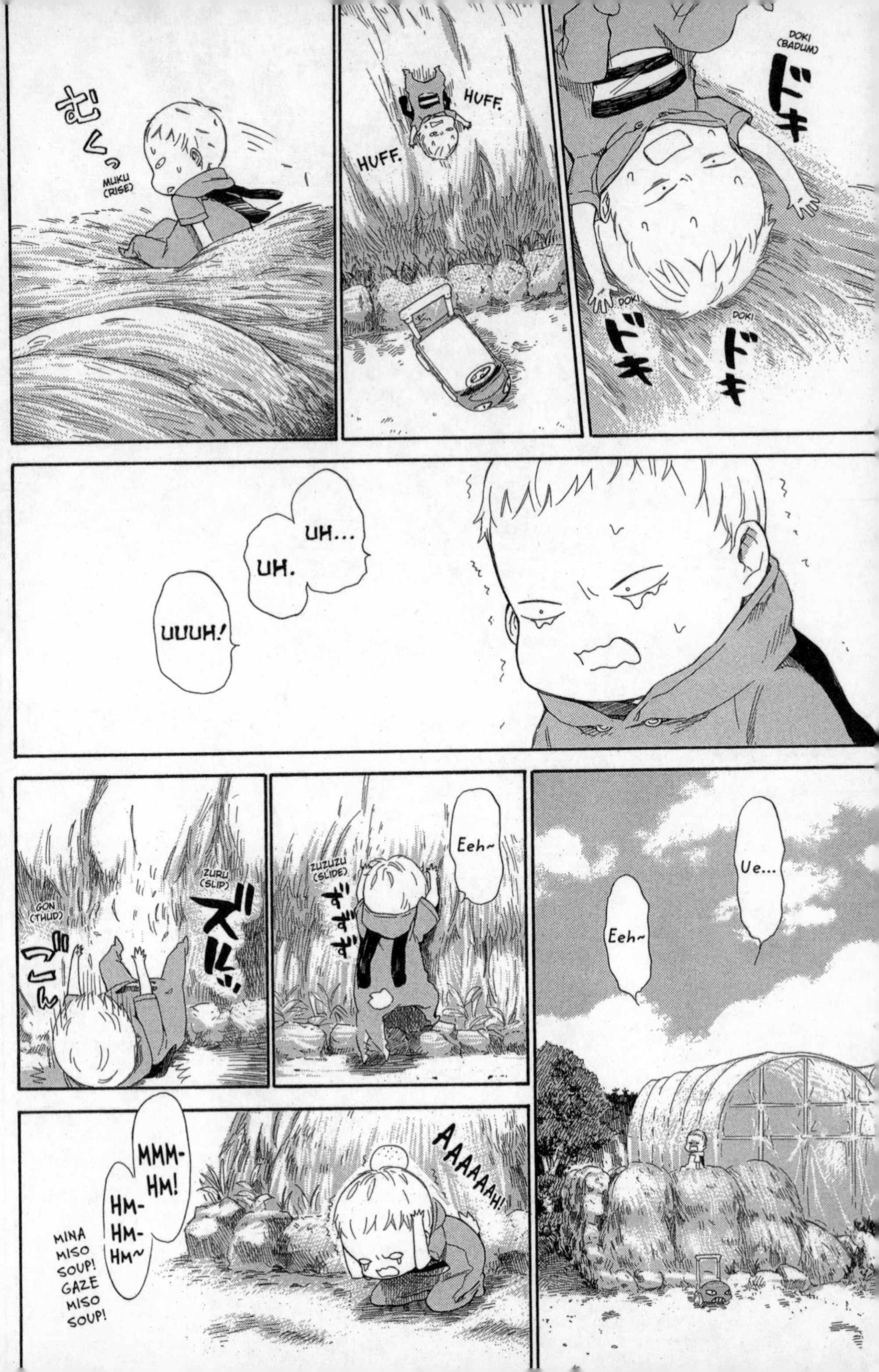

DOKI (BADUM)
ドキ
DOKI
ドキ
DOKI
ドキ
HUFF.
HUFF.
むくっ
MUKU (RISE)
UH... UH.
UUUH!
Ue...
Eeh~
Eeh~
Eeh~
ずずず
ZUZUZU (SLIDE)
ズルッ
ZURU (SLIP)
ごーん
GON (THUD)
AAAAAAH!
MMM-HM! HM-HM-HM~
MINA MISO SOUP! GAZE MISO SOUP!

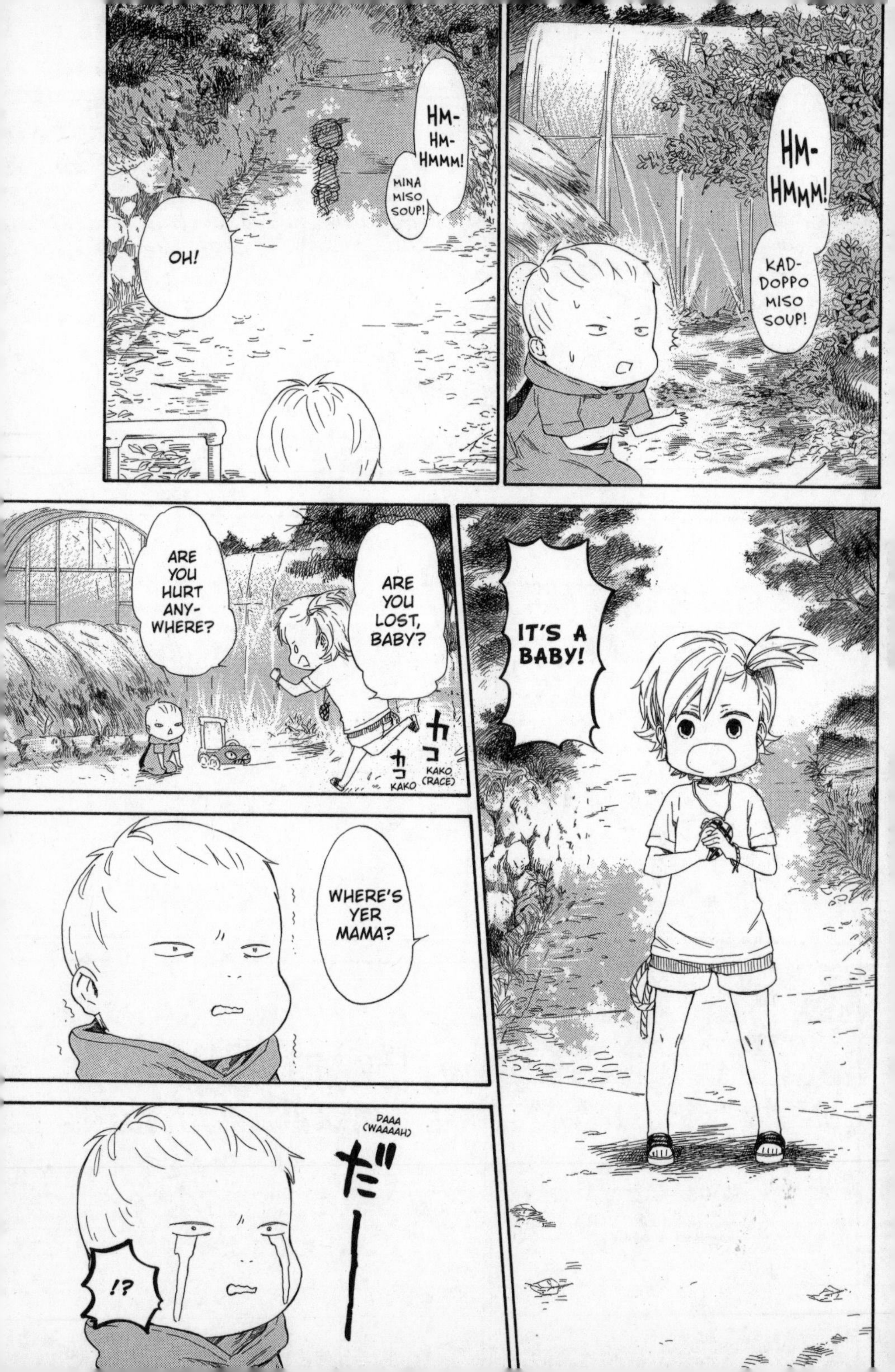
HM-HMMM!
KAD-DOPPO MISO SOUP!
HM-HM-HMMM!
MINA MISO SOUP!
OH!
IT'S A BABY!
ARE YOU LOST, BABY?
ARE YOU HURT ANY-WHERE?
カコ KAKO (RACE)
カコ KAKO
WHERE'S YER MAMA?
だー DAAA (WAAAAH)
!?

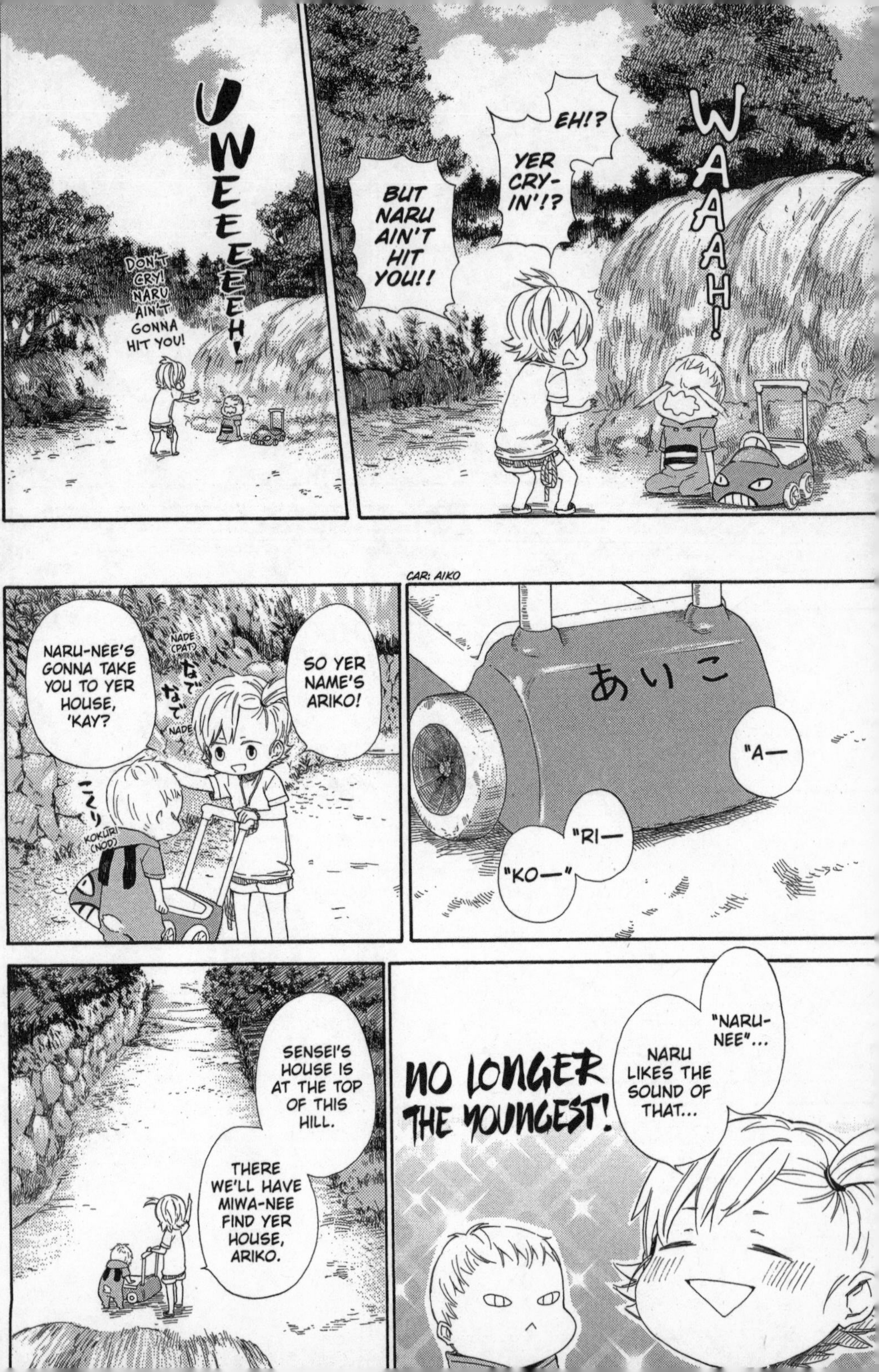
WAAAAH!
EH!?
YER CRY-IN'!?
BUT NARU AIN'T HIT YOU!!
UWEEEEEEH!
DON'T CRY! NARU AIN'T GONNA HIT YOU!
CAR: AIKO
あいこ
"A—
"RI—
"KO—"
SO YER NAME'S ARIKO!
NADE (PAT) なでなで NADE
NARU-NEE'S GONNA TAKE YOU TO YER HOUSE, 'KAY?
こくり KOKURI (NOD)
"NARU-NEE"...
NARU LIKES THE SOUND OF THAT...
NO LONGER THE YOUNGEST!
SENSEI'S HOUSE IS AT THE TOP OF THIS HILL.
THERE WE'LL HAVE MIWA-NEE FIND YER HOUSE, ARIKO.

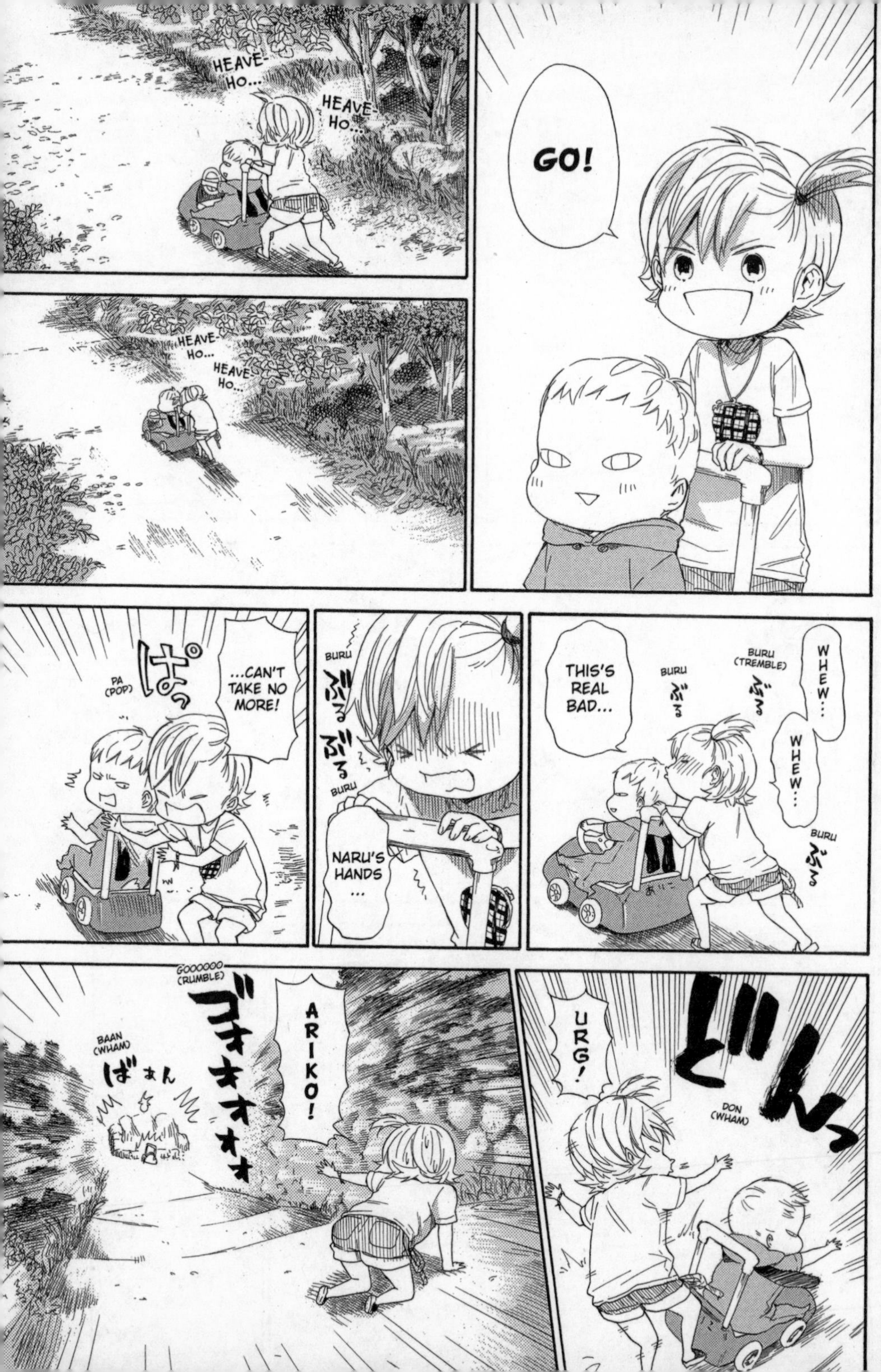

GO!
HEAVE-HO...
HEAVE-HO...
HEAVE-HO...
HEAVE-HO...
WHEW... WHEW...
BURU (TREMBLE) ぶる
BURU ぶる
THIS'S REAL BAD...
BURU ぶる
BURU ぶる
ぶる BURU
NARU'S HANDS ...
...CAN'T TAKE NO MORE!
PA (POP) ぱっ
どんっ DON (WHAM)
URG!
ARIKO!
GOOOOOO (RUMBLE) ゴォオオオオ
BAAN (WHAM) ばぁん

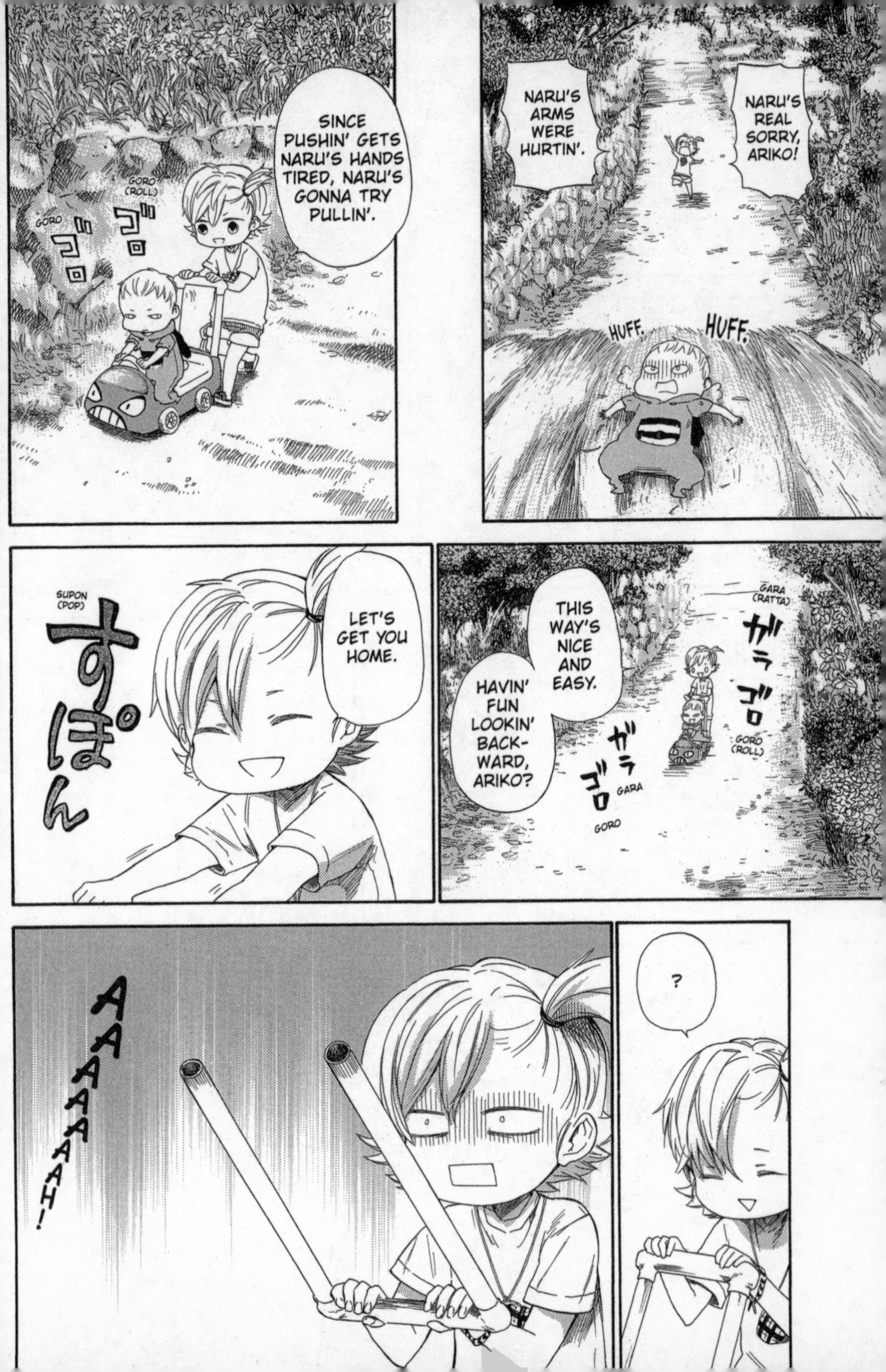
NARU'S REAL SORRY, ARIKO!
NARU'S ARMS WERE HURTIN'.
HUFF.
HUFF.
SINCE PUSHIN' GETS NARU'S HANDS TIRED, NARU'S GONNA TRY PULLIN'.
GORO (ROLL)
ゴロ
GORO
ゴロ
GARA (RATTA)
ガラ
ゴロ
GORO (ROLL)
THIS WAY'S NICE AND EASY.
HAVIN' FUN LOOKIN' BACKWARD, ARIKO?
ガラ
GARA
ゴロ
GORO
LET'S GET YOU HOME.
SUPON (POP)
すぽん
?
AAAAAAAAH!

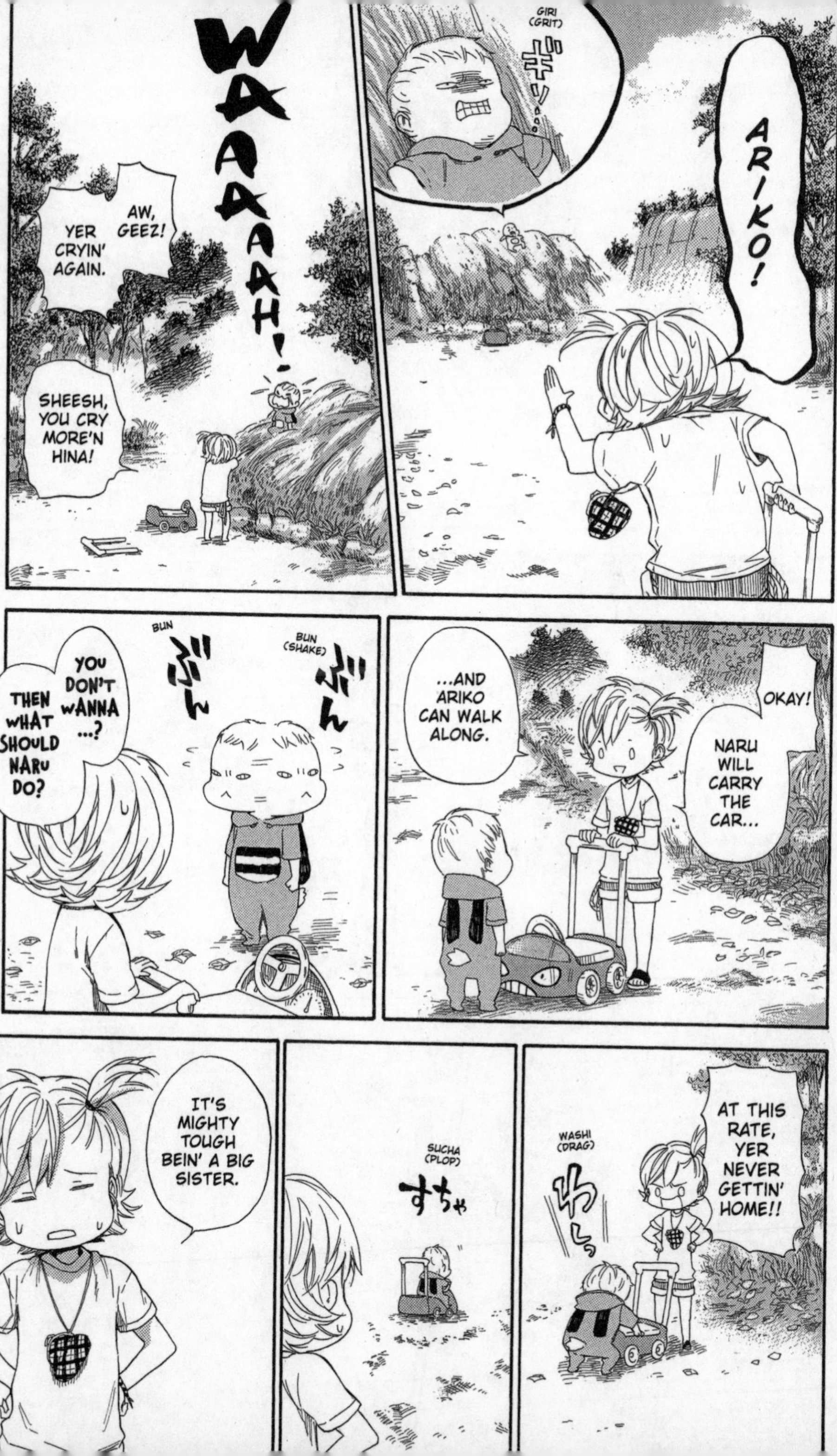
ARIKO!
GIRI (GRIT)
ギリッ...
WAAAAAAH!
AW, GEEZ!
YER CRYIN' AGAIN.
SHEESH, YOU CRY MORE'N HINA!
OKAY!
NARU WILL CARRY THE CAR...
...AND ARIKO CAN WALK ALONG.
BUN (SHAKE)
ぶん
BUN
ぶん
YOU DON'T WANNA...?
THEN WHAT SHOULD NARU DO?
AT THIS RATE, YER NEVER GETTIN' HOME!!
WASHI (DRAG)
わしっ
SUCHA (PLOP)
すちゃ
IT'S MIGHTY TOUGH BEIN' A BIG SISTER.

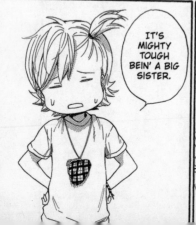

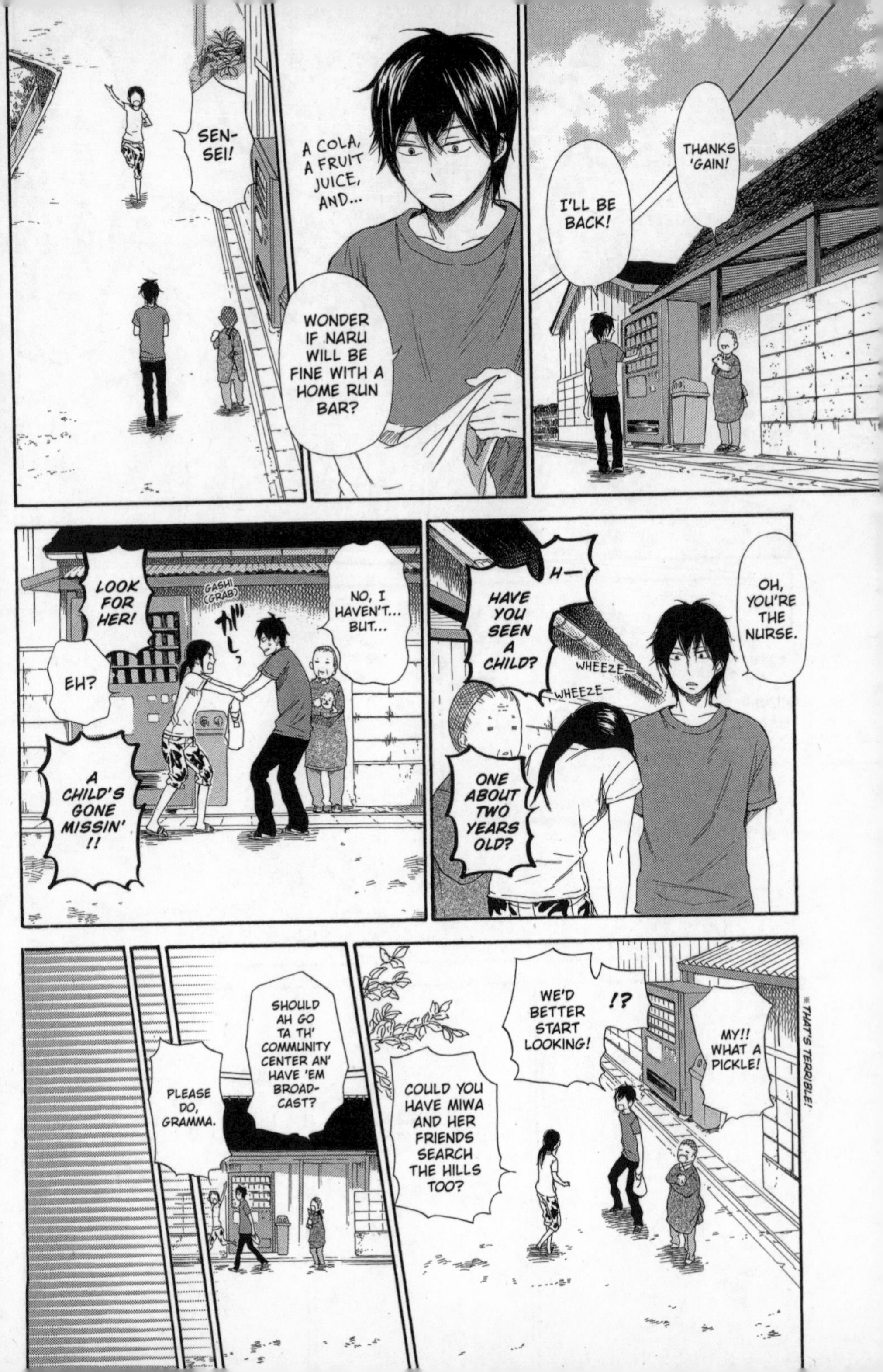
THANKS 'GAIN!
I'LL BE BACK!
A COLA, A FRUIT JUICE, AND...
WONDER IF NARU WILL BE FINE WITH A HOME RUN BAR?
SEN-SEI!
OH, YOU'RE THE NURSE.
H— HAVE YOU SEEN A CHILD?
WHEEZE
WHEEZE—
ONE ABOUT TWO YEARS OLD?
NO, I HAVEN'T... BUT...
GASHI (GRAB)
がしっ
LOOK FOR HER!
EH?
A CHILD'S GONE MISSIN'!!
MY!! WHAT A PICKLE!
*THAT'S TERRIBLE!
!?
WE'D BETTER START LOOKING!
COULD YOU HAVE MIWA AND HER FRIENDS SEARCH THE HILLS TOO?
SHOULD AH GO TA TH' COMMUNITY CENTER AN' HAVE 'EM BROADCAST?
PLEASE DO, GRAMMA.

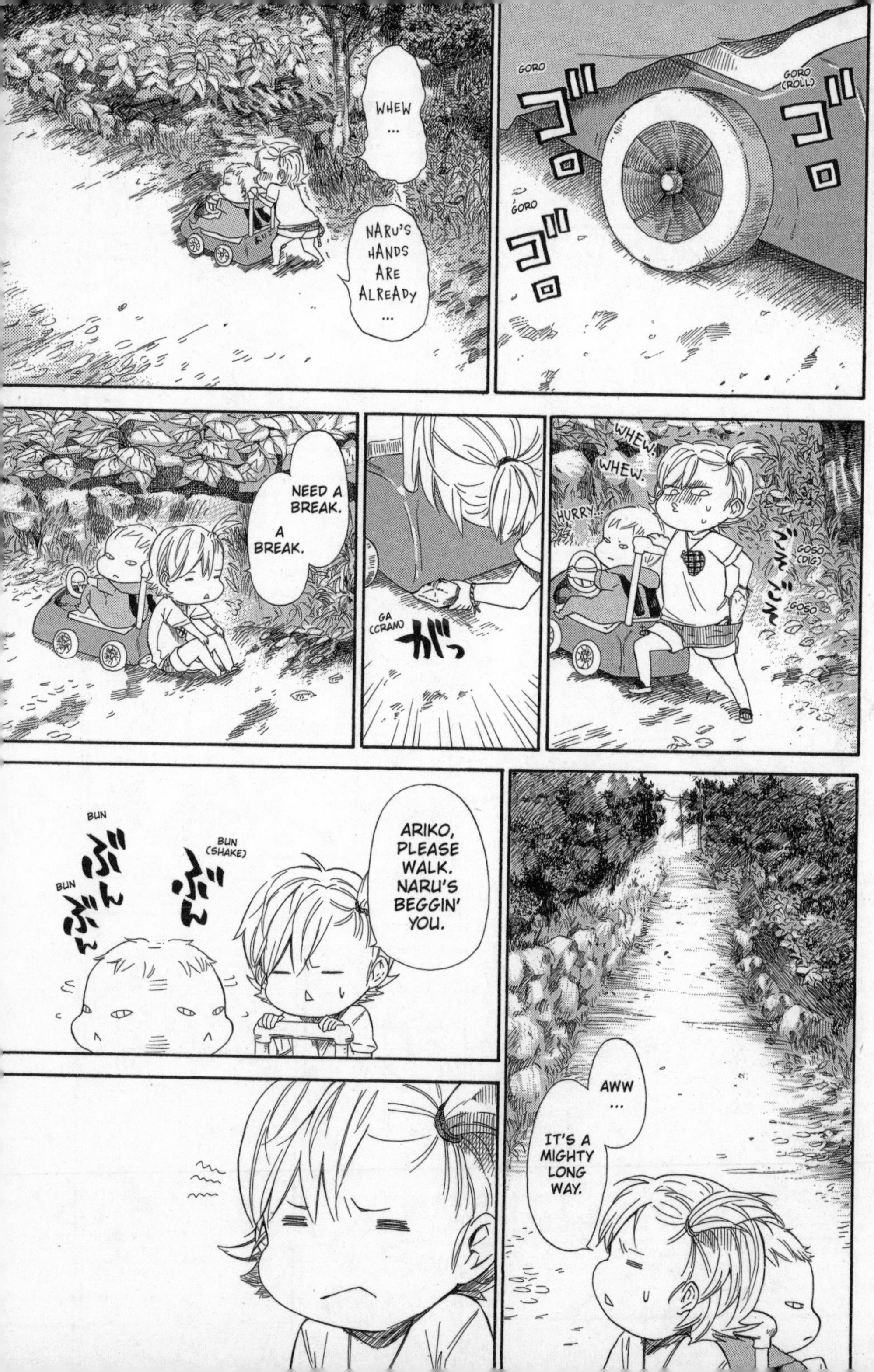

GORO (ROLL)
GORO
GORO
WHEW ...
NARU'S HANDS ARE ALREADY ...
WHEW. WHEW.
HURRY...
GOSO (DIG)
GOSO
GA (CRAM)
NEED A BREAK.
A BREAK.
AWW ...
IT'S A MIGHTY LONG WAY.
ARIKO, PLEASE WALK. NARU'S BEGGIN' YOU.
BUN (SHAKE)
BUN
BUN

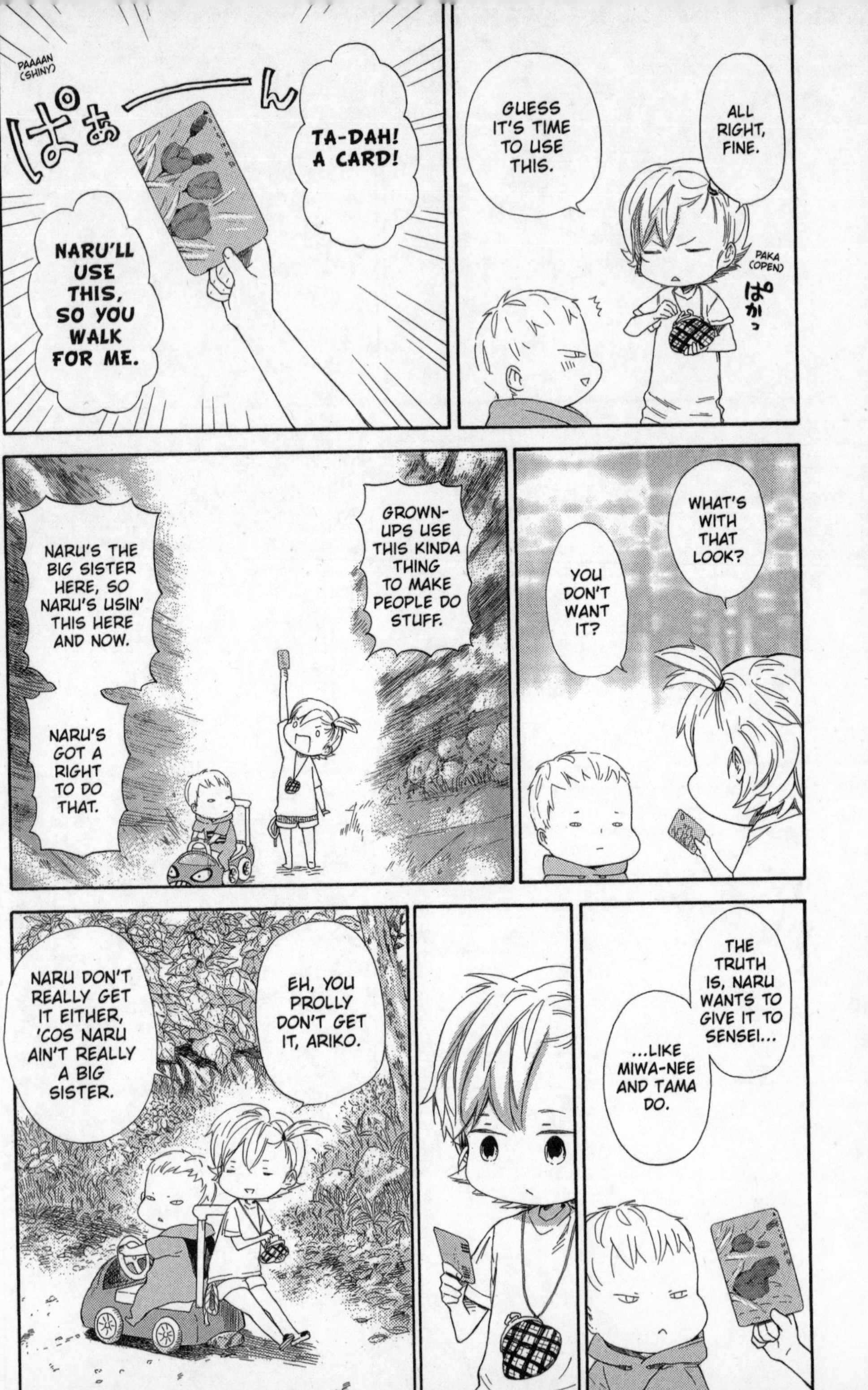
ALL RIGHT, FINE.
GUESS IT'S TIME TO USE THIS.
PAKA (OPEN)
ぱかっ
TA-DAH! A CARD!
PAAAAN (SHINY)
ぱぁーーん
NARU'LL USE THIS, SO YOU WALK FOR ME.
WHAT'S WITH THAT LOOK?
YOU DON'T WANT IT?
GROWN-UPS USE THIS KINDA THING TO MAKE PEOPLE DO STUFF.
NARU'S THE BIG SISTER HERE, SO NARU'S USIN' THIS HERE AND NOW.
NARU'S GOT A RIGHT TO DO THAT.
THE TRUTH IS, NARU WANTS TO GIVE IT TO SENSEI...
...LIKE MIWA-NEE AND TAMA DO.
EH, YOU PROLLY DON'T GET IT, ARIKO.
NARU DON'T REALLY GET IT EITHER, 'COS NARU AIN'T REALLY A BIG SISTER.

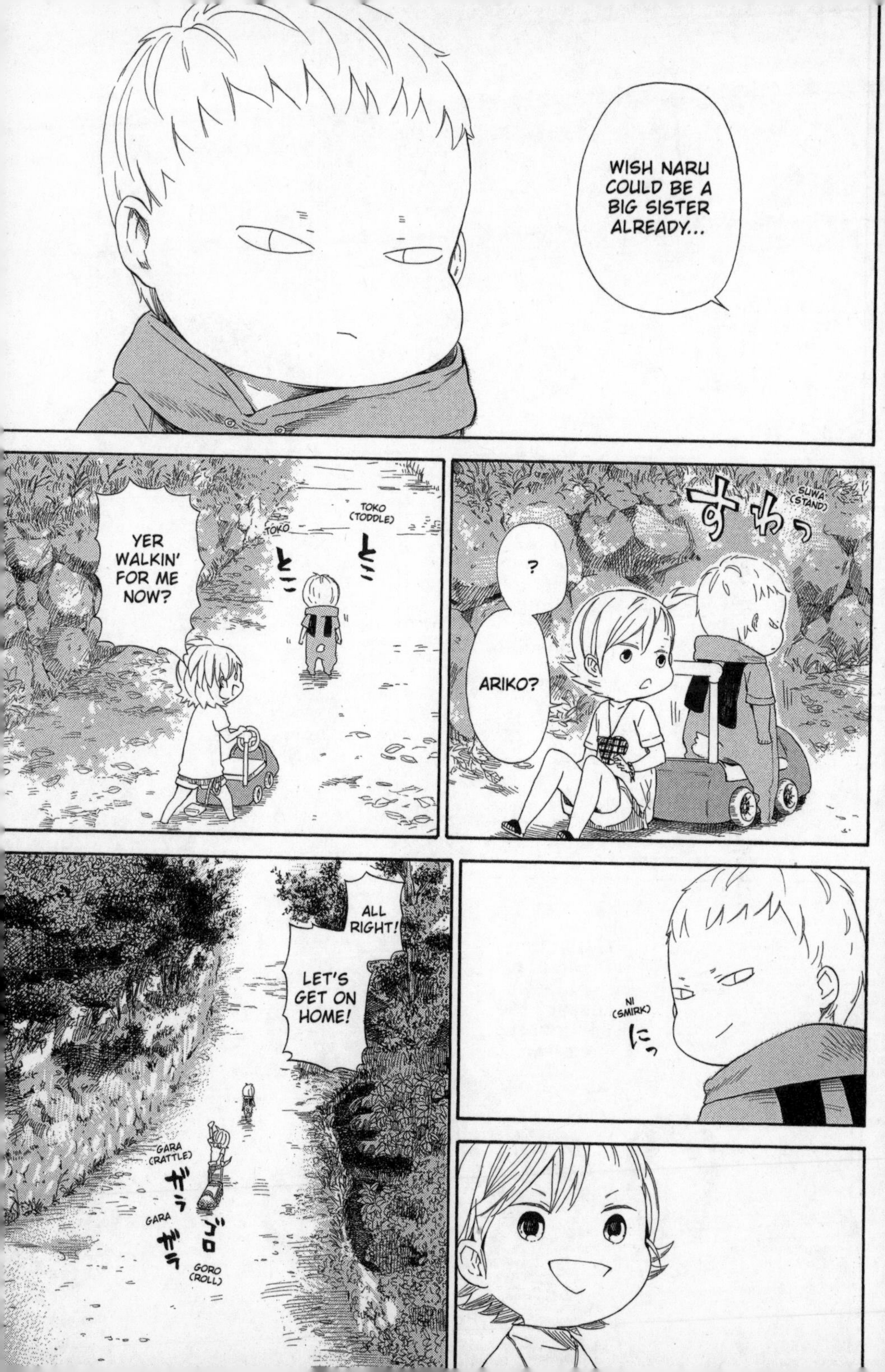
WISH NARU COULD BE A BIG SISTER ALREADY...
SUWA (STAND)
すわっ
?
ARIKO?
TOKO (TODDLE)
とこ
TOKO
とこ
YER WALKIN' FOR ME NOW?
NI (SMIRK)
にっ
ALL RIGHT!
LET'S GET ON HOME!
GARA (RATTLE)
ガラ
GORO (ROLL)
ゴロ
GARA
ガラ

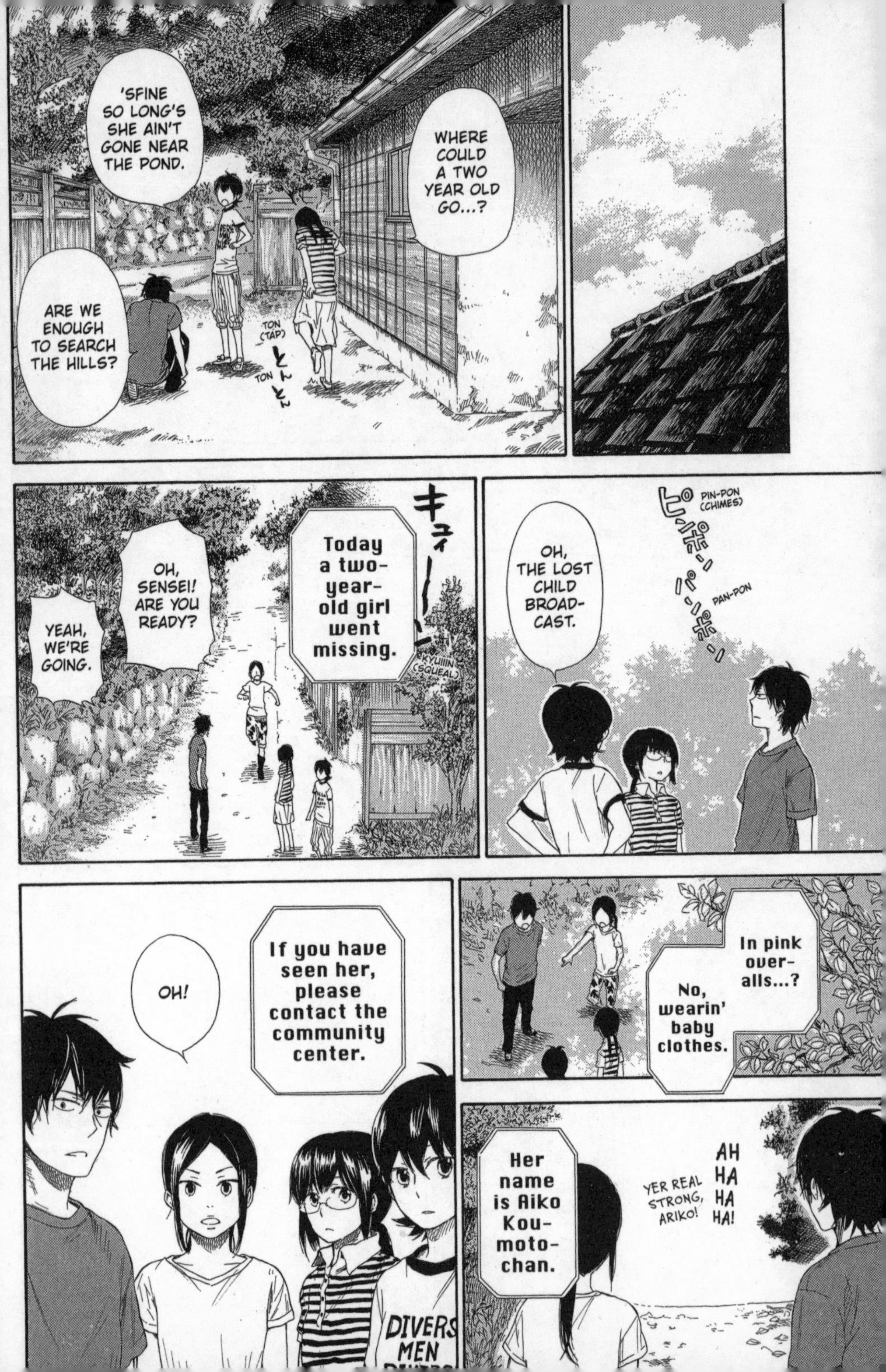
WHERE COULD A TWO YEAR OLD GO...?
'SFINE SO LONG'S SHE AIN'T GONE NEAR THE POND.
TON (TAP)
TON
ARE WE ENOUGH TO SEARCH THE HILLS?
PIN-PON (CHIMES)
PAN-PON
OH, THE LOST CHILD BROADCAST.
KYUIIIN (SQUEAL)
Today a two-year-old girl went missing.
OH, SENSEI! ARE YOU READY?
YEAH, WE'RE GOING.
In pink overalls...?
No, wearin' baby clothes.
AH HA HA HA!
YER REAL STRONG, ARIKO!
Her name is Aiko Koumoto-chan.
If you have seen her, please contact the community center.
OH!
DIVERS MEN

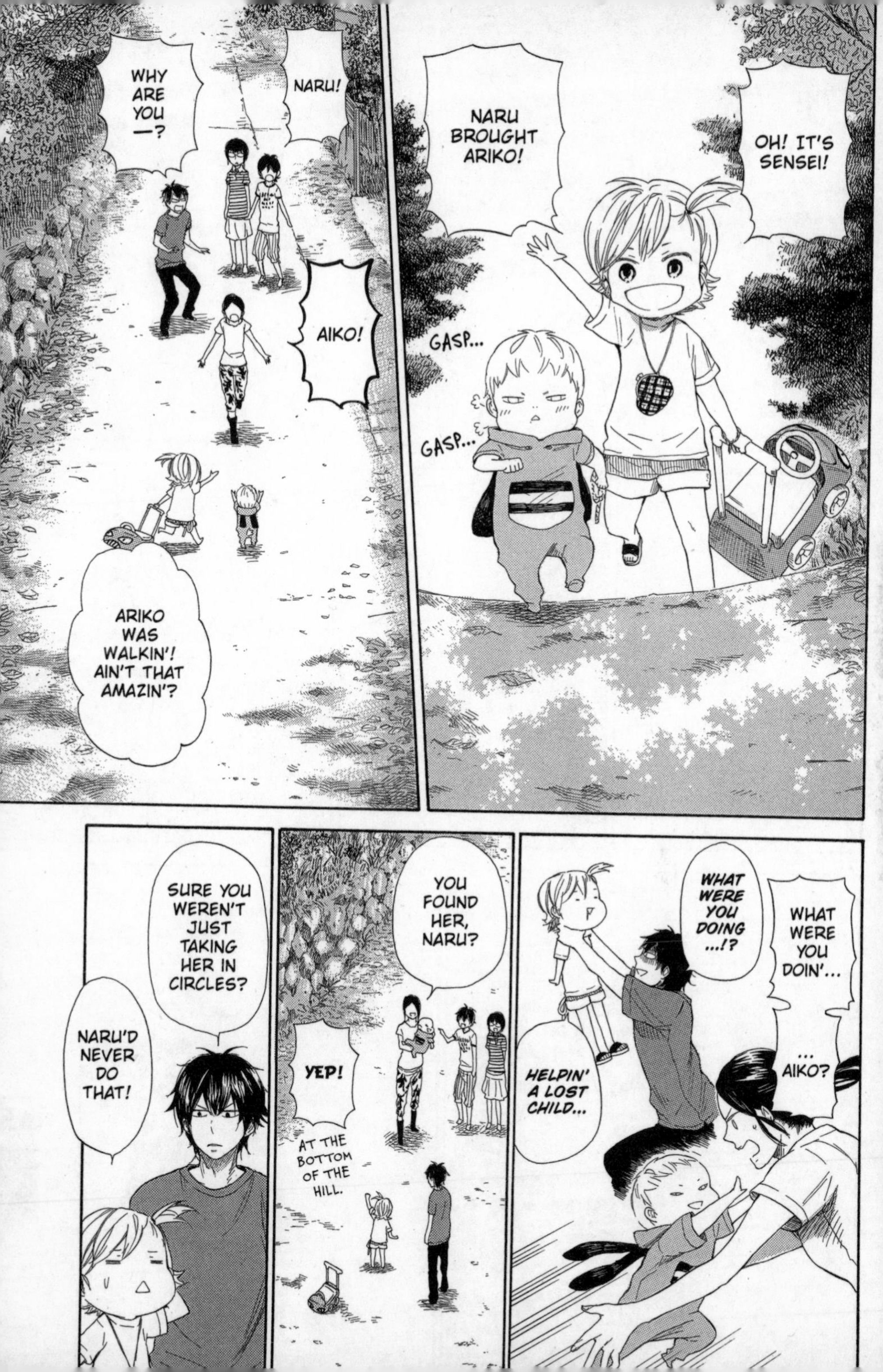
OH! IT'S SENSEI!
NARU BROUGHT ARIKO!
GASP...
GASP...
NARU!
WHY ARE YOU—?
AIKO!
ARIKO WAS WALKIN'! AIN'T THAT AMAZIN'?
WHAT WERE YOU DOIN'...
WHAT WERE YOU DOING...!?
HELPIN' A LOST CHILD...
...AIKO?
YOU FOUND HER, NARU?
YEP!
AT THE BOTTOM OF THE HILL.
SURE YOU WEREN'T JUST TAKING HER IN CIRCLES?
NARU'D NEVER DO THAT!

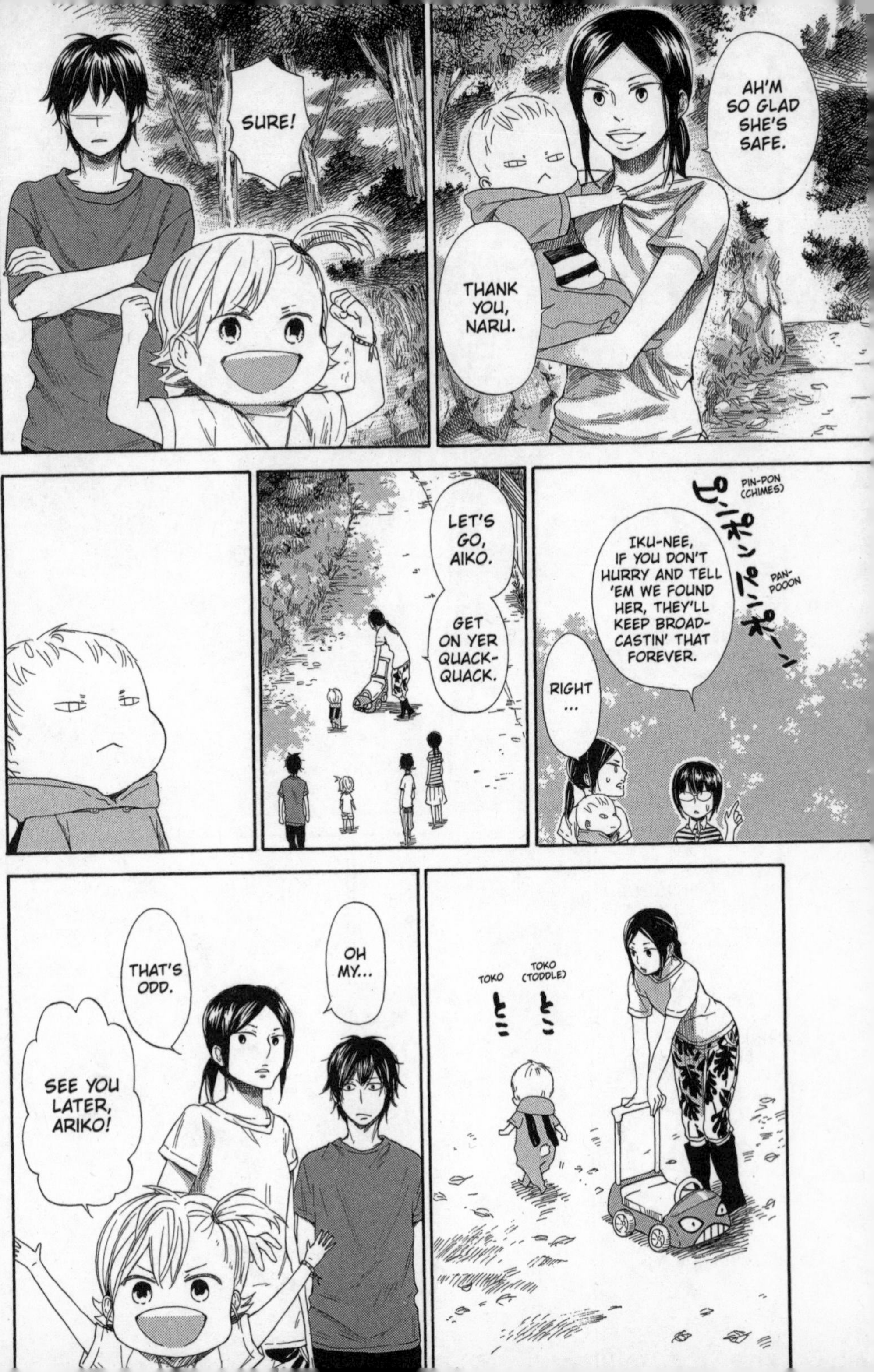
AH'M SO GLAD SHE'S SAFE.
THANK YOU, NARU.
SURE!
ピンポンパンポーン
PIN-PON (CHIMES)
PAN-POOON
IKU-NEE, IF YOU DON'T HURRY AND TELL 'EM WE FOUND HER, THEY'LL KEEP BROAD-CASTIN' THAT FOREVER.
RIGHT ...
LET'S GO, AIKO.
GET ON YER QUACK-QUACK.
とこ
TOKO (TODDLE)
とこ
TOKO
OH MY...
THAT'S ODD.
SEE YOU LATER, ARIKO!

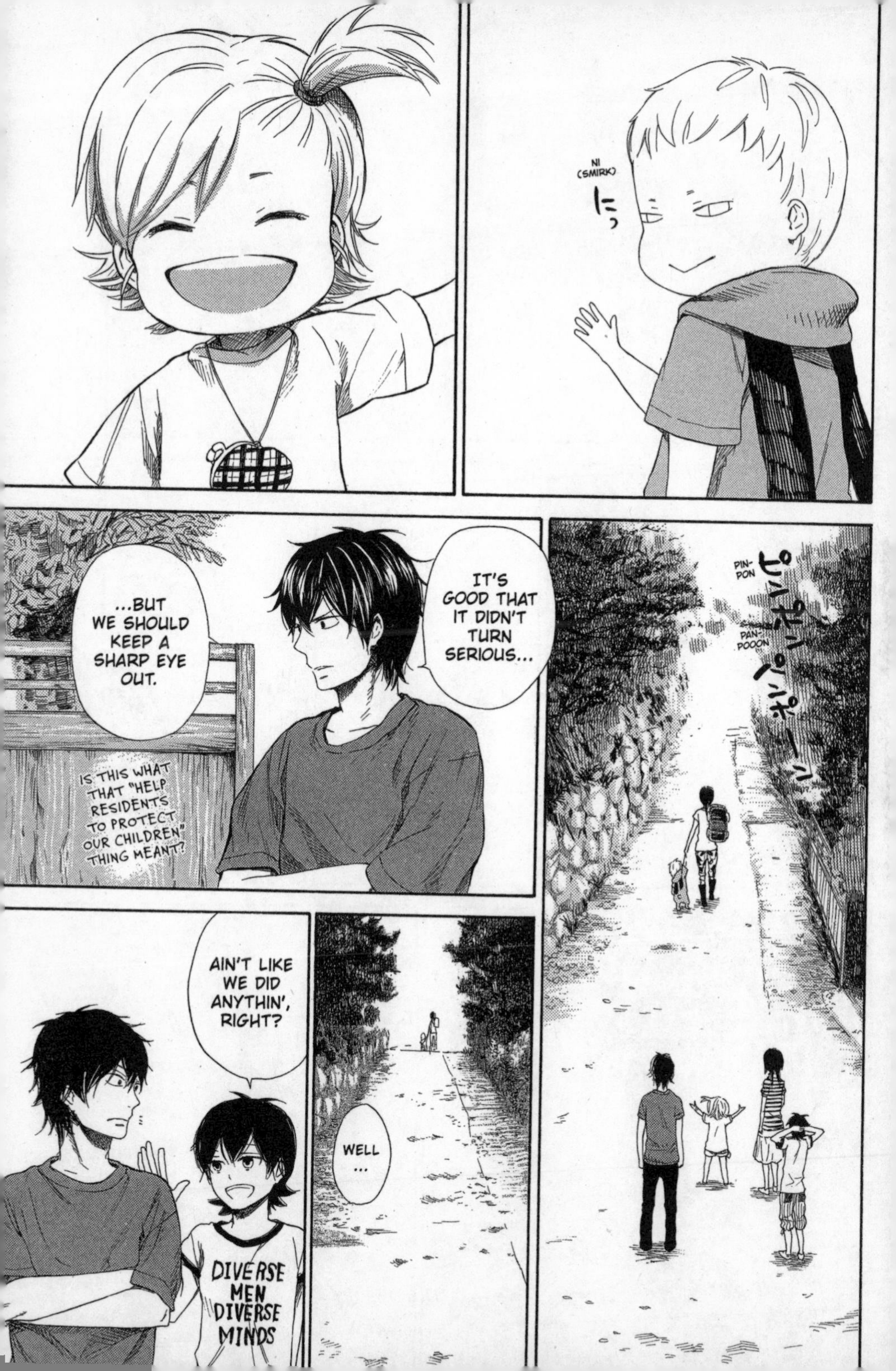
NI (SMIRK)
にっ
PIN-PON
ピンポン
PAN-POOON
パンポーン
IT'S GOOD THAT IT DIDN'T TURN SERIOUS...
...BUT WE SHOULD KEEP A SHARP EYE OUT.
IS THIS WHAT THAT "HELP RESIDENTS TO PROTECT OUR CHILDREN" THING MEANT?
WELL ...
AIN'T LIKE WE DID ANYTHIN', RIGHT?
DIVERSE MEN DIVERSE MINDS

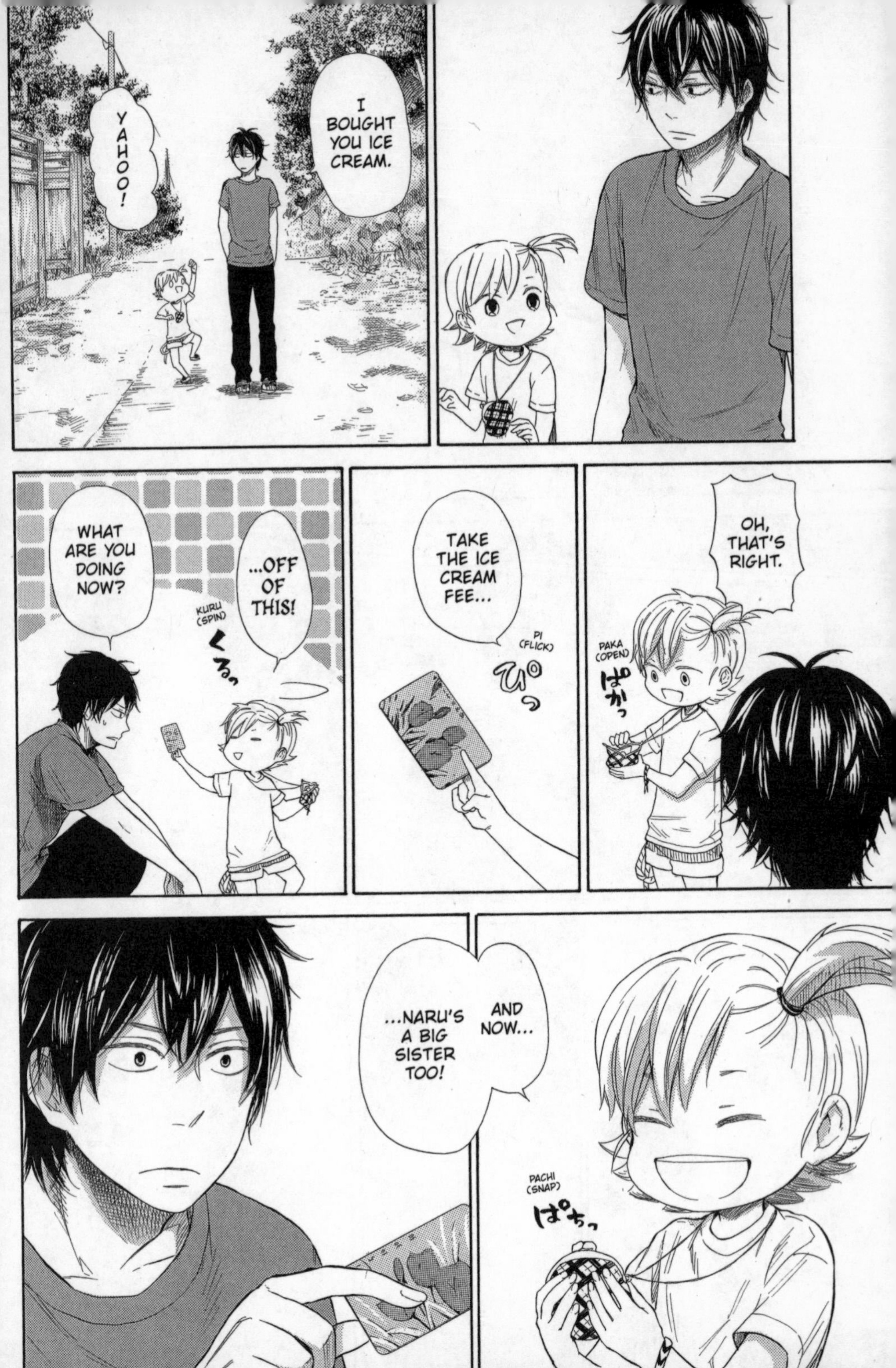
I BOUGHT YOU ICE CREAM.
YAHOO!
OH, THAT'S RIGHT.
PAKA (OPEN)
ぱかっ
TAKE THE ICE CREAM FEE...
PI (FLICK)
ぴっ
...OFF OF THIS!
KURU (SPIN)
くるっ
WHAT ARE YOU DOING NOW?
AND NOW...
...NARU'S A BIG SISTER TOO!
PACHI (SNAP)
ぱちっ

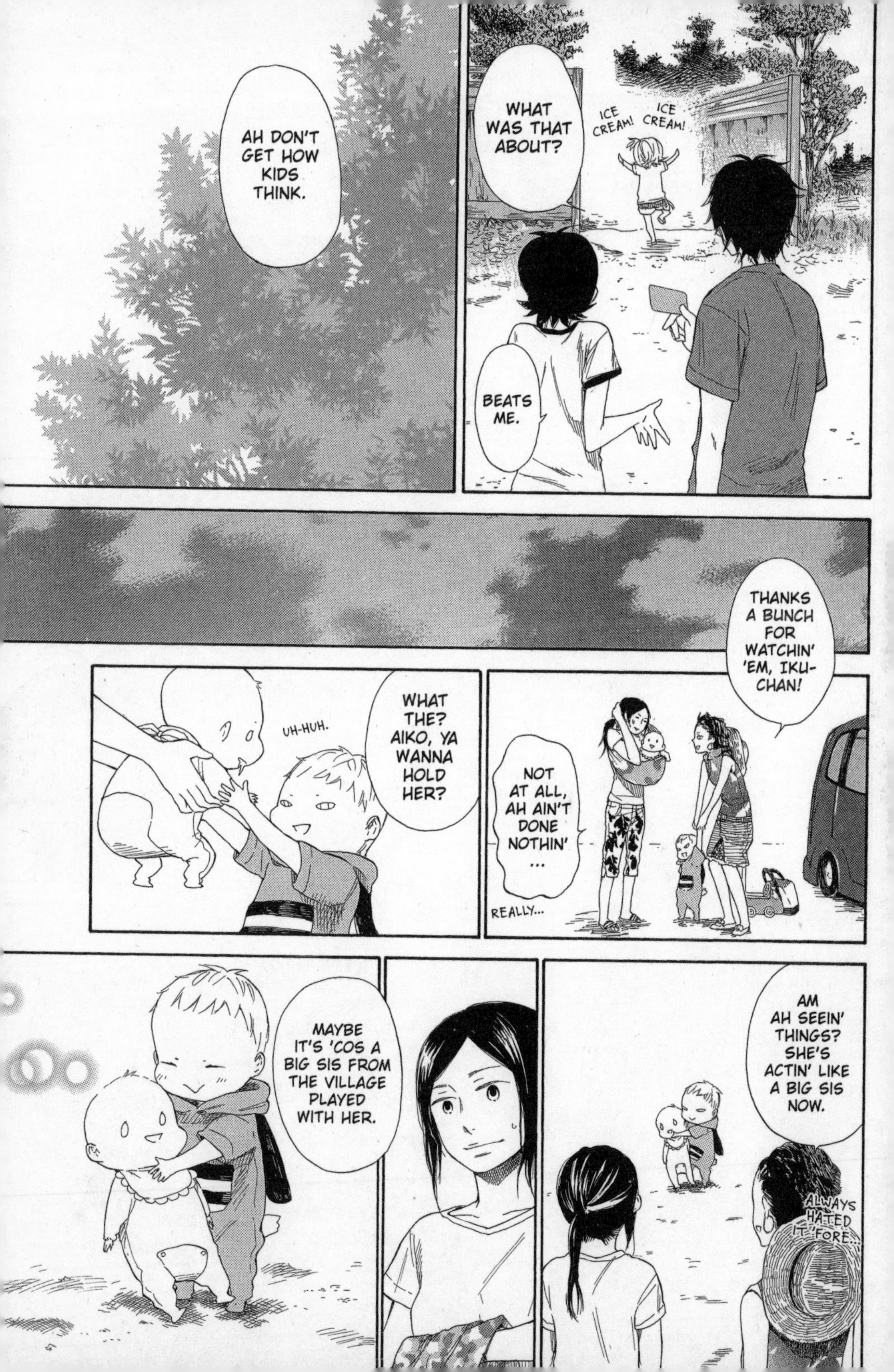
WHAT WAS THAT ABOUT?
ICE CREAM!
ICE CREAM!
BEATS ME.
AH DON'T GET HOW KIDS THINK.
THANKS A BUNCH FOR WATCHIN' 'EM, IKU-CHAN!
NOT AT ALL, AH AIN'T DONE NOTHIN' ...
REALLY...
WHAT THE? AIKO, YA WANNA HOLD HER?
UH-HUH.
AM AH SEEIN' THINGS? SHE'S ACTIN' LIKE A BIG SIS NOW.
ALWAYS HATED IT 'FORE...
MAYBE IT'S 'COS A BIG SIS FROM THE VILLAGE PLAYED WITH HER.

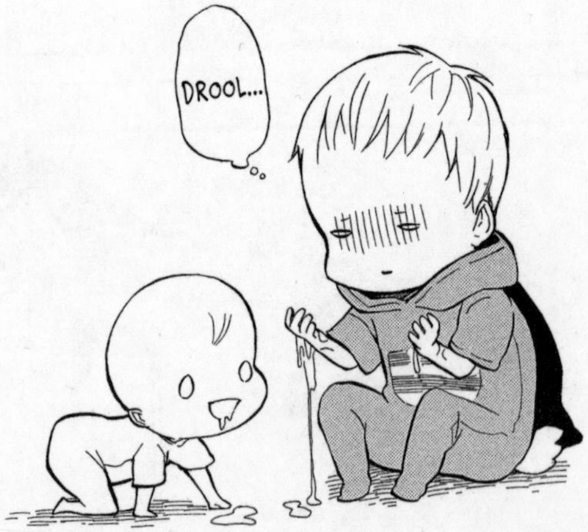
DROOL...

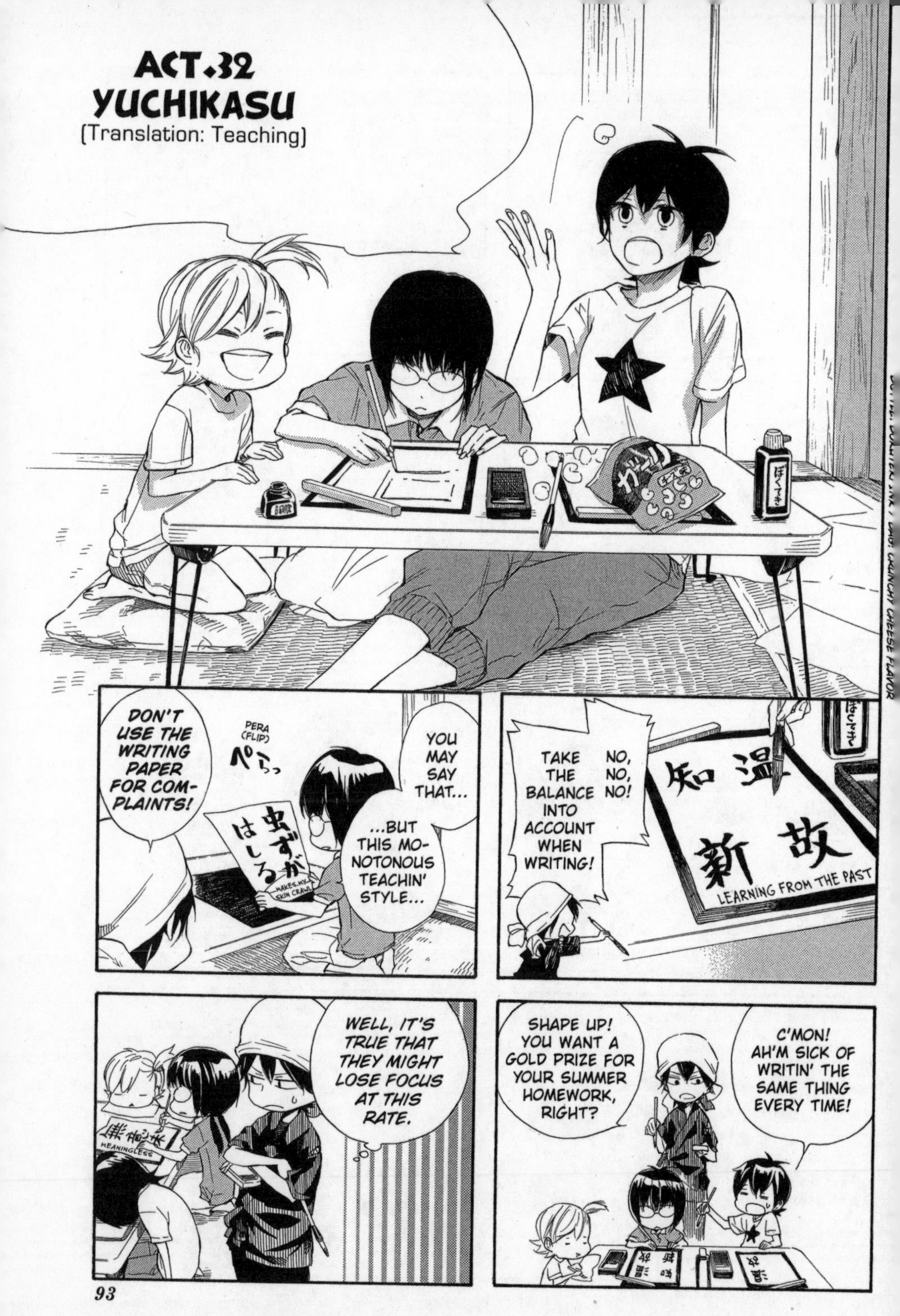
ACT.32
YUCHIKASU
(Translation: Teaching)
CRUNCHY CHEESE FLAVOR
知 温
新 故
LEARNING FROM THE PAST
NO, NO, NO!
TAKE THE BALANCE INTO ACCOUNT WHEN WRITING!
YOU MAY SAY THAT...
...BUT THIS MONOTONOUS TEACHIN' STYLE...
PERA (FLIP)
ぺらっ
虫ずがはしる
MAKES MY SKIN CRAWL
DON'T USE THE WRITING PAPER FOR COMPLAINTS!
C'MON! AH'M SICK OF WRITIN' THE SAME THING EVERY TIME!
SHAPE UP! YOU WANT A GOLD PRIZE FOR YOUR SUMMER HOMEWORK, RIGHT?
WELL, IT'S TRUE THAT THEY MIGHT LOSE FOCUS AT THIS RATE.
MEANINGLESS

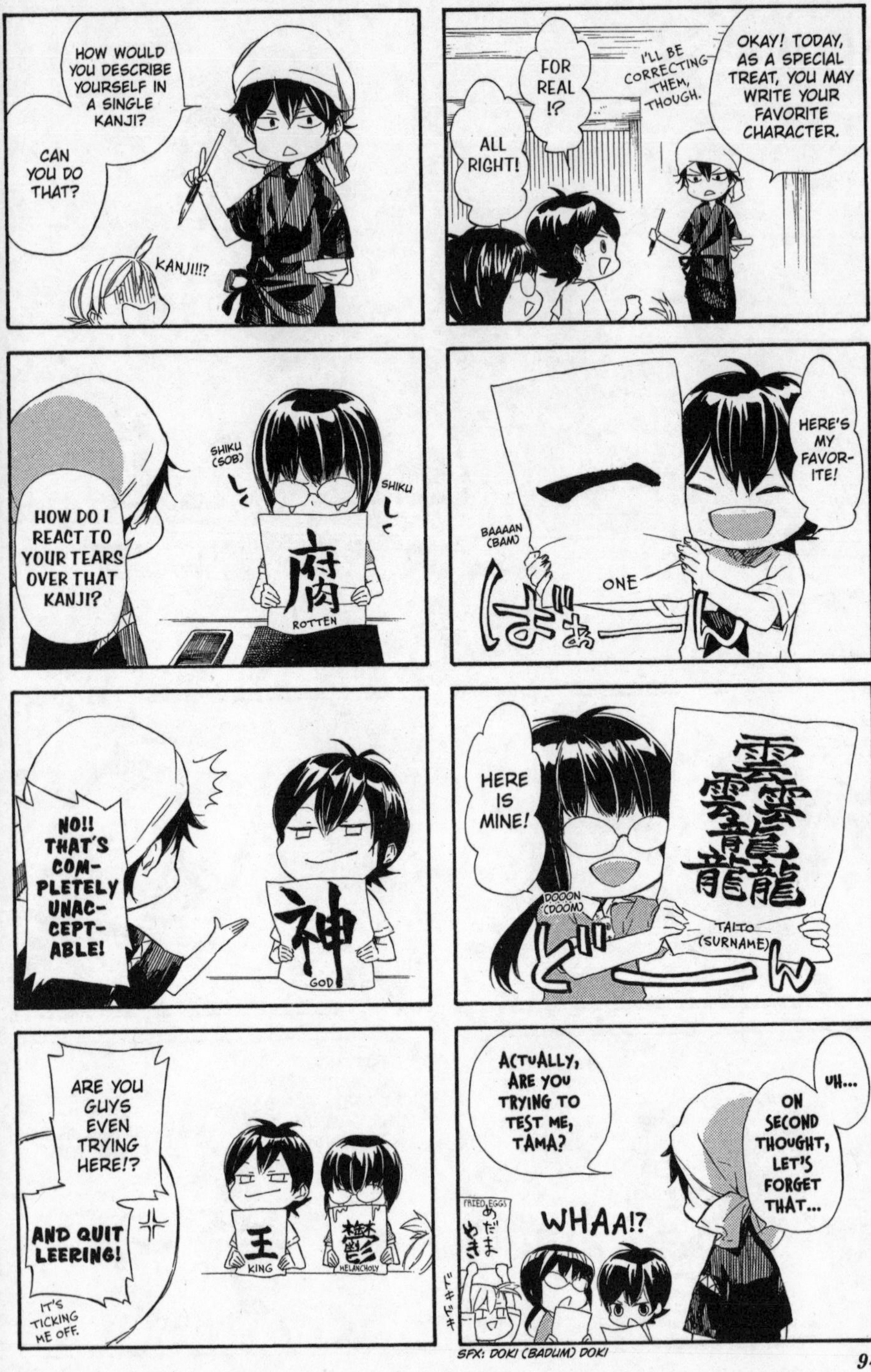
OKAY! TODAY, AS A SPECIAL TREAT, YOU MAY WRITE YOUR FAVORITE CHARACTER.
I'LL BE CORRECTING THEM, THOUGH.
FOR REAL!?
ALL RIGHT!
HOW WOULD YOU DESCRIBE YOURSELF IN A SINGLE KANJI?
CAN YOU DO THAT?
KANJI!!?
HERE'S MY FAVOR-ITE!
BAAAAN (BAM)
ONE
一
ばぁーーん
SHIKU (SOB)
しく
SHIKU
しく
腐
ROTTEN
HOW DO I REACT TO YOUR TEARS OVER THAT KANJI!?
HERE IS MINE!
DOOON (DOOM)
TAITO (SURNAME)
どーーん
神
GOD
NO!! THAT'S COM-PLETELY UNACC-EPT-ABLE!
ACTUALLY, ARE YOU TRYING TO TEST ME, TAMA?
UH...
ON SECOND THOUGHT, LET'S FORGET THAT...
FRIED EGGS
めだまやき
WHAA!?
ドキドキ
ARE YOU GUYS EVEN TRYING HERE!?
AND QUIT LEERING!
王
KING
鬱
MELANCHOLY
IT'S TICKING ME OFF.

SFX: DOKI (BADUM) DOKI

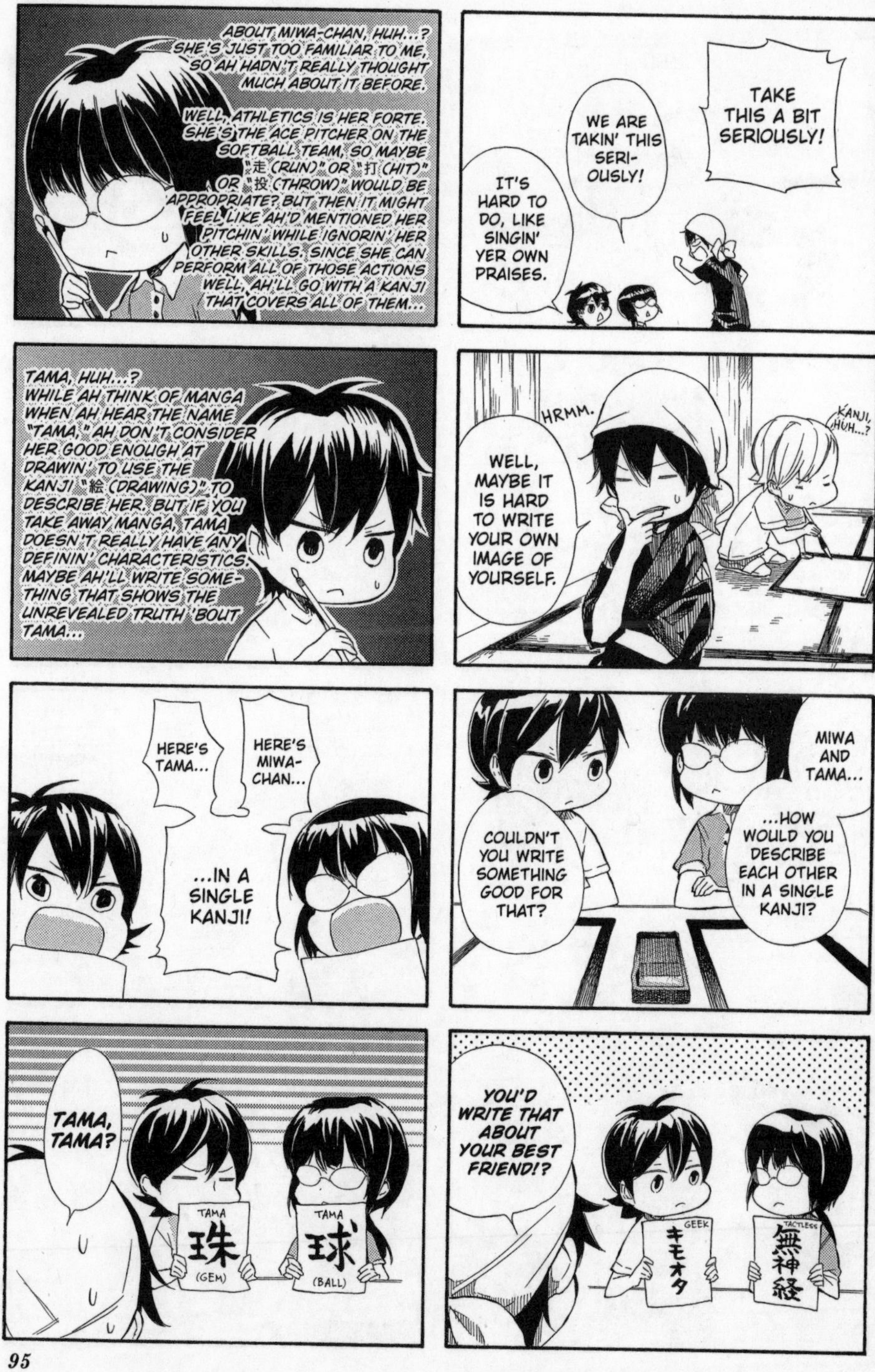
TAKE THIS A BIT SERIOUSLY!
WE ARE TAKIN' THIS SERI-OUSLY!
IT'S HARD TO DO, LIKE SINGIN' YER OWN PRAISES.
ABOUT MIWA-CHAN, HUH...? SHE'S JUST TOO FAMILIAR TO ME, SO AH HADN'T REALLY THOUGHT MUCH ABOUT IT BEFORE.
WELL, ATHLETICS IS HER FORTE. SHE'S THE ACE PITCHER ON THE SOFTBALL TEAM, SO MAYBE "走 (RUN)" OR "打 (HIT)" OR "投 (THROW)" WOULD BE APPROPRIATE? BUT THEN IT MIGHT FEEL LIKE AH'D MENTIONED HER PITCHIN' WHILE IGNORIN' HER OTHER SKILLS. SINCE SHE CAN PERFORM ALL OF THOSE ACTIONS WELL, AH'LL GO WITH A KANJI THAT COVERS ALL OF THEM...
KANJI, HUH...?
HRMM.
WELL, MAYBE IT IS HARD TO WRITE YOUR OWN IMAGE OF YOURSELF.
TAMA, HUH...? WHILE AH THINK OF MANGA WHEN AH HEAR THE NAME "TAMA," AH DON'T CONSIDER HER GOOD ENOUGH AT DRAWIN' TO USE THE KANJI "絵 (DRAWING)" TO DESCRIBE HER. BUT IF YOU TAKE AWAY MANGA, TAMA DOESN'T REALLY HAVE ANY DEFININ' CHARACTERISTICS. MAYBE AH'LL WRITE SOME-THING THAT SHOWS THE UNREVEALED TRUTH 'BOUT TAMA...
MIWA AND TAMA...
...HOW WOULD YOU DESCRIBE EACH OTHER IN A SINGLE KANJI?
COULDN'T YOU WRITE SOMETHING GOOD FOR THAT?
HERE'S MIWA-CHAN...
HERE'S TAMA...
...IN A SINGLE KANJI!
YOU'D WRITE THAT ABOUT YOUR BEST FRIEND!?
TACTLESS
無神経
GEEK
キモオタ
TAMA, TAMA?
TAMA
球
(BALL)
TAMA
珠
(GEM)

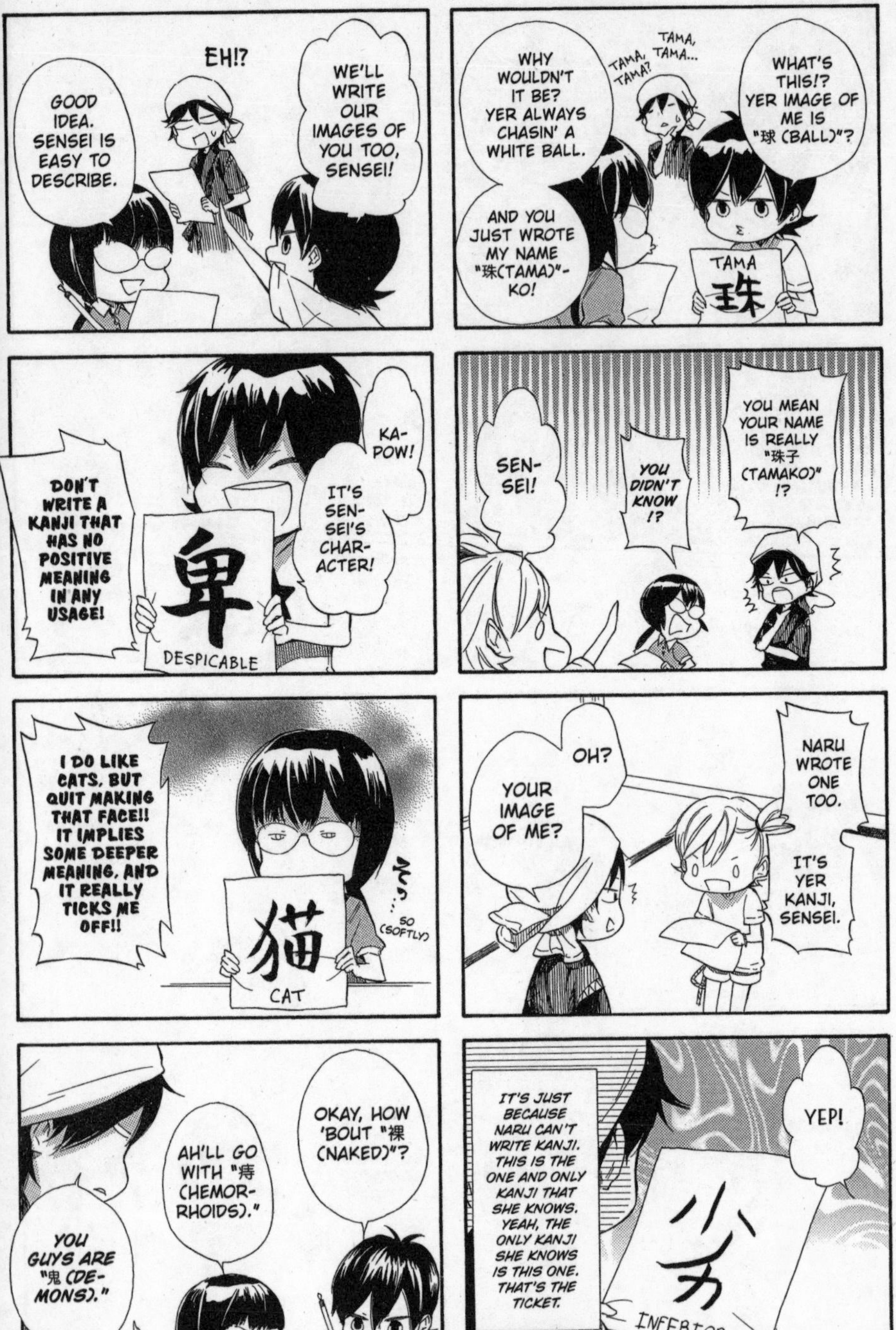
WHAT'S THIS!? YER IMAGE OF ME IS "球 (BALL)"?
TAMA, TAMA...
TAMA, TAMA?
WHY WOULDN'T IT BE? YER ALWAYS CHASIN' A WHITE BALL.
AND YOU JUST WROTE MY NAME "珠(TAMA)"-KO!
TAMA
珠
WE'LL WRITE OUR IMAGES OF YOU TOO, SENSEI!
EH!?
GOOD IDEA. SENSEI IS EASY TO DESCRIBE.
YOU MEAN YOUR NAME IS REALLY "珠子 (TAMAKO)"!?
YOU DIDN'T KNOW!?
SEN-SEI!
KA-POW!
IT'S SEN-SEI'S CHAR-ACTER!
卑
DESPICABLE
DON'T WRITE A KANJI THAT HAS NO POSITIVE MEANING IN ANY USAGE!
NARU WROTE ONE TOO.
IT'S YER KANJI, SENSEI.
OH?
YOUR IMAGE OF ME?
SO (SOFTLY)
猫
CAT
I DO LIKE CATS, BUT QUIT MAKING THAT FACE!! IT IMPLIES SOME DEEPER MEANING, AND IT REALLY TICKS ME OFF!!
YEP!
IT'S JUST BECAUSE NARU CAN'T WRITE KANJI. THIS IS THE ONE AND ONLY KANJI THAT SHE KNOWS. YEAH, THE ONLY KANJI SHE KNOWS IS THIS ONE. THAT'S THE TICKET.
劣
INFERIOR
OKAY, HOW 'BOUT "裸 (NAKED)"?
AH'LL GO WITH "痔 (HEMORRHOIDS)."
YOU GUYS ARE "鬼 (DEMONS)."

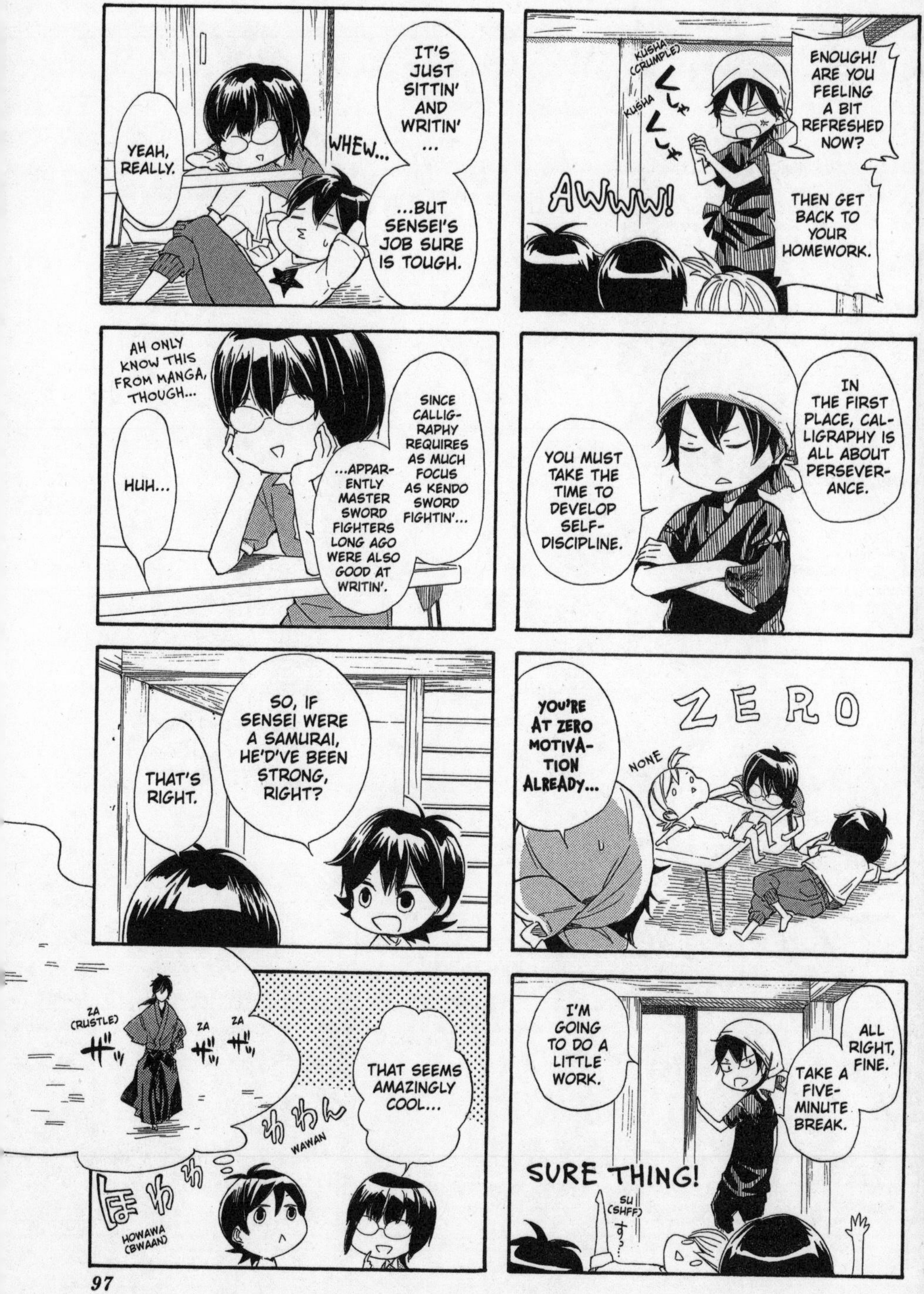
ENOUGH! ARE YOU FEELING A BIT REFRESHED NOW?
KUSHA (CRUMPLE)
くしゃ
KUSHA
くしゃ
THEN GET BACK TO YOUR HOMEWORK.
AWWW!
IN THE FIRST PLACE, CALLIGRAPHY IS ALL ABOUT PERSEVERANCE.
YOU MUST TAKE THE TIME TO DEVELOP SELF-DISCIPLINE.
ZERO
YOU'RE AT ZERO MOTIVATION ALREADY...
NONE
ALL RIGHT, FINE.
TAKE A FIVE-MINUTE BREAK.
I'M GOING TO DO A LITTLE WORK.
SURE THING!
SU (SHFF)
す…
IT'S JUST SITTIN' AND WRITIN' ...
...BUT SENSEI'S JOB SURE IS TOUGH.
WHEW...
YEAH, REALLY.
SINCE CALLIGRAPHY REQUIRES AS MUCH FOCUS AS KENDO SWORD FIGHTIN'...
...APPARENTLY MASTER SWORD FIGHTERS LONG AGO WERE ALSO GOOD AT WRITIN'.
AH ONLY KNOW THIS FROM MANGA, THOUGH...
HUH...
SO, IF SENSEI WERE A SAMURAI, HE'D'VE BEEN STRONG, RIGHT?
THAT'S RIGHT.
THAT SEEMS AMAZINGLY COOL...
わわん
WAWAN
ZA
ザッ
ZA
ザッ
ZA (RUSTLE)
ザッ
ほわわ
HOWAWA (BWAAN)

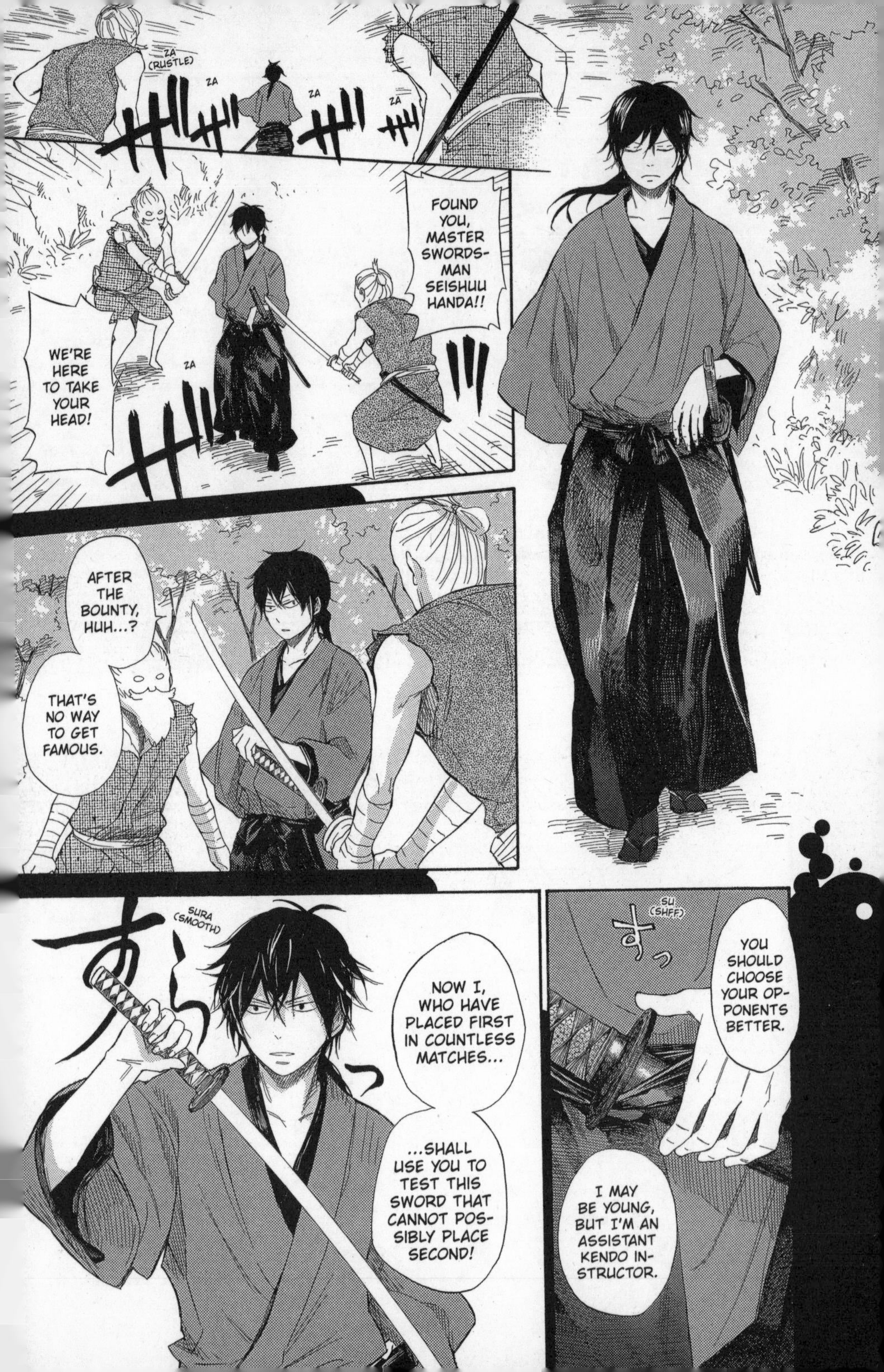
ZA (RUSTLE)
ZA
ZA
ZA
FOUND YOU, MASTER SWORDS-MAN SEISHUU HANDA!!
WE'RE HERE TO TAKE YOUR HEAD!
ZA
AFTER THE BOUNTY, HUH...?
THAT'S NO WAY TO GET FAMOUS.
SU (SHFF)
YOU SHOULD CHOOSE YOUR OP-PONENTS BETTER.
I MAY BE YOUNG, BUT I'M AN ASSISTANT KENDO IN-STRUCTOR.
SURA (SMOOTH)
NOW I, WHO HAVE PLACED FIRST IN COUNTLESS MATCHES...
...SHALL USE YOU TO TEST THIS SWORD THAT CANNOT POS-SIBLY PLACE SECOND!

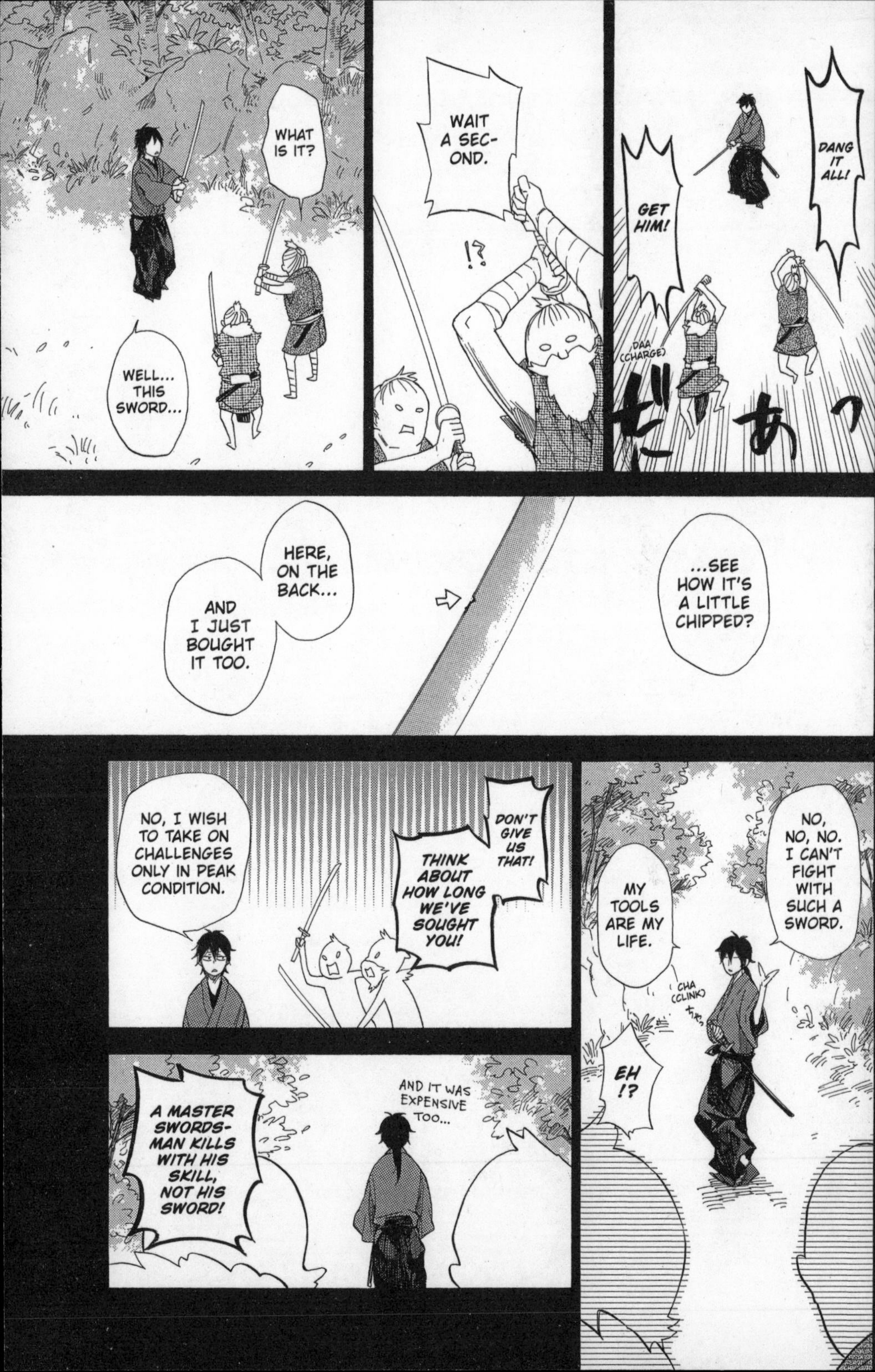
GET HIM!
DANG IT ALL!
DAA (CHARGE)
だあっ
WAIT A SEC-OND.
!?
WHAT IS IT?
WELL... THIS SWORD...
HERE, ON THE BACK...
...SEE HOW IT'S A LITTLE CHIPPED?
AND I JUST BOUGHT IT TOO.
NO, NO, NO. I CAN'T FIGHT WITH SUCH A SWORD.
MY TOOLS ARE MY LIFE.
CHA (CLINK)
EH!?
DON'T GIVE US THAT!
THINK ABOUT HOW LONG WE'VE SOUGHT YOU!
NO, I WISH TO TAKE ON CHALLENGES ONLY IN PEAK CONDITION.
AND IT WAS EXPENSIVE TOO...
A MASTER SWORDS-MAN KILLS WITH HIS SKILL, NOT HIS SWORD!

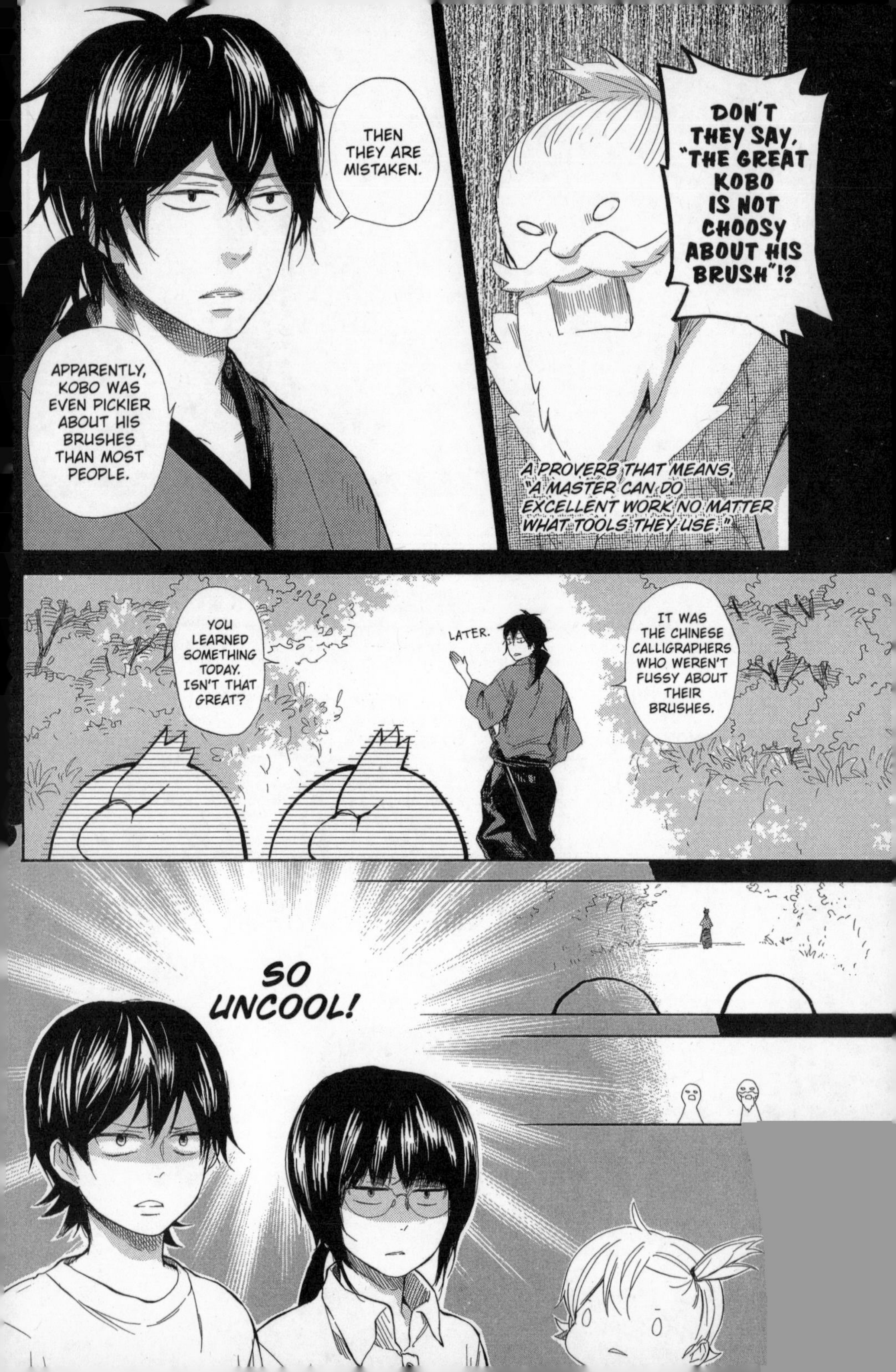
DON'T THEY SAY, "THE GREAT KOBO IS NOT CHOOSY ABOUT HIS BRUSH"!?
A PROVERB THAT MEANS, "A MASTER CAN DO EXCELLENT WORK NO MATTER WHAT TOOLS THEY USE."
THEN THEY ARE MISTAKEN.
APPARENTLY, KOBO WAS EVEN PICKIER ABOUT HIS BRUSHES THAN MOST PEOPLE.
IT WAS THE CHINESE CALLIGRAPHERS WHO WEREN'T FUSSY ABOUT THEIR BRUSHES.
LATER.
YOU LEARNED SOMETHING TODAY. ISN'T THAT GREAT?
SO UNCOOL!

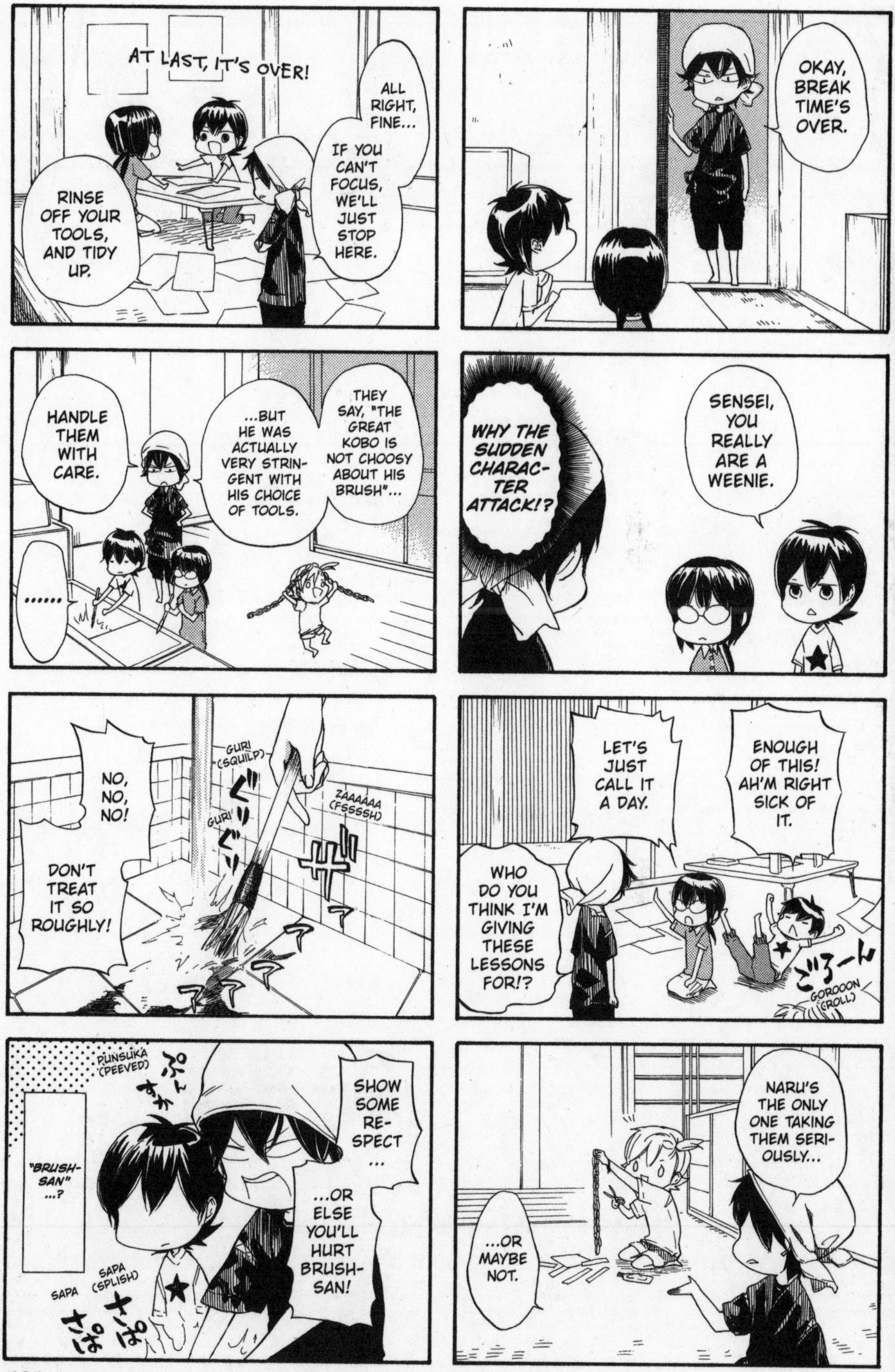
OKAY, BREAK TIME'S OVER.
SENSEI, YOU REALLY ARE A WEENIE.
WHY THE SUDDEN CHARACTER-ATTACK!?
ENOUGH OF THIS! AH'M RIGHT SICK OF IT.
LET'S JUST CALL IT A DAY.
WHO DO YOU THINK I'M GIVING THESE LESSONS FOR!?
ごろーん
GOROOON (ROLL)
NARU'S THE ONLY ONE TAKING THEM SERIOUSLY...
...OR MAYBE NOT.
ALL RIGHT, FINE...
IF YOU CAN'T FOCUS, WE'LL JUST STOP HERE.
AT LAST, IT'S OVER!
RINSE OFF YOUR TOOLS, AND TIDY UP.
THEY SAY, "THE GREAT KOBO IS NOT CHOOSY ABOUT HIS BRUSH"...
...BUT HE WAS ACTUALLY VERY STRINGENT WITH HIS CHOICE OF TOOLS.
HANDLE THEM WITH CARE.
......
GURI (SQUILP)
GURI
ZAAAAAA (FSSSSH)
NO, NO, NO!
DON'T TREAT IT SO ROUGHLY!
SHOW SOME RESPECT...
...OR ELSE YOU'LL HURT BRUSH-SAN!
PUNSUKA (PEEVED)
ぷんすか
"BRUSH-SAN"...?
SAPA (SPLISH)
SAPA
さぱさぱ

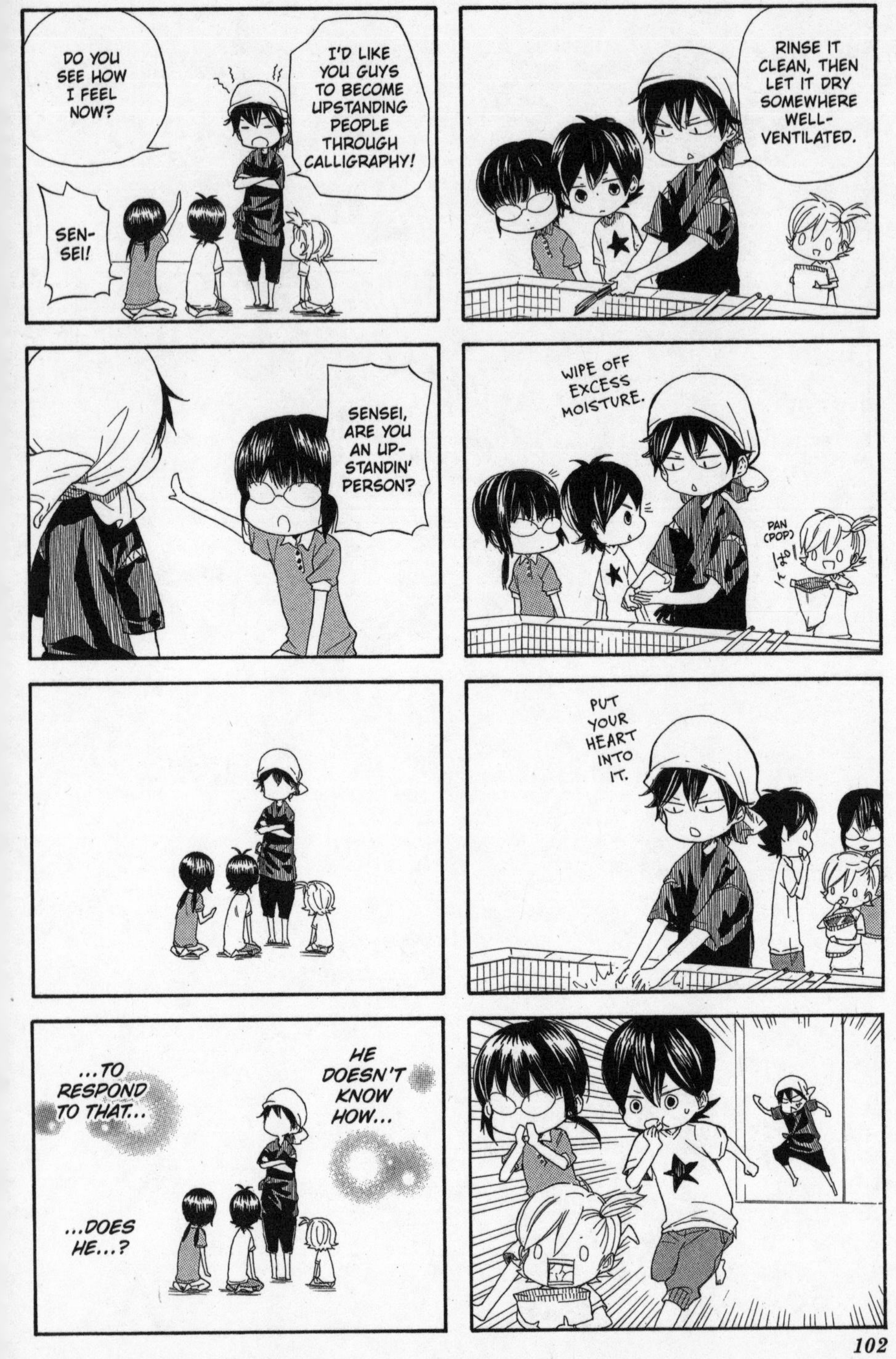
RINSE IT CLEAN, THEN LET IT DRY SOMEWHERE WELL-VENTILATED.
I'D LIKE YOU GUYS TO BECOME UPSTANDING PEOPLE THROUGH CALLIGRAPHY!
DO YOU SEE HOW I FEEL NOW?
SEN-SEI!
WIPE OFF EXCESS MOISTURE.
PAN (POP)
SENSEI, ARE YOU AN UP-STANDIN' PERSON?
PUT YOUR HEART INTO IT.
HE DOESN'T KNOW HOW...
...TO RESPOND TO THAT...
...DOES HE...?

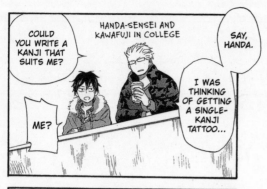

BONUS

HANDA-SENSEI AND KAWAFUJI IN COLLEGE
SAY, HANDA.
I WAS THINKING OF GETTING A SINGLE-KANJI TATTOO...
COULD YOU WRITE A KANJI THAT SUITS ME?
ME?
MAKE IT A COOL ONE.
PI (SNAP)
GEEZ, WHAT A PAIN.
SU (SHFF)
MY ONE AND ONLY FRIEND IS MAKING A LIFE-CHANGING REQUEST.
I CAN'T MESS THIS UP.
BUT WHAT SINGLE KANJI WOULD SUIT HIM? I CAN'T GO WITH THE SUPERFICIAL "眼 (EYE)" FROM "眼鏡 (EYEGLASSES)." AND A KANJI LIKE "龍 (DRAGON)" OR "虎 (TIGER)" WOULD BE OVERDOING IT SO MUCH THAT IT TURNS AROUND AND BECOMES UNCOOL.
HE HAS A GENTLER PERSONALITY, SO A KANJI WITH MANY STROKES WOULD FEEL AWKWARD. I NEED A KANJI THAT'S SIMPLE BUT HAS WIDE-SPREAD APPEAL... ESPECIALLY SINCE KAWAFUJI'S POPULAR...
HOW ABOUT THIS?
犬
DOG
A SMALL RIFT FORMED BETWEEN THEM.

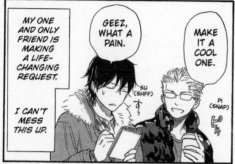

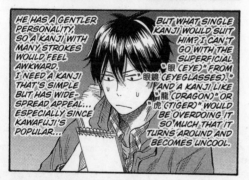

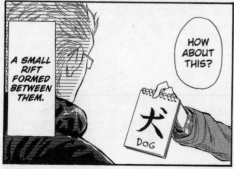

NOW JUST TRY TO ATTACK ME! MY SWORD IS THE WORK OF THE MASTER CRAFTSMAN CHIYOGIKU. IT'S A FINE BLADE THAT APPEARED IN THIS WORLD THREE YEARS AGO, BUT AFTER BOUNCING FROM PLACE TO PLACE...

...IT HAS NOW BECOME A MYSTICAL SWORD. WITH THIS BLADE IN HAND, I AM NOW UNSTOPPABLE! HOWEVER, I DON'T KNOW MY OWN STATS VERY WELL YET. DO SAMURAI REALLY HAVE TO KILL PEOPLE SO READILY? IN ANY CASE, I HATE SMELLING TOO MUCH OF BLOOD, SO WOULD YOU JUST LEAVE ALREADY!? DON'T MAKE ME GET SERIOUS HERE!

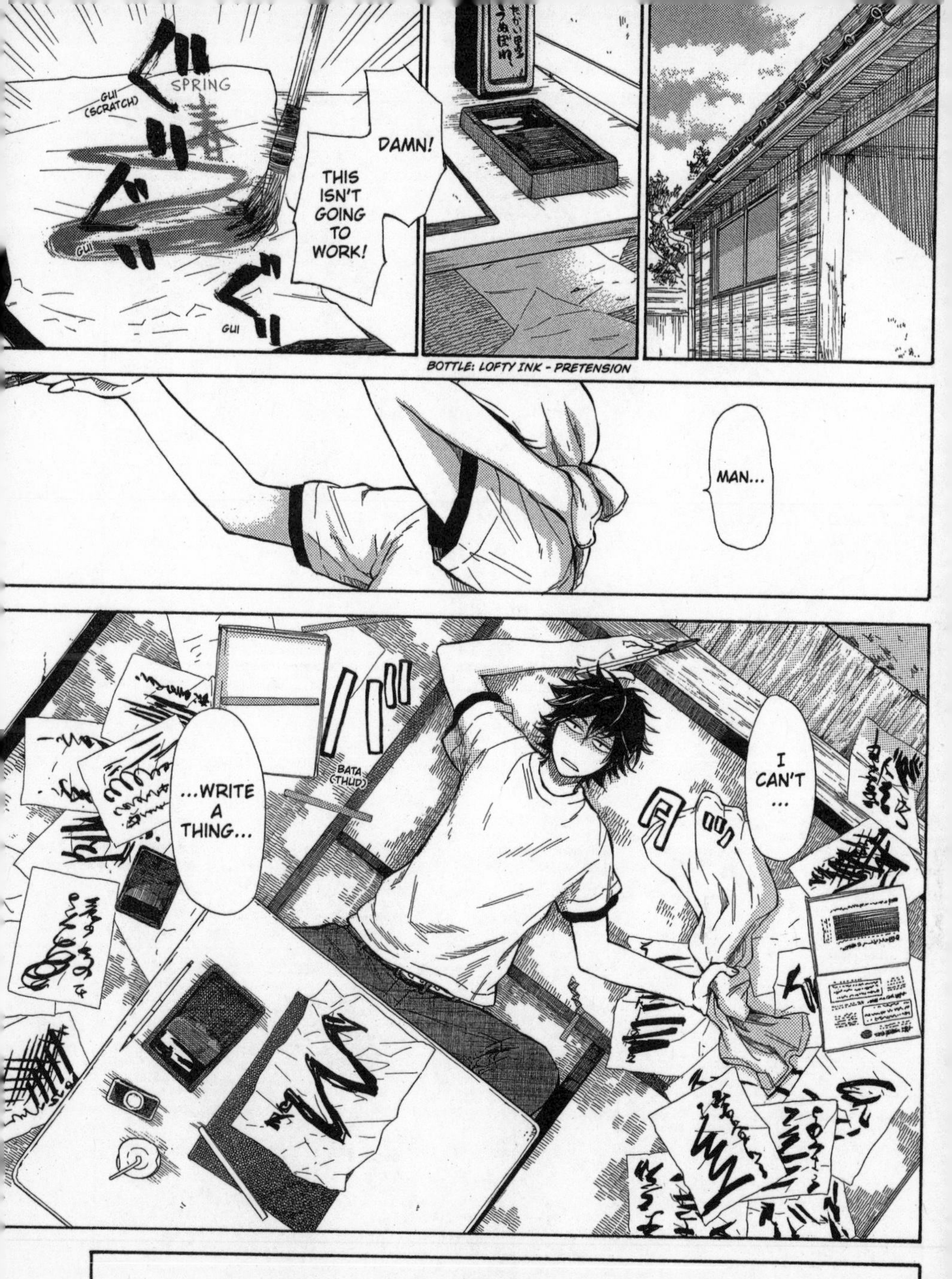
DAMN!
THIS ISN'T GOING TO WORK!
SPRING
GUI (SCRATCH)
GUI
GUI
BOTTLE: LOFTY INK - PRETENSION
MAN...
I CAN'T ...
BATA (THUD)
...WRITE A THING...

ACT.33 MENOHA

(Translation: Wakame Seaweed)

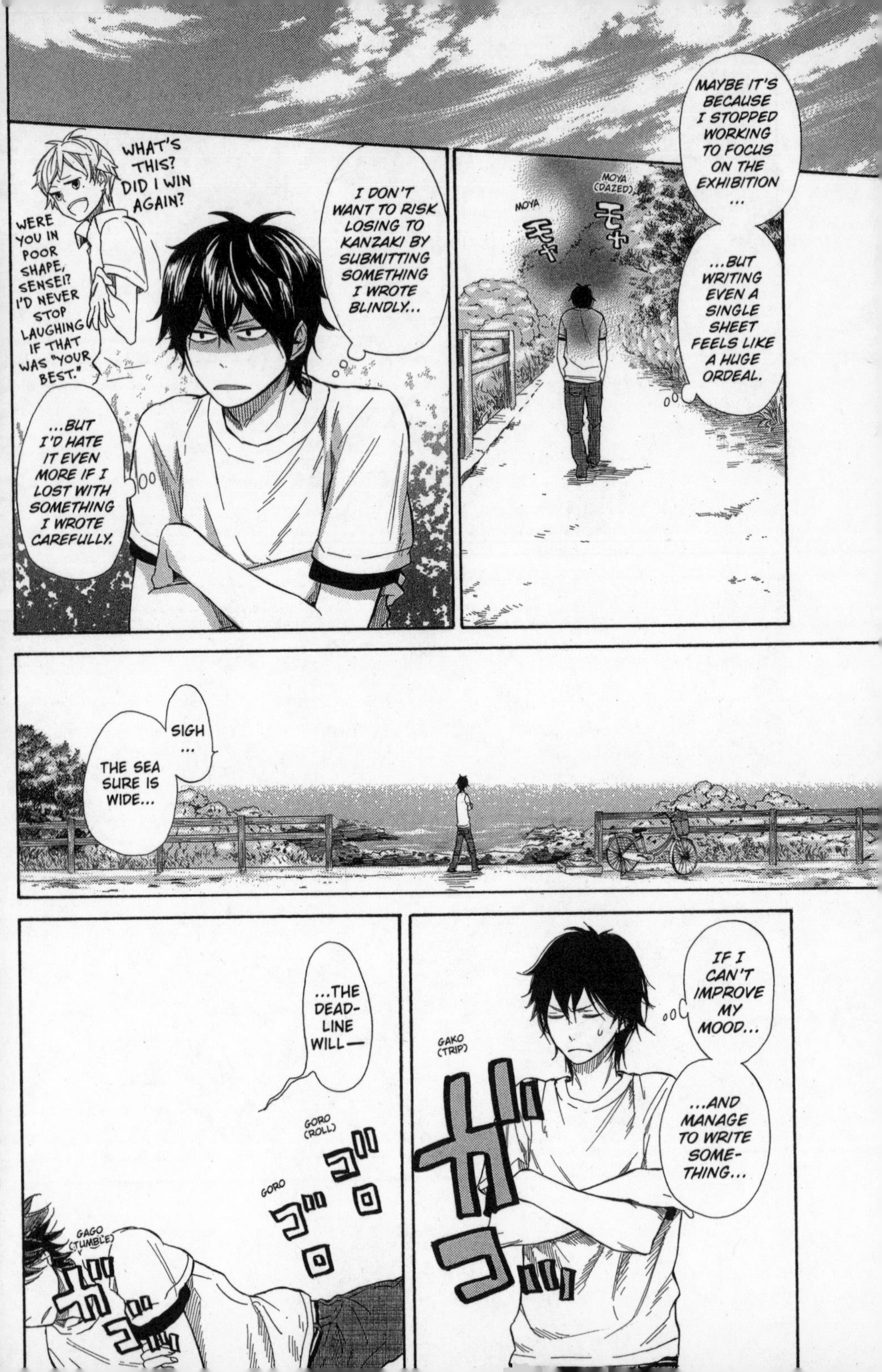
MAYBE IT'S BECAUSE I STOPPED WORKING TO FOCUS ON THE EXHIBITION...
...BUT WRITING EVEN A SINGLE SHEET FEELS LIKE A HUGE ORDEAL.
MOYA (DAZED)
MOYA
I DON'T WANT TO RISK LOSING TO KANZAKI BY SUBMITTING SOMETHING I WROTE BLINDLY...
WHAT'S THIS? DID I WIN AGAIN?
WERE YOU IN POOR SHAPE, SENSEI? I'D NEVER STOP LAUGHING IF THAT WAS "YOUR BEST."
...BUT I'D HATE IT EVEN MORE IF I LOST WITH SOMETHING I WROTE CAREFULLY.
SIGH...
THE SEA SURE IS WIDE...
IF I CAN'T IMPROVE MY MOOD...
...AND MANAGE TO WRITE SOME-THING...
GAKO (TRIP)
...THE DEAD-LINE WILL—
GORO (ROLL)
GORO
GAGO (TUMBLE)

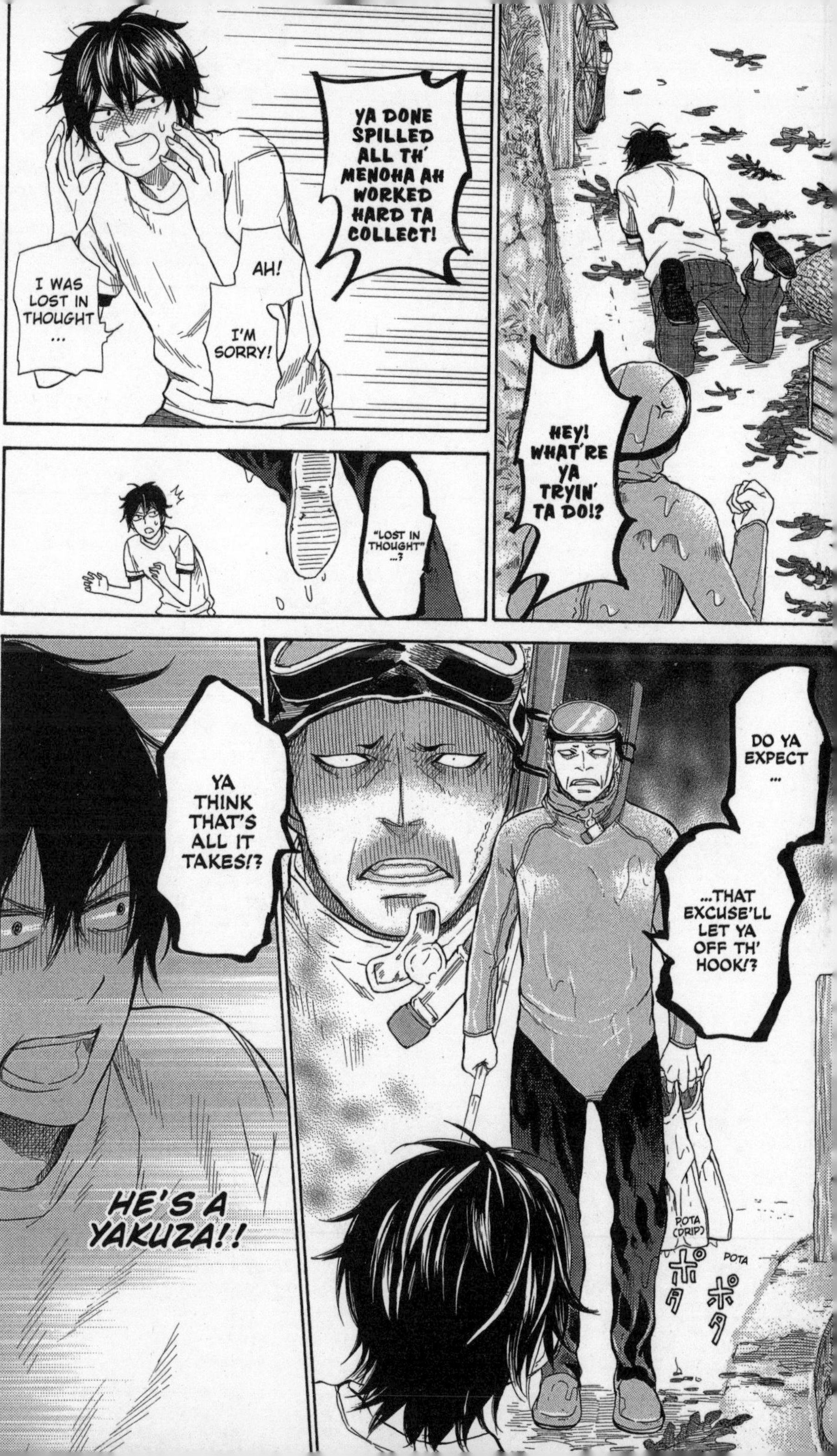
HEY! WHAT'RE YA TRYIN' TA DO!?
YA DONE SPILLED ALL TH' MENOHA AH WORKED HARD TA COLLECT!
AH!
I'M SORRY!
I WAS LOST IN THOUGHT ...
"LOST IN THOUGHT" ...?
DO YA EXPECT ...
...THAT EXCUSE'LL LET YA OFF TH' HOOK!?
POTA (DRIP)
POTA
YA THINK THAT'S ALL IT TAKES!?
HE'S A YAKUZA!!

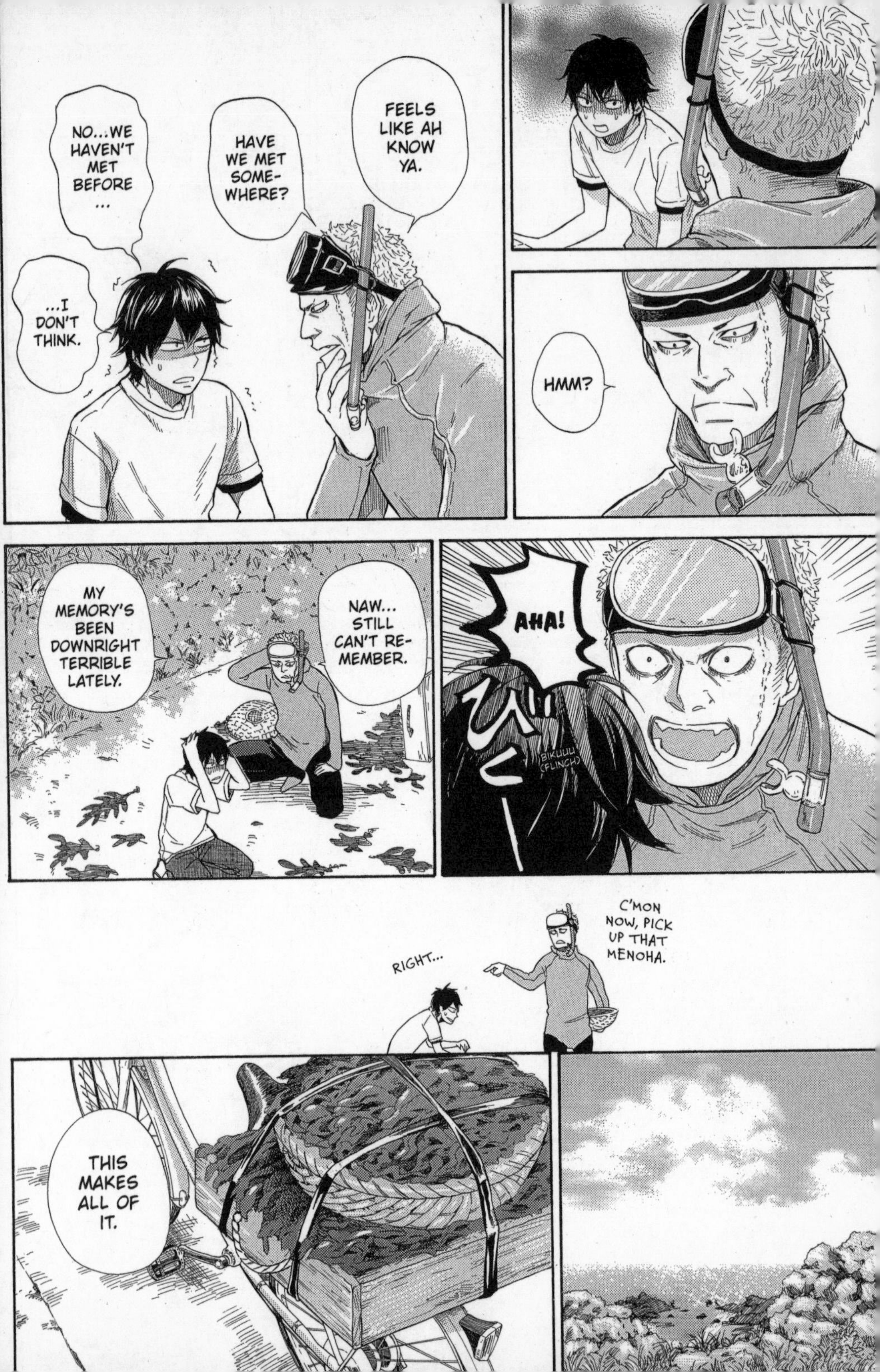
HMM?
FEELS LIKE AH KNOW YA.
HAVE WE MET SOME-WHERE?
NO...WE HAVEN'T MET BEFORE...
...I DON'T THINK.
AHA!
BIKUUU (FLINCH)
NAW... STILL CAN'T RE-MEMBER.
MY MEMORY'S BEEN DOWNRIGHT TERRIBLE LATELY.
C'MON NOW, PICK UP THAT MENOHA.
RIGHT...
THIS MAKES ALL OF IT.

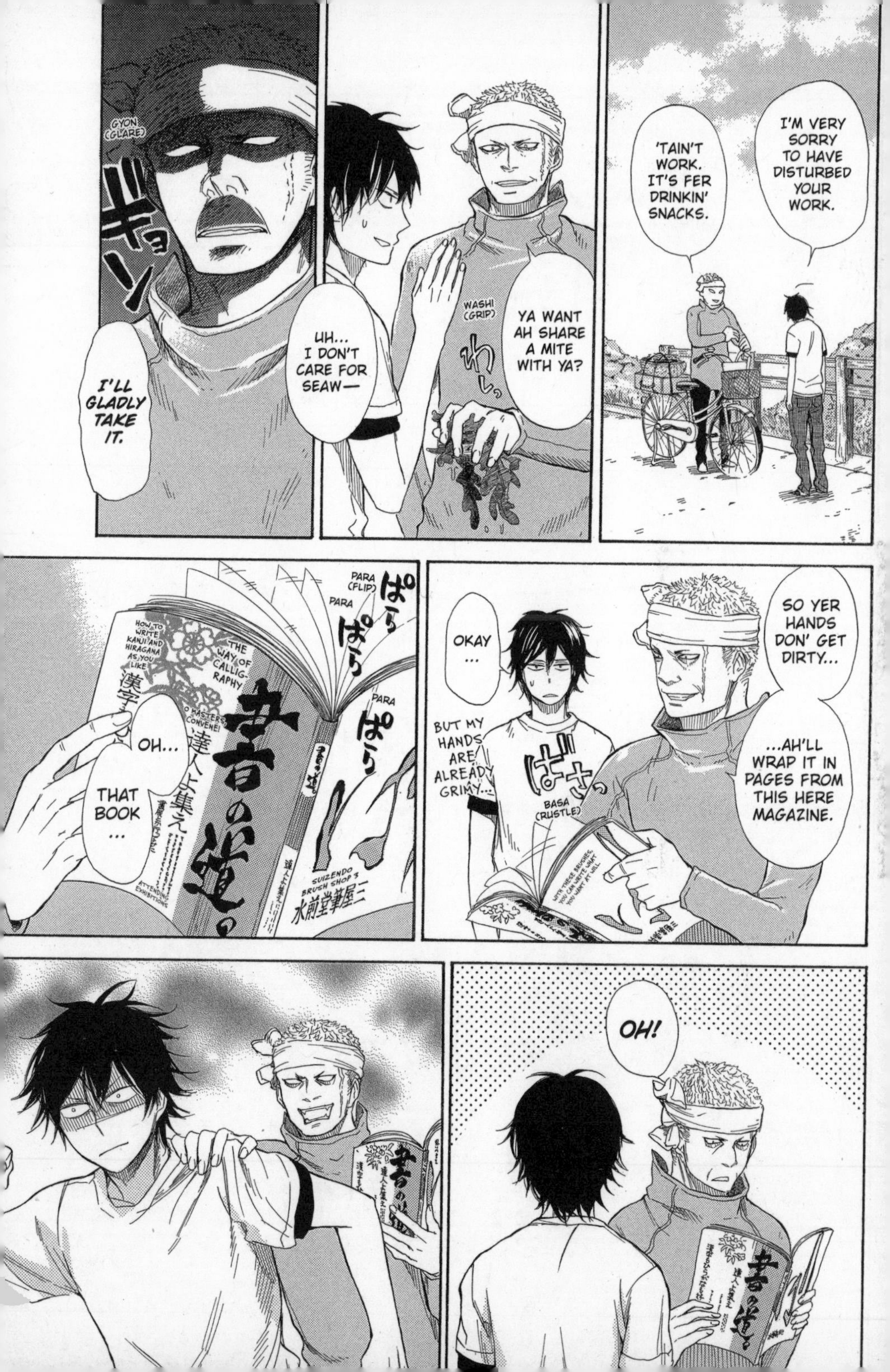
I'M VERY SORRY TO HAVE DISTURBED YOUR WORK.
'TAIN'T WORK. IT'S FER DRINKIN' SNACKS.
YA WANT AH SHARE A MITE WITH YA?
WASHI (GRIP)
わしっ
UH... I DON'T CARE FOR SEAW—
GYON (GLARE)
ギョン
I'LL GLADLY TAKE IT.
SO YER HANDS DON' GET DIRTY...
OKAY ...
...AH'LL WRAP IT IN PAGES FROM THIS HERE MAGAZINE.
BUT MY HANDS ARE ALREADY GRIMY...
BASA (RUSTLE)
ばさっ
WITH THESE BRUSHES, YOU CAN WRITE WHAT YOU WANT AT WILL
PARA (FLIP)
ぱら
PARA
ぱら
PARA
ぱら
THE WAY OF CALLIGRAPHY
書の道
HOW TO WRITE KANJI AND HIRAGANA AS YOU LIKE
O MASTERS, CONVENE!
達人よ集え
ATTENDING EXHIBITIONS
SUIZENDO BRUSH SHOP 3
水前堂筆屋三
OH...
THAT BOOK ...
OH!

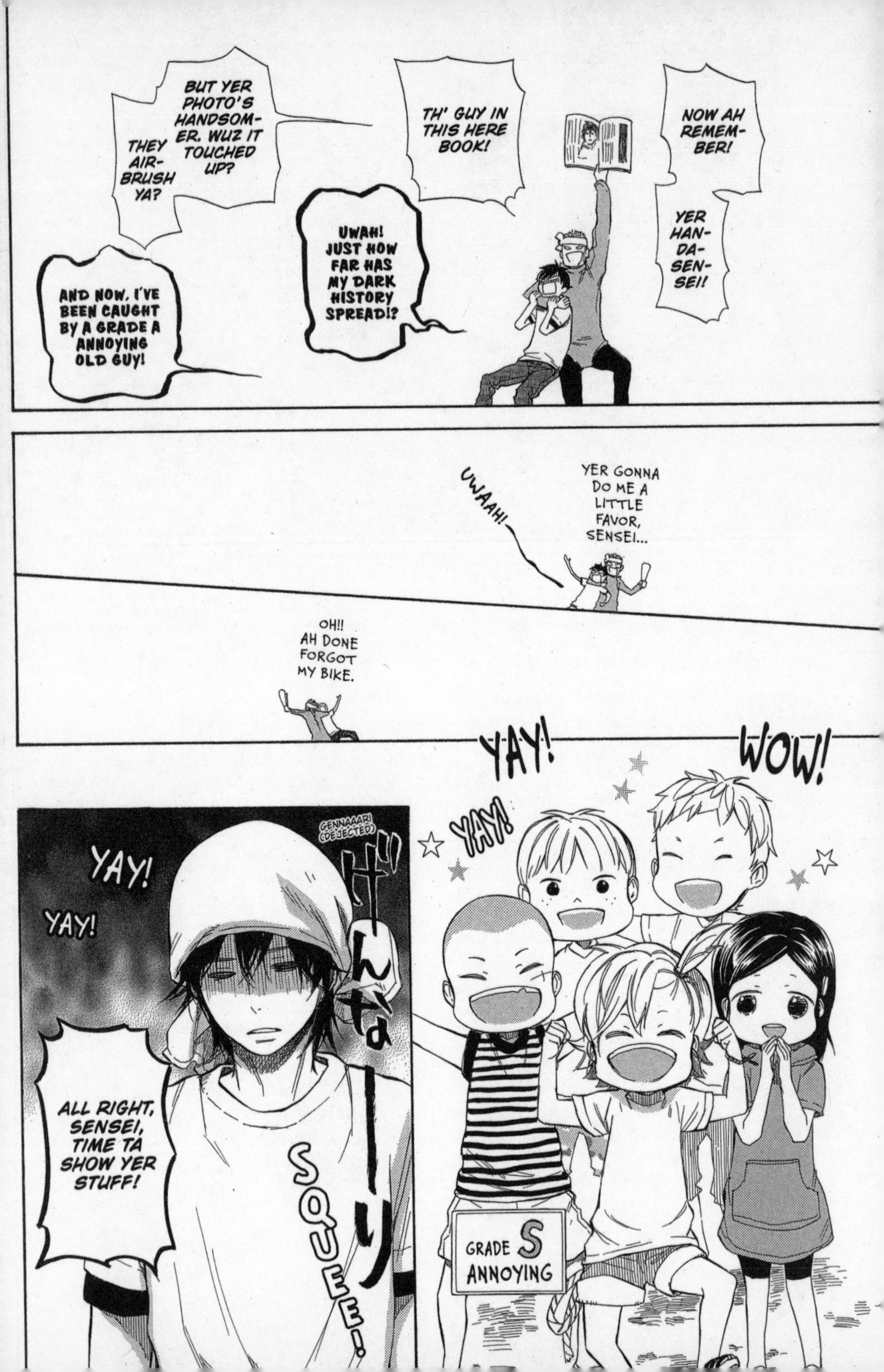
NOW AH REMEMBER!
YER HANDA-SENSEI!
TH' GUY IN THIS HERE BOOK!
BUT YER PHOTO'S HANDSOMER. WUZ IT TOUCHED UP?
THEY AIRBRUSH YA?
UWAH! JUST HOW FAR HAS MY DARK HISTORY SPREAD!?
AND NOW, I'VE BEEN CAUGHT BY A GRADE A ANNOYING OLD GUY!
YER GONNA DO ME A LITTLE FAVOR, SENSEI...
UWAAH!
OH!! AH DONE FORGOT MY BIKE.
WOW!
YAY!
YAY!
GRADE S ANNOYING
GENNAAARI (DEJECTED)
SQUEEE!
YAY!
YAY!
ALL RIGHT, SENSEI, TIME TA SHOW YER STUFF!

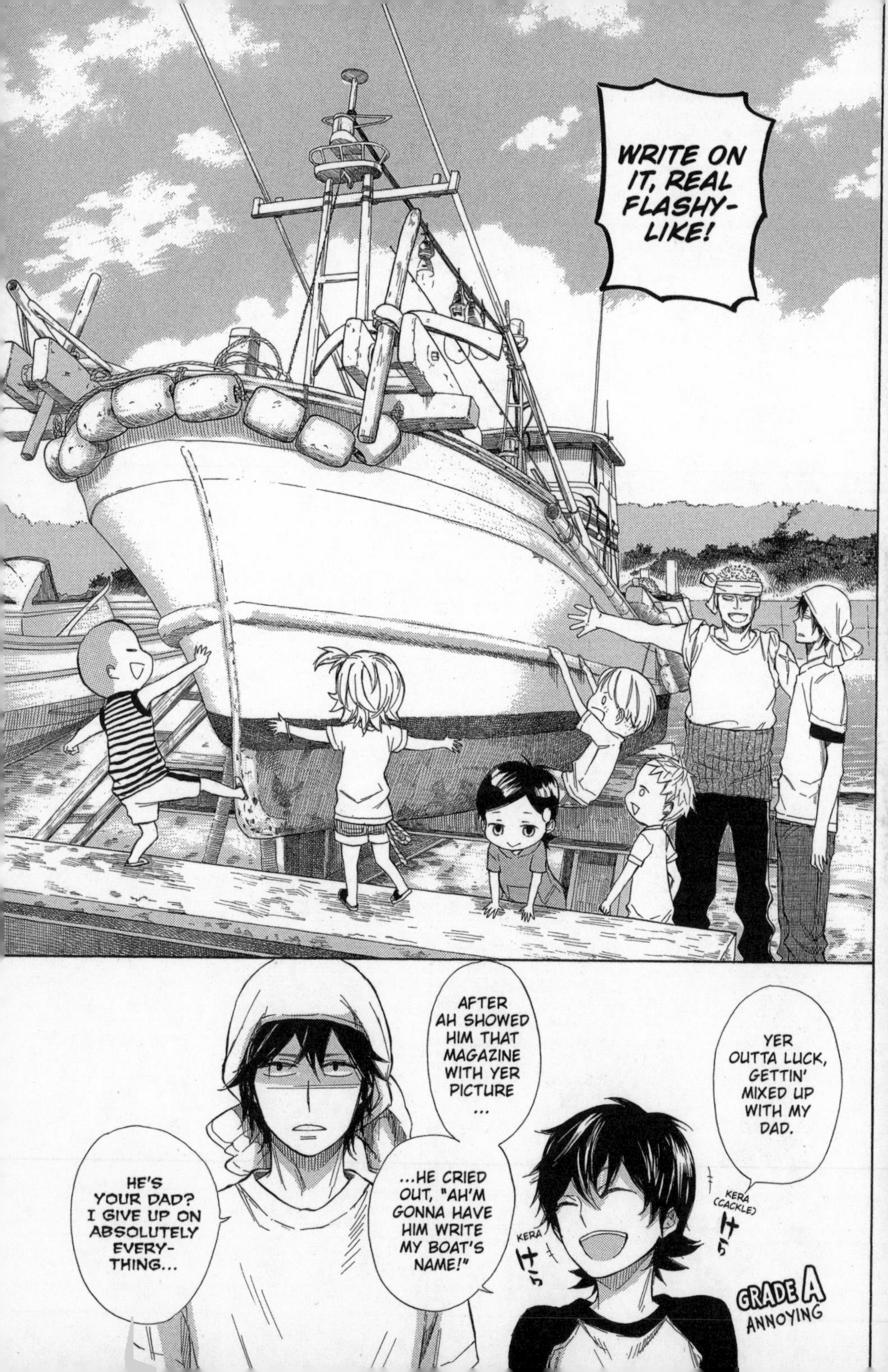

WRITE ON IT, REAL FLASHY-LIKE!
YER OUTTA LUCK, GETTIN' MIXED UP WITH MY DAD.
KERA (CACKLE)
KERA
GRADE A ANNOYING
AFTER AH SHOWED HIM THAT MAGAZINE WITH YER PICTURE ...
...HE CRIED OUT, "AH'M GONNA HAVE HIM WRITE MY BOAT'S NAME!"
HE'S YOUR DAD? I GIVE UP ON ABSOLUTELY EVERY-THING...

DAD'S A LIQUOR SELLER AND JUST BOUGHT THE BOAT FOR FUN.

WHAT'S THE NAME?

IS IT "MIWA-MARU," AS THE CUSTOM GOES?

IT AIN'T GETTIN' MY NAME.

WHAT'S THIS FEELING...? HE SEEMS LIKE HE'D NEVER FORGIVE ANY FAILURE.

HEH-HEH-HEH... AH CAN'T WAIT...

DAD DOES GET MIGHTY SCARY WHEN MAD.

Small Craft Registration Form

Boat Name:		
唯我独尊丸 Yuigadokuson-Maru (I Alone Am Holy)		
	Model #:	
Owner:	BA-10080030-30	
Iwao Yamamura		
	Personal Use	
Anchorage Port:	Anchored at Port Nearest to Current Address	
...utake Village 100-300-2		

THANK HEAVEN MOM PICKED MY NAME...

HE HAS... VERY UNIQUE TASTE.

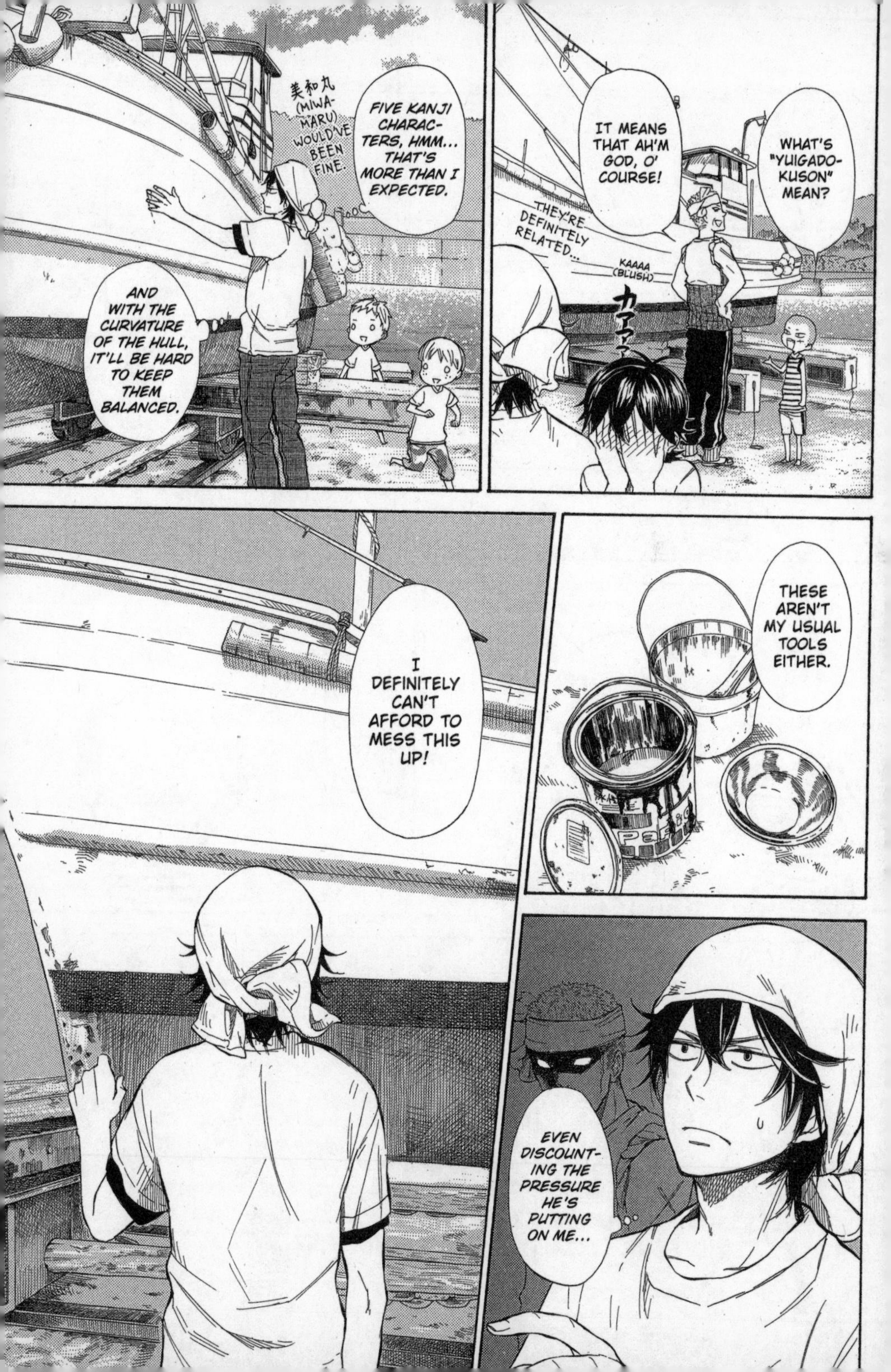
WHAT'S "YUIGADOKUSON" MEAN?
IT MEANS THAT AH'M GOD, O' COURSE!
THEY'RE DEFINITELY RELATED...
KAAAA (BLUSH)
FIVE KANJI CHARACTERS, HMM... THAT'S MORE THAN I EXPECTED.
美和丸 (MIWA-MARU) WOULD'VE BEEN FINE.
AND WITH THE CURVATURE OF THE HULL, IT'LL BE HARD TO KEEP THEM BALANCED.
THESE AREN'T MY USUAL TOOLS EITHER.
EVEN DISCOUNTING THE PRESSURE HE'S PUTTING ON ME...
I DEFINITELY CAN'T AFFORD TO MESS THIS UP!

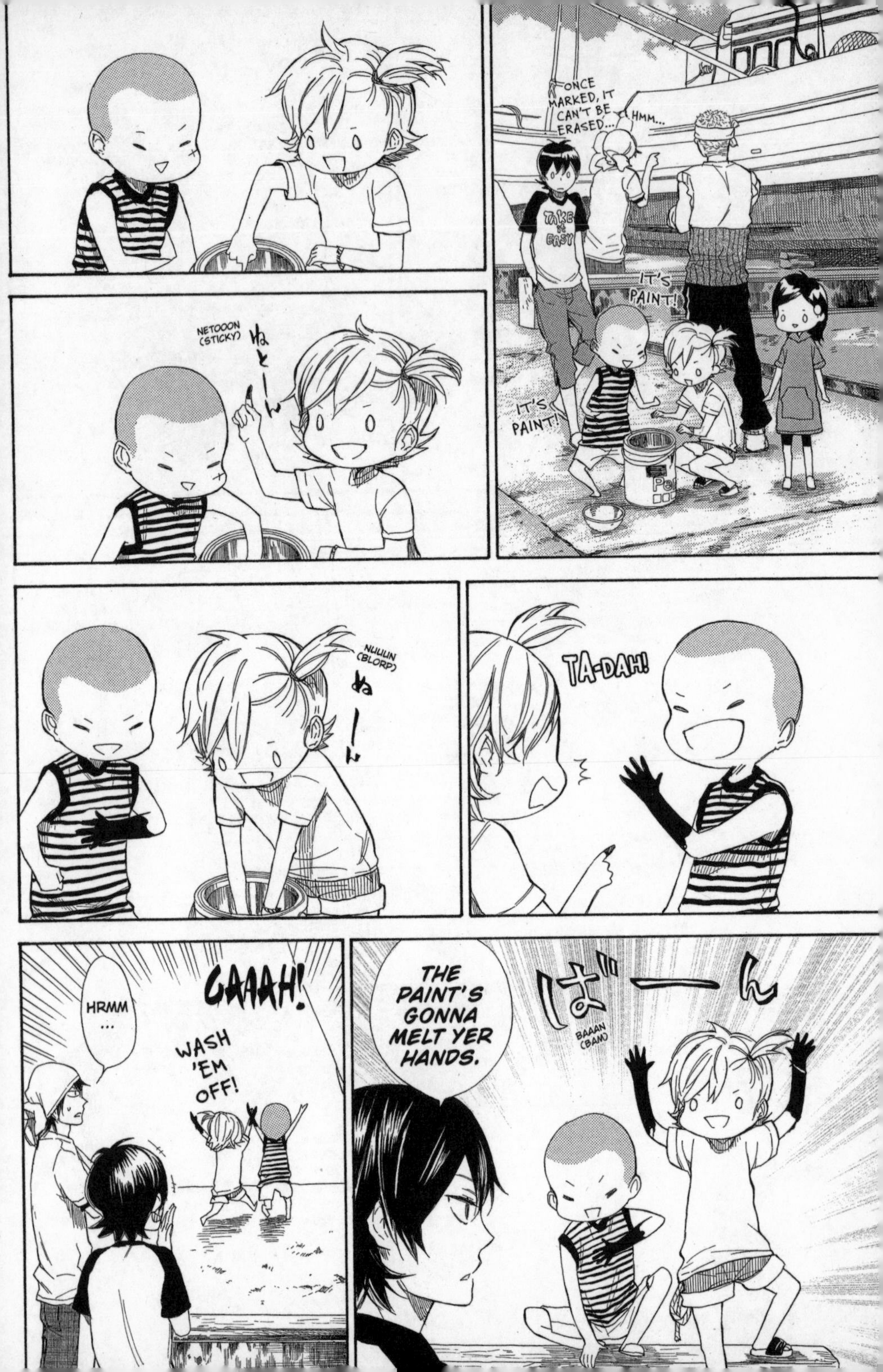

ONCE MARKED, IT CAN'T BE ERASED...
HMM...
IT'S PAINT!
IT'S PAINT!
NETOOON (STICKY)
ねとーん
TA-DAH!
NUULIN (BLORP)
ぬーん
THE PAINT'S GONNA MELT YER HANDS.
ばーーん
BAAAN (BAM)
GAAAH!
WASH 'EM OFF!
HRMM ...

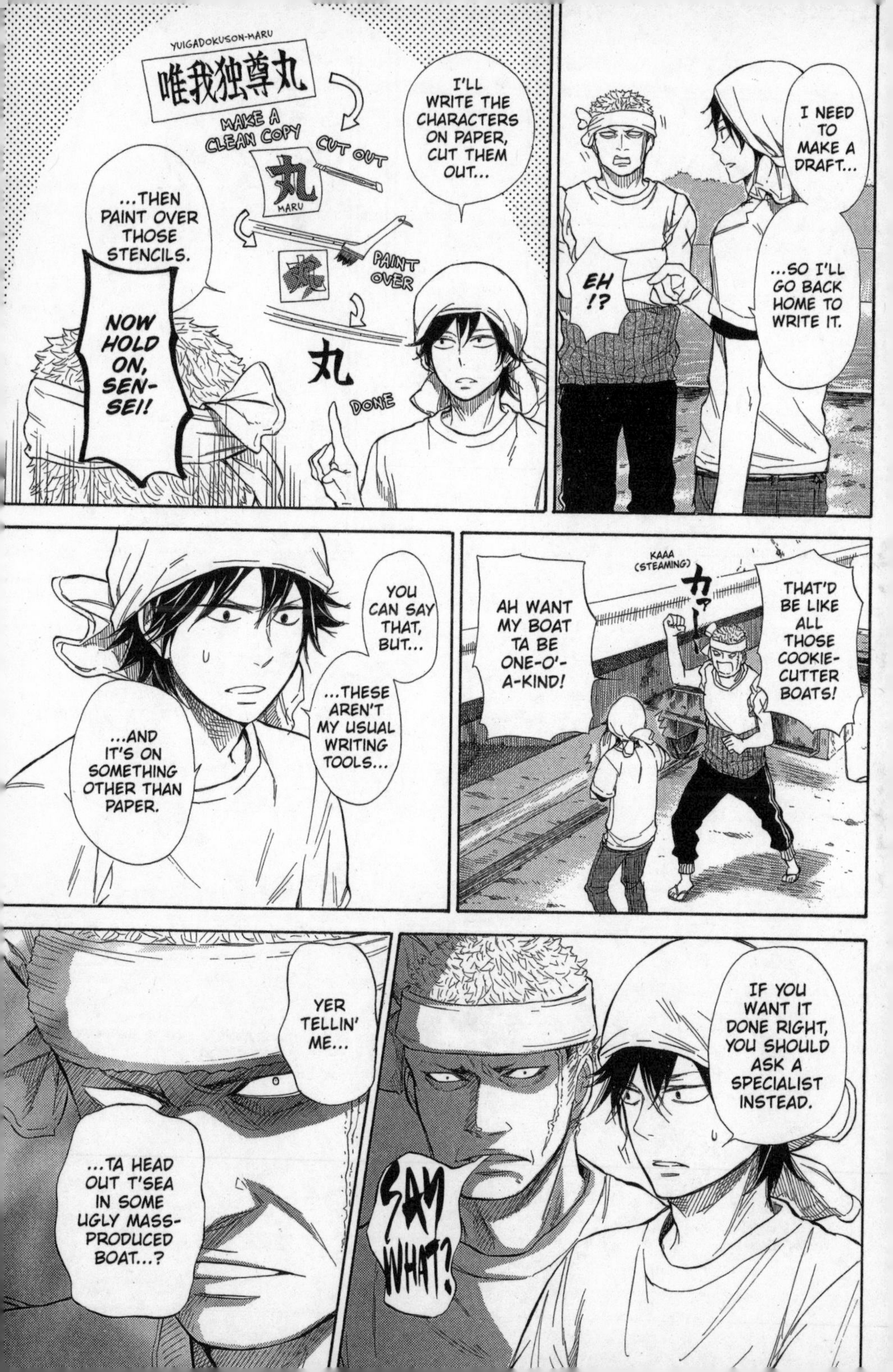
I NEED TO MAKE A DRAFT...
EH!?
...SO I'LL GO BACK HOME TO WRITE IT.
I'LL WRITE THE CHARACTERS ON PAPER, CUT THEM OUT...
YUIGADOKUSON-MARU
唯我独尊丸
MAKE A CLEAN COPY
CUT OUT
丸
MARU
PAINT OVER
丸
DONE
...THEN PAINT OVER THOSE STENCILS.
NOW HOLD ON, SENSEI!
KAAA (STEAMING)
カァー
THAT'D BE LIKE ALL THOSE COOKIE-CUTTER BOATS!
AH WANT MY BOAT TA BE ONE-O'-A-KIND!
YOU CAN SAY THAT, BUT...
...THESE AREN'T MY USUAL WRITING TOOLS...
...AND IT'S ON SOMETHING OTHER THAN PAPER.
IF YOU WANT IT DONE RIGHT, YOU SHOULD ASK A SPECIALIST INSTEAD.
SAY WHAT?
YER TELLIN' ME...
...TA HEAD OUT T'SEA IN SOME UGLY MASS-PRODUCED BOAT...?

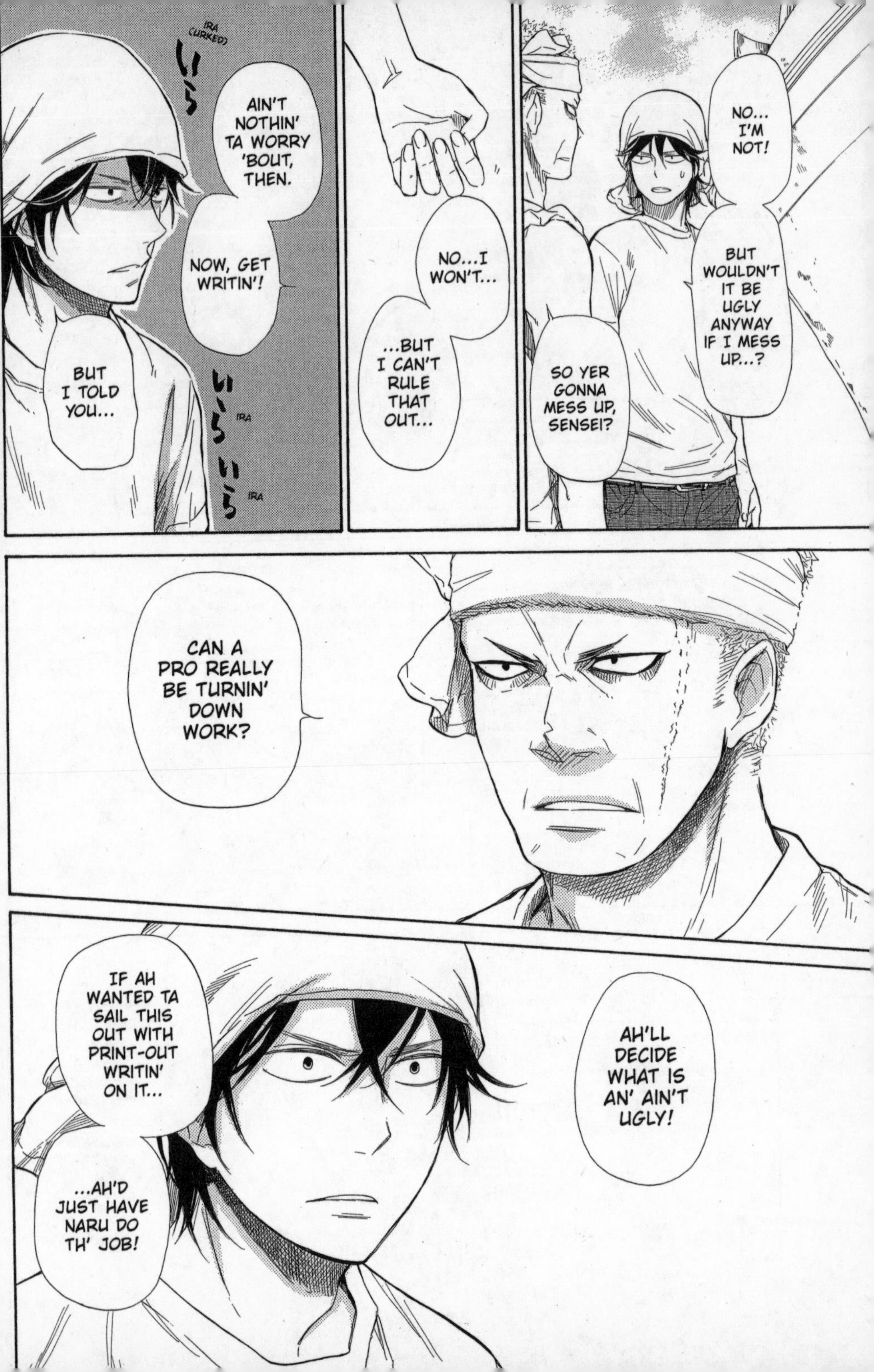
NO... I'M NOT!
BUT WOULDN'T IT BE UGLY ANYWAY IF I MESS UP...?
SO YER GONNA MESS UP, SENSEI?
NO...I WON'T...
...BUT I CAN'T RULE THAT OUT...
IRA (IRKED)
いら
AIN'T NOTHIN' TA WORRY 'BOUT, THEN.
NOW, GET WRITIN'!
いら いら
IRA
IRA
BUT I TOLD YOU...
CAN A PRO REALLY BE TURNIN' DOWN WORK?
AH'LL DECIDE WHAT IS AN' AIN'T UGLY!
IF AH WANTED TA SAIL THIS OUT WITH PRINT-OUT WRITIN' ON IT...
...AH'D JUST HAVE NARU DO TH' JOB!

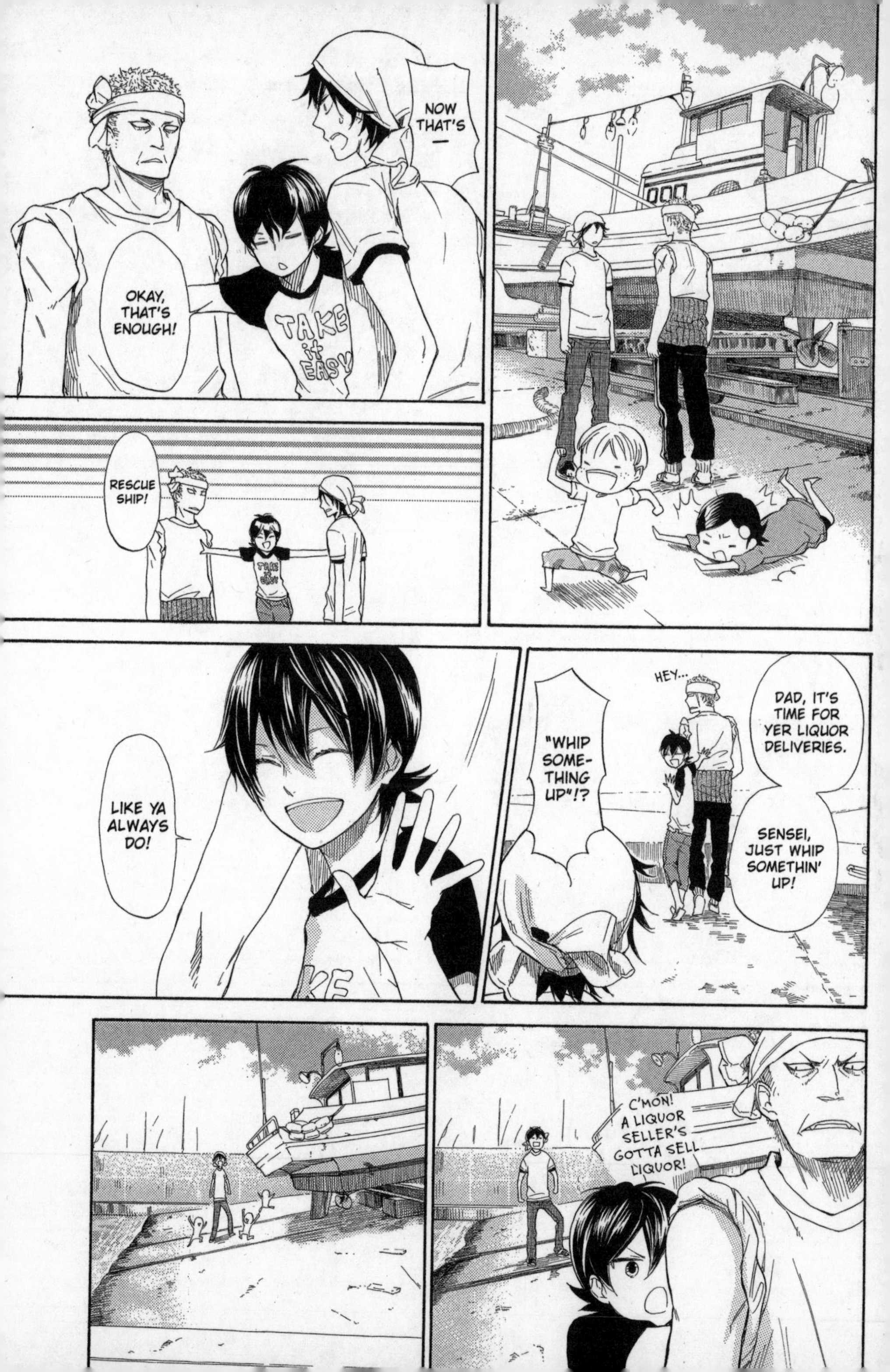
NOW THAT'S —
OKAY, THAT'S ENOUGH!
RESCUE SHIP!
DAD, IT'S TIME FOR YER LIQUOR DELIVERIES.
HEY...
SENSEI, JUST WHIP SOMETHIN' UP!
"WHIP SOMETHING UP"!?
LIKE YA ALWAYS DO!
C'MON! A LIQUOR SELLER'S GOTTA SELL LIQUOR!

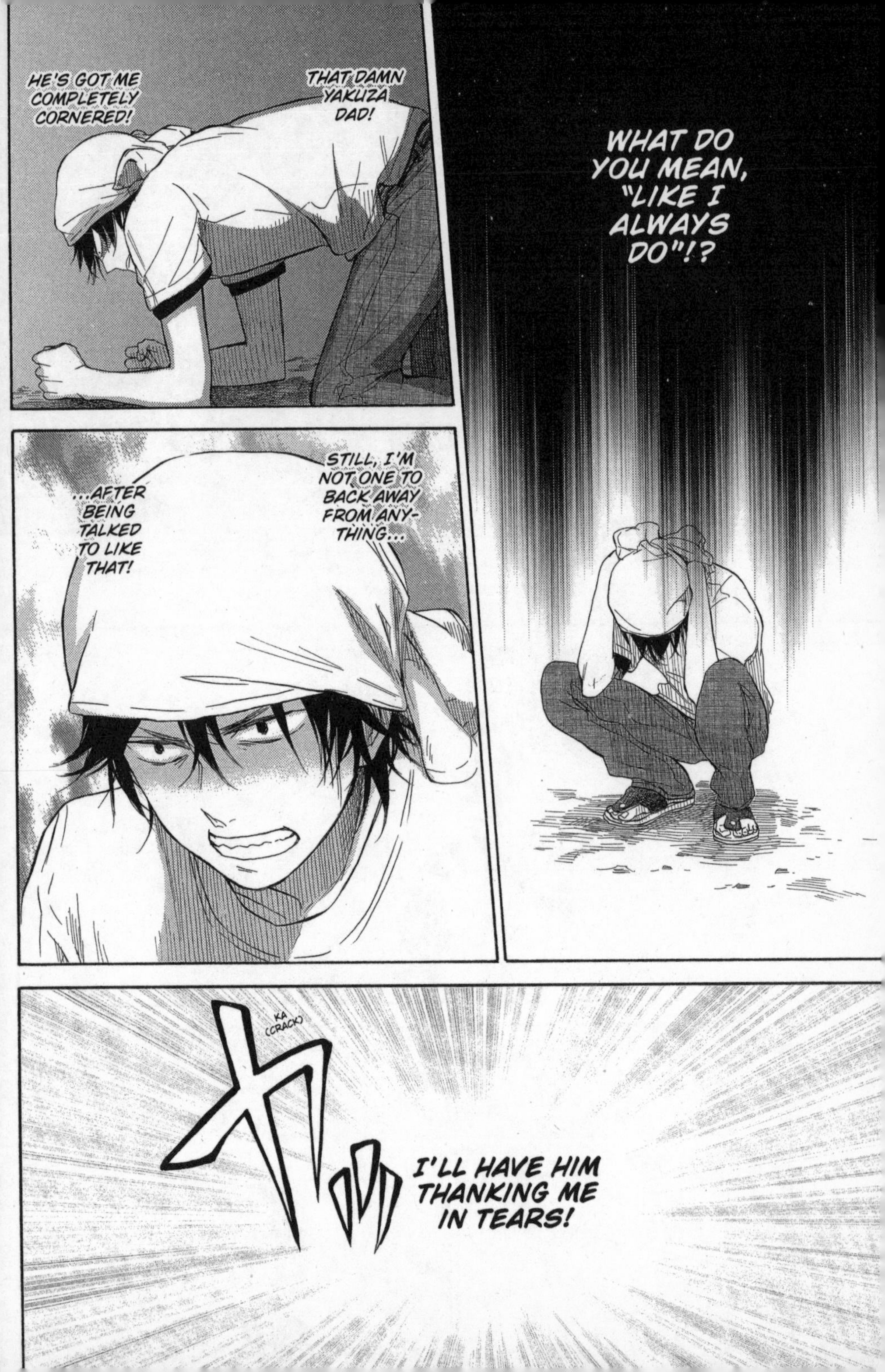
WHAT DO YOU MEAN, "LIKE I ALWAYS DO"!?
THAT DAMN YAKUZA DAD!
HE'S GOT ME COMPLETELY CORNERED!
STILL, I'M NOT ONE TO BACK AWAY FROM ANY-THING...
...AFTER BEING TALKED TO LIKE THAT!
KA (CRACK)
I'LL HAVE HIM THANKING ME IN TEARS!

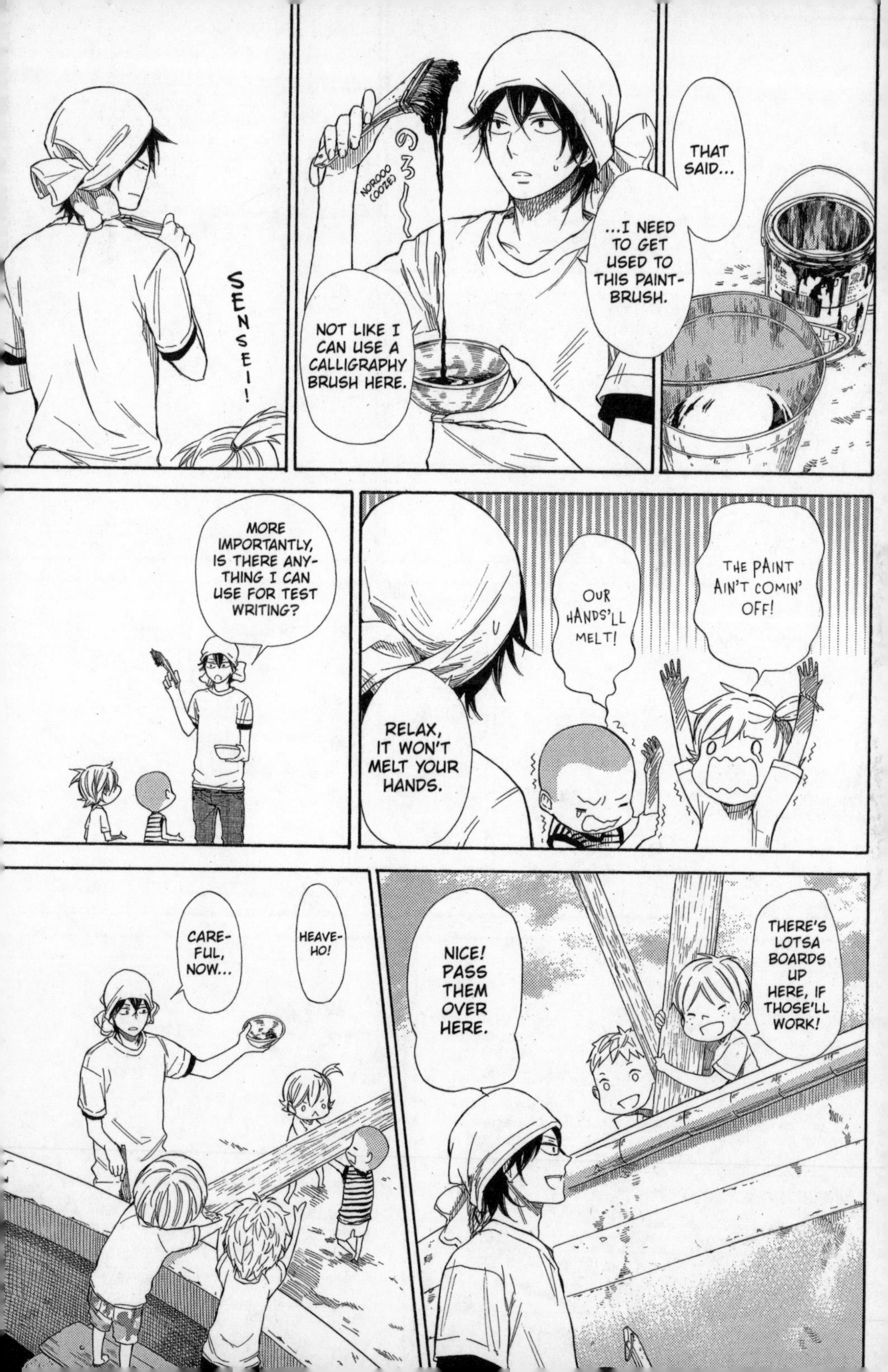
THAT SAID...
...I NEED TO GET USED TO THIS PAINT-BRUSH.
のろ～～
NOROOO (OOZE)
NOT LIKE I CAN USE A CALLIGRAPHY BRUSH HERE.
SENSEI!
THE PAINT AIN'T COMIN' OFF!
OUR HANDS'LL MELT!
RELAX, IT WON'T MELT YOUR HANDS.
MORE IMPORTANTLY, IS THERE ANY-THING I CAN USE FOR TEST WRITING?
THERE'S LOTSA BOARDS UP HERE, IF THOSE'LL WORK!
NICE! PASS THEM OVER HERE.
HEAVE-HO!
CARE-FUL, NOW...

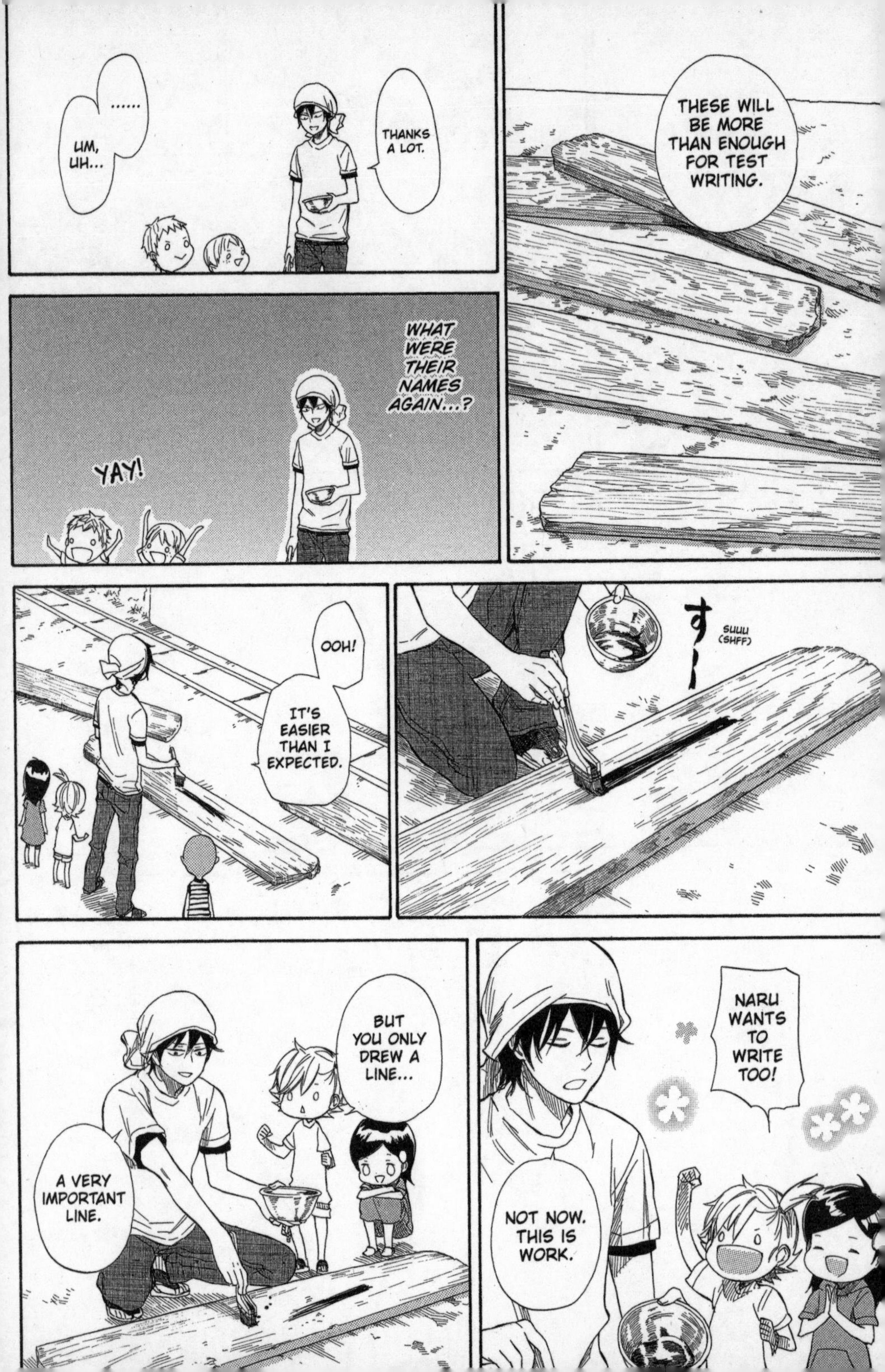

THESE WILL BE MORE THAN ENOUGH FOR TEST WRITING.
THANKS A LOT.
......
UM, UH...
WHAT WERE THEIR NAMES AGAIN...?
YAY!
すー
SUUU (SHFF)
OOH!
IT'S EASIER THAN I EXPECTED.
NARU WANTS TO WRITE TOO!
NOT NOW. THIS IS WORK.
BUT YOU ONLY DREW A LINE...
A VERY IMPORTANT LINE.

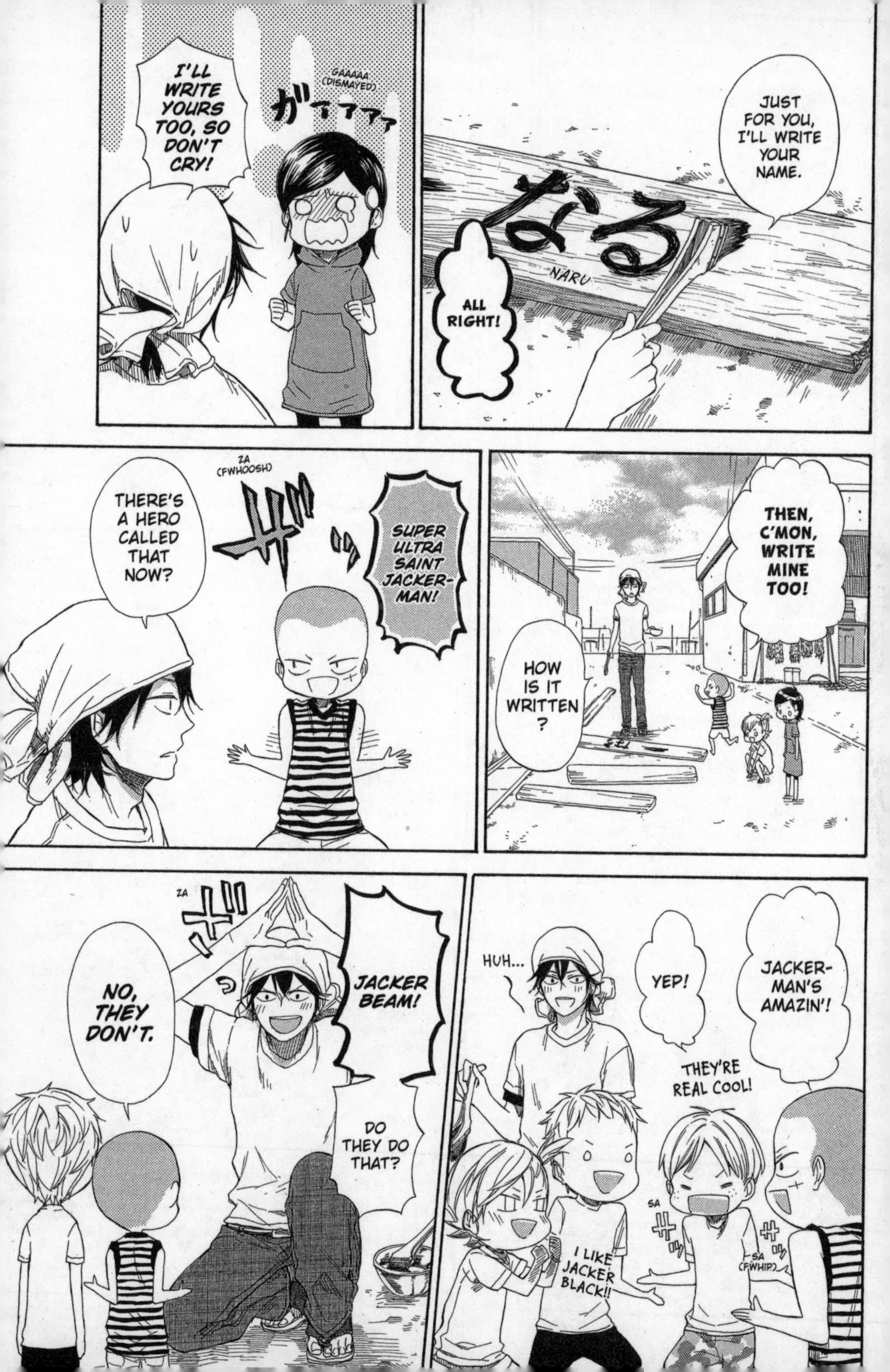
JUST FOR YOU, I'LL WRITE YOUR NAME.
なる
NARU
ALL RIGHT!
GAAAAA (DISMAYED)
I'LL WRITE YOURS TOO, SO DON'T CRY!
THEN, C'MON, WRITE MINE TOO!
HOW IS IT WRITTEN?
SUPER ULTRA SAINT JACKER-MAN!
ZA (FWHOOSH)
THERE'S A HERO CALLED THAT NOW?
JACKER-MAN'S AMAZIN'!
YEP!
HUH...
THEY'RE REAL COOL!
SA (FWHIP)
SA
I LIKE JACKER BLACK!!
JACKER BEAM!
ZA
NO, THEY DON'T.
DO THEY DO THAT?

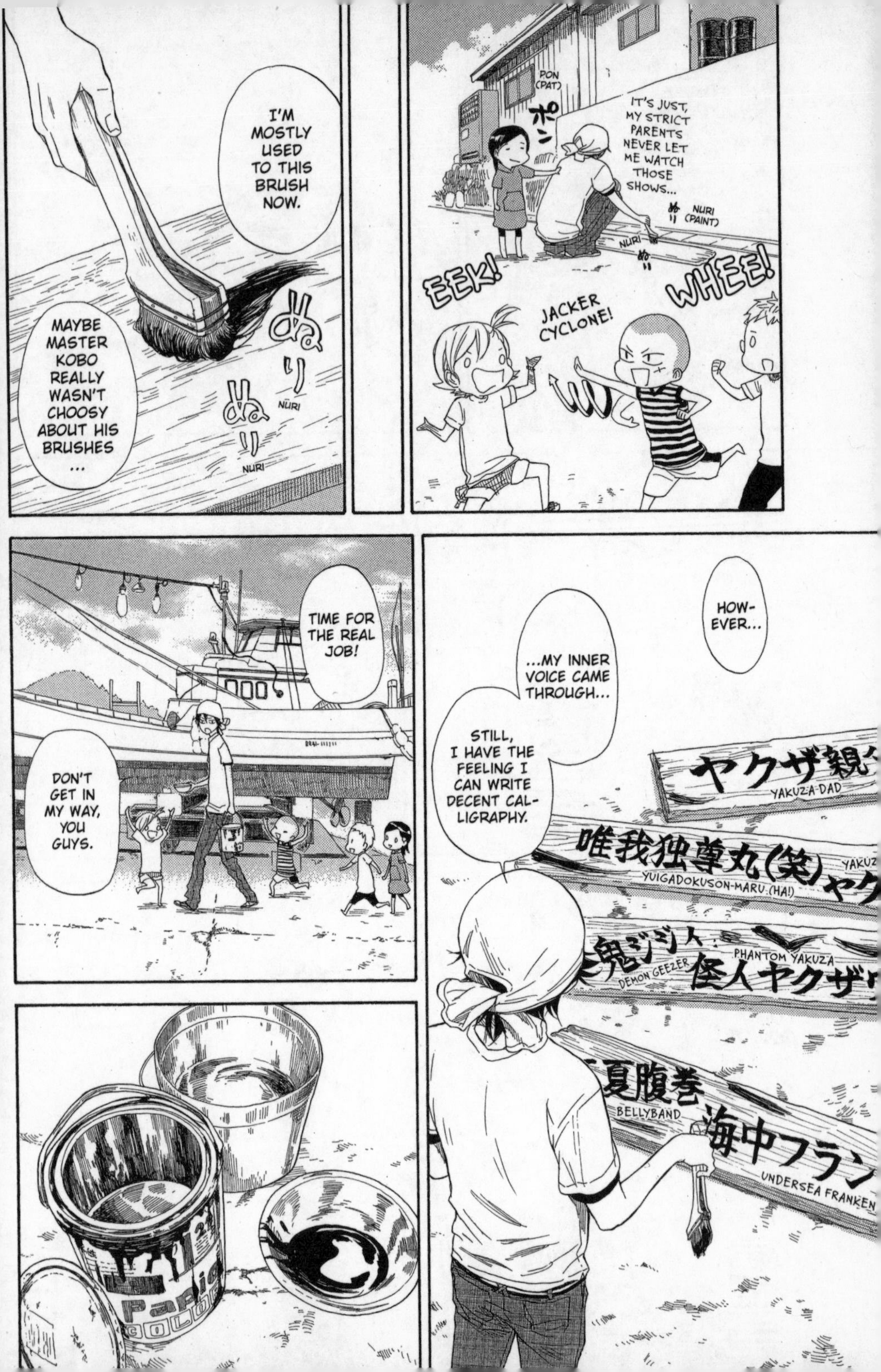

PON (PAT)
ポン
IT'S JUST, MY STRICT PARENTS NEVER LET ME WATCH THOSE SHOWS...
ぬり
NURI (PAINT)
NURI
ぬり
EEK!
WHEE!
JACKER CYCLONE!
I'M MOSTLY USED TO THIS BRUSH NOW.
MAYBE MASTER KOBO REALLY WASN'T CHOOSY ABOUT HIS BRUSHES ...
ぬり
NURI
ぬり
NURI
HOW-EVER...
...MY INNER VOICE CAME THROUGH...
STILL, I HAVE THE FEELING I CAN WRITE DECENT CAL-LIGRAPHY.
ヤクザ親
YAKUZA DAD
唯我独尊丸(笑)
YUIGADOKUSON-MARU (HA!)
YAKU
怪人ヤクザ
PHANTOM YAKUZA
DEMON GEEZER
夏腹巻
BELLYBAND
海中フラン
UNDERSEA FRANKEN
TIME FOR THE REAL JOB!
DON'T GET IN MY WAY, YOU GUYS.

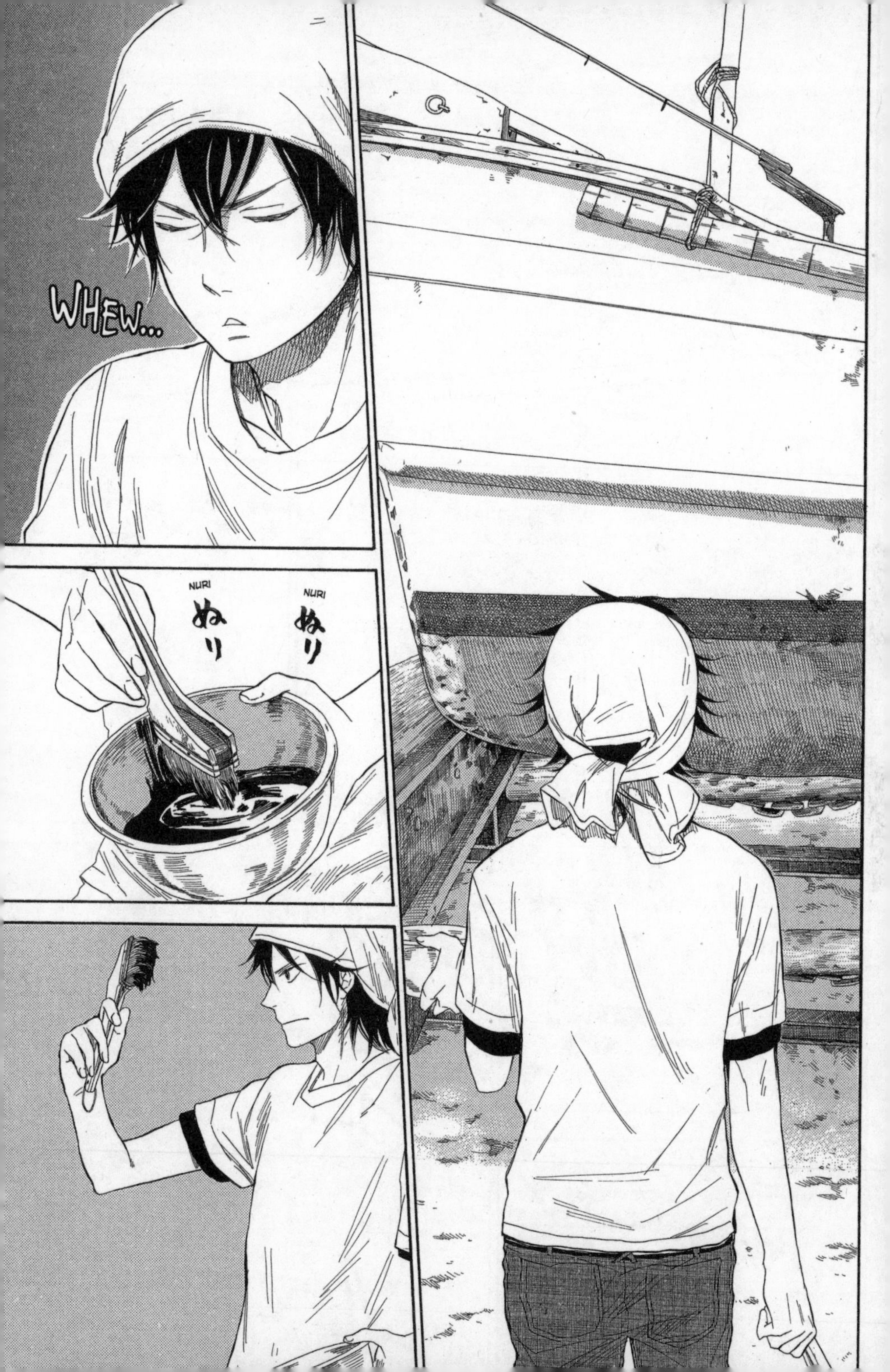
WHEW...
NURI
ぬり
NURI
ぬり

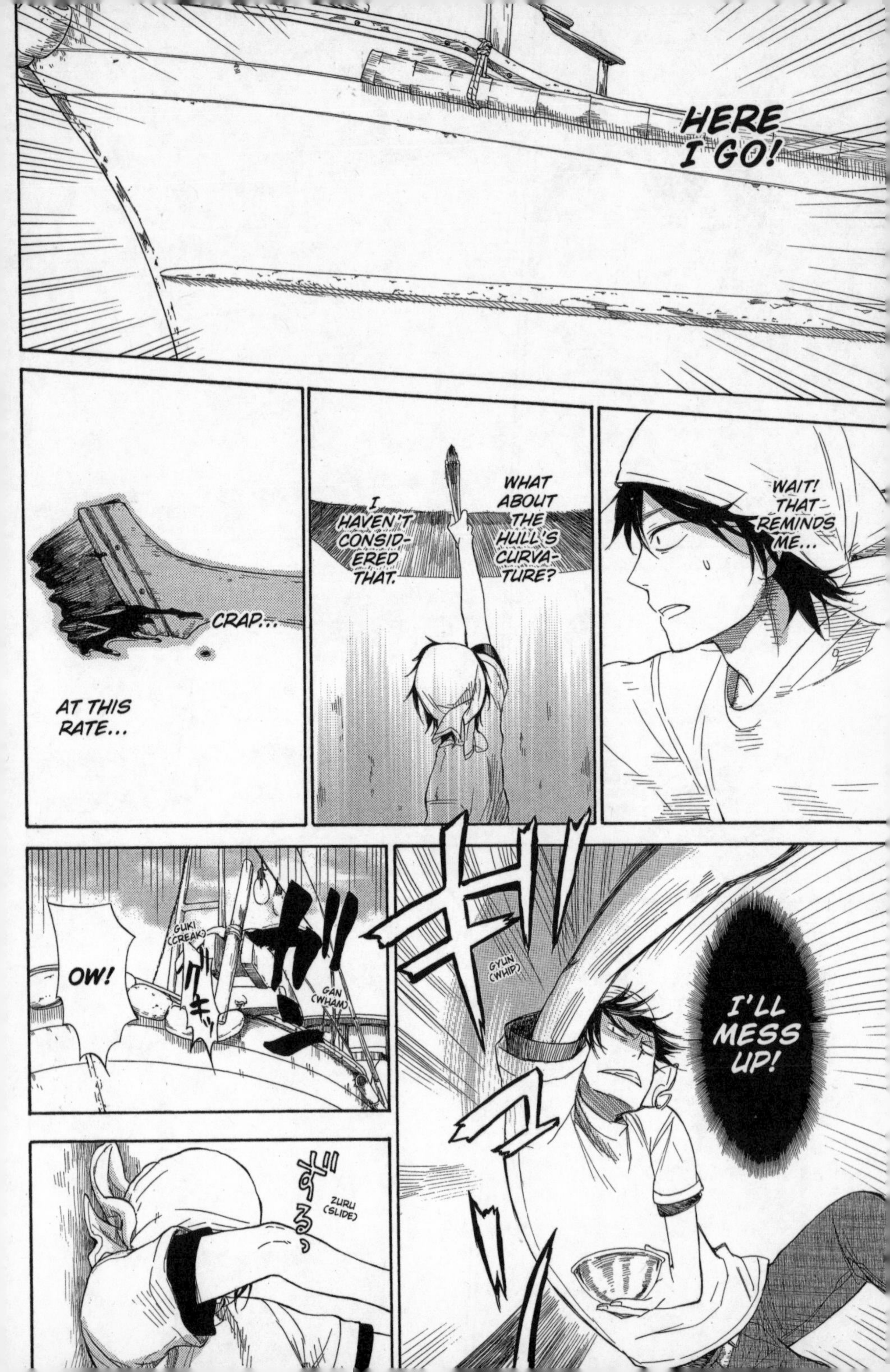
HERE I GO!
WAIT! THAT REMINDS ME...
WHAT ABOUT THE HULL'S CURVA-TURE?
I HAVEN'T CONSID-ERED THAT.
CRAP...
AT THIS RATE...
I'LL MESS UP!
GYUN (WHIP)
GAN (WHAM)
GUKI (CREAK)
OW!
ずるっ
ZURU (SLIDE)

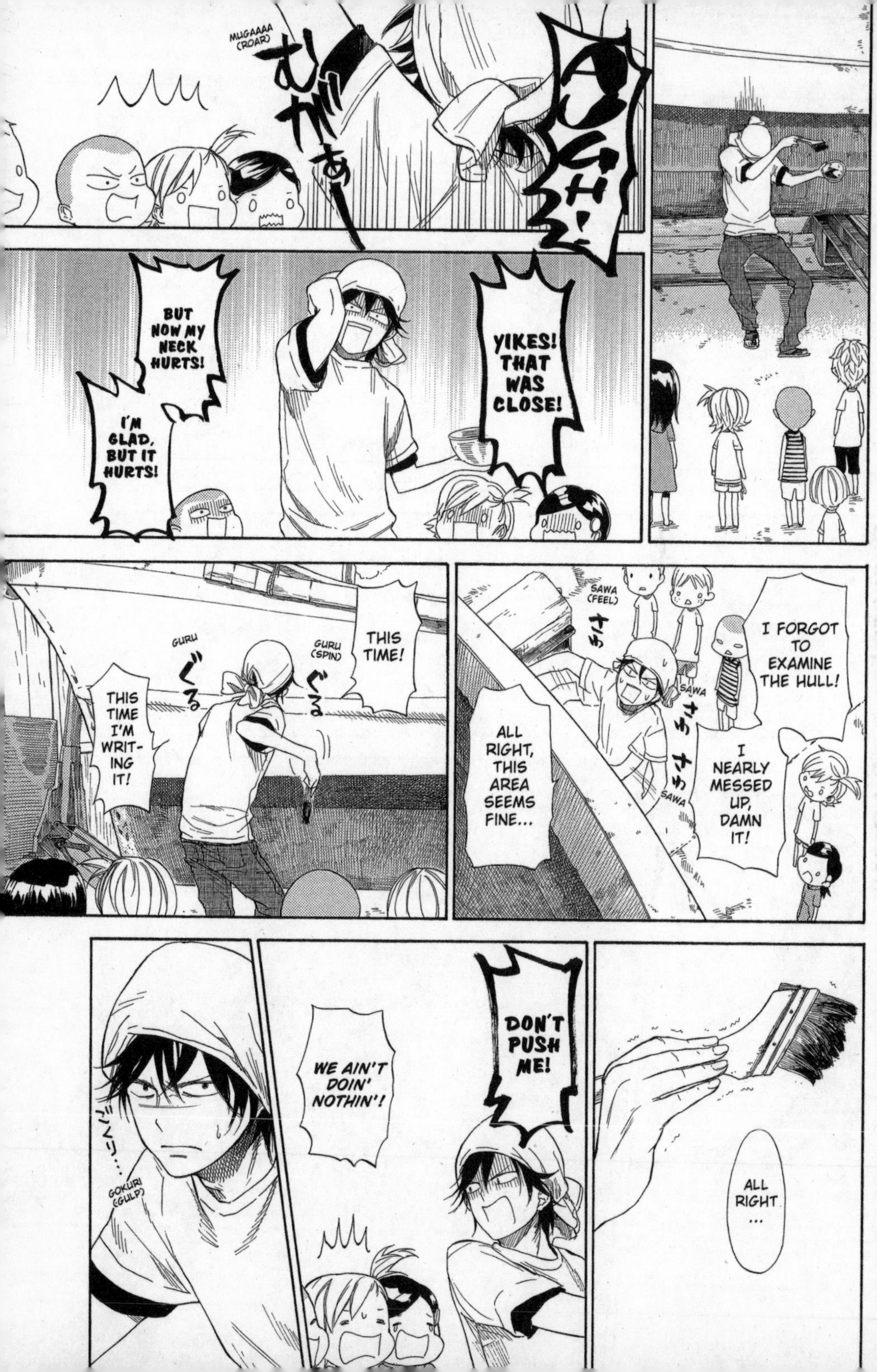
AUGH!
MUGAAAA (ROAR)
むがあー
YIKES! THAT WAS CLOSE!
BUT NOW MY NECK HURTS!
I'M GLAD, BUT IT HURTS!
I FORGOT TO EXAMINE THE HULL!
SAWA (FEEL)
さわ
SAWA
さわ
さわ
SAWA
I NEARLY MESSED UP, DAMN IT!
ALL RIGHT, THIS AREA SEEMS FINE...
THIS TIME!
GURU (SPIN)
ぐる
GURU
ぐる
THIS TIME I'M WRITING IT!
ALL RIGHT...
DON'T PUSH ME!
WE AIN'T DOIN' NOTHIN'!
GOKURI (GULP)
ごくり…

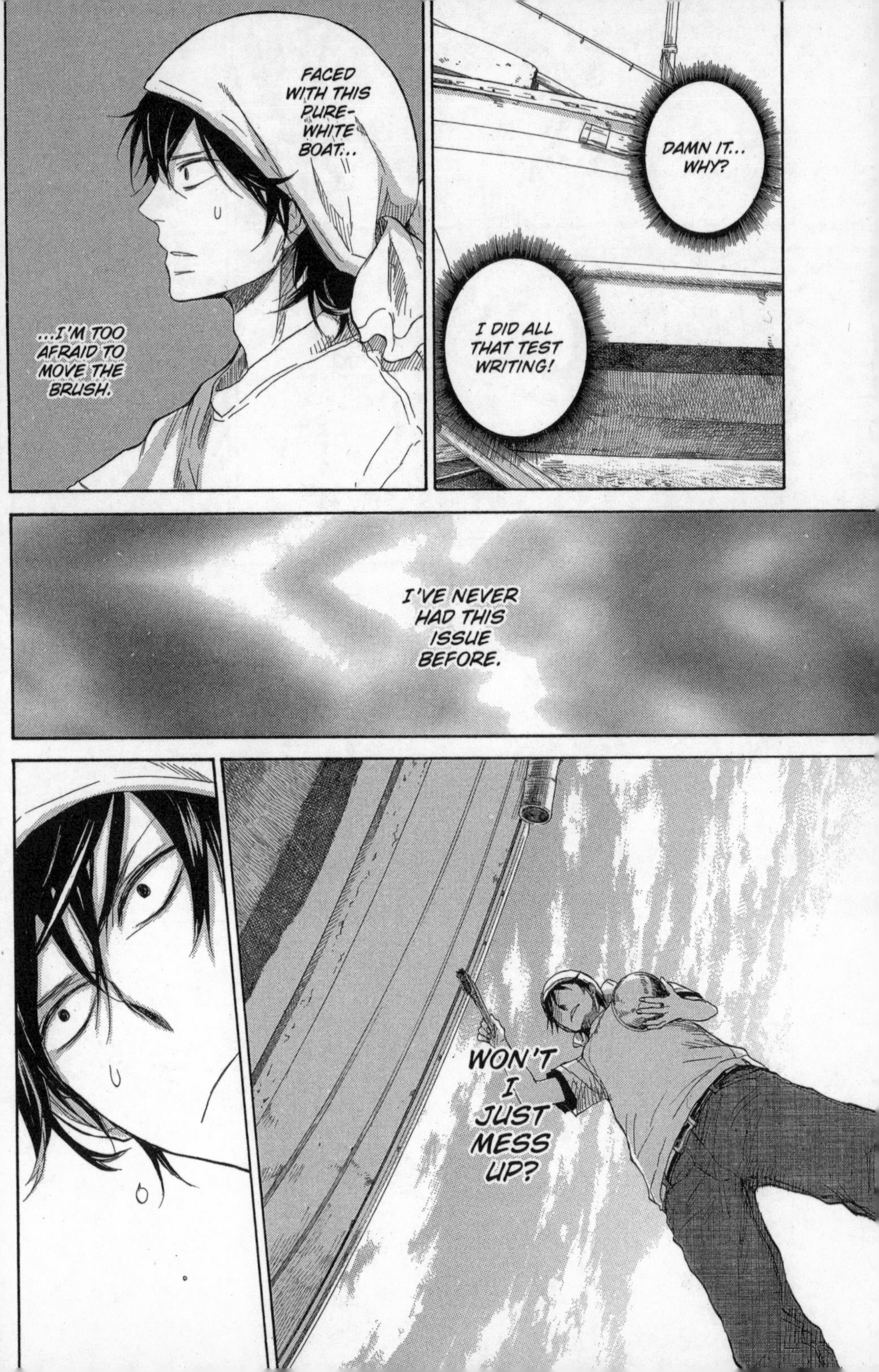
DAMN IT... WHY?
I DID ALL THAT TEST WRITING!
FACED WITH THIS PURE-WHITE BOAT...
...I'M TOO AFRAID TO MOVE THE BRUSH.
I'VE NEVER HAD THIS ISSUE BEFORE.
WON'T I JUST MESS UP?

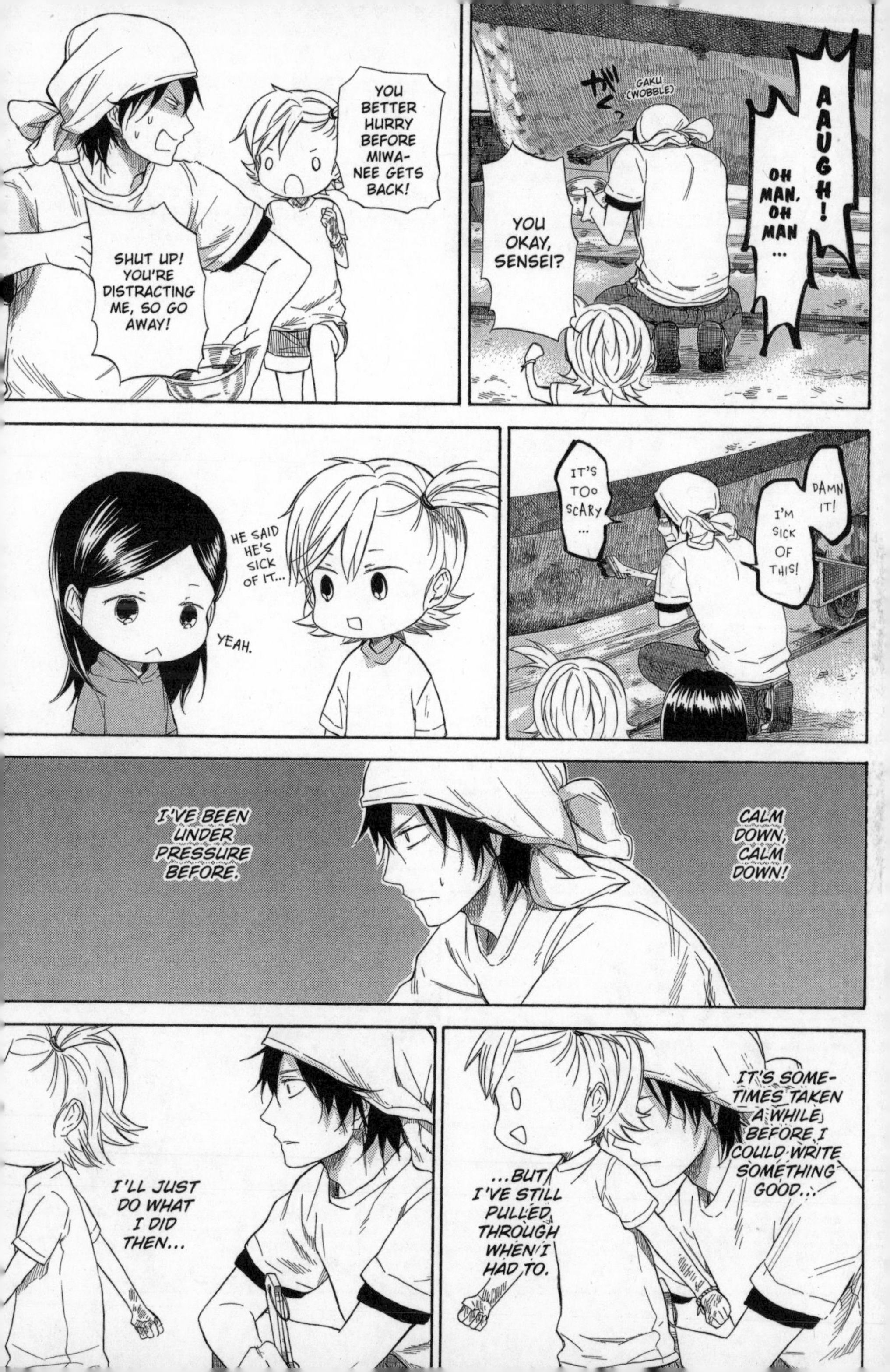
AAUGH!
OH MAN, OH MAN...
GAKU (WOBBLE)
YOU OKAY, SENSEI?
YOU BETTER HURRY BEFORE MIWA-NEE GETS BACK!
SHUT UP! YOU'RE DISTRACTING ME, SO GO AWAY!
DAMN IT!
I'M SICK OF THIS!
IT'S TOO SCARY...
HE SAID HE'S SICK OF IT...
YEAH.
CALM DOWN, CALM DOWN!
I'VE BEEN UNDER PRESSURE BEFORE.
IT'S SOMETIMES TAKEN A WHILE BEFORE I COULD WRITE SOMETHING GOOD...
...BUT I'VE STILL PULLED THROUGH WHEN I HAD TO.
I'LL JUST DO WHAT I DID THEN...

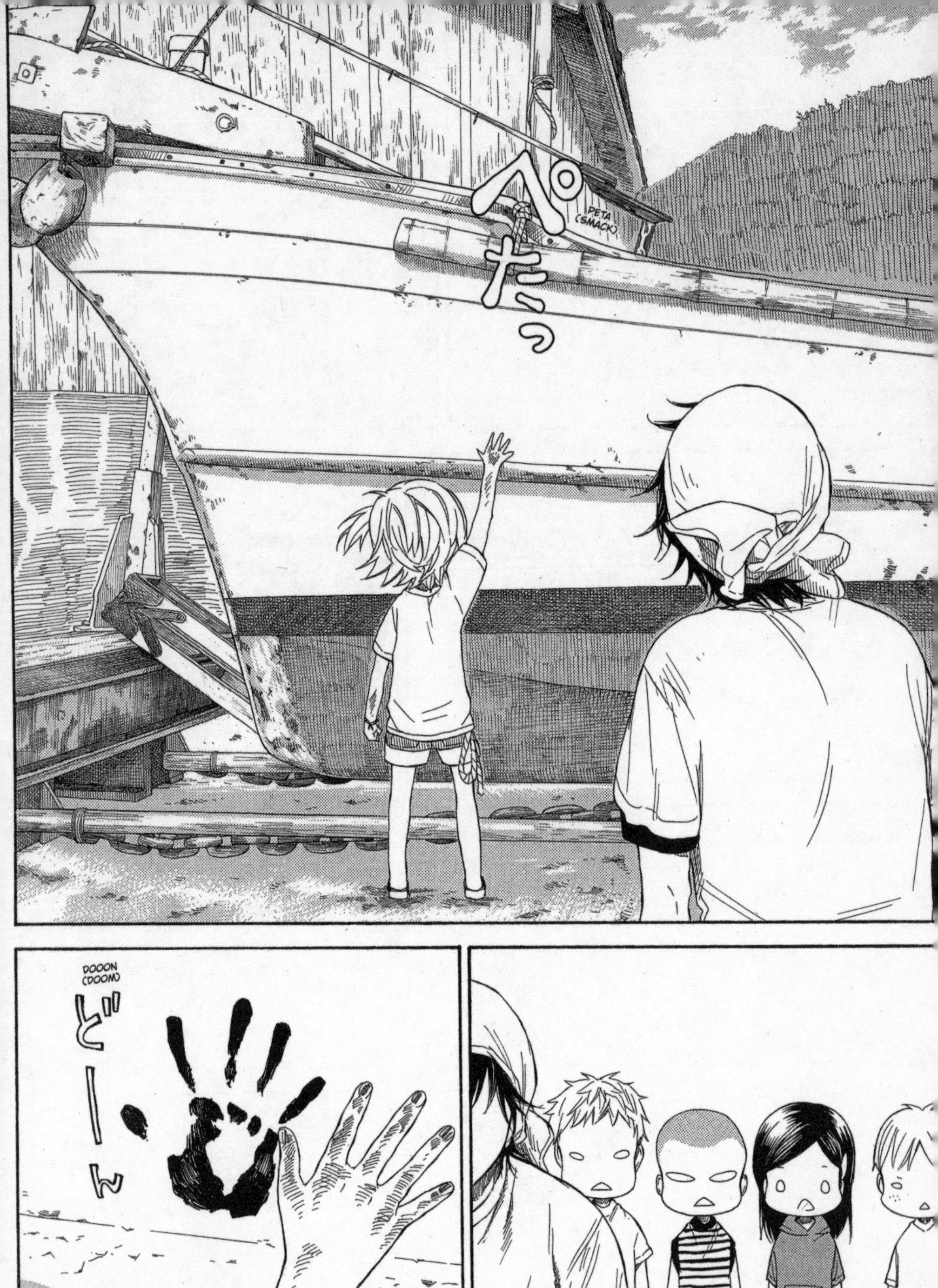
ぺたっ
PETA (SMACK)
DOOON (DOOM)
どーーん

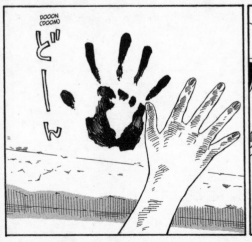

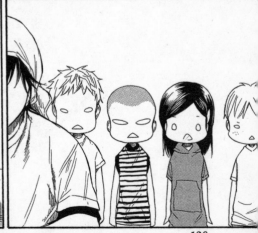

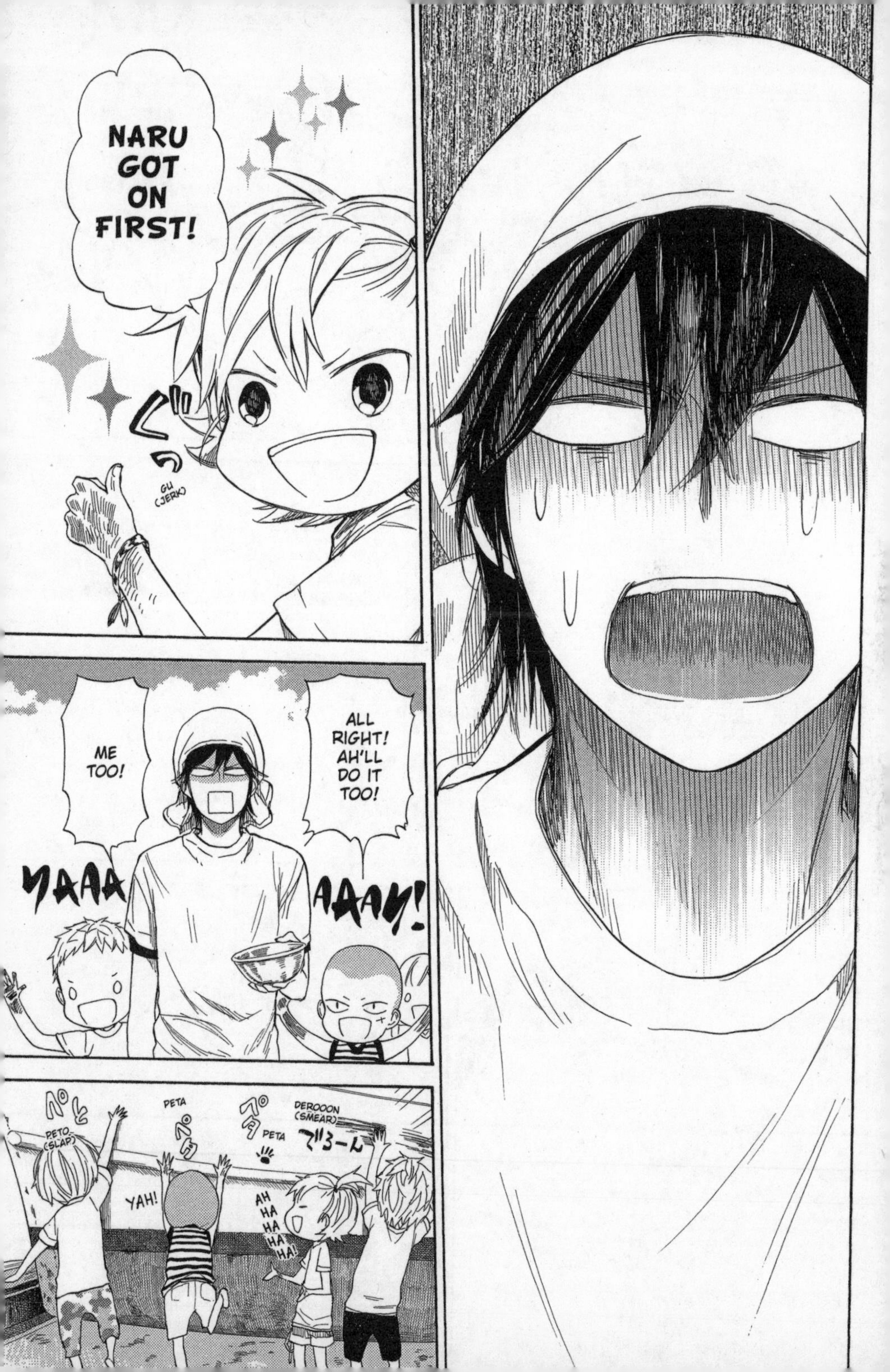
NARU GOT ON FIRST!
GU (JERK)
ALL RIGHT! AH'LL DO IT TOO!
ME TOO!
YAAA AAAN!
でろーん DEROOON (SMEAR)
ぺタ PETA
PETA
ぺタ PETA
ぺと PETO (SLAP)
AH HA HA HA HA!
YAH!

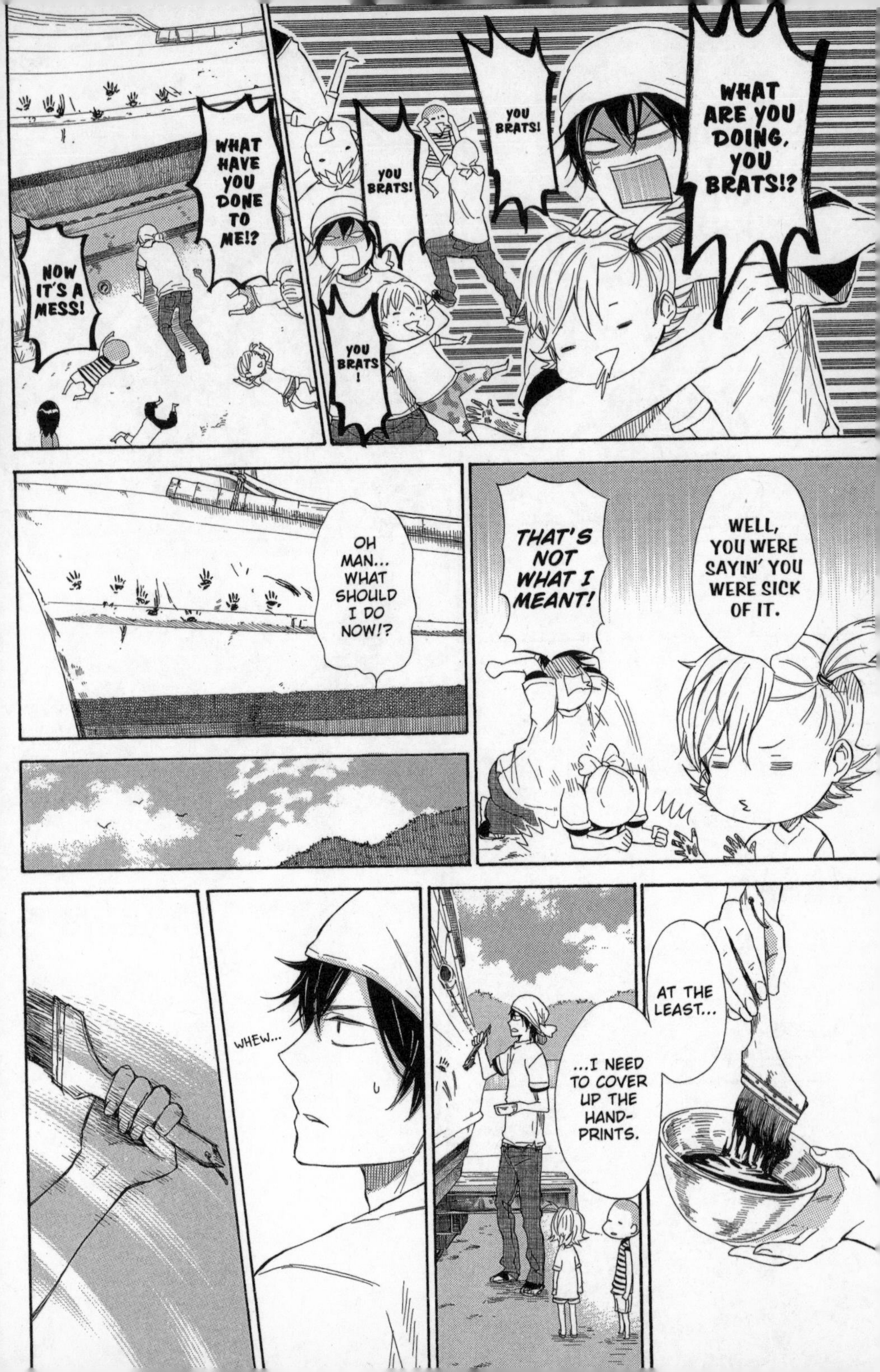
WHAT ARE YOU DOING, YOU BRATS!?
YOU BRATS!
YOU BRATS!
YOU BRATS!
WHAT HAVE YOU DONE TO ME!?
NOW IT'S A MESS!
WELL, YOU WERE SAYIN' YOU WERE SICK OF IT.
THAT'S NOT WHAT I MEANT!
OH MAN... WHAT SHOULD I DO NOW!?
AT THE LEAST...
...I NEED TO COVER UP THE HAND-PRINTS.
WHEW...

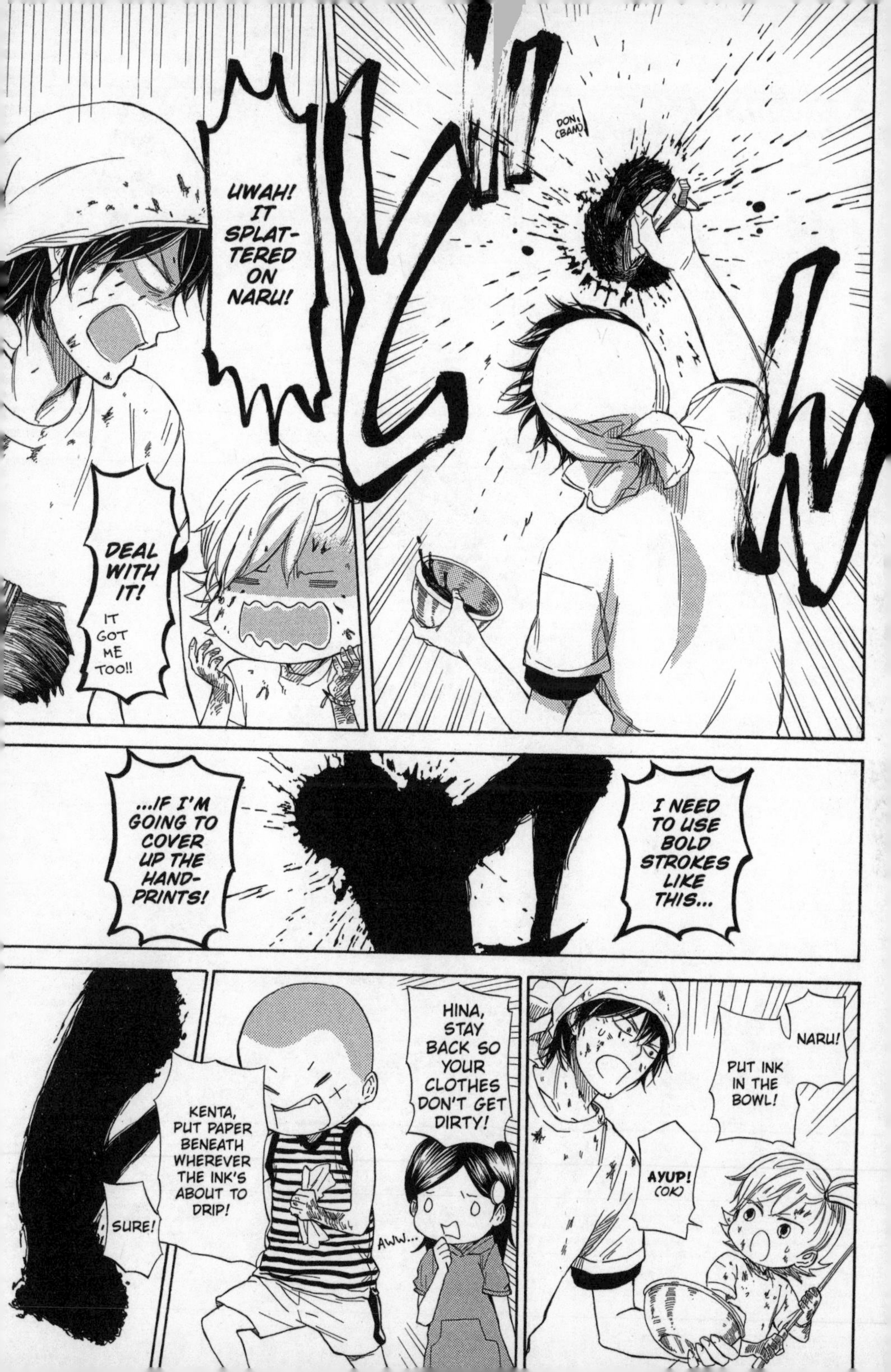
DON (BAM)
UWAH! IT SPLATTERED ON NARU!
DEAL WITH IT!
IT GOT ME TOO!!
I NEED TO USE BOLD STROKES LIKE THIS...
...IF I'M GOING TO COVER UP THE HAND-PRINTS!
NARU!
PUT INK IN THE BOWL!
AYUP! (OK)
HINA, STAY BACK SO YOUR CLOTHES DON'T GET DIRTY!
AWW...
KENTA, PUT PAPER BENEATH WHEREVER THE INK'S ABOUT TO DRIP!
SURE!

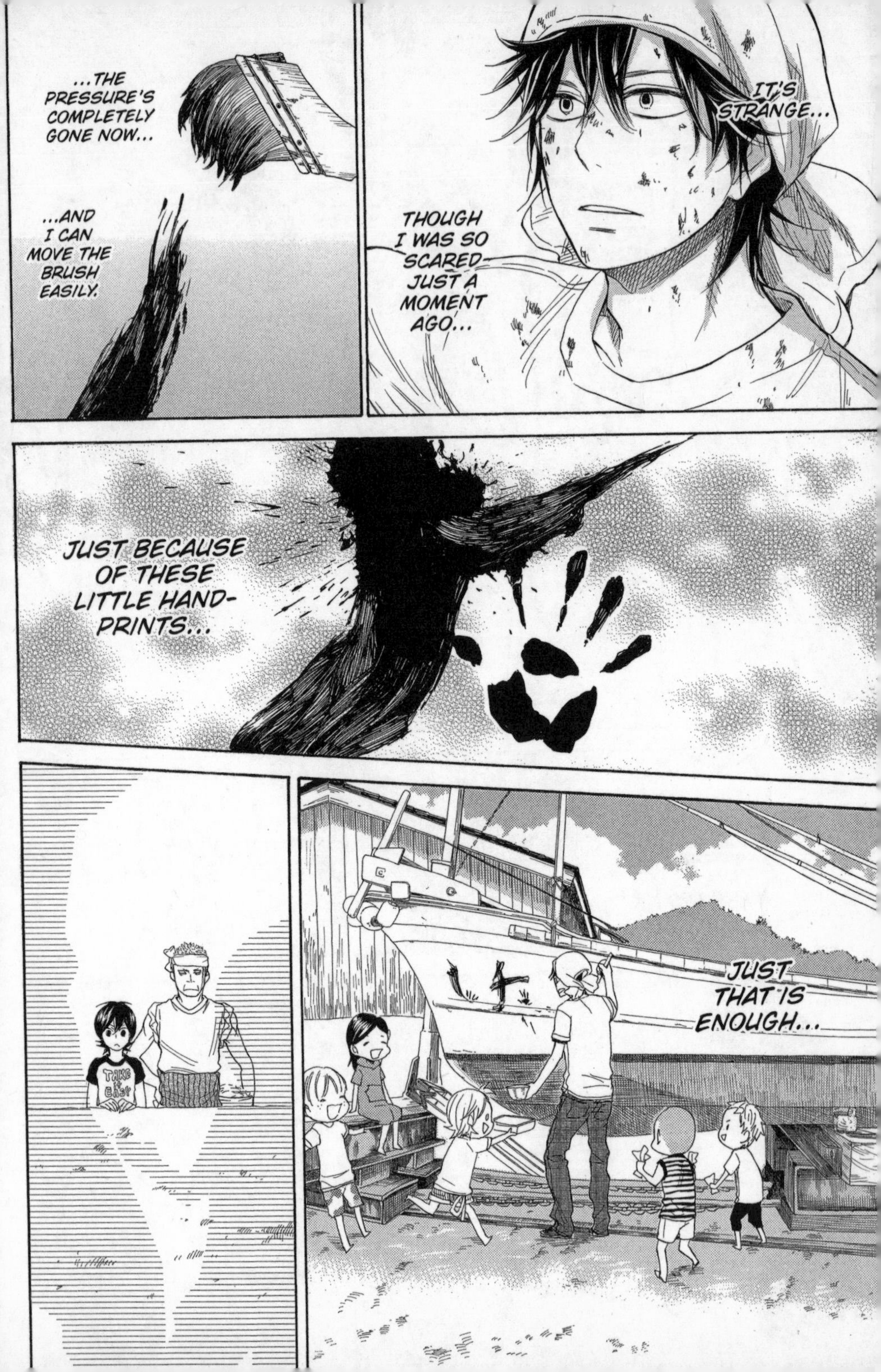
IT'S STRANGE...
THOUGH I WAS SO SCARED JUST A MOMENT AGO...
...THE PRESSURE'S COMPLETELY GONE NOW...
...AND I CAN MOVE THE BRUSH EASILY.
JUST BECAUSE OF THESE LITTLE HAND-PRINTS...
JUST THAT IS ENOUGH...

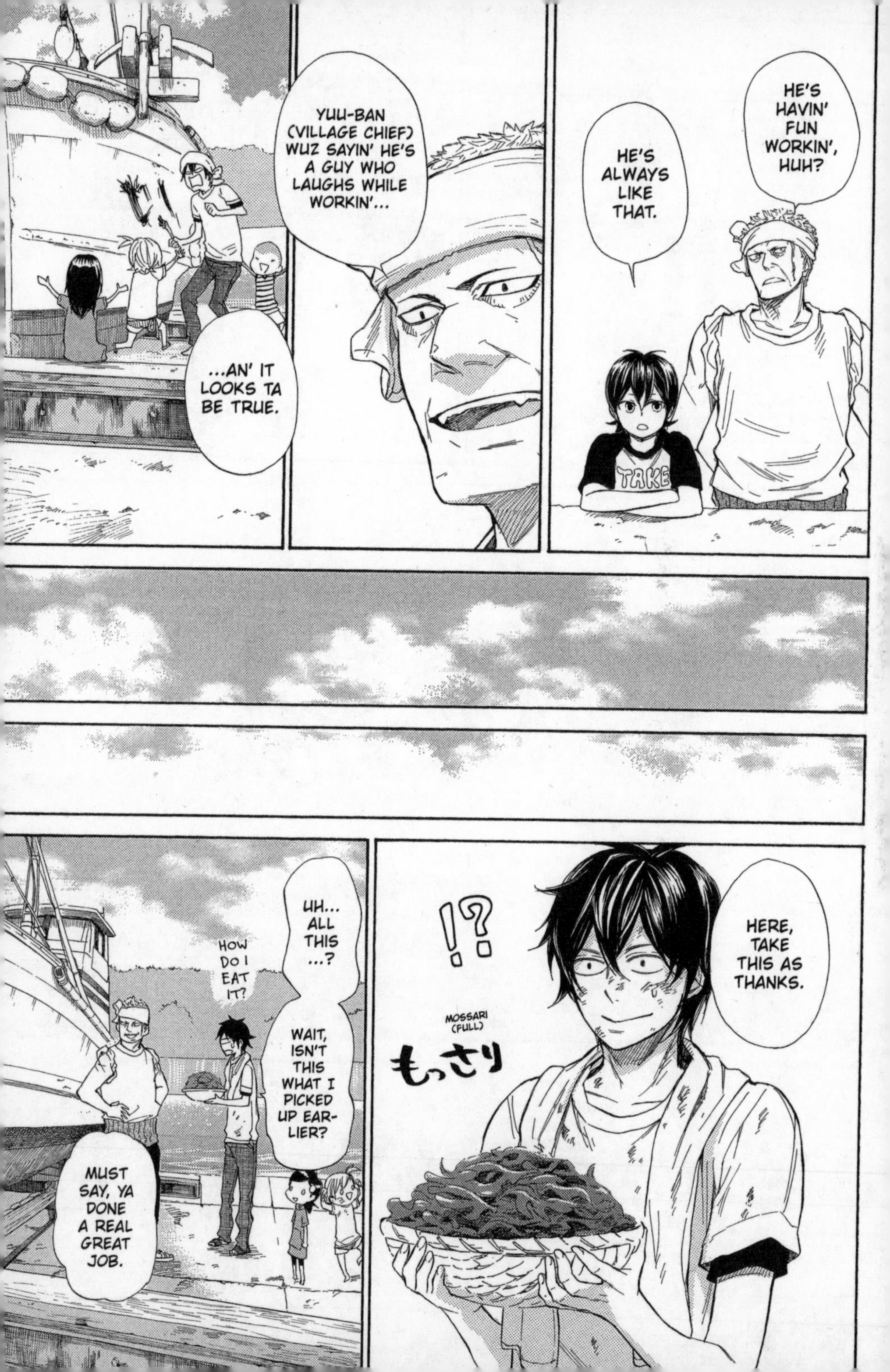
HE'S HAVIN' FUN WORKIN', HUH?
HE'S ALWAYS LIKE THAT.
YUU-BAN (VILLAGE CHIEF) WUZ SAYIN' HE'S A GUY WHO LAUGHS WHILE WORKIN'...
...AN' IT LOOKS TA BE TRUE.
HERE, TAKE THIS AS THANKS.
!?
MOSSARI (FULL)
もっさり
UH... ALL THIS ...?
HOW DO I EAT IT?
WAIT, ISN'T THIS WHAT I PICKED UP EARLIER?
MUST SAY, YA DONE A REAL GREAT JOB.

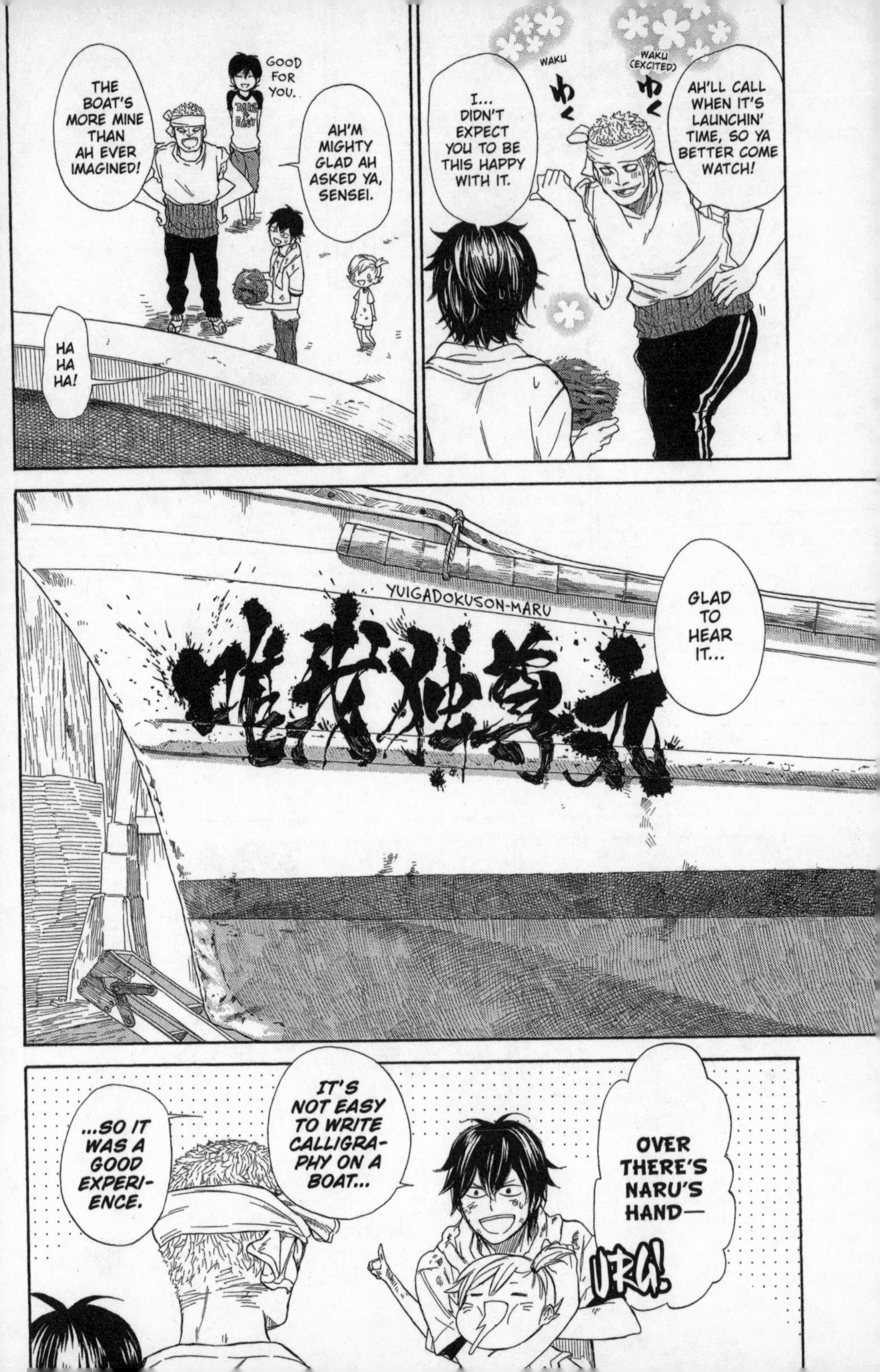
WAKU (EXCITED)
わく
AH'LL CALL WHEN IT'S LAUNCHIN' TIME, SO YA BETTER COME WATCH!
WAKU
わく
I... DIDN'T EXPECT YOU TO BE THIS HAPPY WITH IT.
AH'M MIGHTY GLAD AH ASKED YA, SENSEI.
GOOD FOR YOU..
THE BOAT'S MORE MINE THAN AH EVER IMAGINED!
HA HA HA!
GLAD TO HEAR IT...
YUIGADOKUSON-MARU
唯我独尊丸
OVER THERE'S NARU'S HAND—
URG!
IT'S NOT EASY TO WRITE CALLIGRAPHY ON A BOAT...
...SO IT WAS A GOOD EXPERIENCE.

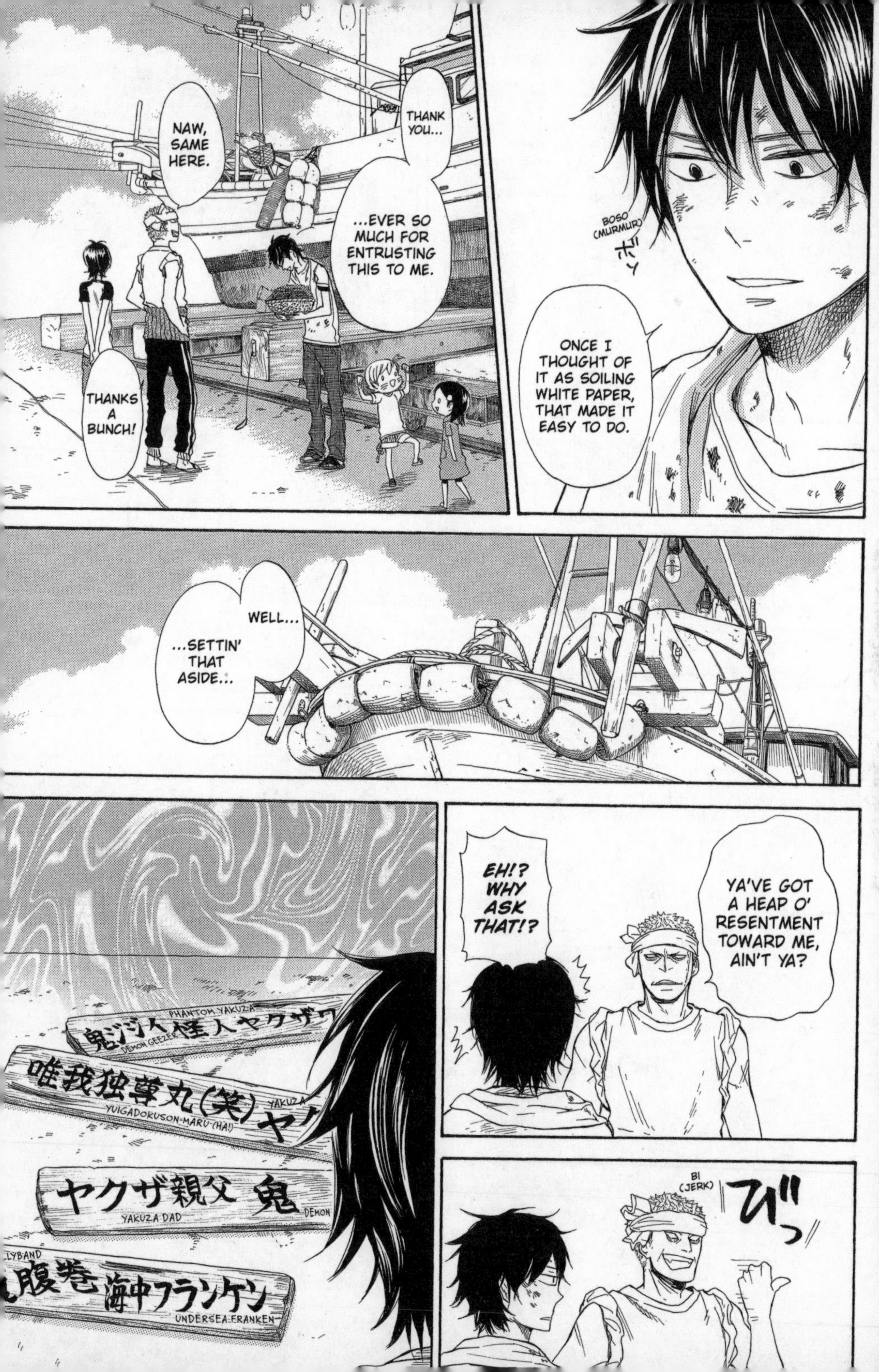

BOSO (MURMUR)
ボソ
ONCE I THOUGHT OF IT AS SOILING WHITE PAPER, THAT MADE IT EASY TO DO.
THANK YOU...
...EVER SO MUCH FOR ENTRUSTING THIS TO ME.
NAW, SAME HERE.
THANKS A BUNCH!
WELL...
...SETTIN' THAT ASIDE...
YA'VE GOT A HEAP O' RESENTMENT TOWARD ME, AIN'T YA?
EH!? WHY ASK THAT!?
BI (JERK)
びっ
PHANTOM YAKUZA
DEMON GEEZER
唯我独尊丸(笑)
YUIGADOKUSON-MARU (HA!)
YAKUZA
ヤクザ親父 鬼
YAKUZA DAD
DEMON
腹巻 海中フランケン
UNDERSEA FRANKEN

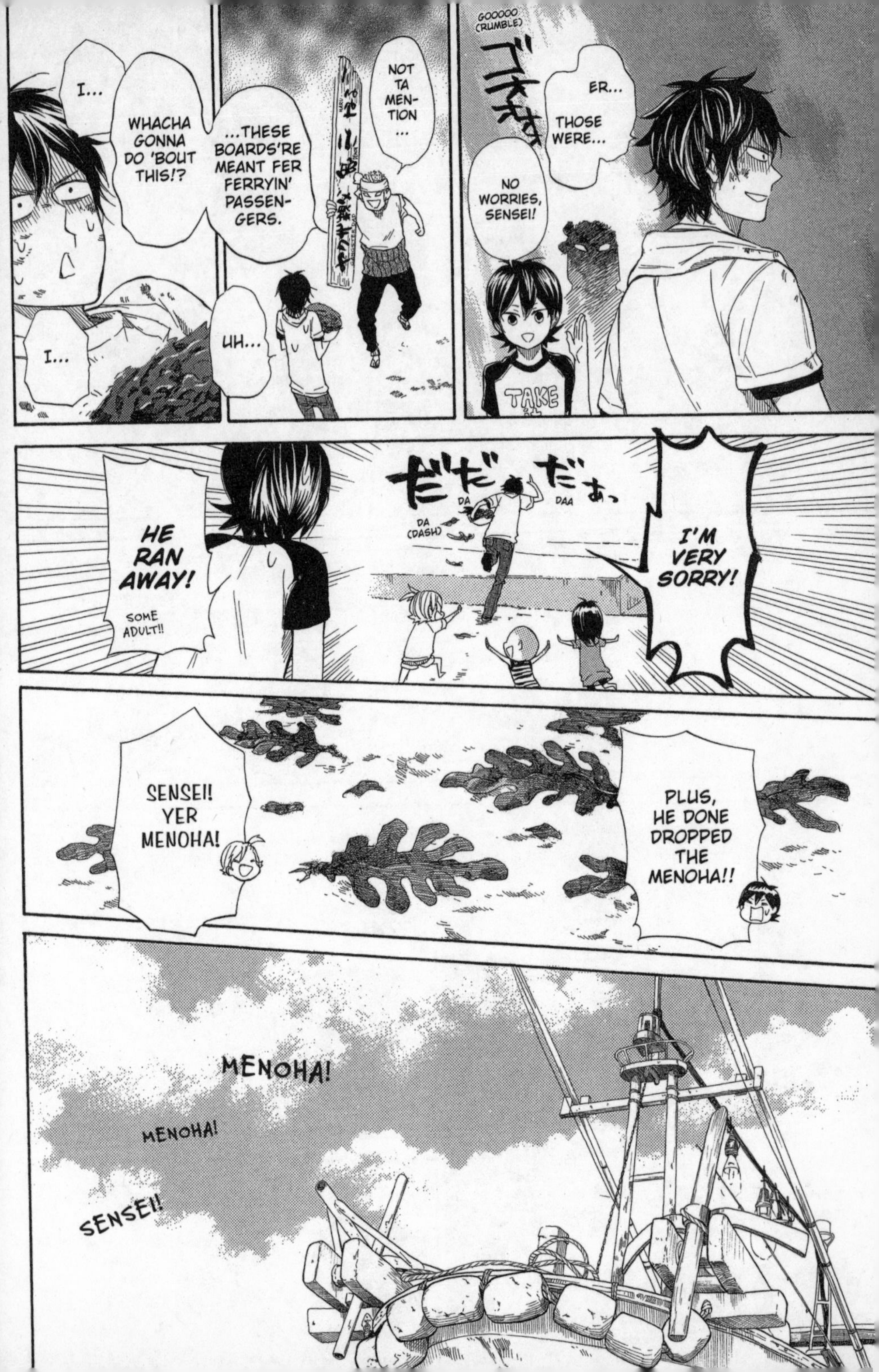
GOOOGO (RUMBLE)
ER... THOSE WERE...
NO WORRIES, SENSEI!
NOT TA MENTION...
...THESE BOARDS'RE MEANT FER FERRYIN' PASSENGERS.
WHACHA GONNA DO 'BOUT THIS!?
UH...
I...
I...
I'M VERY SORRY!
だだ だぁっ
DA DA (DASH) DAA
HE RAN AWAY!
SOME ADULT!!
PLUS, HE DONE DROPPED THE MENOHA!!
SENSEI! YER MENOHA!
MENOHA!
MENOHA!
SENSEI!

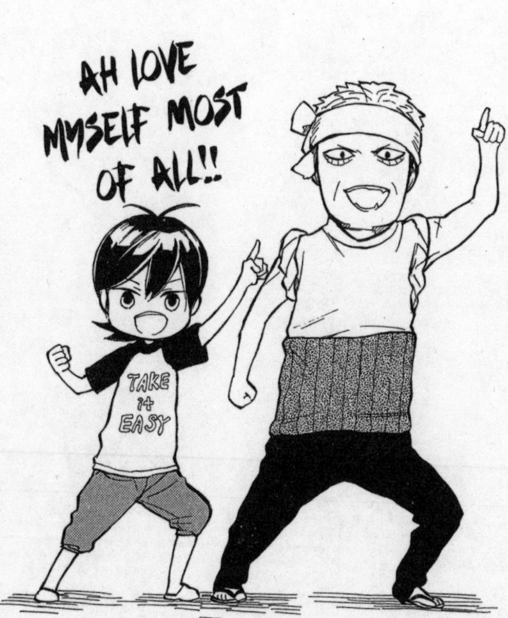
AH LOVE MYSELF MOST OF ALL!!
TAKE it EASY

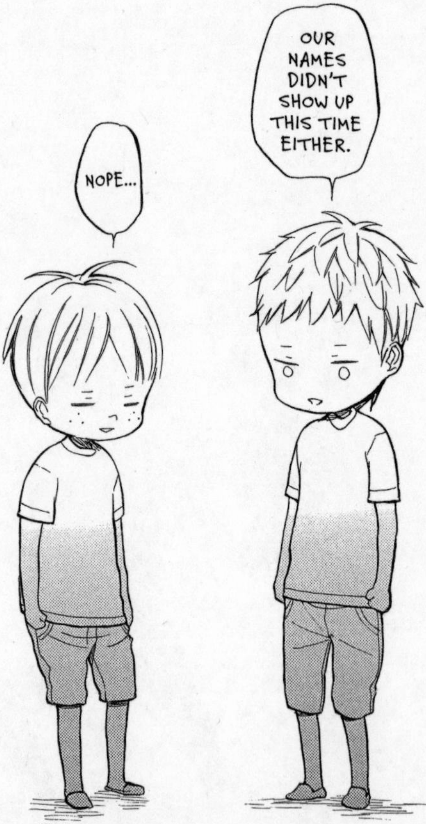
OUR NAMES DIDN'T SHOW UP THIS TIME EITHER.
NOPE...

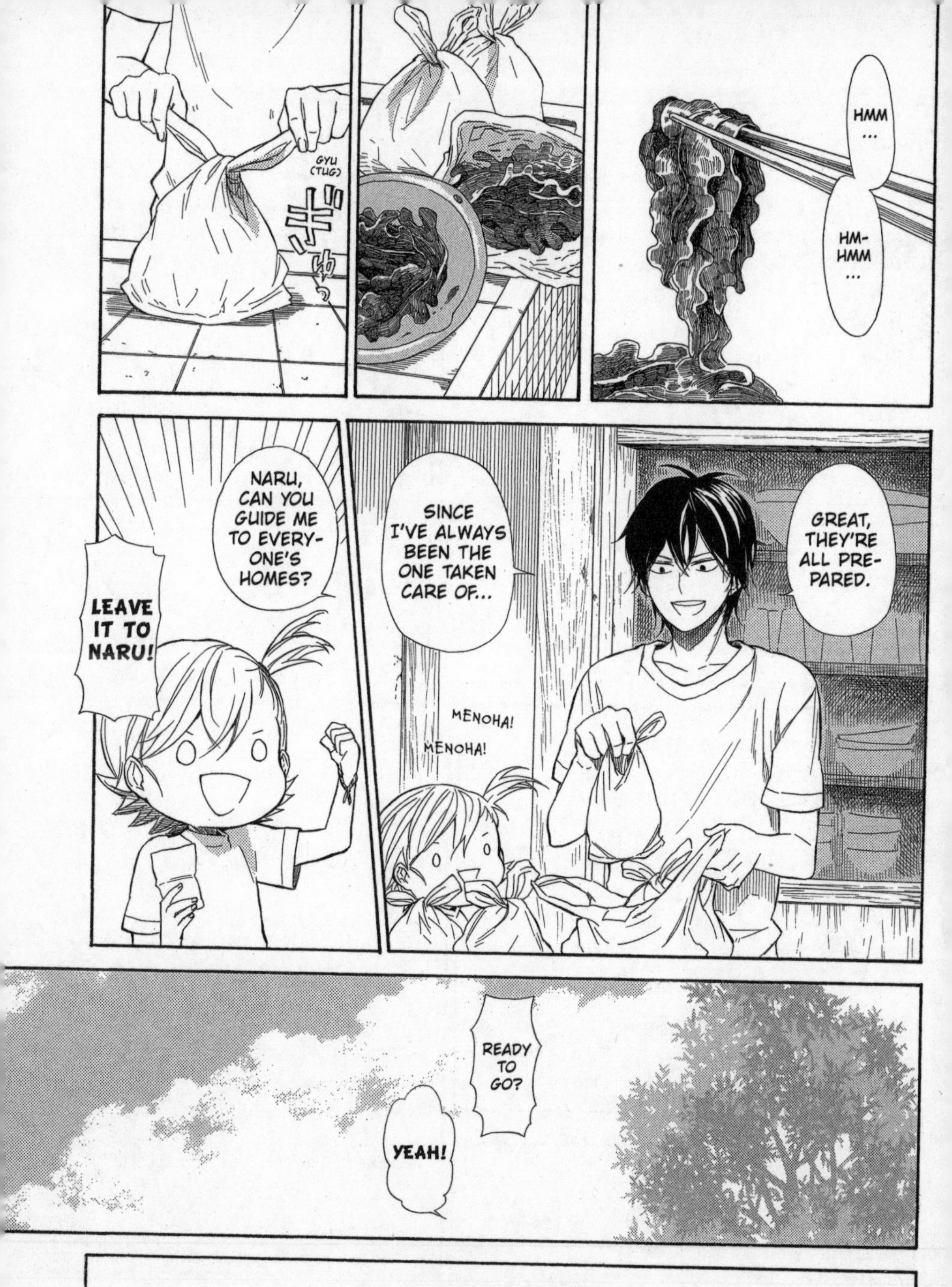
HMM...
HM-HMM...
GYU (TUG)
ぎゅっ
GREAT, THEY'RE ALL PREPARED.
SINCE I'VE ALWAYS BEEN THE ONE TAKEN CARE OF...
MENOHA!
MENOHA!
NARU, CAN YOU GUIDE ME TO EVERYONE'S HOMES?
LEAVE IT TO NARU!
READY TO GO?
YEAH!

ACT.34 MOTTEMAWA

(Translation: Sharing Around)

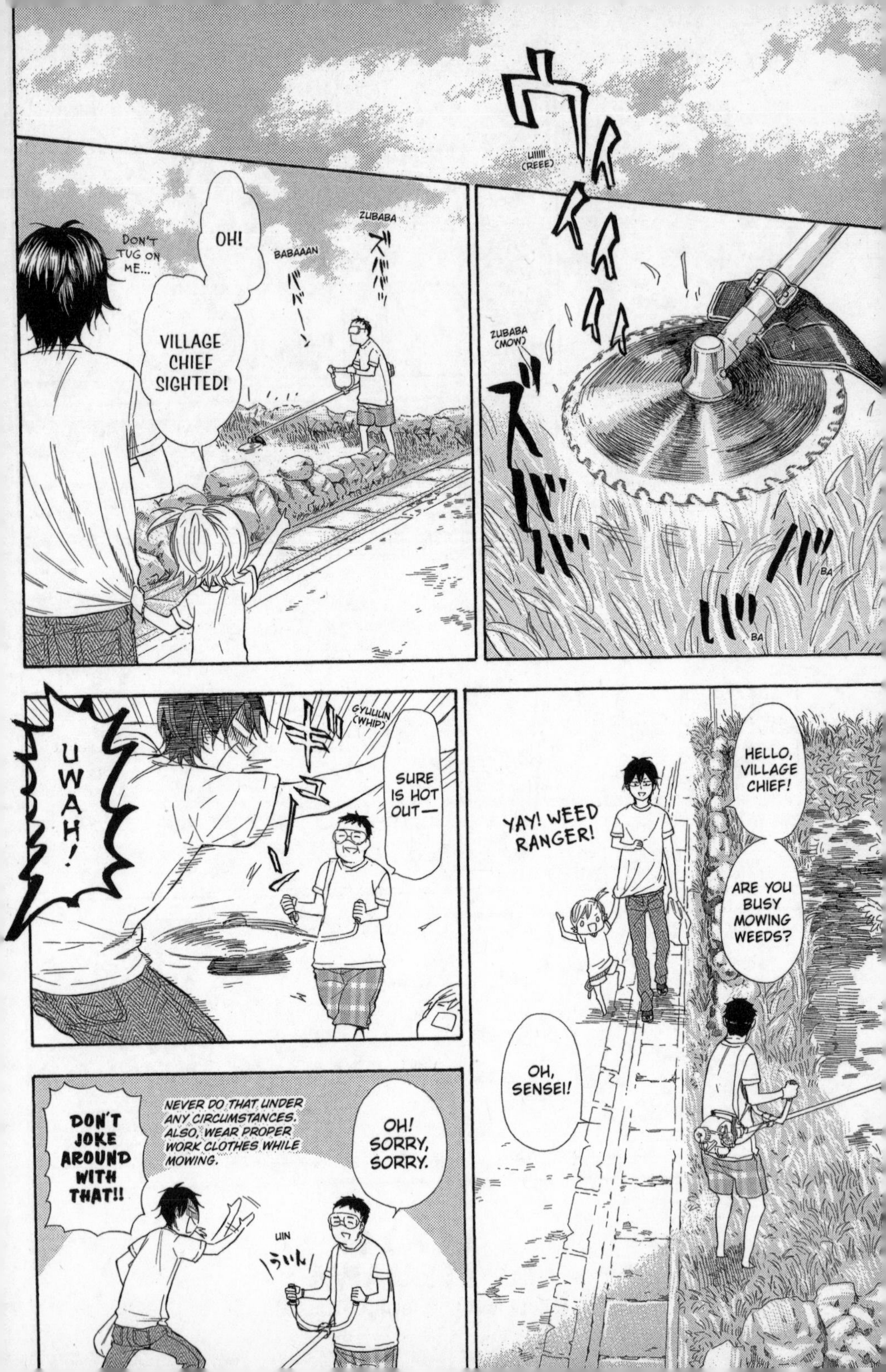
UIIIII (REEE)
ZUBABA (MOW)
BA
BA
ZUBABA
BABAAAN
OH!
VILLAGE CHIEF SIGHTED!
DON'T TUG ON ME...
HELLO, VILLAGE CHIEF!
ARE YOU BUSY MOWING WEEDS?
YAY! WEED RANGER!
OH, SENSEI!
GYUUUN (WHIP)
SURE IS HOT OUT—
UWAH!
OH! SORRY, SORRY.
NEVER DO THAT UNDER ANY CIRCUMSTANCES. ALSO, WEAR PROPER WORK CLOTHES WHILE MOWING.
DON'T JOKE AROUND WITH THAT!!
UIN

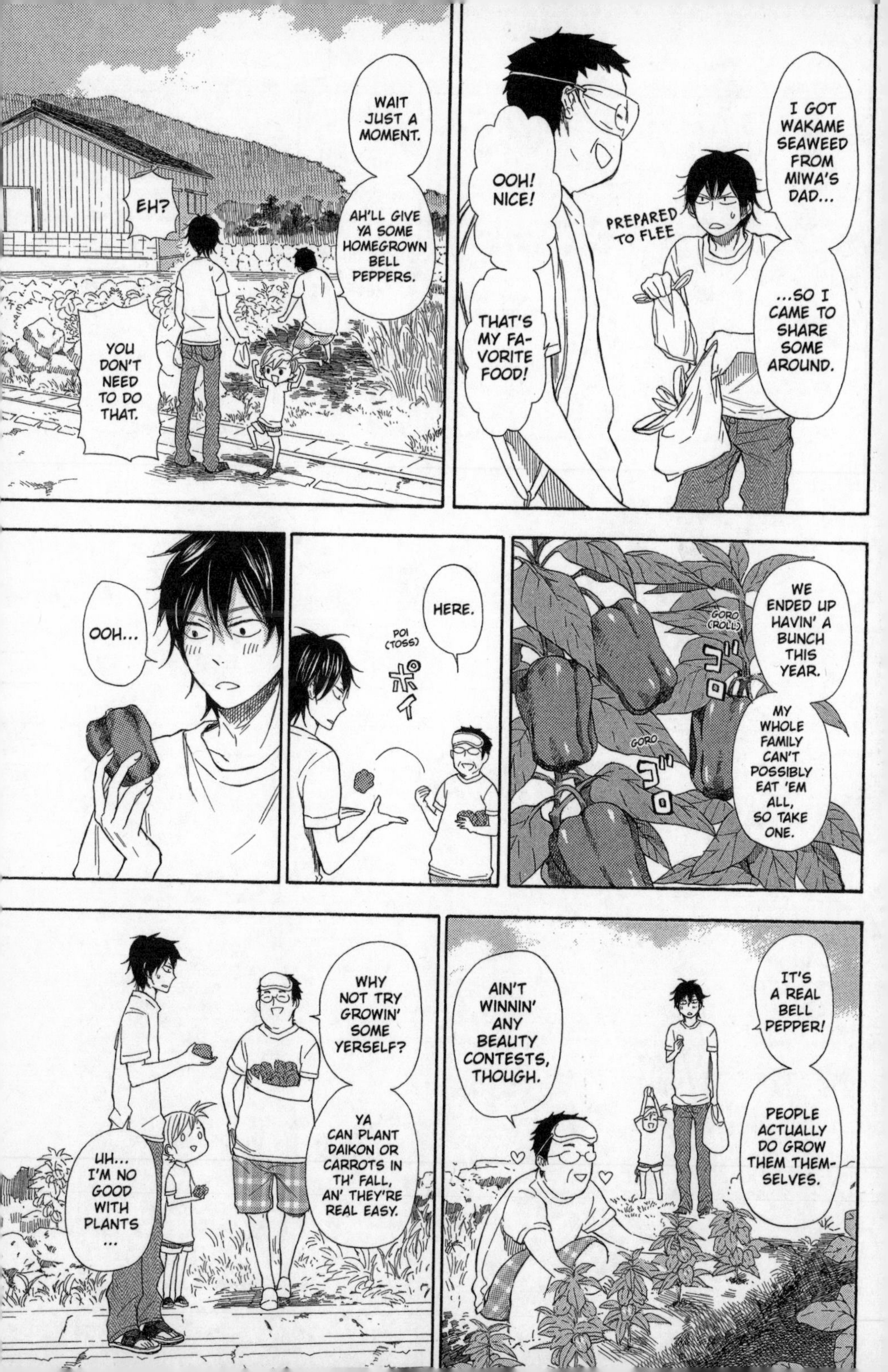
I GOT WAKAME SEAWEED FROM MIWA'S DAD...
PREPARED TO FLEE
...SO I CAME TO SHARE SOME AROUND.
OOH! NICE!
THAT'S MY FA-VORITE FOOD!
WAIT JUST A MOMENT.
AH'LL GIVE YA SOME HOMEGROWN BELL PEPPERS.
EH?
YOU DON'T NEED TO DO THAT.
WE ENDED UP HAVIN' A BUNCH THIS YEAR.
GORO (ROLL)
MY WHOLE FAMILY CAN'T POSSIBLY EAT 'EM ALL, SO TAKE ONE.
GORO
HERE.
POI (TOSS)
OOH...
IT'S A REAL BELL PEPPER!
PEOPLE ACTUALLY DO GROW THEM THEM-SELVES.
AIN'T WINNIN' ANY BEAUTY CONTESTS, THOUGH.
WHY NOT TRY GROWIN' SOME YERSELF?
YA CAN PLANT DAIKON OR CARROTS IN TH' FALL, AN' THEY'RE REAL EASY.
UH... I'M NO GOOD WITH PLANTS ...

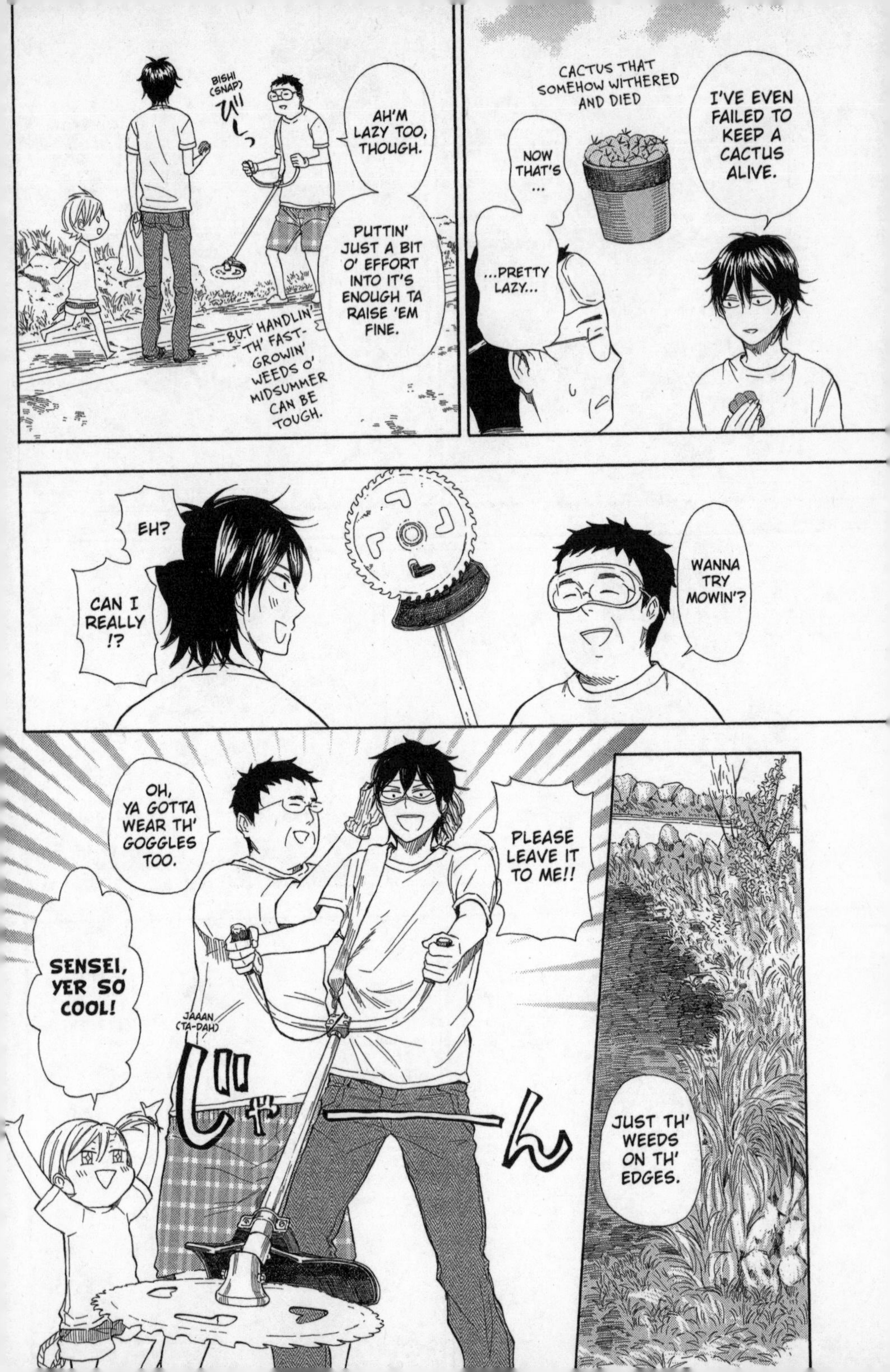
I'VE EVEN FAILED TO KEEP A CACTUS ALIVE.
CACTUS THAT SOMEHOW WITHERED AND DIED
NOW THAT'S ...
...PRETTY LAZY...
AH'M LAZY TOO, THOUGH.
PUTTIN' JUST A BIT O' EFFORT INTO IT'S ENOUGH TA RAISE 'EM FINE.
BISHI (SNAP)
びしっ
BUT HANDLIN' TH' FAST-GROWIN' WEEDS O' MIDSUMMER CAN BE TOUGH.
WANNA TRY MOWIN'?
EH?
CAN I REALLY !?
JUST TH' WEEDS ON TH' EDGES.
PLEASE LEAVE IT TO ME!!
OH, YA GOTTA WEAR TH' GOGGLES TOO.
JAAAN (TA-DAH)
じゃーん
SENSEI, YER SO COOL!

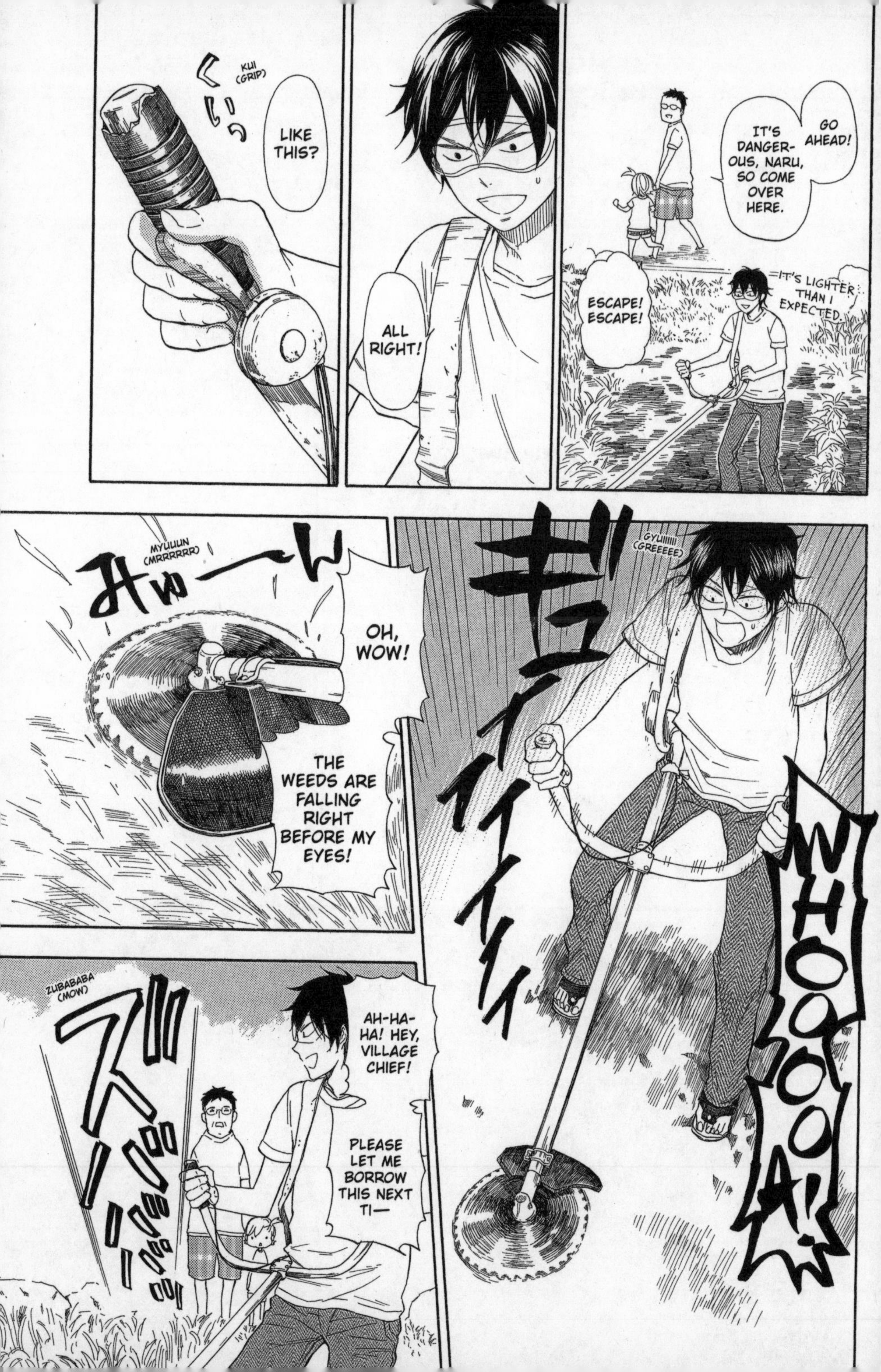
GO AHEAD!
IT'S DANGEROUS, NARU, SO COME OVER HERE.
ESCAPE! ESCAPE!
IT'S LIGHTER THAN I EXPECTED.
ALL RIGHT!
KUI (GRIP)
LIKE THIS?
GYUIIIIIII (GREEEEEE)
WHOOOOA!!
MYUUUN (MRRRRRR)
OH, WOW!
THE WEEDS ARE FALLING RIGHT BEFORE MY EYES!
ZUBABABA (MOW)
AH-HA-HA! HEY, VILLAGE CHIEF!
PLEASE LET ME BORROW THIS NEXT TI—

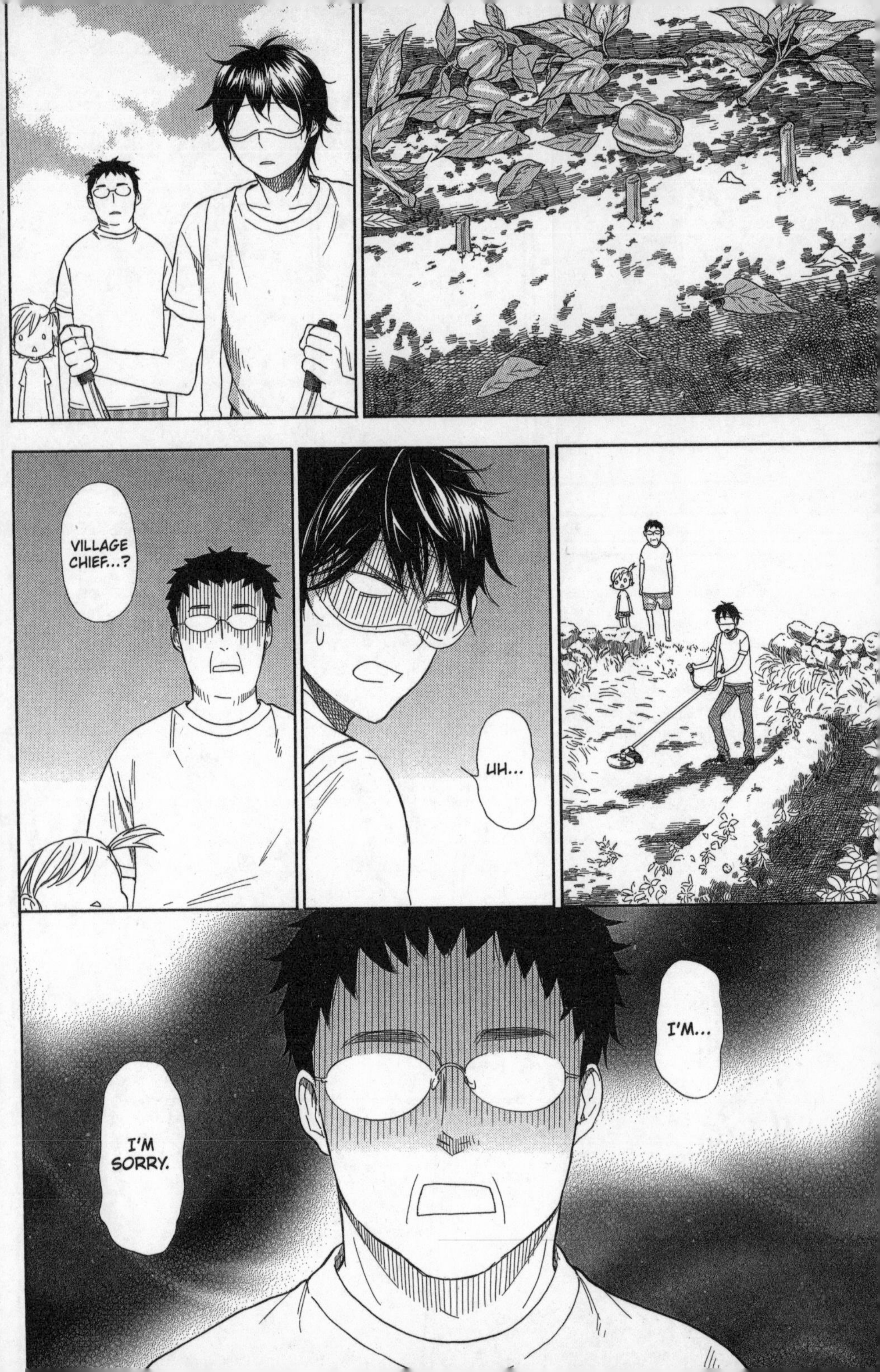
UH...
VILLAGE CHIEF...?
I'M...
I'M SORRY.

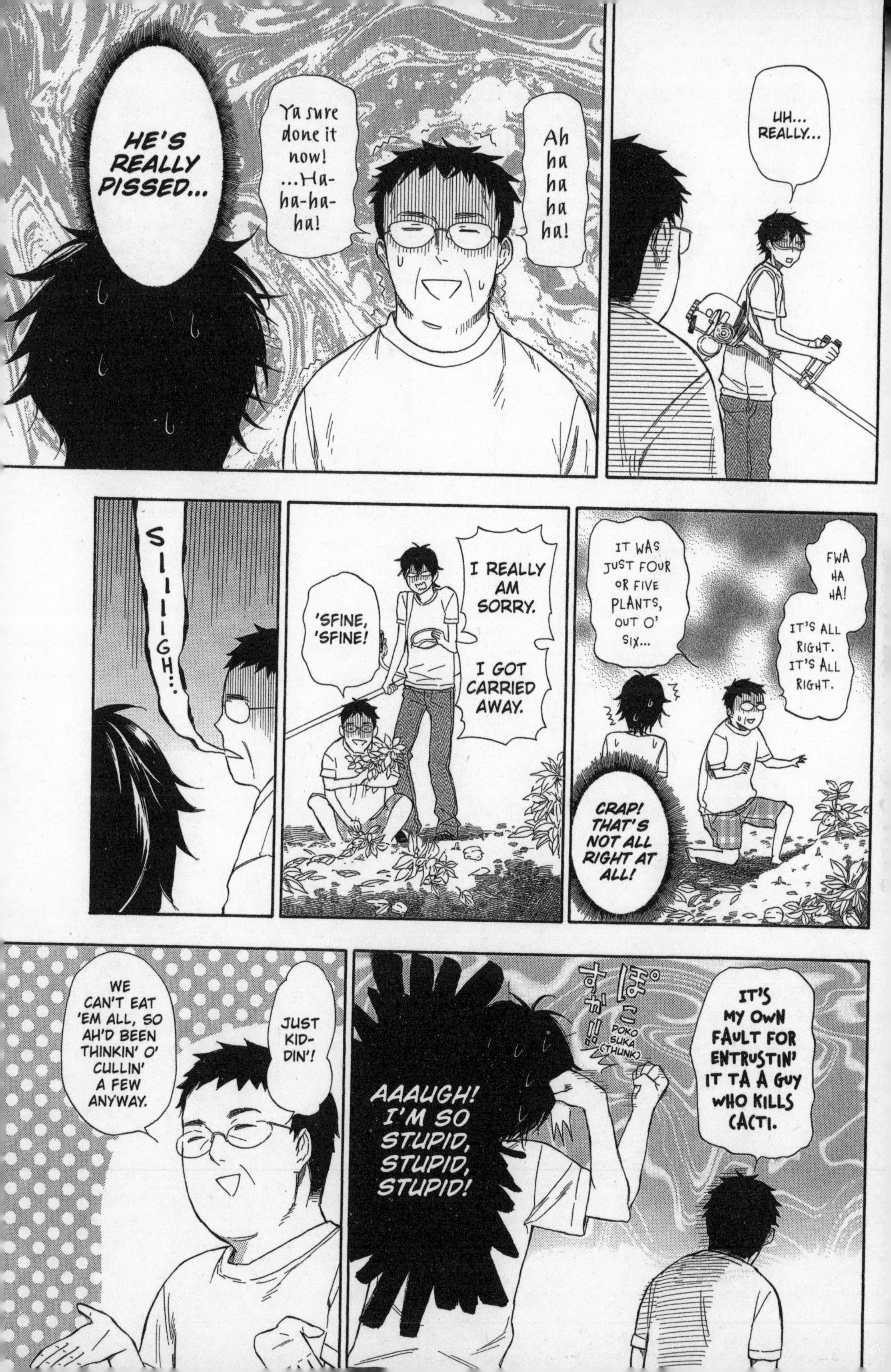
UH... REALLY...
Ah ha ha ha ha!
Ya sure done it now! ...Ha-ha-ha-ha!
HE'S REALLY PISSED...
FWA HA HA!
IT'S ALL RIGHT. IT'S ALL RIGHT.
IT WAS JUST FOUR OR FIVE PLANTS, OUT O' SIX...
CRAP! THAT'S NOT ALL RIGHT AT ALL!
I REALLY AM SORRY.
I GOT CARRIED AWAY.
'SFINE, 'SFINE!
SIIIIIGH...
IT'S MY OWN FAULT FOR ENTRUSTIN' IT TA A GUY WHO KILLS CACTI.
ぽこすか!!
POKO SUKA (THUNK)
AAAUGH! I'M SO STUPID, STUPID, STUPID!
JUST KID-DIN'!
WE CAN'T EAT 'EM ALL, SO AH'D BEEN THINKIN' O' CULLIN' A FEW ANYWAY.

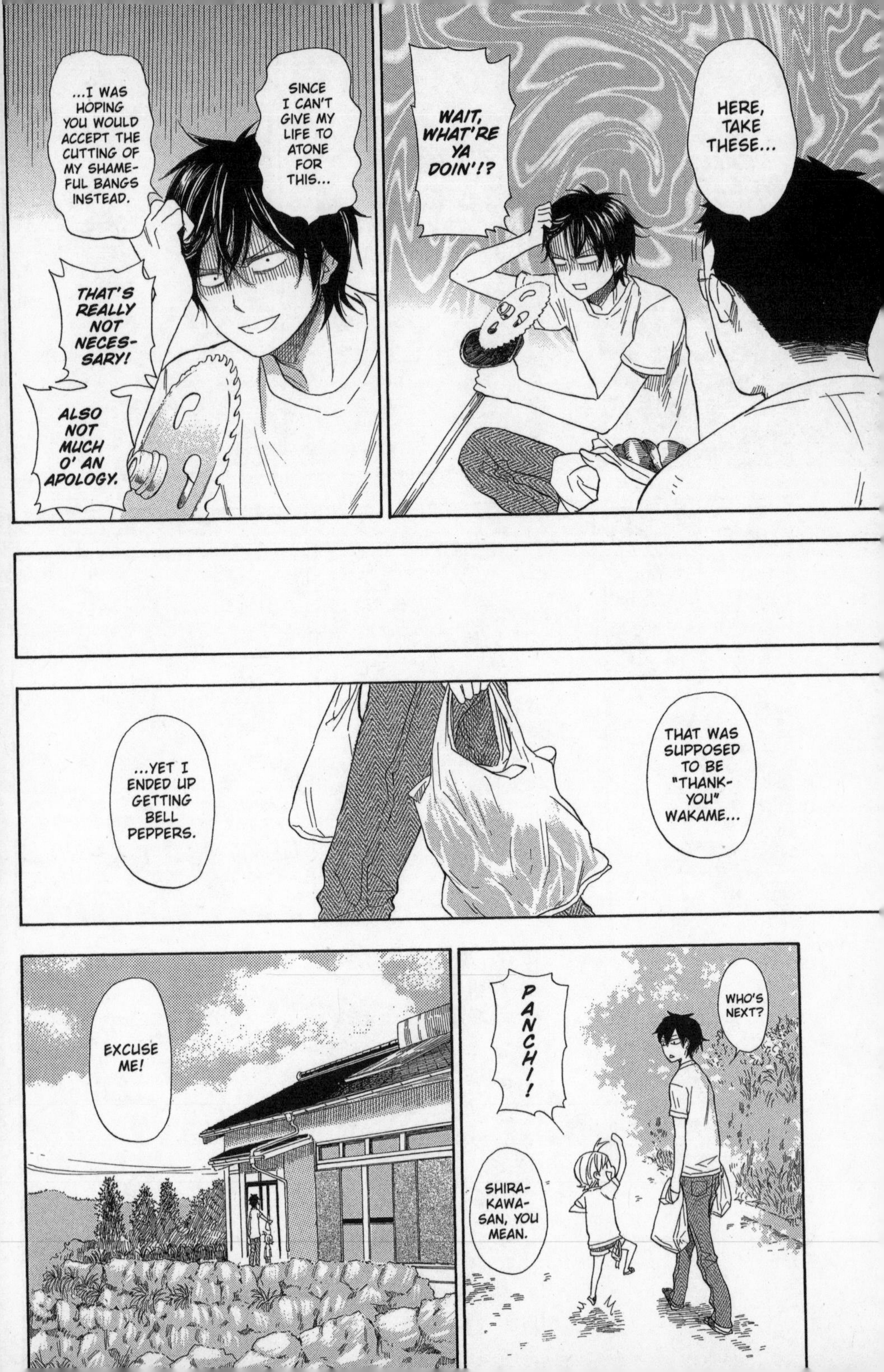
HERE, TAKE THESE...
WAIT, WHAT'RE YA DOIN'!?
SINCE I CAN'T GIVE MY LIFE TO ATONE FOR THIS...
...I WAS HOPING YOU WOULD ACCEPT THE CUTTING OF MY SHAMEFUL BANGS INSTEAD.
THAT'S REALLY NOT NECESSARY!
ALSO NOT MUCH O' AN APOLOGY.
THAT WAS SUPPOSED TO BE "THANK-YOU" WAKAME...
...YET I ENDED UP GETTING BELL PEPPERS.
WHO'S NEXT?
PANCHI!
SHIRAKAWA-SAN, YOU MEAN.
EXCUSE ME!

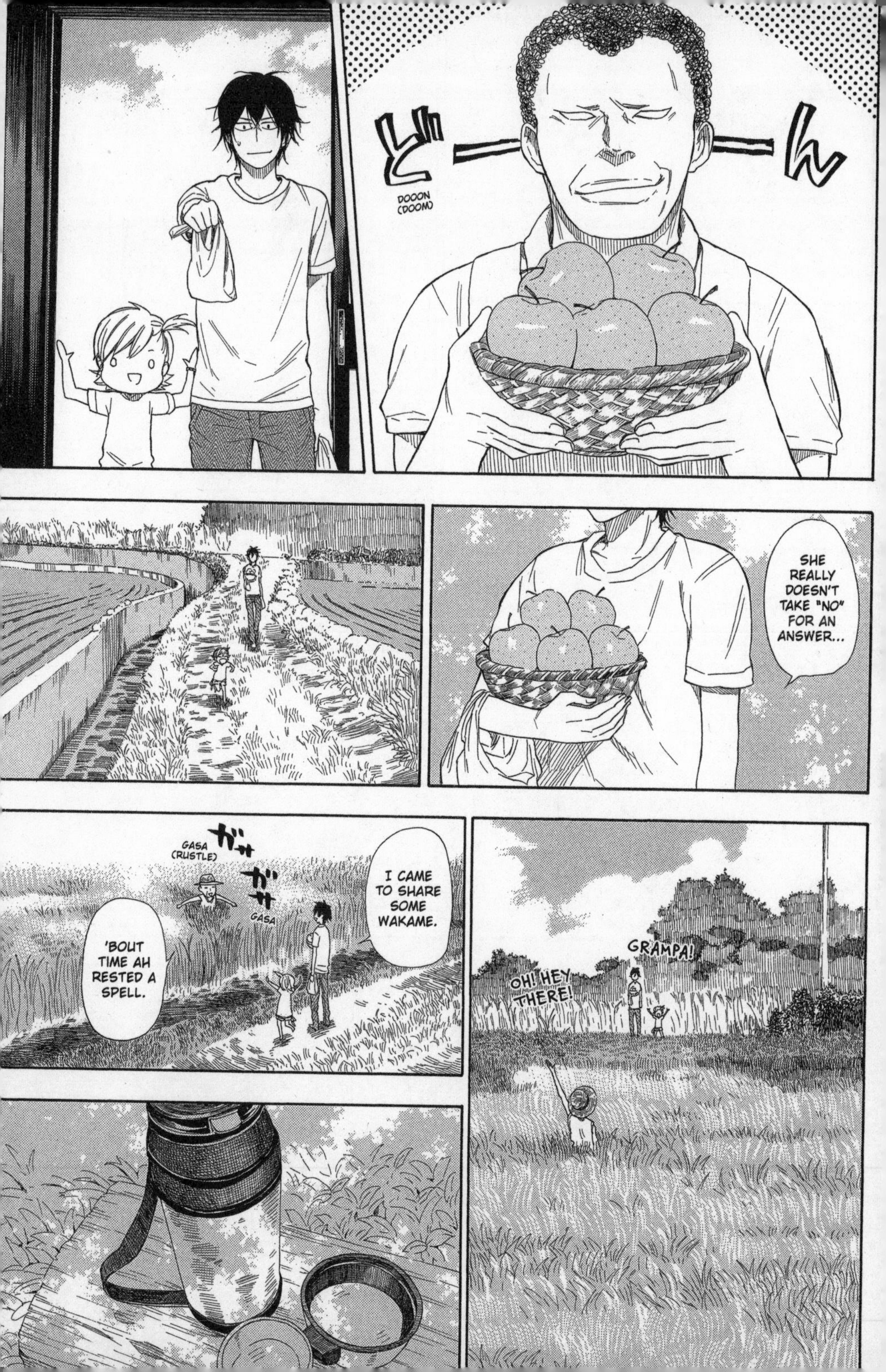
DOOON (DOOM)
SHE REALLY DOESN'T TAKE "NO" FOR AN ANSWER...
GRAMPA!
OH! HEY THERE!
I CAME TO SHARE SOME WAKAME.
GASA
GASA (RUSTLE)
'BOUT TIME AH RESTED A SPELL.

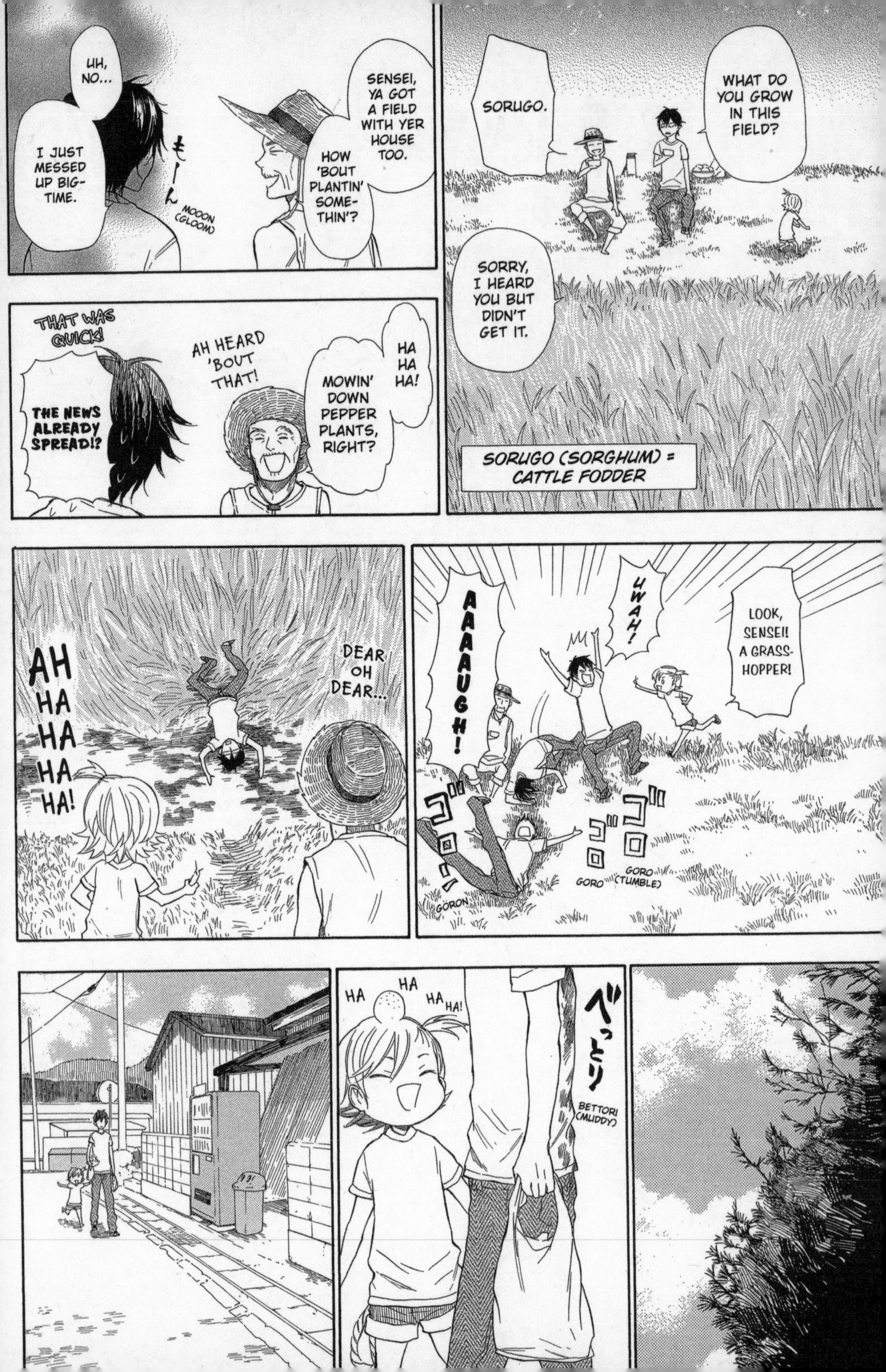
WHAT DO YOU GROW IN THIS FIELD?
SORUGO.
SORRY, I HEARD YOU BUT DIDN'T GET IT.
SORUGO (SORGHUM) = CATTLE FODDER
SENSEI, YA GOT A FIELD WITH YER HOUSE TOO.
HOW 'BOUT PLANTIN' SOME-THIN'?
UH, NO...
I JUST MESSED UP BIG-TIME.
もーん
MOOON (GLOOM)
HA HA HA!
AH HEARD 'BOUT THAT!
MOWIN' DOWN PEPPER PLANTS, RIGHT?
THAT WAS QUICK!
THE NEWS ALREADY SPREAD!?
LOOK, SENSEI! A GRASS-HOPPER!
UWAH!
AAAAAUGH!
ゴロ
ゴロ
GORO
GORO (TUMBLE)
ゴロン
GORON
DEAR OH DEAR...
AH HA HA HA HA!
HA HA HA HA!
べっとり
BETTORI (MUDDY)

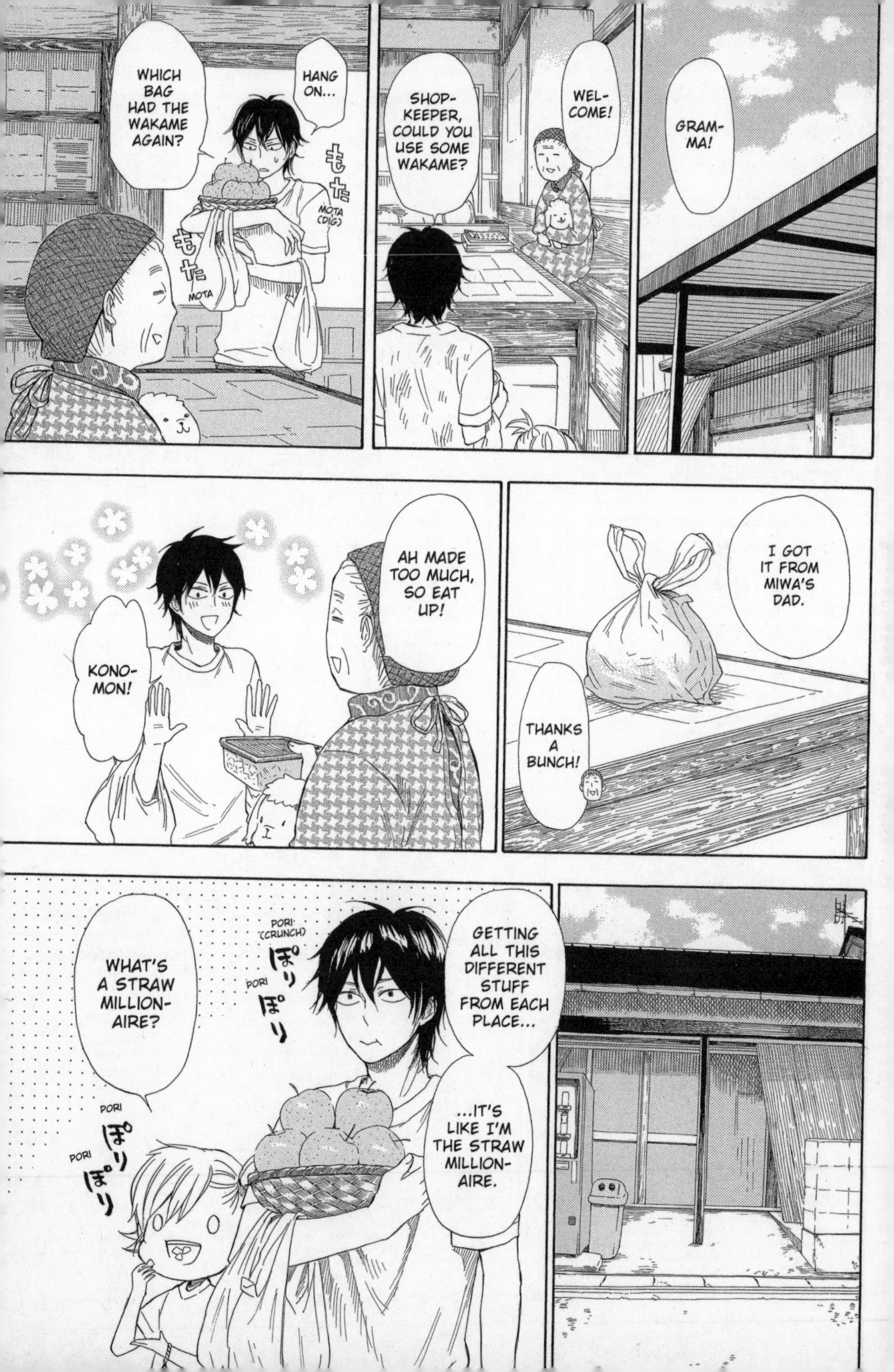
GRAM-MA!
WEL-COME!
SHOP-KEEPER, COULD YOU USE SOME WAKAME?
HANG ON...
WHICH BAG HAD THE WAKAME AGAIN?
もた MOTA (DIG)
もた MOTA
I GOT IT FROM MIWA'S DAD.
THANKS A BUNCH!
AH MADE TOO MUCH, SO EAT UP!
KONO-MON!
GETTING ALL THIS DIFFERENT STUFF FROM EACH PLACE...
...IT'S LIKE I'M THE STRAW MILLION-AIRE.
ぽり PORI (CRUNCH)
ぽり PORI
WHAT'S A STRAW MILLION-AIRE?
ぽり PORI
ぽり PORI

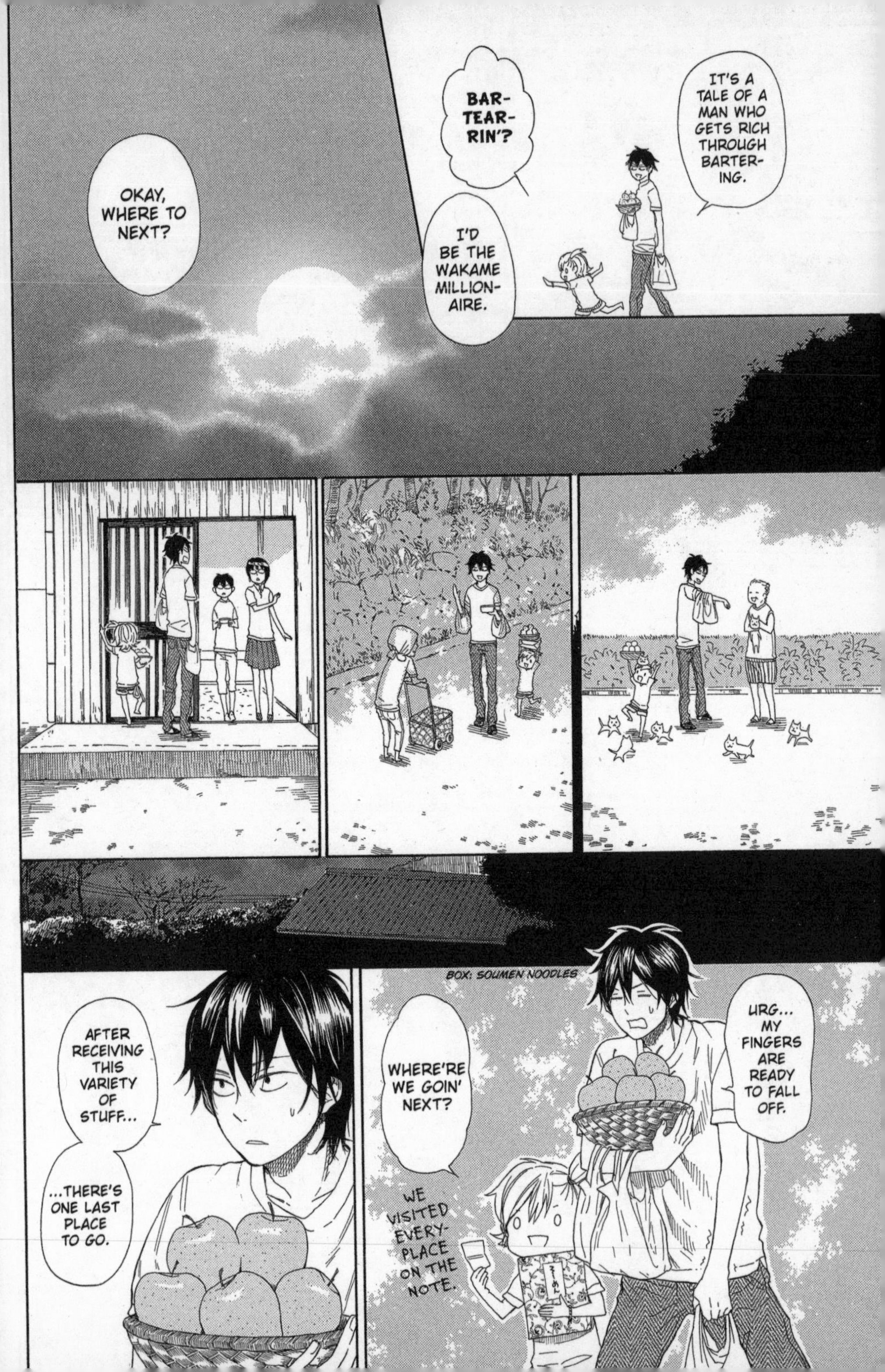
IT'S A TALE OF A MAN WHO GETS RICH THROUGH BARTER-ING.
BAR-TEAR-RIN'?
I'D BE THE WAKAME MILLION-AIRE.
OKAY, WHERE TO NEXT?
BOX: SOUMEN NOODLES
URG... MY FINGERS ARE READY TO FALL OFF.
WHERE'RE WE GOIN' NEXT?
WE VISITED EVERY-PLACE ON THE NOTE.
AFTER RECEIVING THIS VARIETY OF STUFF...
...THERE'S ONE LAST PLACE TO GO.

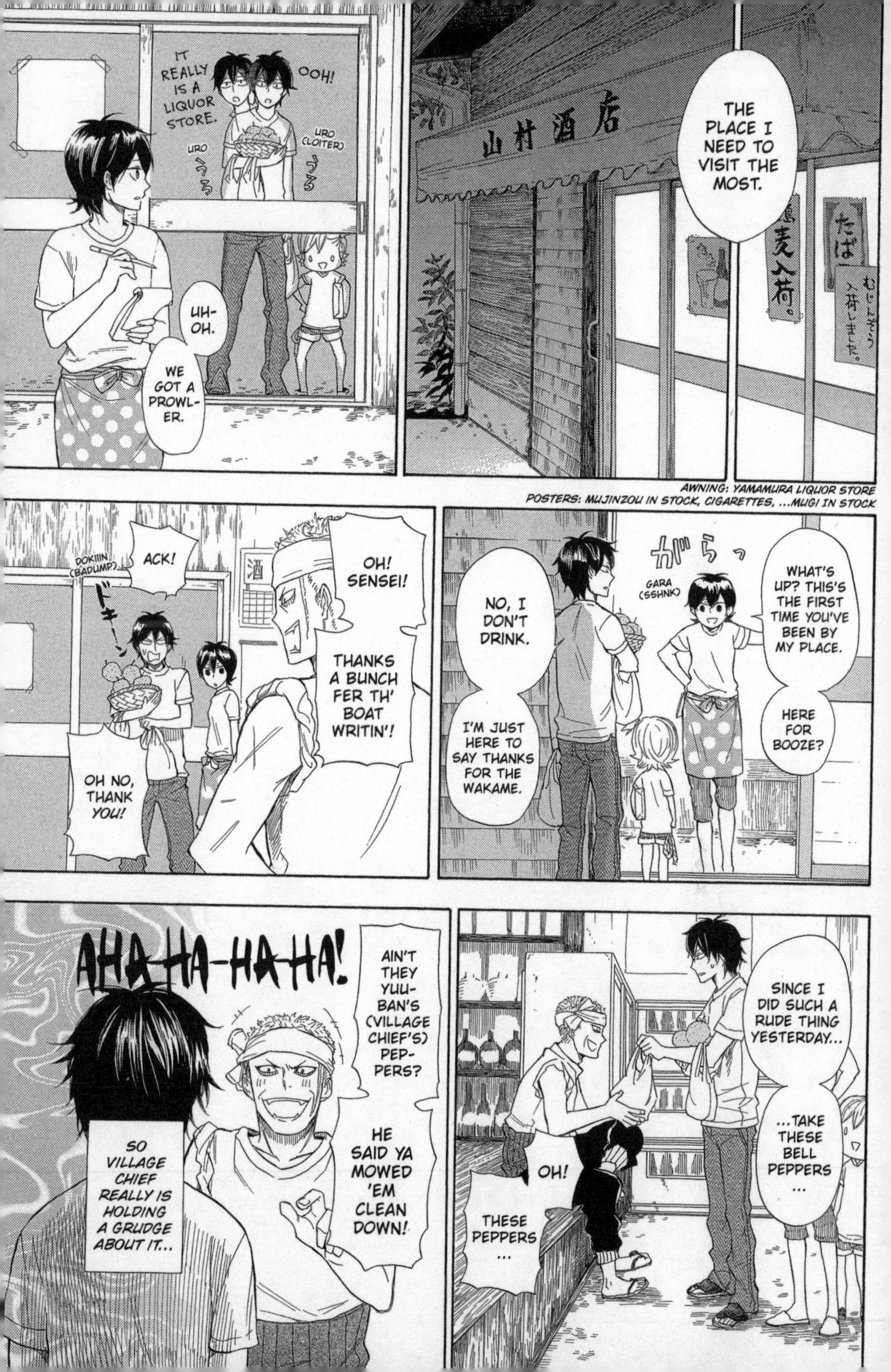
山村酒店
むじんぞう入荷しました。
麦入荷。
THE PLACE I NEED TO VISIT THE MOST.
IT REALLY IS A LIQUOR STORE.
OOH!
URO (LOITER) うろ
URO うろ
UH-OH.
WE GOT A PROWLER.
AWNING: YAMAMURA LIQUOR STORE
POSTERS: MUJINZOU IN STOCK, CIGARETTES, ...MUGI IN STOCK
WHAT'S UP? THIS'S THE FIRST TIME YOU'VE BEEN BY MY PLACE.
HERE FOR BOOZE?
がらっ
GARA (SSHNK)
NO, I DON'T DRINK.
I'M JUST HERE TO SAY THANKS FOR THE WAKAME.
OH! SENSEI!
THANKS A BUNCH FER TH' BOAT WRITIN'!
ACK!
DOKIIN (BADUMP)
ドキーン
OH NO, THANK YOU!
SINCE I DID SUCH A RUDE THING YESTERDAY...
...TAKE THESE BELL PEPPERS...
OH!
THESE PEPPERS...
AIN'T THEY YUU-BAN'S (VILLAGE CHIEF'S) PEP-PERS?
HE SAID YA MOWED 'EM CLEAN DOWN!
AHA-HA-HA-HA!
SO VILLAGE CHIEF REALLY IS HOLDING A GRUDGE ABOUT IT...

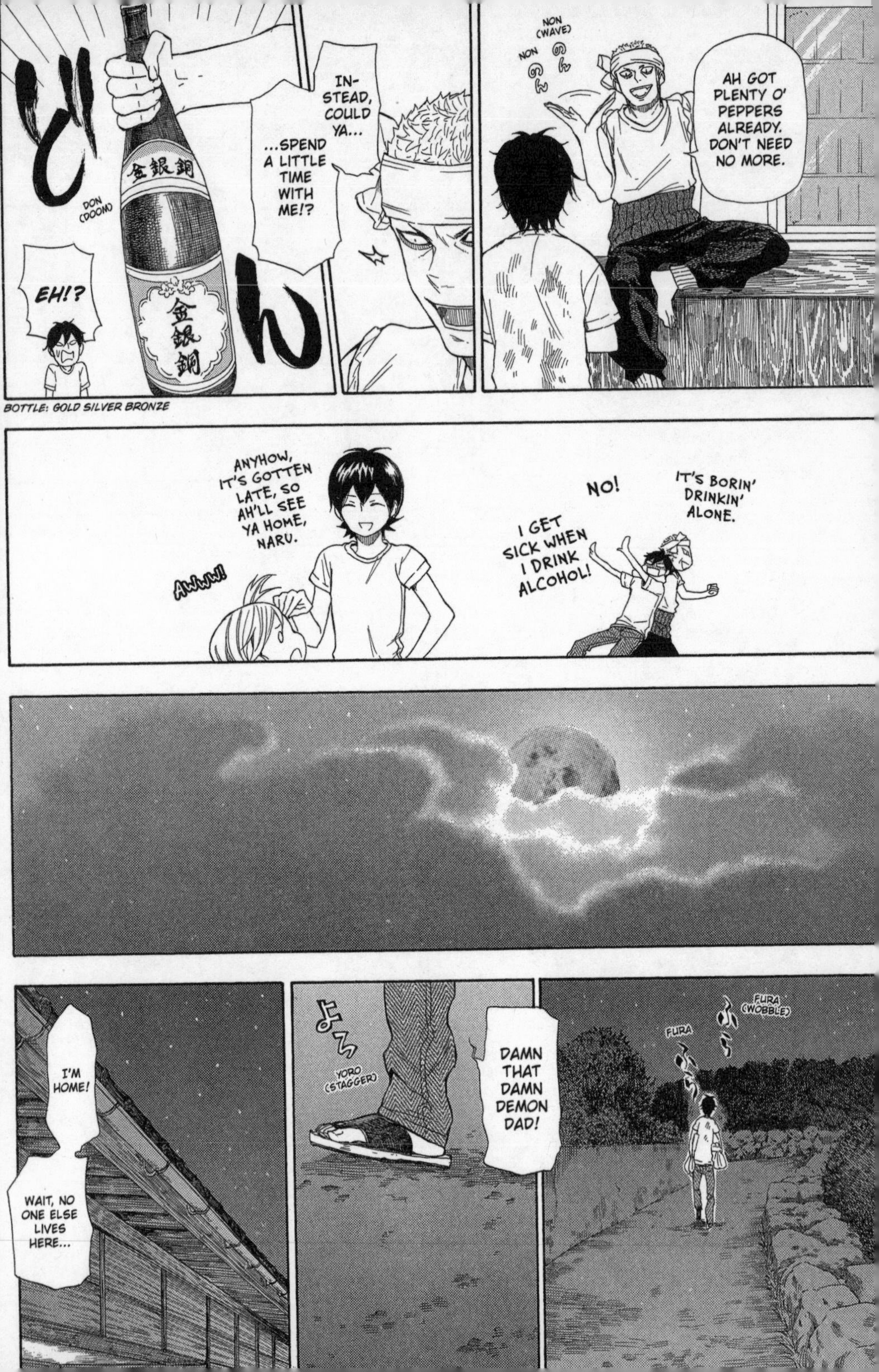
NON (WAVE)
NON
AH GOT PLENTY O' PEPPERS ALREADY. DON'T NEED NO MORE.
IN-STEAD, COULD YA...
...SPEND A LITTLE TIME WITH ME!?
DON (DOOM)
金銀銅
金銀銅
EH!?
BOTTLE: GOLD SILVER BRONZE
IT'S BORIN' DRINKIN' ALONE.
NO!
I GET SICK WHEN I DRINK ALCOHOL!
ANYHOW, IT'S GOTTEN LATE, SO AH'LL SEE YA HOME, NARU.
AWWW!
FURA (WOBBLE)
FURA
DAMN THAT DAMN DEMON DAD!
YORO (STAGGER)
I'M HOME!
WAIT, NO ONE ELSE LIVES HERE...

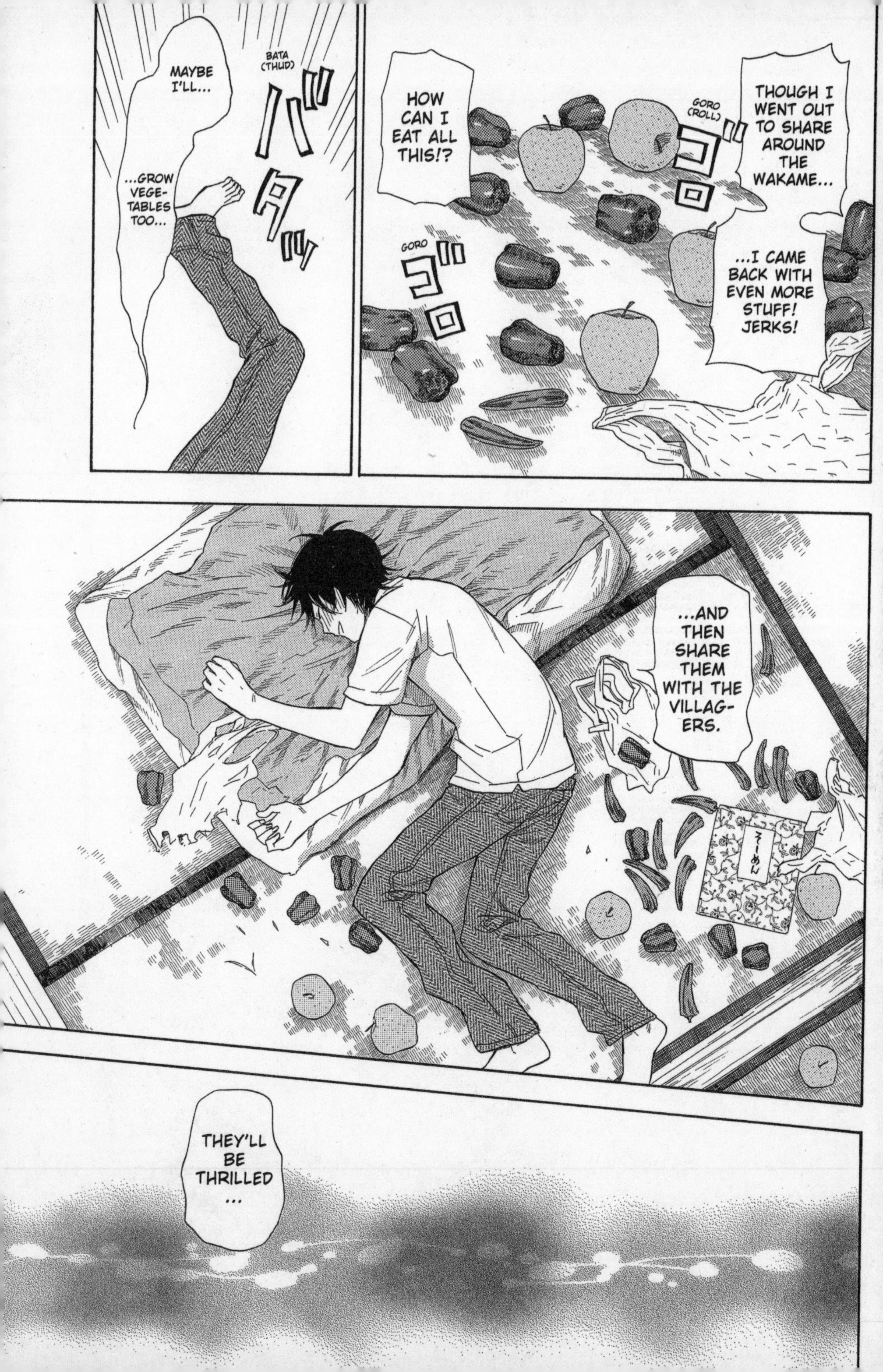
THOUGH I WENT OUT TO SHARE AROUND THE WAKAME...
GORO (ROLL)
...I CAME BACK WITH EVEN MORE STUFF! JERKS!
HOW CAN I EAT ALL THIS!?
GORO
BATA (THUD)
MAYBE I'LL...
...GROW VEGE-TABLES TOO...
...AND THEN SHARE THEM WITH THE VILLAG-ERS.
そーめん
THEY'LL BE THRILLED ...

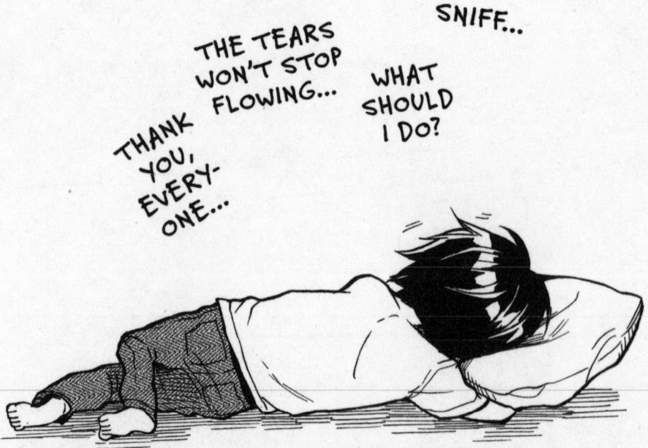
SNIFF...
WHAT SHOULD I DO?
THE TEARS WON'T STOP FLOWING...
THANK YOU, EVERY-ONE...

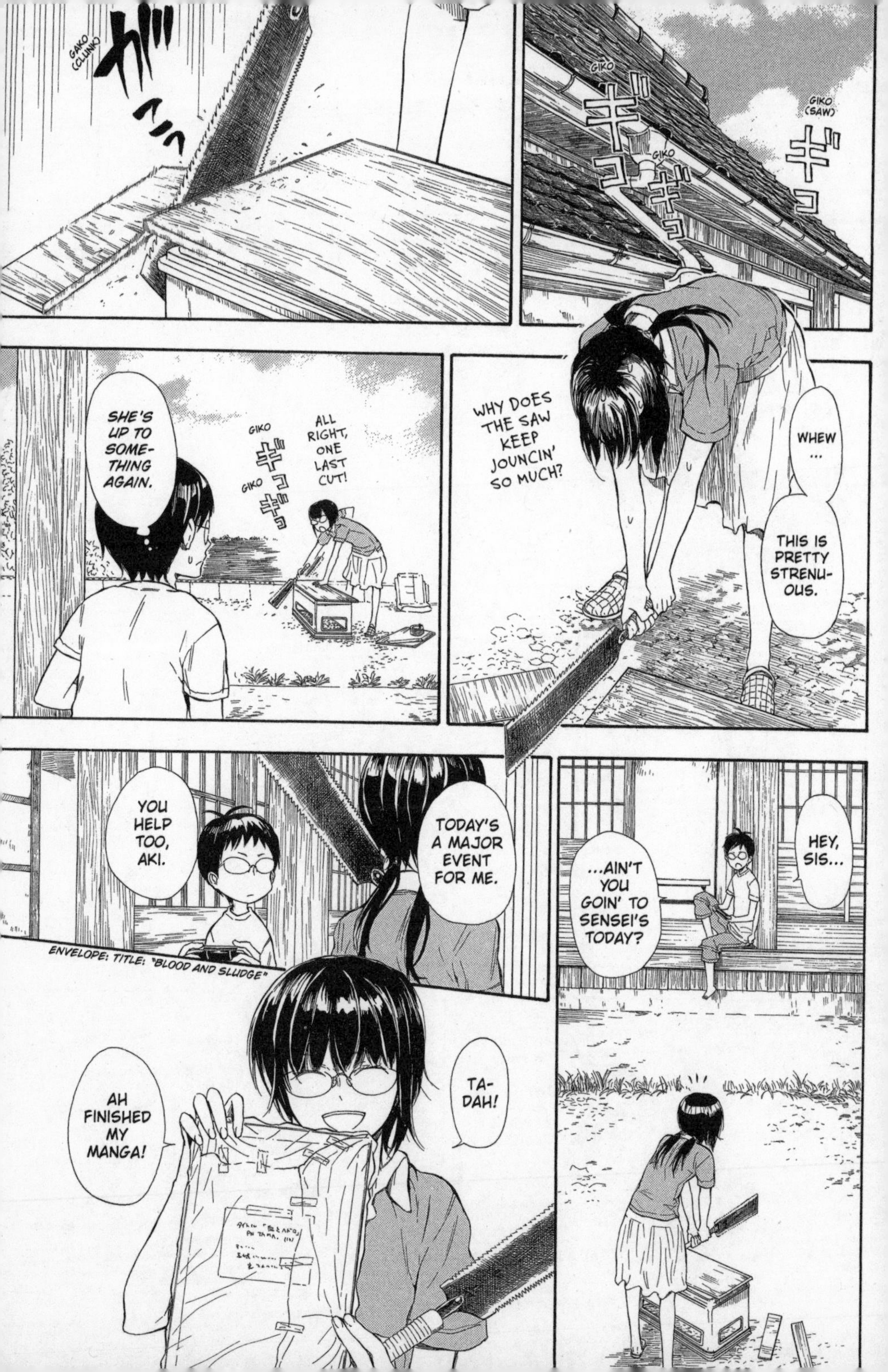
GIKO
GIKO (SAW)
GIKO
GAKO (CLUNK)
WHEW...
THIS IS PRETTY STRENU-OUS.
WHY DOES THE SAW KEEP JOUNCIN' SO MUCH?
ALL RIGHT, ONE LAST CUT!
GIKO
GIKO
SHE'S UP TO SOME-THING AGAIN.
HEY, SIS...
...AIN'T YOU GOIN' TO SENSEI'S TODAY?
TODAY'S A MAJOR EVENT FOR ME.
YOU HELP TOO, AKI.
ENVELOPE: TITLE: "BLOOD AND SLUDGE"
TA-DAH!
AH FINISHED MY MANGA!

ACT.35
OKU
(Translation: Sending Off)

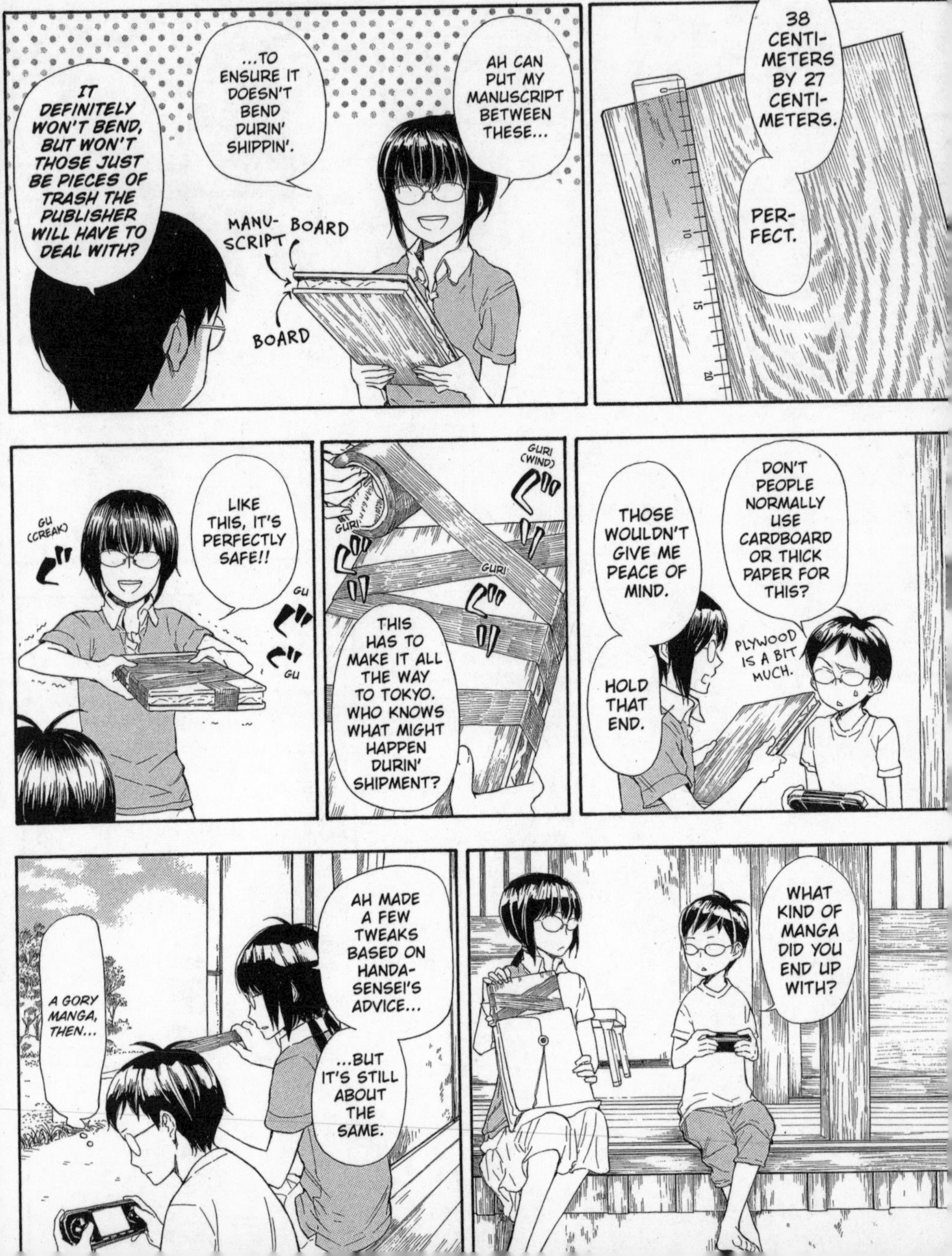
38 CENTIMETERS BY 27 CENTIMETERS.
PERFECT.
AH CAN PUT MY MANUSCRIPT BETWEEN THESE...
...TO ENSURE IT DOESN'T BEND DURIN' SHIPPIN'.
BOARD
MANUSCRIPT
BOARD
IT DEFINITELY WON'T BEND, BUT WON'T THOSE JUST BE PIECES OF TRASH THE PUBLISHER WILL HAVE TO DEAL WITH?
DON'T PEOPLE NORMALLY USE CARDBOARD OR THICK PAPER FOR THIS?
PLYWOOD IS A BIT MUCH.
THOSE WOULDN'T GIVE ME PEACE OF MIND.
HOLD THAT END.
GURI (WIND)
GURI
GURI
THIS HAS TO MAKE IT ALL THE WAY TO TOKYO. WHO KNOWS WHAT MIGHT HAPPEN DURIN' SHIPMENT?
LIKE THIS, IT'S PERFECTLY SAFE!!
GU (CREAK)
GU
GU
WHAT KIND OF MANGA DID YOU END UP WITH?
AH MADE A FEW TWEAKS BASED ON HANDA-SENSEI'S ADVICE...
...BUT IT'S STILL ABOUT THE SAME.
A GORY MANGA, THEN...

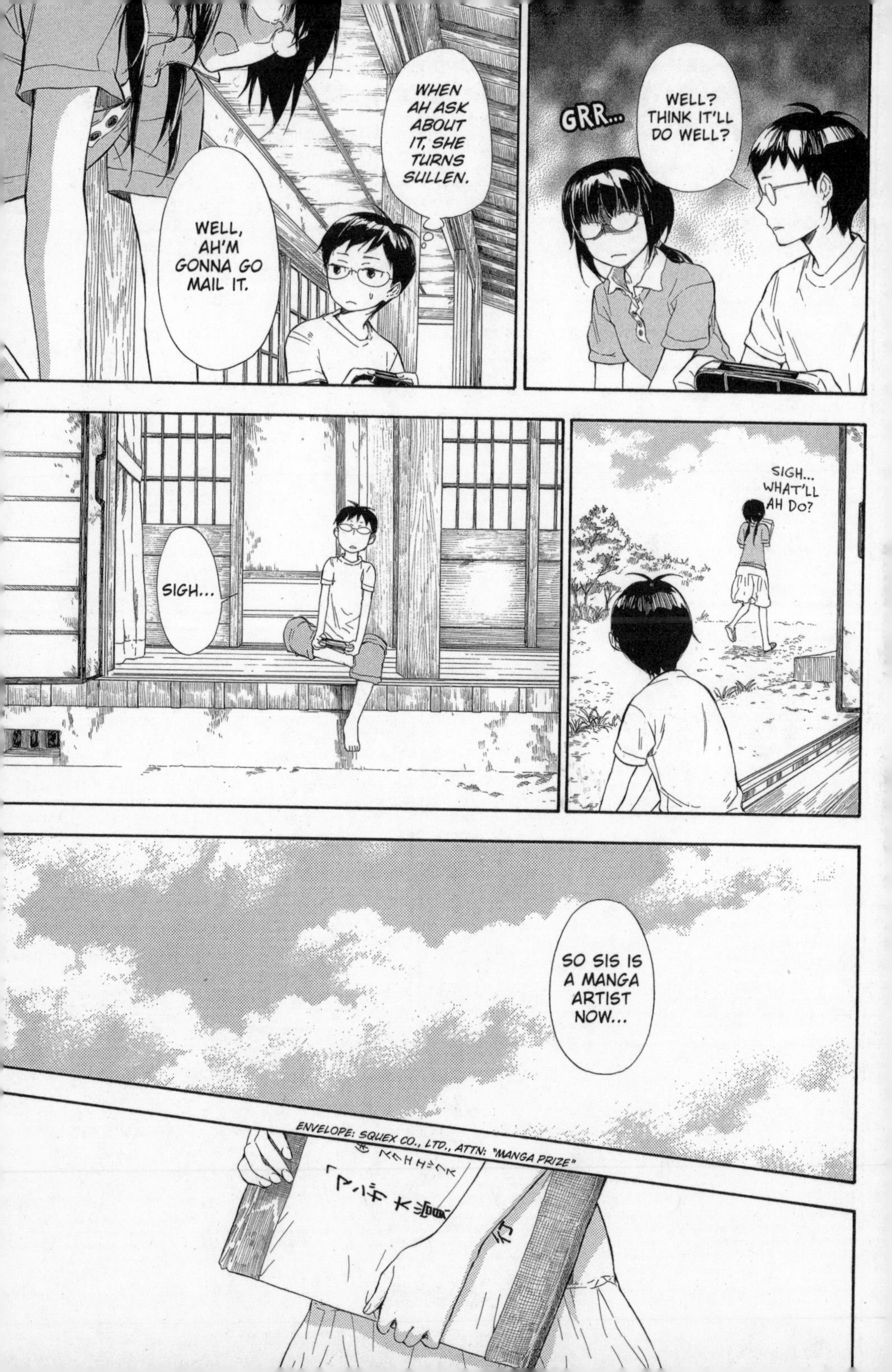
GRR...
WELL? THINK IT'LL DO WELL?
WHEN AH ASK ABOUT IT, SHE TURNS SULLEN.
WELL, AH'M GONNA GO MAIL IT.
SIGH... WHAT'LL AH DO?
SIGH...
SO SIS IS A MANGA ARTIST NOW...
ENVELOPE: SQUEX CO., LTD., ATTN: "MANGA PRIZE"

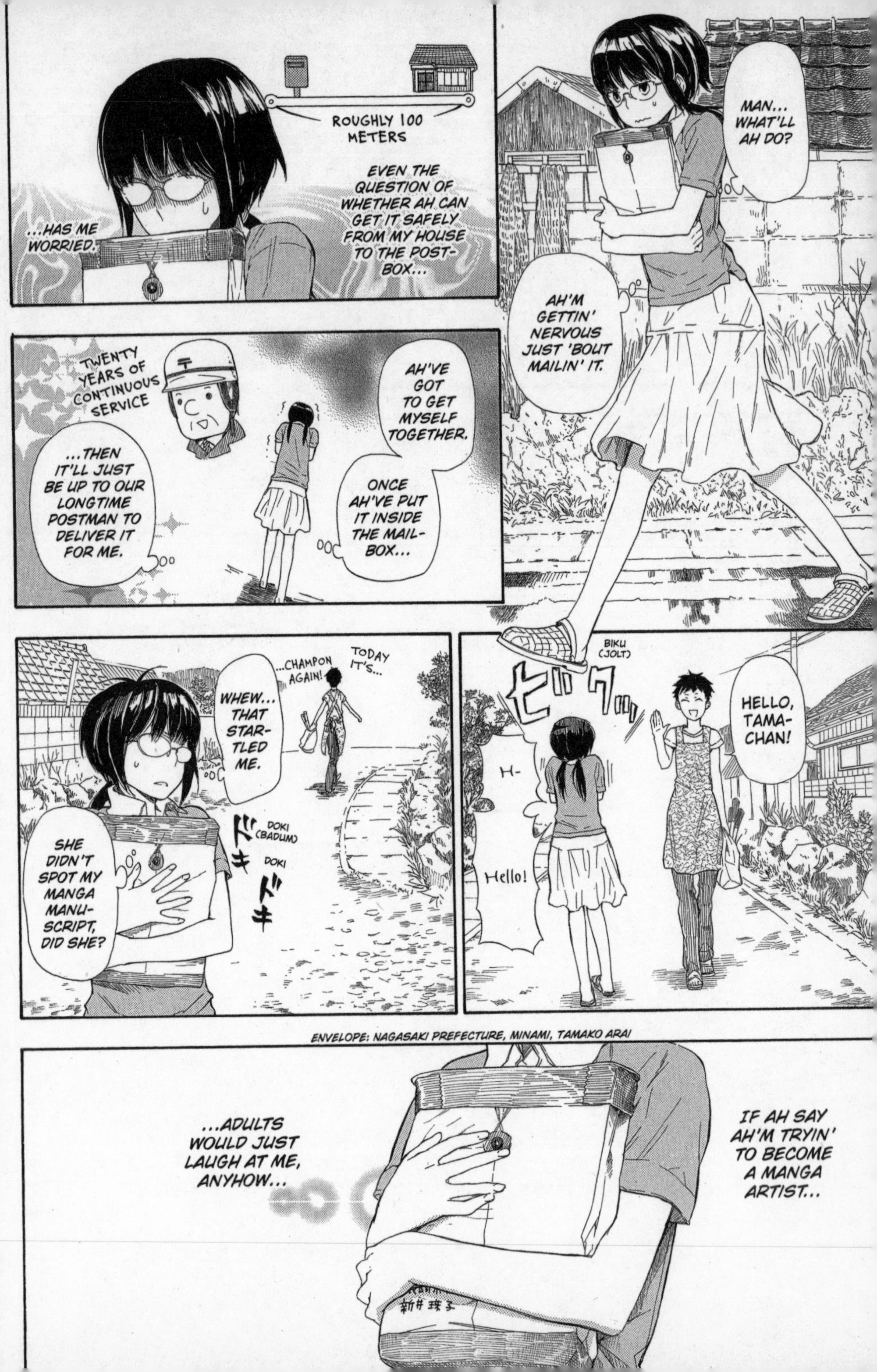
MAN... WHAT'LL AH DO?
AH'M GETTIN' NERVOUS JUST 'BOUT MAILIN' IT.
ROUGHLY 100 METERS
EVEN THE QUESTION OF WHETHER AH CAN GET IT SAFELY FROM MY HOUSE TO THE POST-BOX...
...HAS ME WORRIED.
AH'VE GOT TO GET MYSELF TOGETHER.
ONCE AH'VE PUT IT INSIDE THE MAIL-BOX...
TWENTY YEARS OF CONTINUOUS SERVICE
...THEN IT'LL JUST BE UP TO OUR LONGTIME POSTMAN TO DELIVER IT FOR ME.
BIKU (JOLT)
HELLO, TAMA-CHAN!
H-
Hello!
TODAY IT'S...
...CHAMPON AGAIN!
WHEW... THAT STARTLED ME.
DOKI (BADUM)
DOKI
SHE DIDN'T SPOT MY MANGA MANU-SCRIPT, DID SHE?
ENVELOPE: NAGASAKI PREFECTURE, MINAMI, TAMAKO ARAI
IF AH SAY AH'M TRYIN' TO BECOME A MANGA ARTIST...
...ADULTS WOULD JUST LAUGH AT ME, ANYHOW...
新井珠子

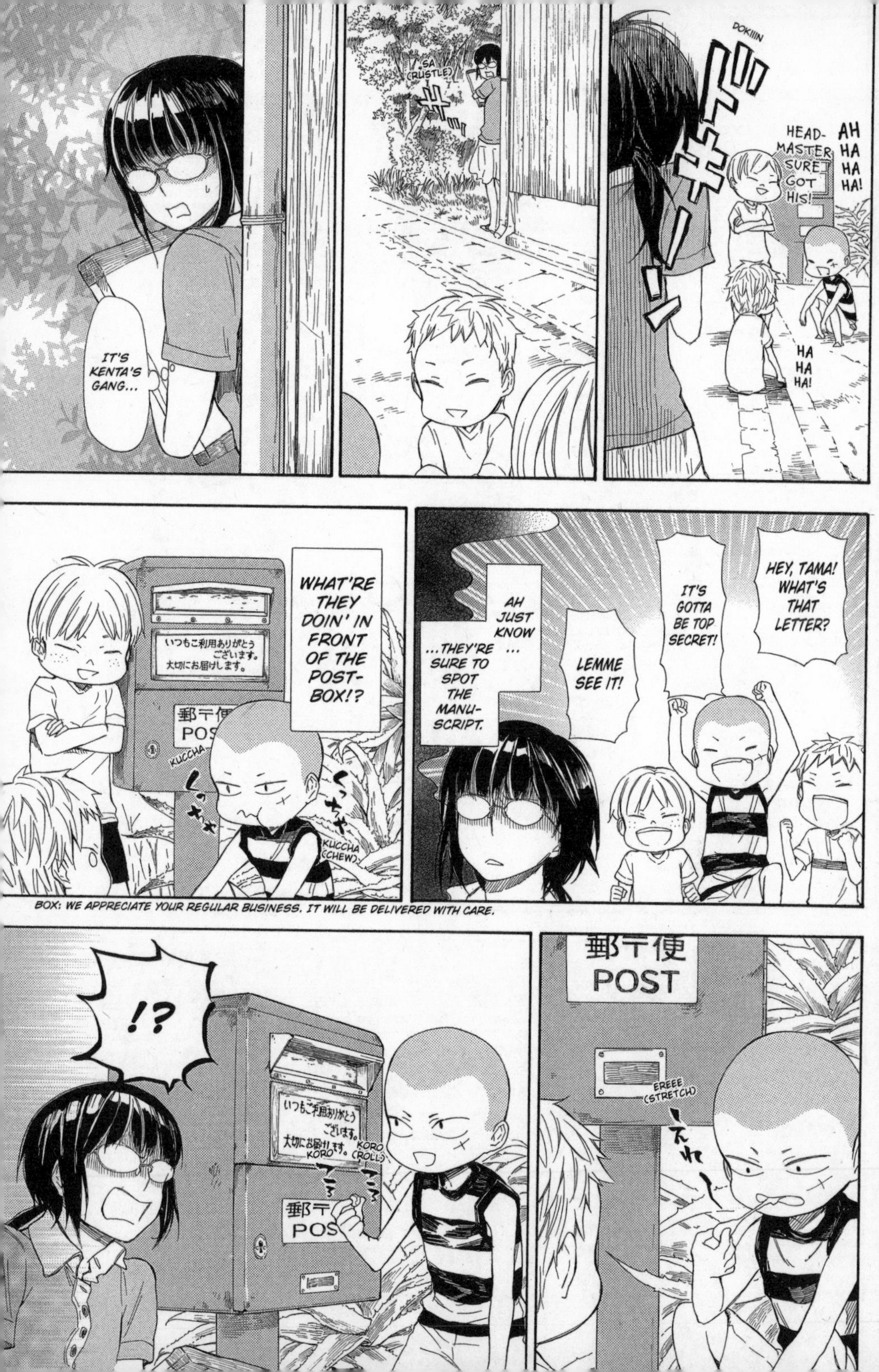
DOKIIN
HEAD-MASTER SURE GOT HIS!
AH HA HA HA!
HA HA HA!
SA (RUSTLE)
IT'S KENTA'S GANG...
HEY, TAMA! WHAT'S THAT LETTER?
IT'S GOTTA BE TOP SECRET!
LEMME SEE IT!
AH JUST KNOW ...
...THEY'RE SURE TO SPOT THE MANU-SCRIPT.
WHAT'RE THEY DOIN' IN FRONT OF THE POST-BOX!?
いつもご利用ありがとうございます。大切にお届けします。
郵〒便 POST
KUCCHA
KUCCHA (CHEW)
BOX: WE APPRECIATE YOUR REGULAR BUSINESS. IT WILL BE DELIVERED WITH CARE.
郵〒便 POST
EREEE (STRETCH)
!?
いつもご利用ありがとうございます。大切にお届けします。
郵〒便 POS
KORO KORO (ROLL)

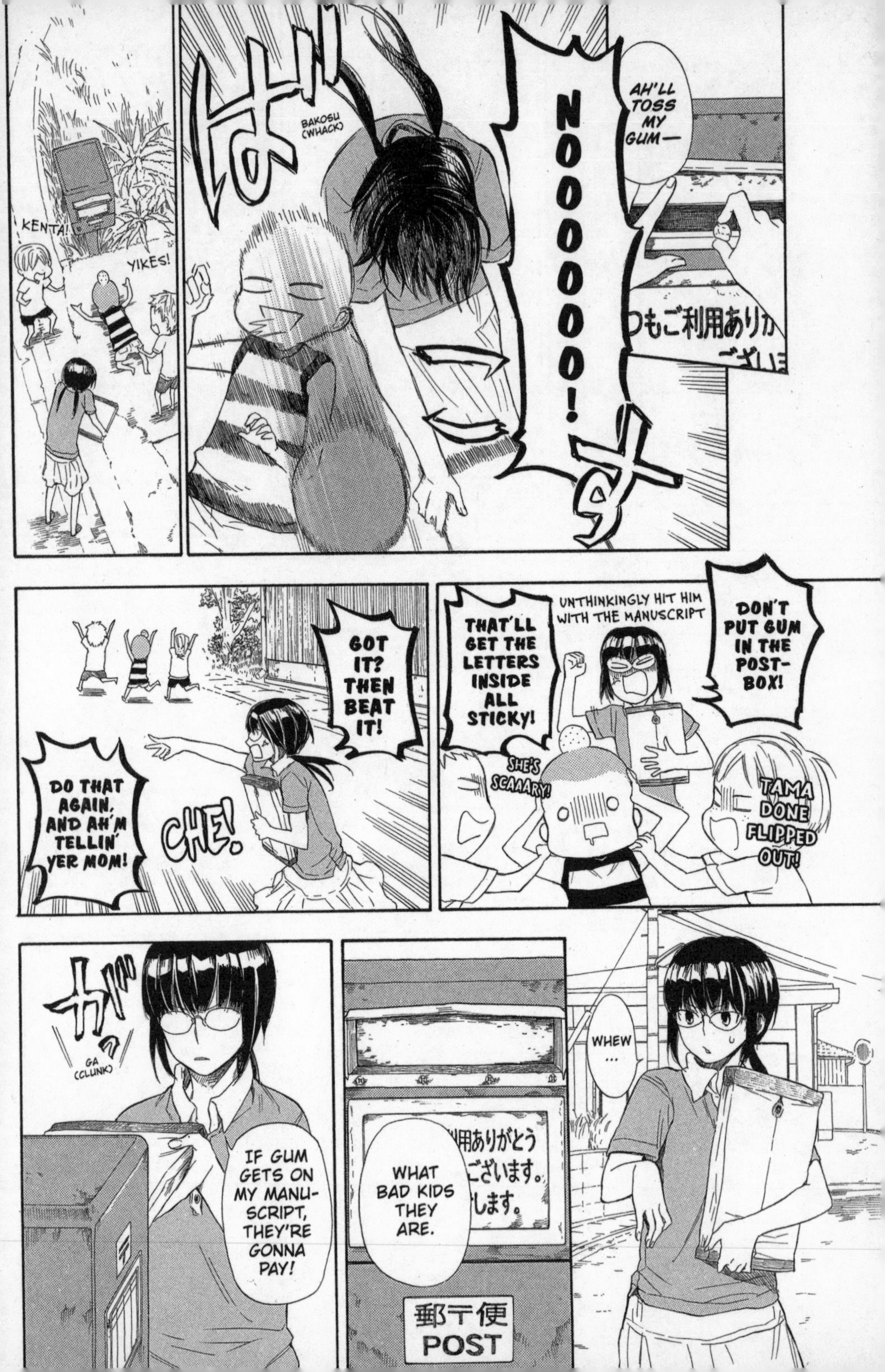
AH'LL TOSS MY GUM—
つもご利用ありが
NOOOOOOO!
BAKOSU (WHACK)
KENTA!
YIKES!
DON'T PUT GUM IN THE POST-BOX!
UNTHINKINGLY HIT HIM WITH THE MANUSCRIPT
THAT'LL GET THE LETTERS INSIDE ALL STICKY!
SHE'S SCAAARY!
TAMA DONE FLIPPED OUT!
GOT IT? THEN BEAT IT!
CHE!
DO THAT AGAIN, AND AH'M TELLIN' YER MOM!
WHEW ...
WHAT BAD KIDS THEY ARE.
利用ありがとう
ございます。
します。
郵〒便
POST
GA (CLUNK)
IF GUM GETS ON MY MANU-SCRIPT, THEY'RE GONNA PAY!

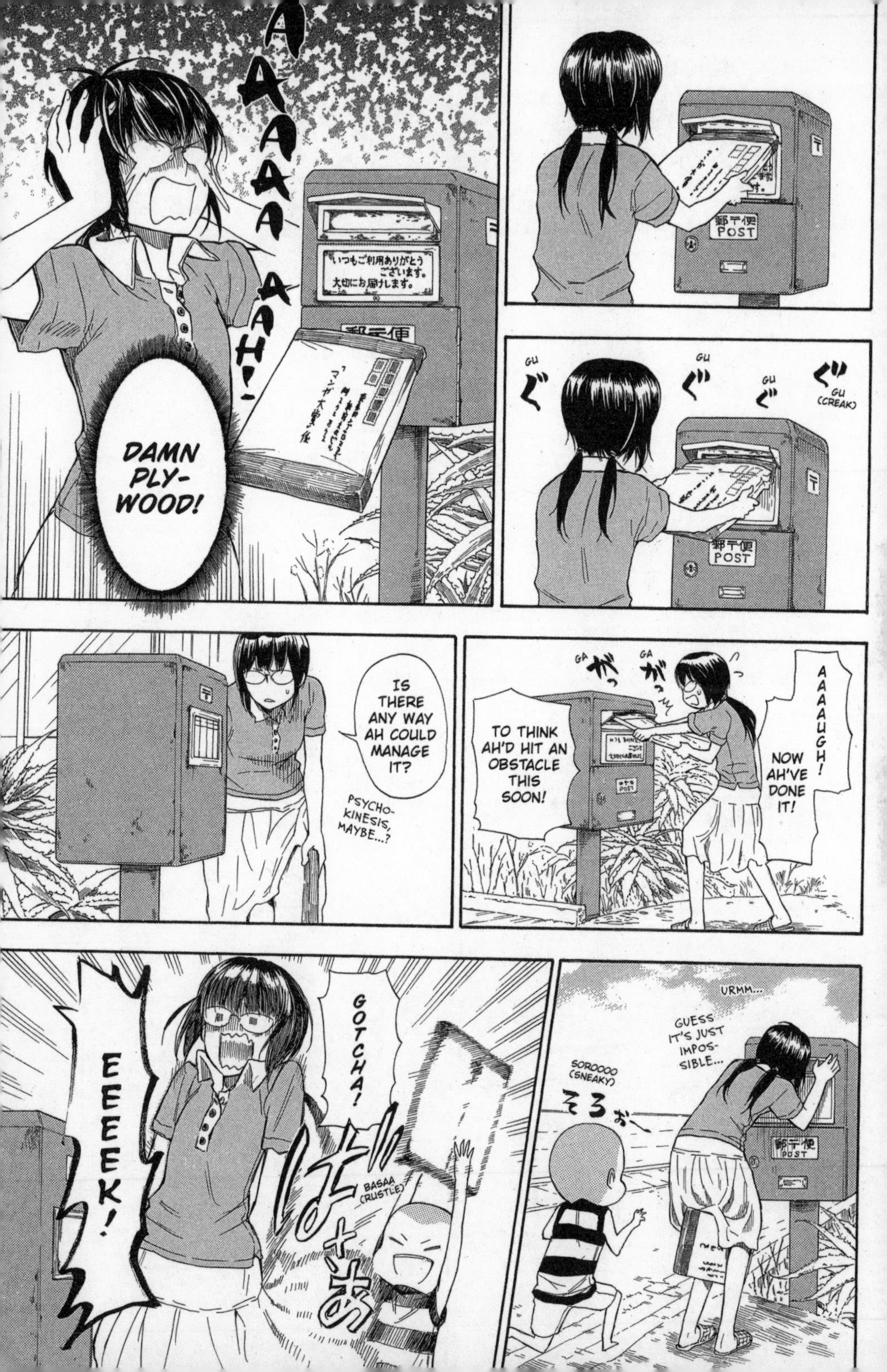
郵便
POST
GU
ぐ
GU
ぐ
GU
ぐ
GU
ぐ
(CREAK)
郵便
POST
AAAA
AAH!
DAMN PLYWOOD!
いつもご利用ありがとうございます。大切にお届けします。
郵便
マンガ大賞係
GA
がっ
GA
がっ
AAAAUGH!
NOW AH'VE DONE IT!
TO THINK AH'D HIT AN OBSTACLE THIS SOON!
IS THERE ANY WAY AH COULD MANAGE IT?
PSYCHO-KINESIS, MAYBE...?
URMM...
GUESS IT'S JUST IMPOSSIBLE...
SOROOOO
(SNEAKY)
そろぉ~
郵便
POST
GOTCHA!
EEEEEK!
BASAA
(RUSTLE)
ばさぁ

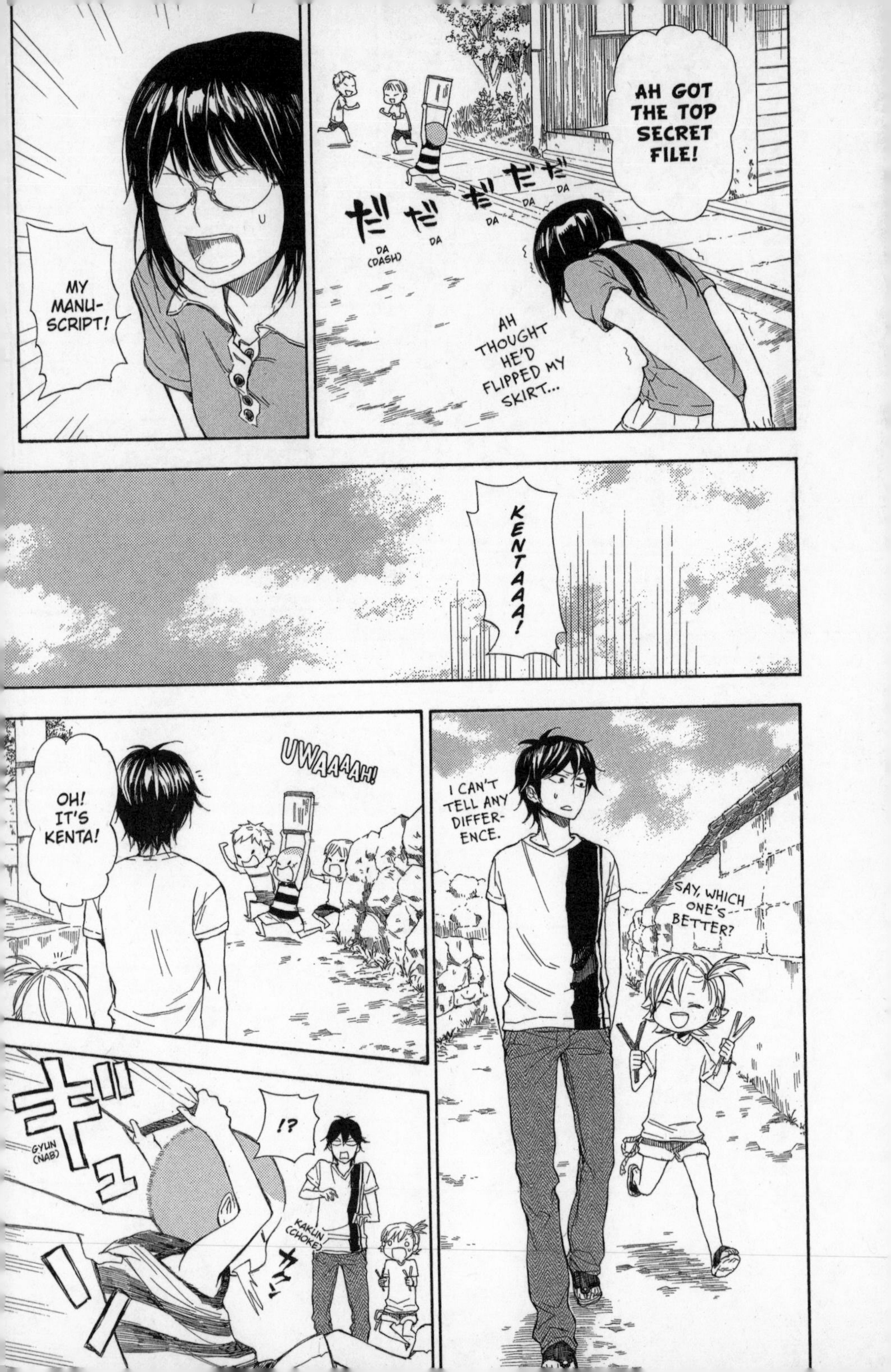
AH GOT THE TOP SECRET FILE!
だ だ だ だ
DA (DASH)
DA
DA
DA
DA
AH THOUGHT HE'D FLIPPED MY SKIRT...
MY MANU-SCRIPT!
KENTAAAA!
SAY, WHICH ONE'S BETTER?
I CAN'T TELL ANY DIFFERENCE.
UWAAAAH!
OH! IT'S KENTA!
!?
ギュン
GYUN (NAB)
KAKUN (CHOKE)

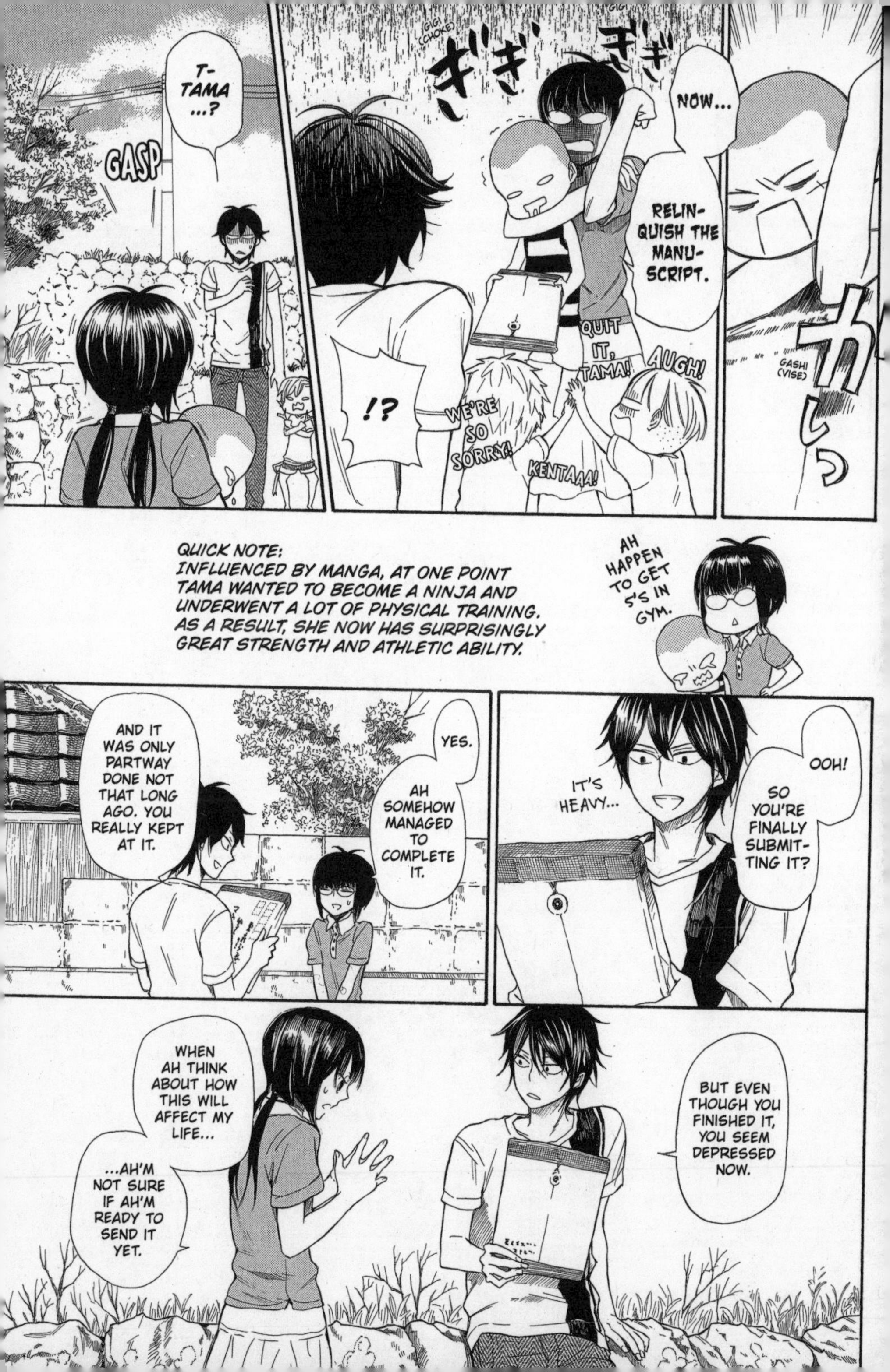
NOW...
RELINQUISH THE MANUSCRIPT.
GASHI (VISE)
GIGI (CHOKE)
GIGI
!?
QUIT IT, TAMA!
AUGH!
WE'RE SO SORRY!
KENTAAA!
T-TAMA...?
GASP
AH HAPPEN TO GET 5'S IN GYM.
QUICK NOTE: INFLUENCED BY MANGA, AT ONE POINT TAMA WANTED TO BECOME A NINJA AND UNDERWENT A LOT OF PHYSICAL TRAINING. AS A RESULT, SHE NOW HAS SURPRISINGLY GREAT STRENGTH AND ATHLETIC ABILITY.
OOH!
SO YOU'RE FINALLY SUBMITTING IT?
IT'S HEAVY...
YES.
AH SOMEHOW MANAGED TO COMPLETE IT.
AND IT WAS ONLY PARTWAY DONE NOT THAT LONG AGO. YOU REALLY KEPT AT IT.
BUT EVEN THOUGH YOU FINISHED IT, YOU SEEM DEPRESSED NOW.
WHEN AH THINK ABOUT HOW THIS WILL AFFECT MY LIFE...
...AH'M NOT SURE IF AH'M READY TO SEND IT YET.

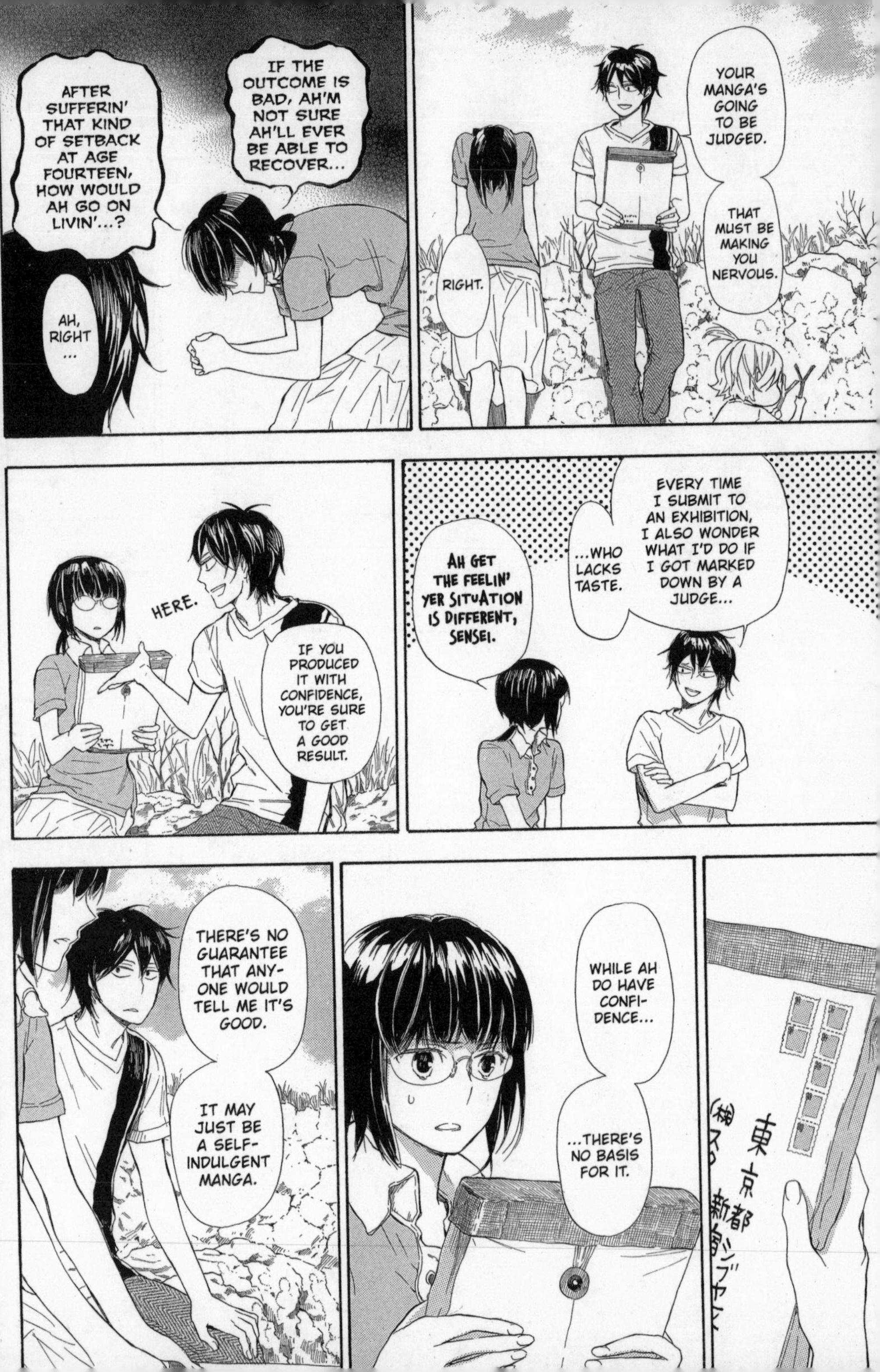
YOUR MANGA'S GOING TO BE JUDGED.
THAT MUST BE MAKING YOU NERVOUS.
RIGHT.
IF THE OUTCOME IS BAD, AH'M NOT SURE AH'LL EVER BE ABLE TO RECOVER...
AFTER SUFFERIN' THAT KIND OF SETBACK AT AGE FOURTEEN, HOW WOULD AH GO ON LIVIN'...?
AH, RIGHT...
EVERY TIME I SUBMIT TO AN EXHIBITION, I ALSO WONDER WHAT I'D DO IF I GOT MARKED DOWN BY A JUDGE...
...WHO LACKS TASTE.
AH GET THE FEELIN' YER SITUATION IS DIFFERENT, SENSEI.
HERE.
IF YOU PRODUCED IT WITH CONFIDENCE, YOU'RE SURE TO GET A GOOD RESULT.
WHILE AH DO HAVE CONFIDENCE...
...THERE'S NO BASIS FOR IT.
THERE'S NO GUARANTEE THAT ANYONE WOULD TELL ME IT'S GOOD.
IT MAY JUST BE A SELF-INDULGENT MANGA.

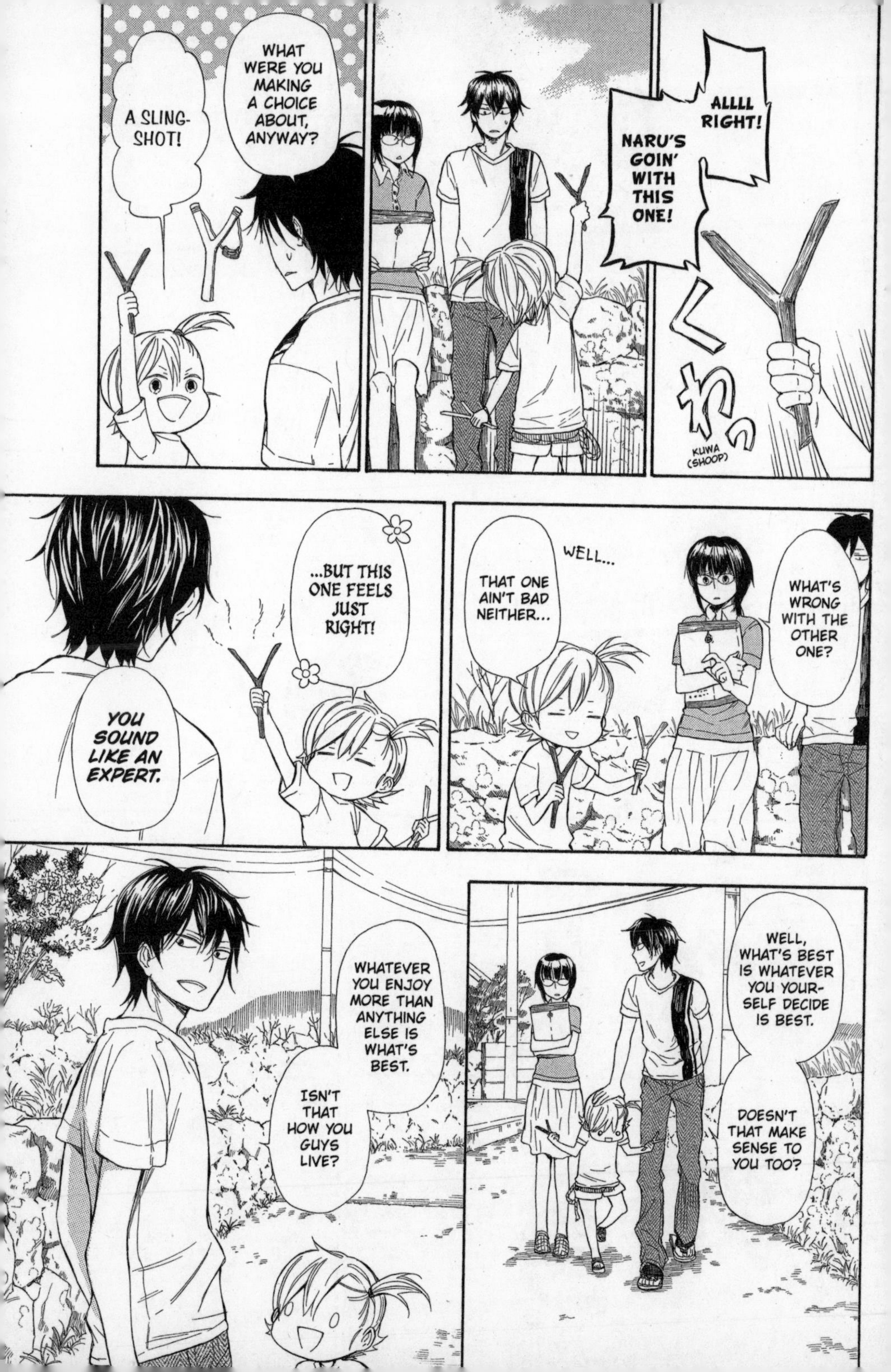
ALLLL RIGHT!
NARU'S GOIN' WITH THIS ONE!
くわっ
KUWA (SHOOP)
WHAT WERE YOU MAKING A CHOICE ABOUT, ANYWAY?
A SLING-SHOT!
WHAT'S WRONG WITH THE OTHER ONE?
WELL...
THAT ONE AIN'T BAD NEITHER...
...BUT THIS ONE FEELS JUST RIGHT!
YOU SOUND LIKE AN EXPERT.
WELL, WHAT'S BEST IS WHATEVER YOU YOUR-SELF DECIDE IS BEST.
DOESN'T THAT MAKE SENSE TO YOU TOO?
WHATEVER YOU ENJOY MORE THAN ANYTHING ELSE IS WHAT'S BEST.
ISN'T THAT HOW YOU GUYS LIVE?

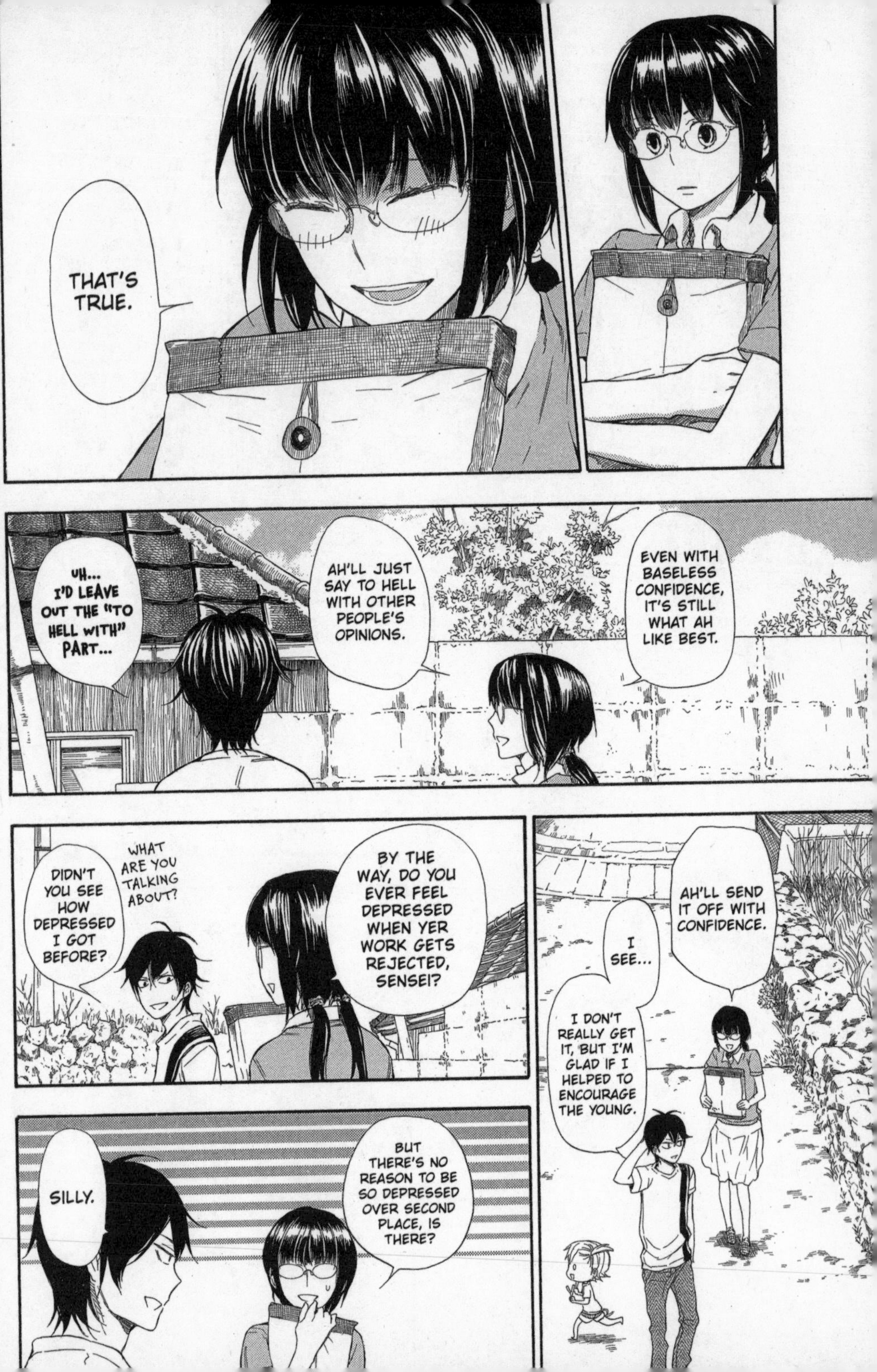
THAT'S TRUE.
EVEN WITH BASELESS CONFIDENCE, IT'S STILL WHAT AH LIKE BEST.
AH'LL JUST SAY TO HELL WITH OTHER PEOPLE'S OPINIONS.
UH... I'D LEAVE OUT THE "TO HELL WITH" PART...
AH'LL SEND IT OFF WITH CONFIDENCE.
I SEE...
I DON'T REALLY GET IT, BUT I'M GLAD IF I HELPED TO ENCOURAGE THE YOUNG.
BY THE WAY, DO YOU EVER FEEL DEPRESSED WHEN YER WORK GETS REJECTED, SENSEI?
WHAT ARE YOU TALKING ABOUT?
DIDN'T YOU SEE HOW DEPRESSED I GOT BEFORE?
BUT THERE'S NO REASON TO BE SO DEPRESSED OVER SECOND PLACE, IS THERE?
SILLY.

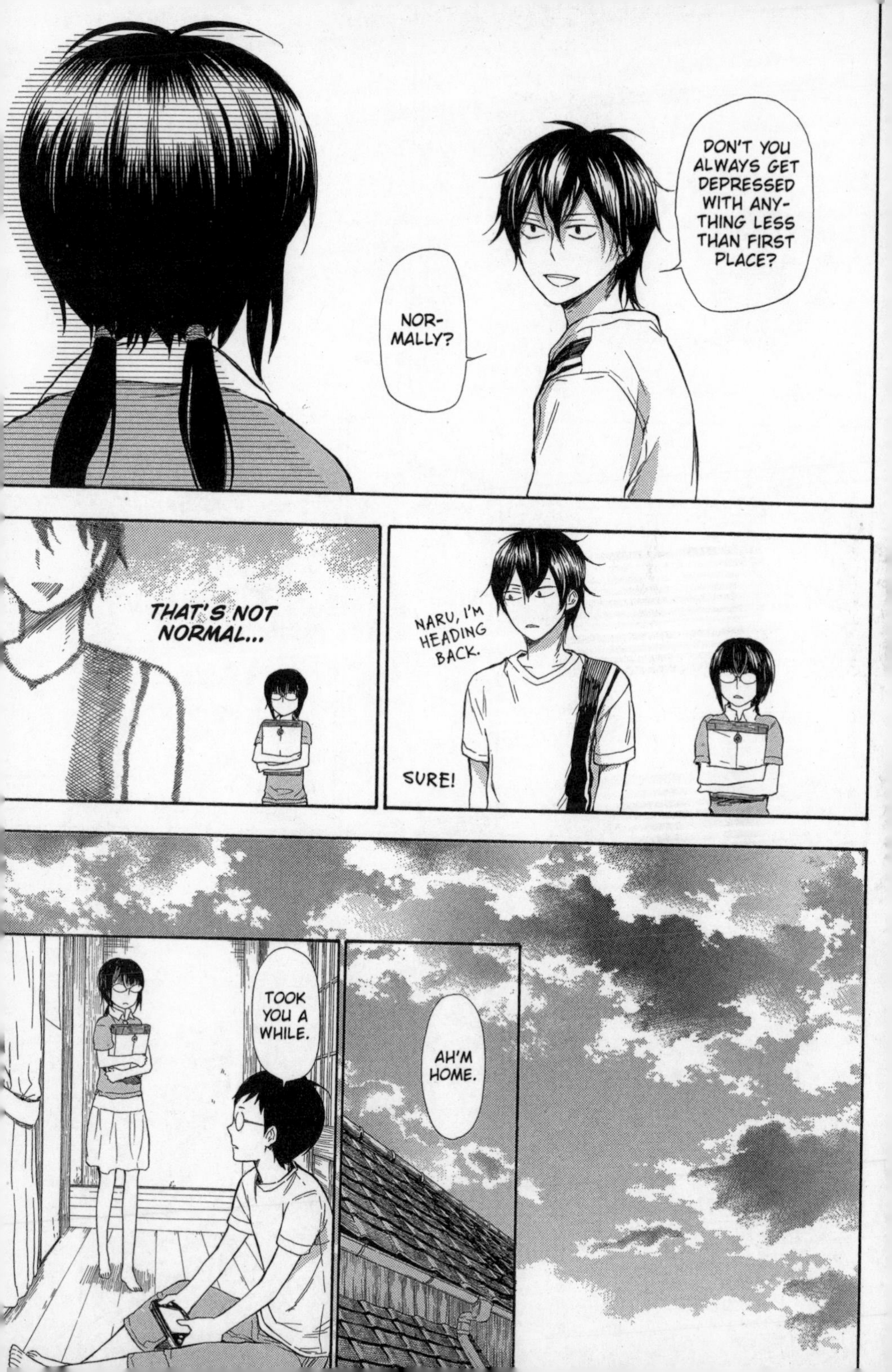
DON'T YOU ALWAYS GET DEPRESSED WITH ANY-THING LESS THAN FIRST PLACE?
NOR-MALLY?
NARU, I'M HEADING BACK.
SURE!
THAT'S NOT NORMAL...
AH'M HOME.
TOOK YOU A WHILE.

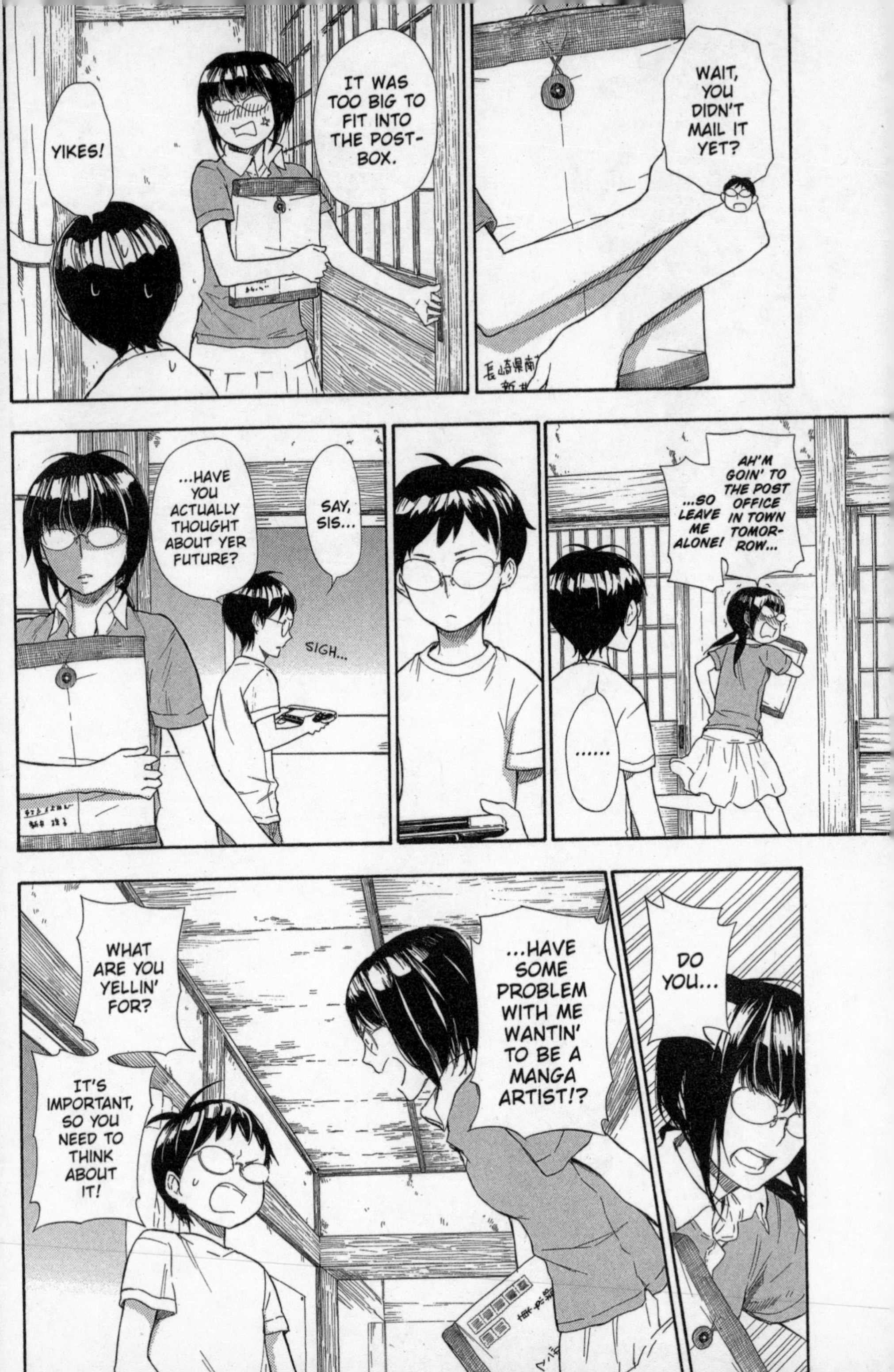
WAIT, YOU DIDN'T MAIL IT YET?
IT WAS TOO BIG TO FIT INTO THE POST-BOX.
YIKES!
AH'M GOIN' TO THE POST OFFICE IN TOWN TOMOR-ROW...
...SO LEAVE ME ALONE!
......
SAY, SIS...
...HAVE YOU ACTUALLY THOUGHT ABOUT YER FUTURE?
SIGH...
DO YOU...
...HAVE SOME PROBLEM WITH ME WANTIN' TO BE A MANGA ARTIST!?
WHAT ARE YOU YELLIN' FOR?
IT'S IMPORTANT, SO YOU NEED TO THINK ABOUT IT!

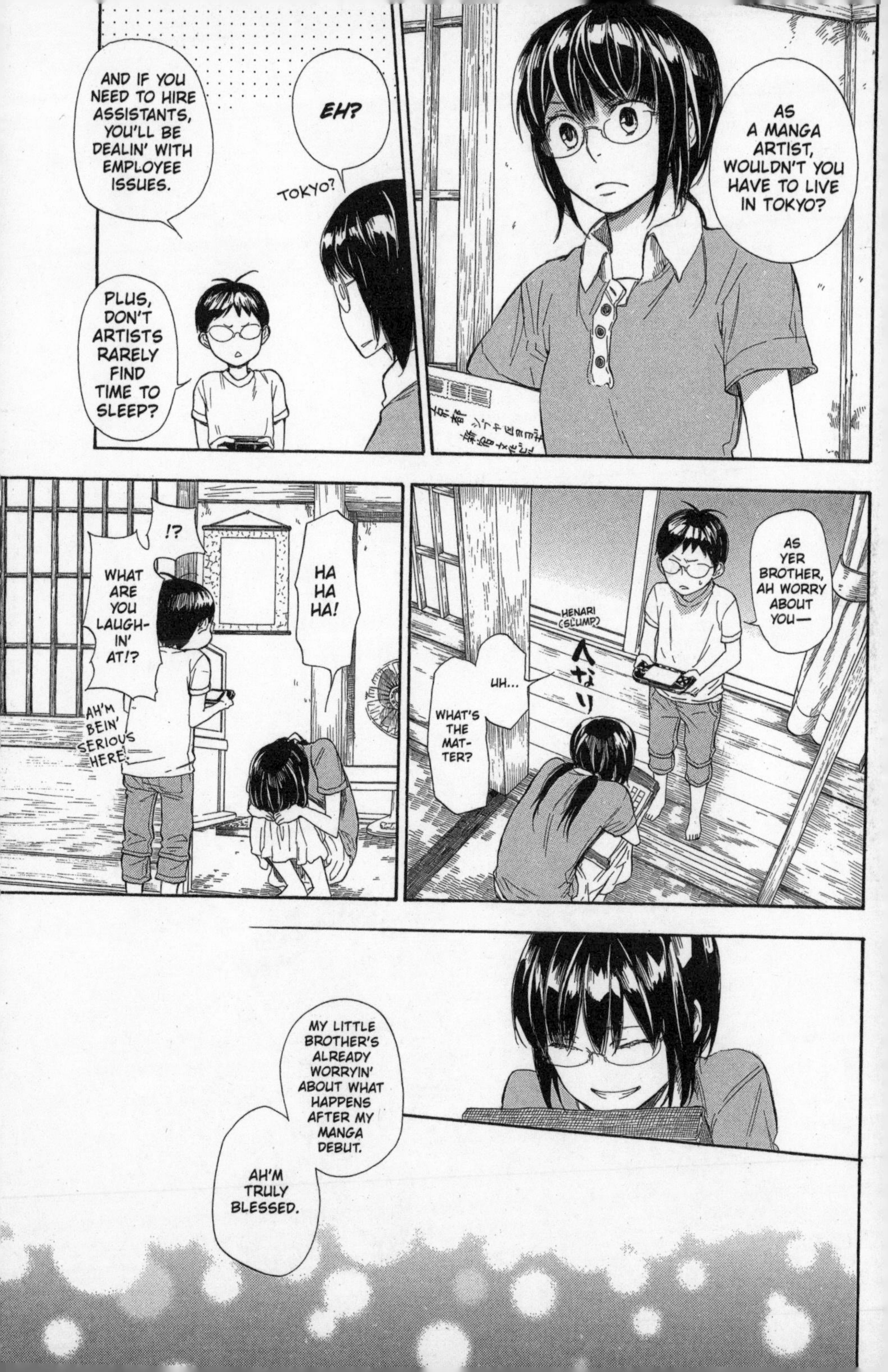
AS A MANGA ARTIST, WOULDN'T YOU HAVE TO LIVE IN TOKYO?
EH?
TOKYO?
AND IF YOU NEED TO HIRE ASSISTANTS, YOU'LL BE DEALIN' WITH EMPLOYEE ISSUES.
PLUS, DON'T ARTISTS RARELY FIND TIME TO SLEEP?
AS YER BROTHER, AH WORRY ABOUT YOU—
HENARI (SLUMP)
へなり
UH...
WHAT'S THE MATTER?
HA HA HA!
!?
WHAT ARE YOU LAUGHIN' AT!?
AH'M BEIN' SERIOUS HERE!
MY LITTLE BROTHER'S ALREADY WORRYIN' ABOUT WHAT HAPPENS AFTER MY MANGA DEBUT.
AH'M TRULY BLESSED.

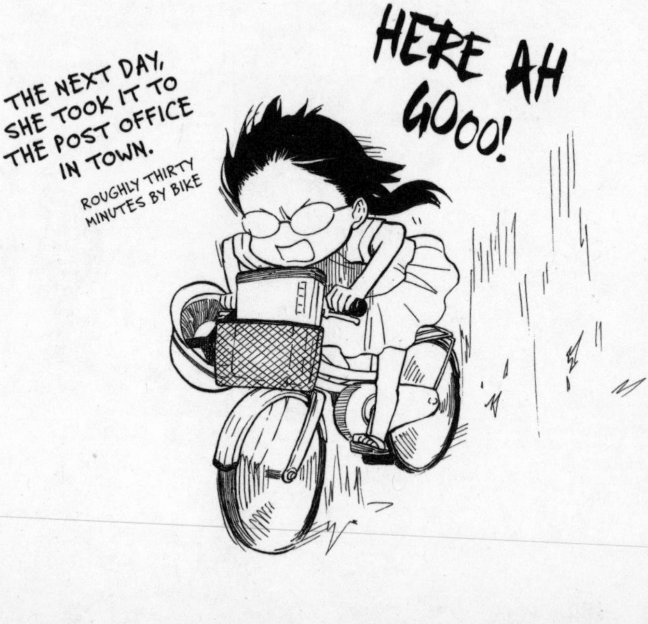
HERE AH GOOO!
THE NEXT DAY, SHE TOOK IT TO THE POST OFFICE IN TOWN.
ROUGHLY THIRTY MINUTES BY BIKE

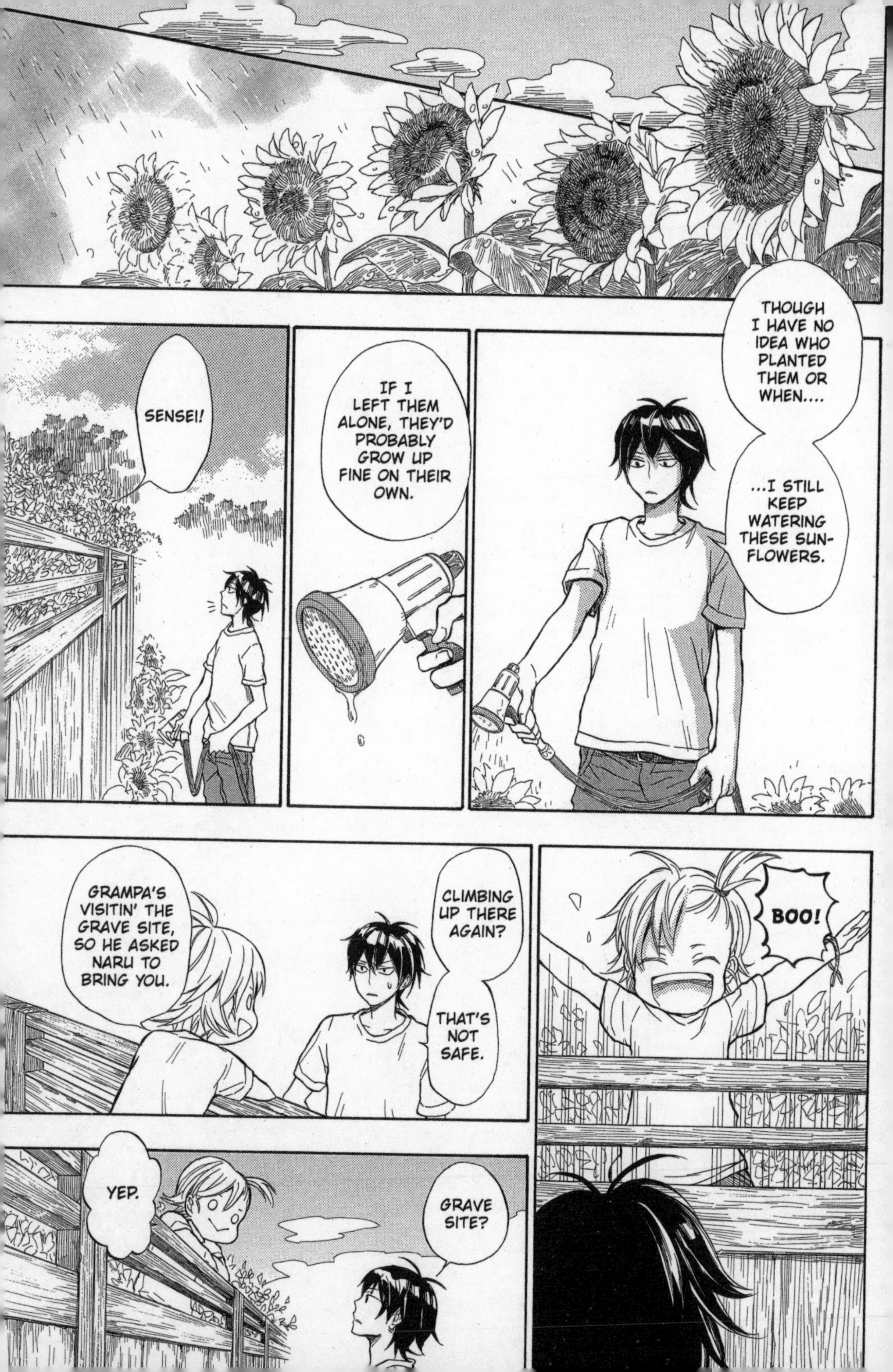
THOUGH I HAVE NO IDEA WHO PLANTED THEM OR WHEN....
...I STILL KEEP WATERING THESE SUN-FLOWERS.
IF I LEFT THEM ALONE, THEY'D PROBABLY GROW UP FINE ON THEIR OWN.
SENSEI!
BOO!
CLIMBING UP THERE AGAIN?
THAT'S NOT SAFE.
GRAMPA'S VISITIN' THE GRAVE SITE, SO HE ASKED NARU TO BRING YOU.
GRAVE SITE?
YEP.

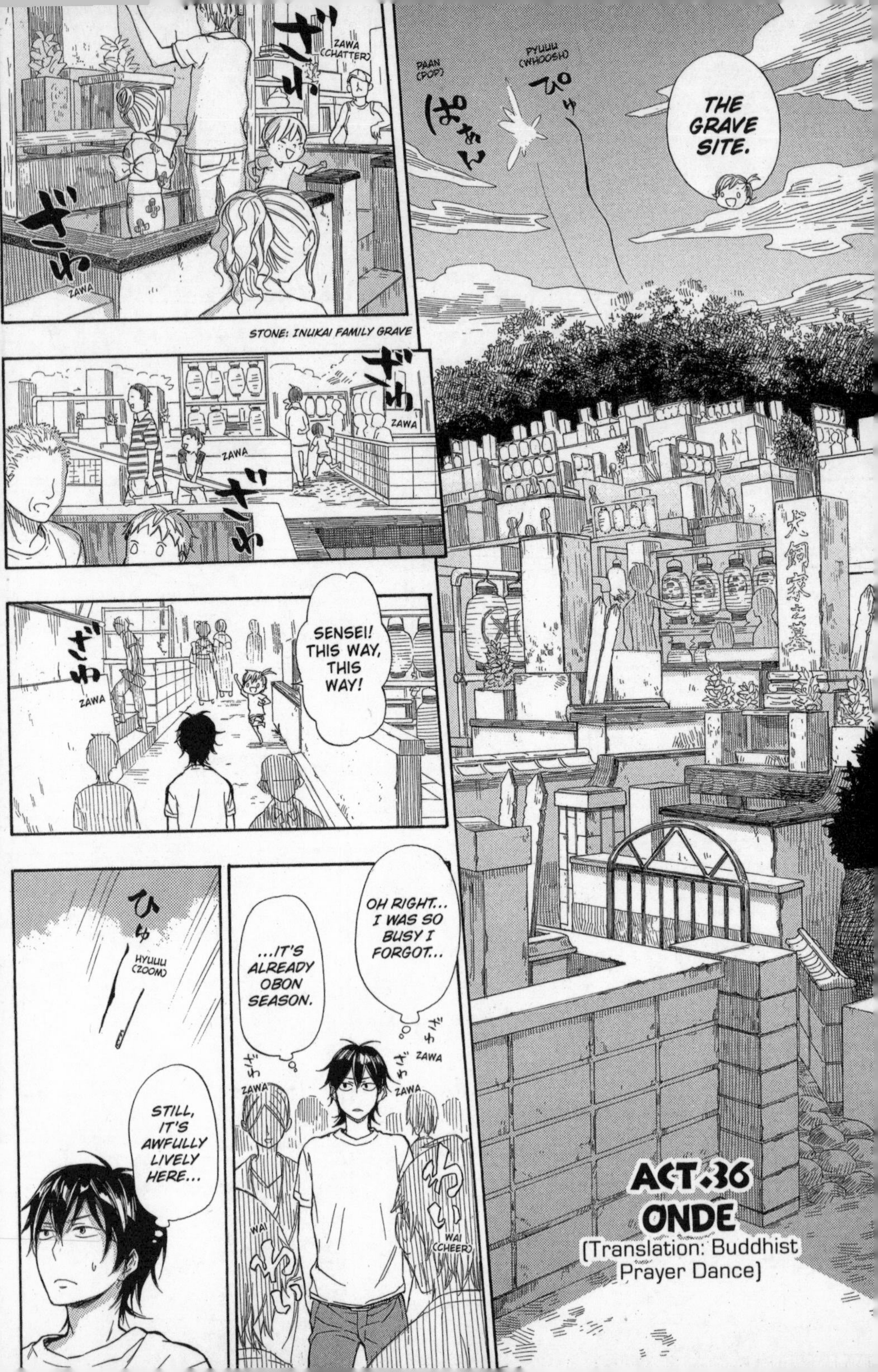
PAAN (POP)
ぱぁん
PYUUU (WHOOSH)
ぴゅ
THE GRAVE SITE.
ACT.36 ONDE
(Translation: Buddhist Prayer Dance)
ZAWA (CHATTER)
ZAWA
STONE: INUKAI FAMILY GRAVE
ZAWA
ZAWA
SENSEI! THIS WAY, THIS WAY!
ZAWA
OH RIGHT... I WAS SO BUSY I FORGOT...
...IT'S ALREADY OBON SEASON.
ZAWA
ZAWA
ZAWA
WAI (CHEER)
WAI
HYUUU (ZOOM)
STILL, IT'S AWFULLY LIVELY HERE...

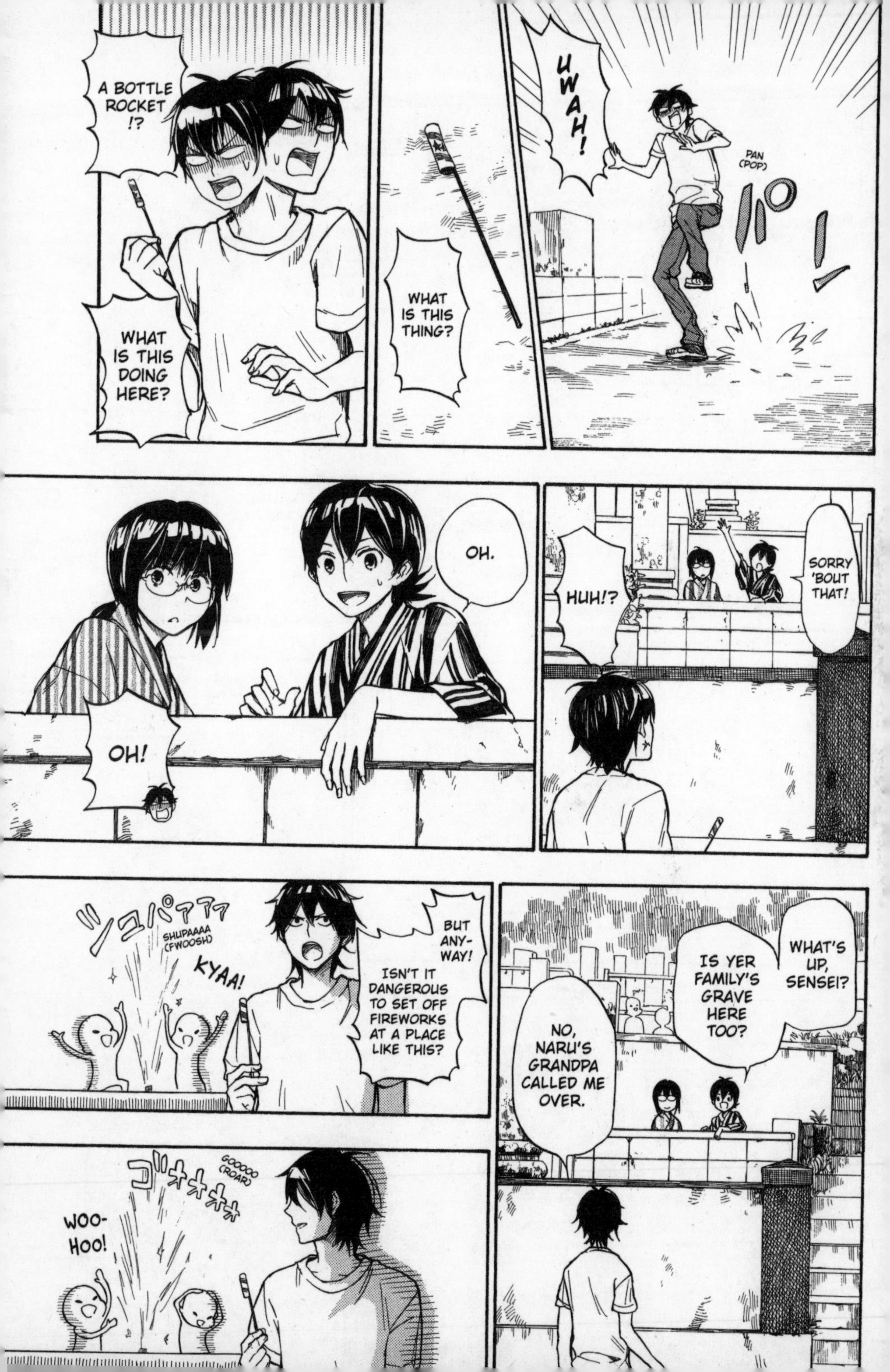
UWAH!
PAN (POP)
パ！
WHAT IS THIS THING?
A BOTTLE ROCKET !?
WHAT IS THIS DOING HERE?
SORRY 'BOUT THAT!
HUH!?
OH.
OH!
WHAT'S UP, SENSEI?
IS YER FAMILY'S GRAVE HERE TOO?
NO, NARU'S GRANDPA CALLED ME OVER.
BUT ANY-WAY!
ISN'T IT DANGEROUS TO SET OFF FIREWORKS AT A PLACE LIKE THIS?
シュパァァァ
SHUPAAAA (FWOOSH)
KYAA!
ゴォォォォォ
GOOOOO (ROAR)
WOO-HOO!

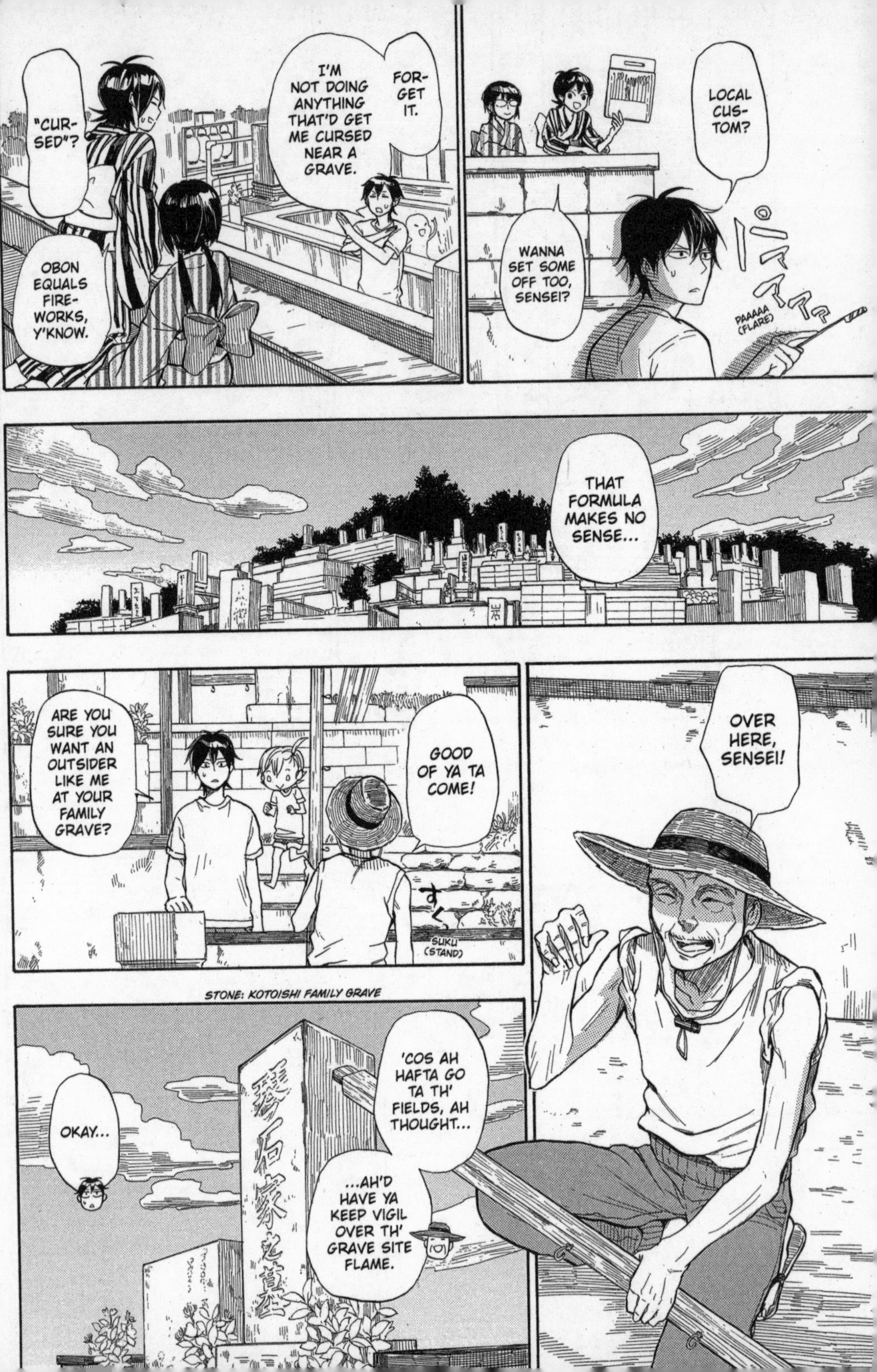
LOCAL CUS-TOM?
WANNA SET SOME OFF TOO, SENSEI?
PAAAAA (FLARE)
FOR-GET IT.
I'M NOT DOING ANYTHING THAT'D GET ME CURSED NEAR A GRAVE.
"CUR-SED"?
OBON EQUALS FIRE-WORKS, Y'KNOW.
THAT FORMULA MAKES NO SENSE...
OVER HERE, SENSEI!
GOOD OF YA TA COME!
ARE YOU SURE YOU WANT AN OUTSIDER LIKE ME AT YOUR FAMILY GRAVE?
すく
SUKU (STAND)
STONE: KOTOISHI FAMILY GRAVE
'COS AH HAFTA GO TA TH' FIELDS, AH THOUGHT...
...AH'D HAVE YA KEEP VIGIL OVER TH' GRAVE SITE FLAME.
OKAY...

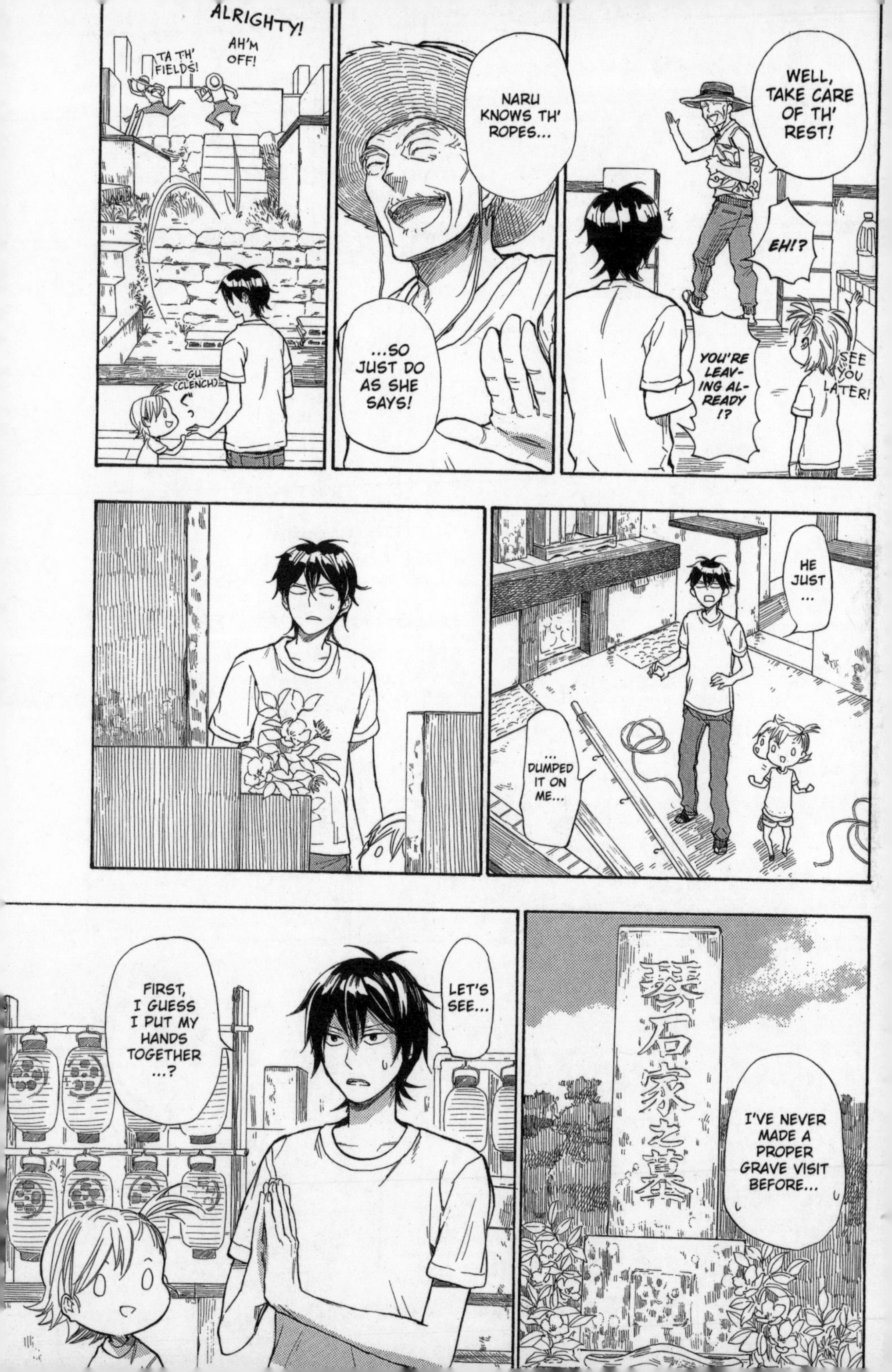
WELL, TAKE CARE OF TH' REST!
EH!?
YOU'RE LEAVING ALREADY!?
SEE YOU LATER!
NARU KNOWS TH' ROPES...
...SO JUST DO AS SHE SAYS!
ALRIGHTY!
AH'M OFF!
TA TH' FIELDS!
GU (CLENCH)
HE JUST ...
...DUMPED IT ON ME...
琴石家之墓
I'VE NEVER MADE A PROPER GRAVE VISIT BEFORE...
LET'S SEE...
FIRST, I GUESS I PUT MY HANDS TOGETHER ...?

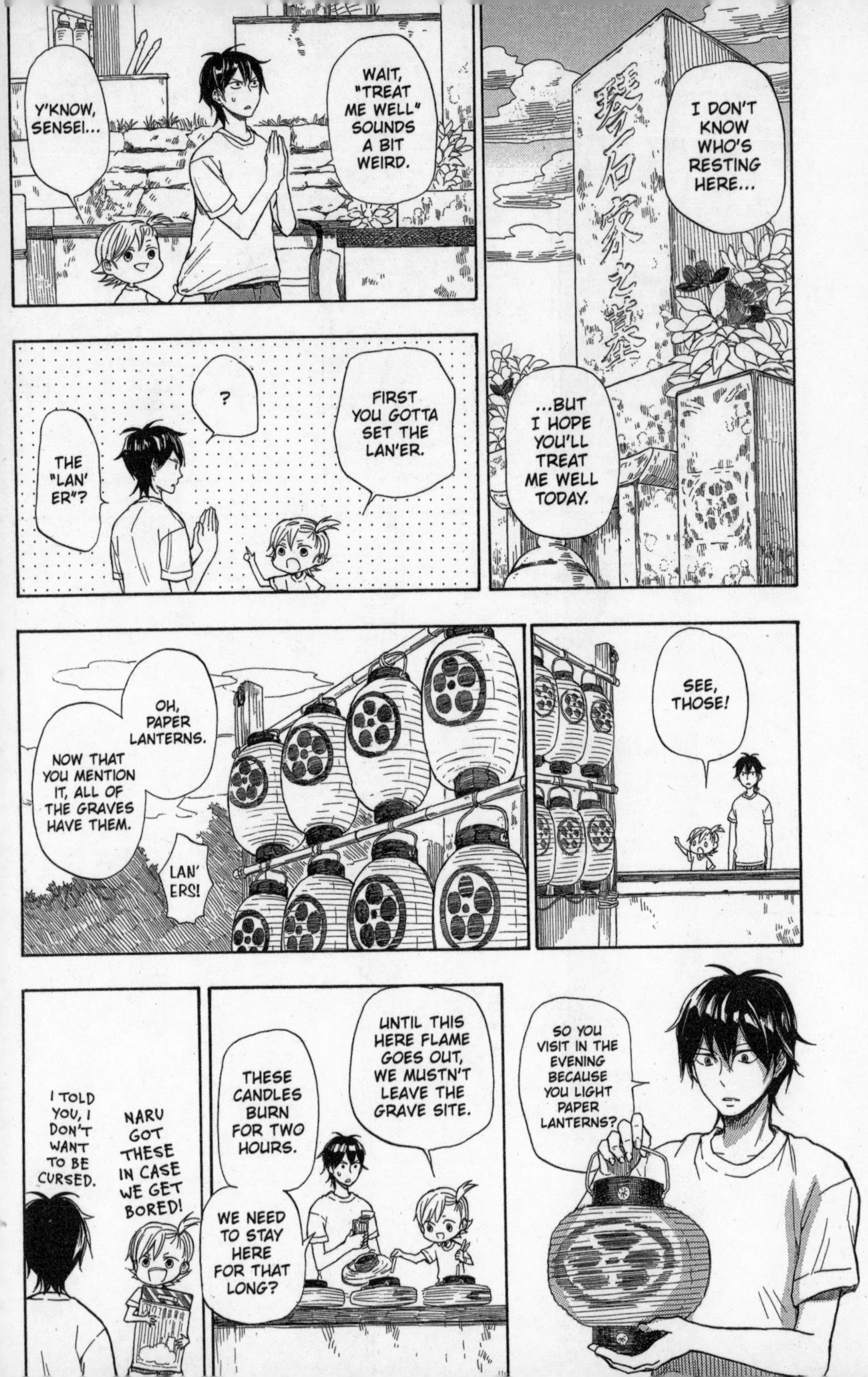
I DON'T KNOW WHO'S RESTING HERE...
...BUT I HOPE YOU'LL TREAT ME WELL TODAY.
WAIT, "TREAT ME WELL" SOUNDS A BIT WEIRD.
Y'KNOW, SENSEI...
FIRST YOU GOTTA SET THE LAN'ER.
?
THE "LAN' ER"?
SEE, THOSE!
OH, PAPER LANTERNS.
NOW THAT YOU MENTION IT, ALL OF THE GRAVES HAVE THEM.
LAN' ERS!
SO YOU VISIT IN THE EVENING BECAUSE YOU LIGHT PAPER LANTERNS?
UNTIL THIS HERE FLAME GOES OUT, WE MUSTN'T LEAVE THE GRAVE SITE.
THESE CANDLES BURN FOR TWO HOURS.
WE NEED TO STAY HERE FOR THAT LONG?
NARU GOT THESE IN CASE WE GET BORED!
I TOLD YOU, I DON'T WANT TO BE CURSED.

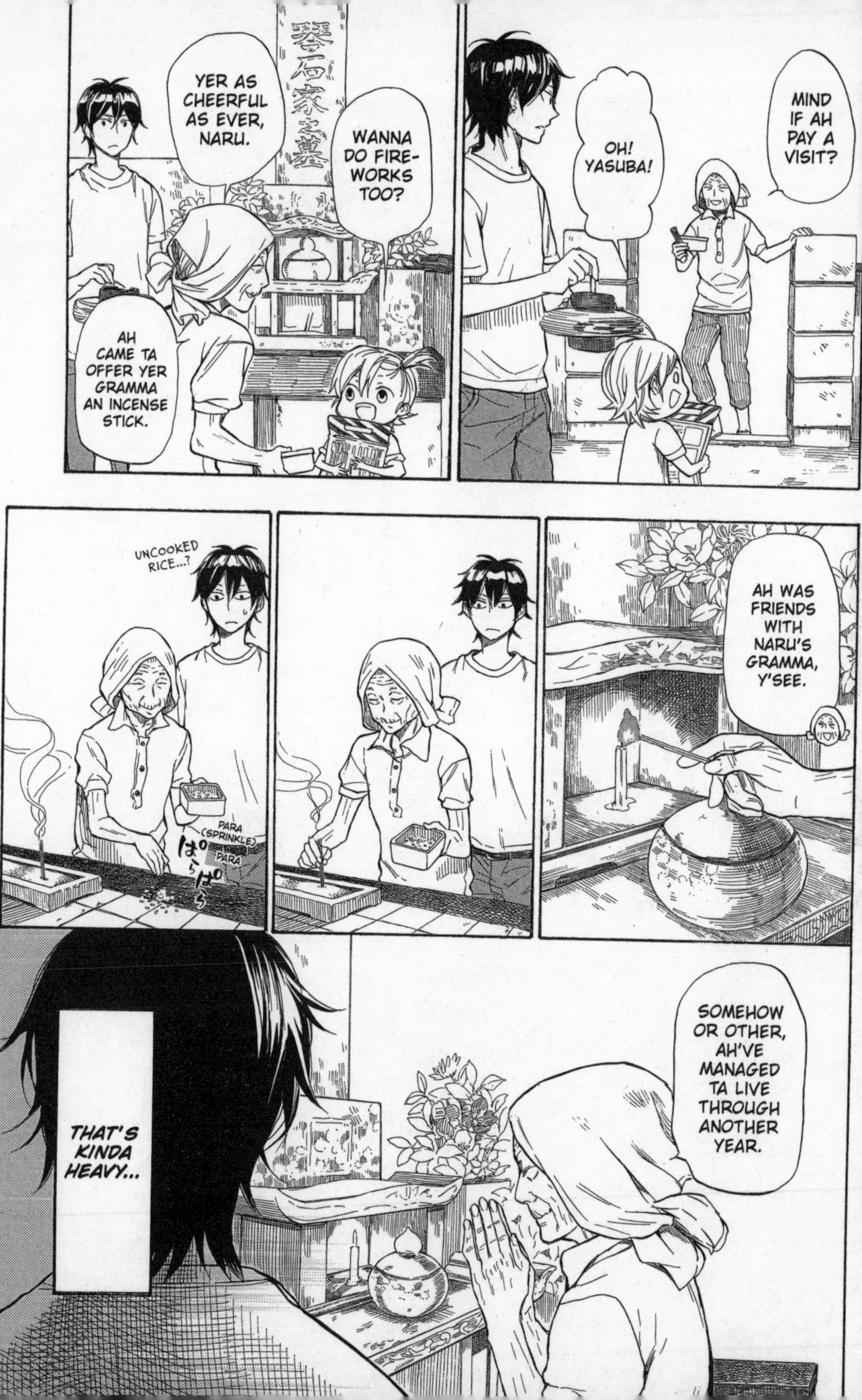
MIND IF AH PAY A VISIT?
OH! YASUBA!
WANNA DO FIRE-WORKS TOO?
琴石家之墓
YER AS CHEERFUL AS EVER, NARU.
AH CAME TA OFFER YER GRAMMA AN INCENSE STICK.
AH WAS FRIENDS WITH NARU'S GRAMMA, Y'SEE.
UNCOOKED RICE...?
PARA (SPRINKLE) PARA
ぱらぱら
SOMEHOW OR OTHER, AH'VE MANAGED TA LIVE THROUGH ANOTHER YEAR.
THAT'S KINDA HEAVY...

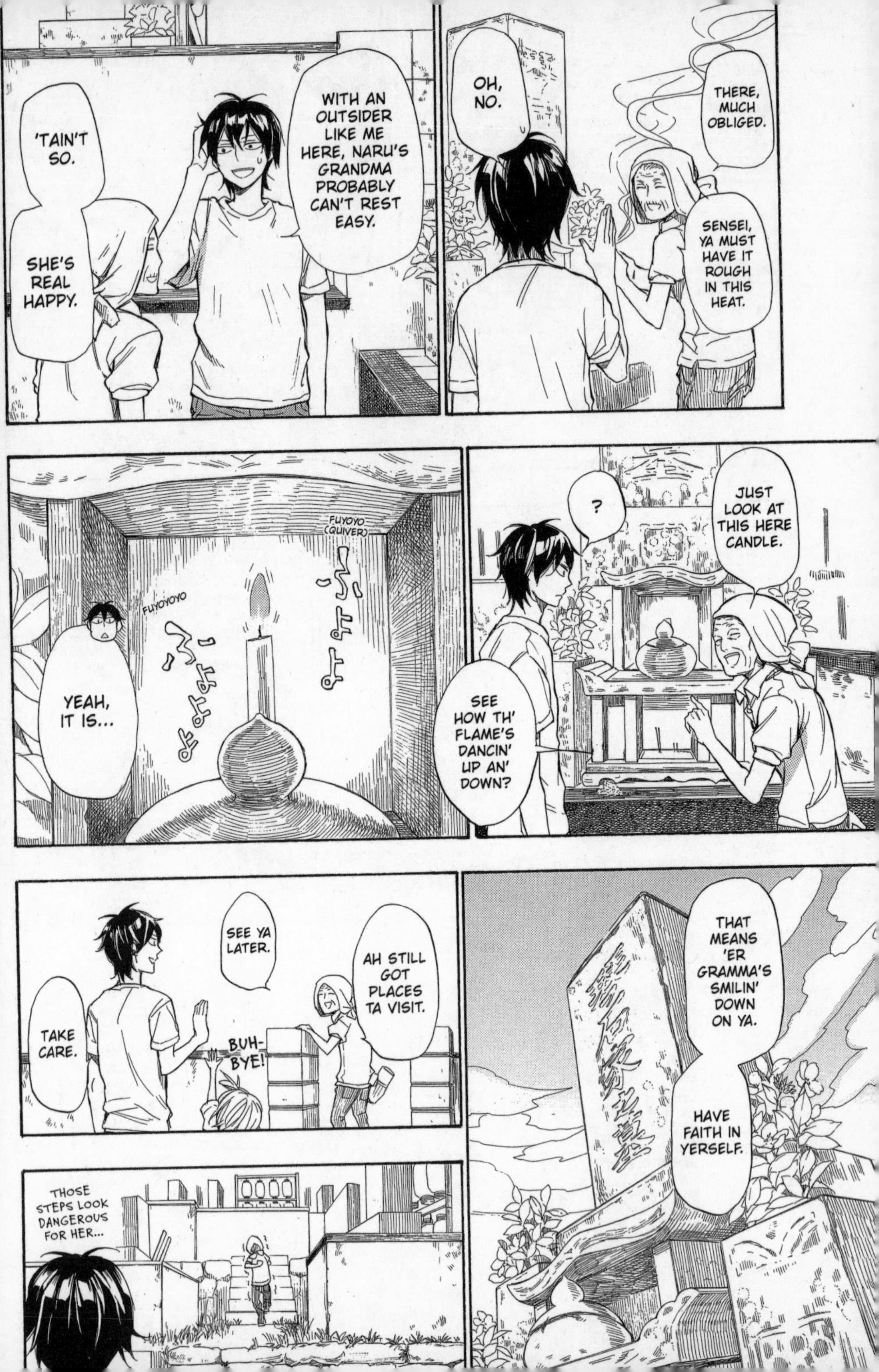
THERE, MUCH OBLIGED.
SENSEI, YA MUST HAVE IT ROUGH IN THIS HEAT.
OH, NO.
WITH AN OUTSIDER LIKE ME HERE, NARU'S GRANDMA PROBABLY CAN'T REST EASY.
'TAIN'T SO.
SHE'S REAL HAPPY.
JUST LOOK AT THIS HERE CANDLE.
?
SEE HOW TH' FLAME'S DANCIN' UP AN' DOWN?
FUYOYO (QUIVER)
ふよよ
FUYOYOYO
ふよよよ
YEAH, IT IS...
THAT MEANS 'ER GRAMMA'S SMILIN' DOWN ON YA.
HAVE FAITH IN YERSELF.
AH STILL GOT PLACES TA VISIT.
SEE YA LATER.
BUH-BYE!
TAKE CARE.
THOSE STEPS LOOK DANGEROUS FOR HER...

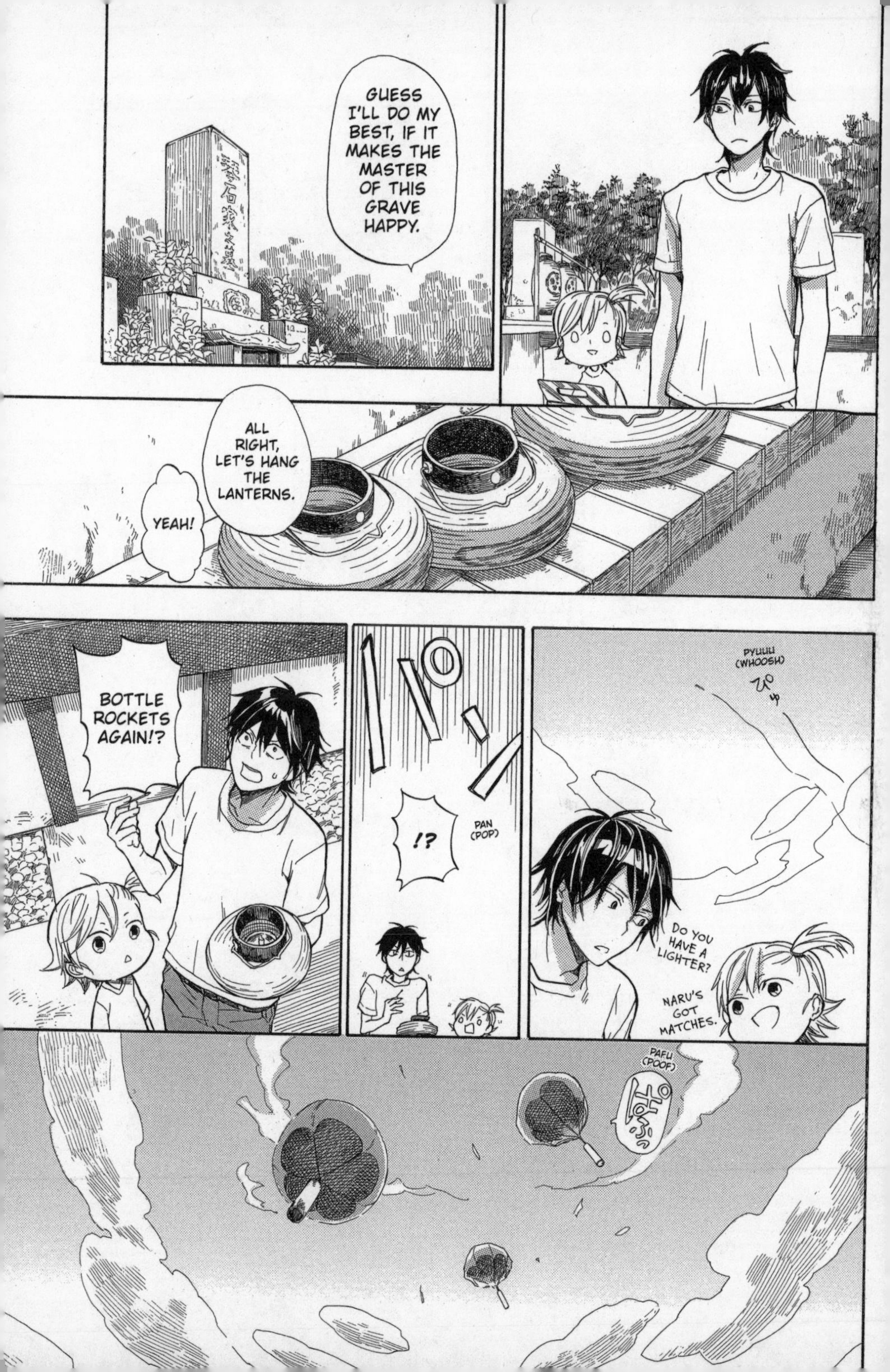
GUESS I'LL DO MY BEST, IF IT MAKES THE MASTER OF THIS GRAVE HAPPY.
ALL RIGHT, LET'S HANG THE LANTERNS.
YEAH!
PYUUU (WHOOSH)
DO YOU HAVE A LIGHTER?
NARU'S GOT MATCHES.
パン
PAN (POP)
!?
BOTTLE ROCKETS AGAIN!?
PAFU (POOF)
ぱふっ

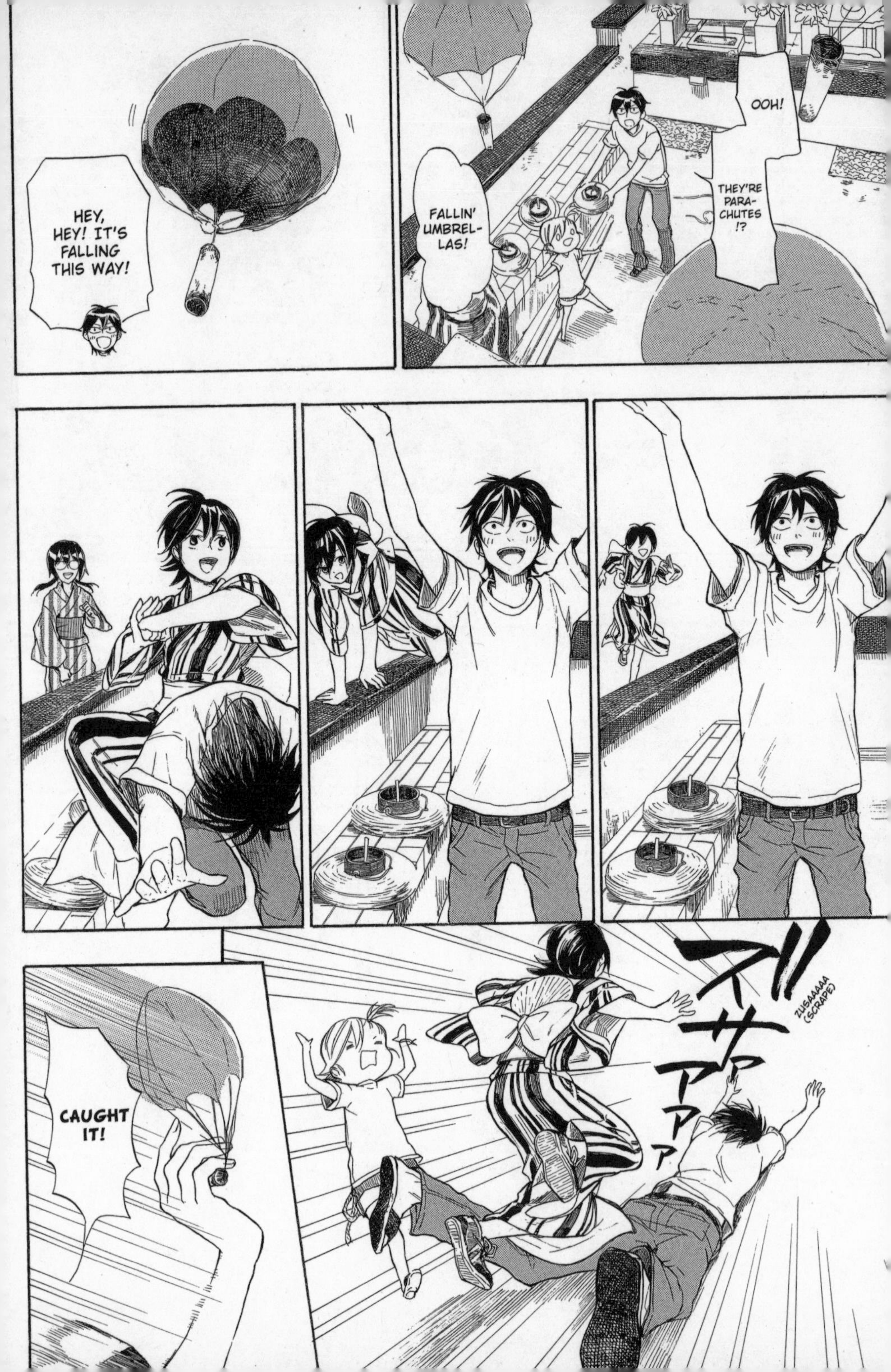
OOH!
THEY'RE PARA-CHUTES !?
FALLIN' UMBREL-LAS!
HEY, HEY! IT'S FALLING THIS WAY!
ズサアアア
ZUSAAAAA (SCRAPE)
CAUGHT IT!

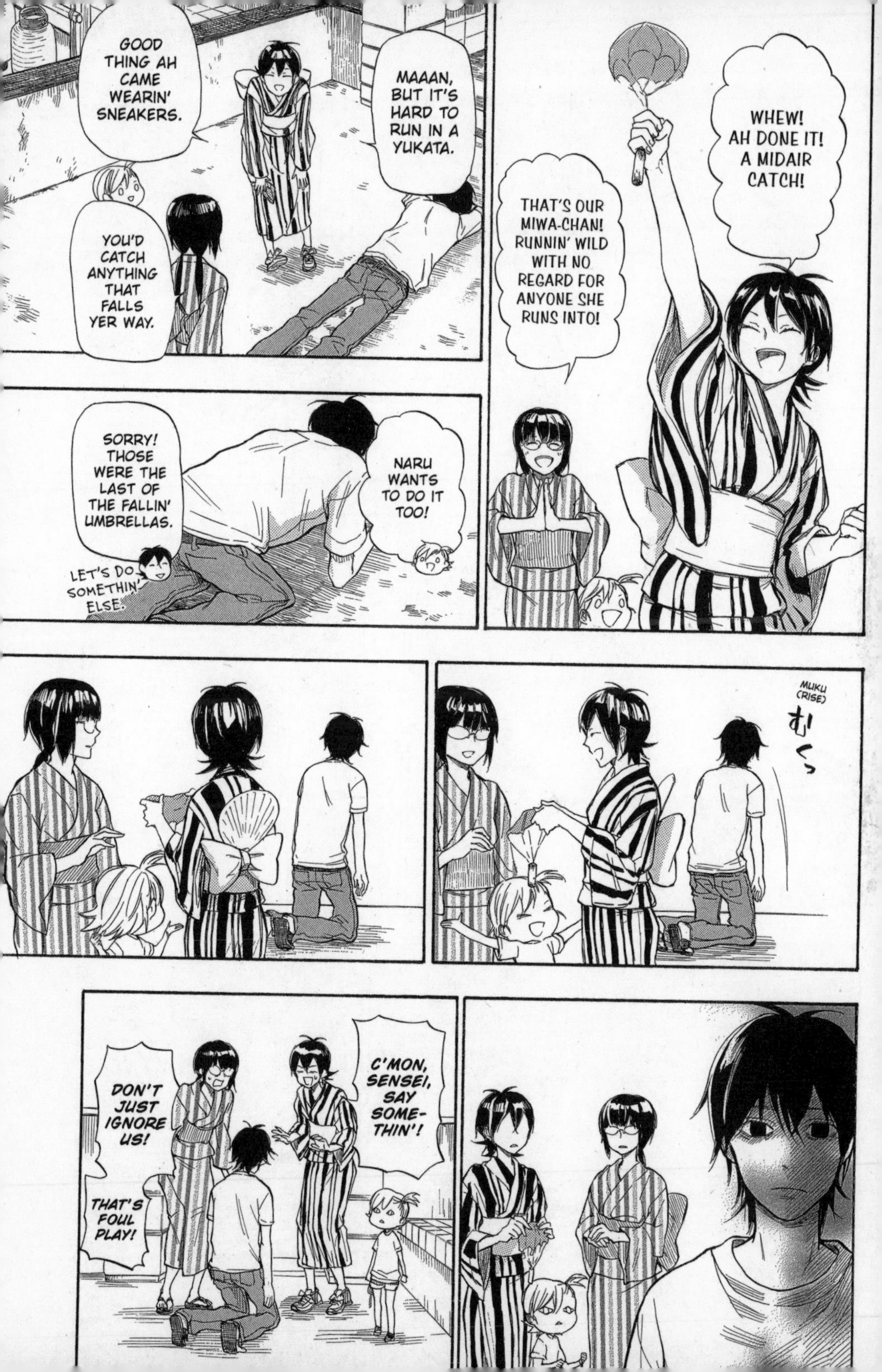
WHEW! AH DONE IT! A MIDAIR CATCH!
THAT'S OUR MIWA-CHAN! RUNNIN' WILD WITH NO REGARD FOR ANYONE SHE RUNS INTO!
MAAAN, BUT IT'S HARD TO RUN IN A YUKATA.
GOOD THING AH CAME WEARIN' SNEAKERS.
YOU'D CATCH ANYTHING THAT FALLS YER WAY.
NARU WANTS TO DO IT TOO!
SORRY! THOSE WERE THE LAST OF THE FALLIN' UMBRELLAS.
LET'S DO SOMETHIN' ELSE.
MUKU (RISE)
むくっ
C'MON, SENSEI, SAY SOME-THIN'!
DON'T JUST IGNORE US!
THAT'S FOUL PLAY!

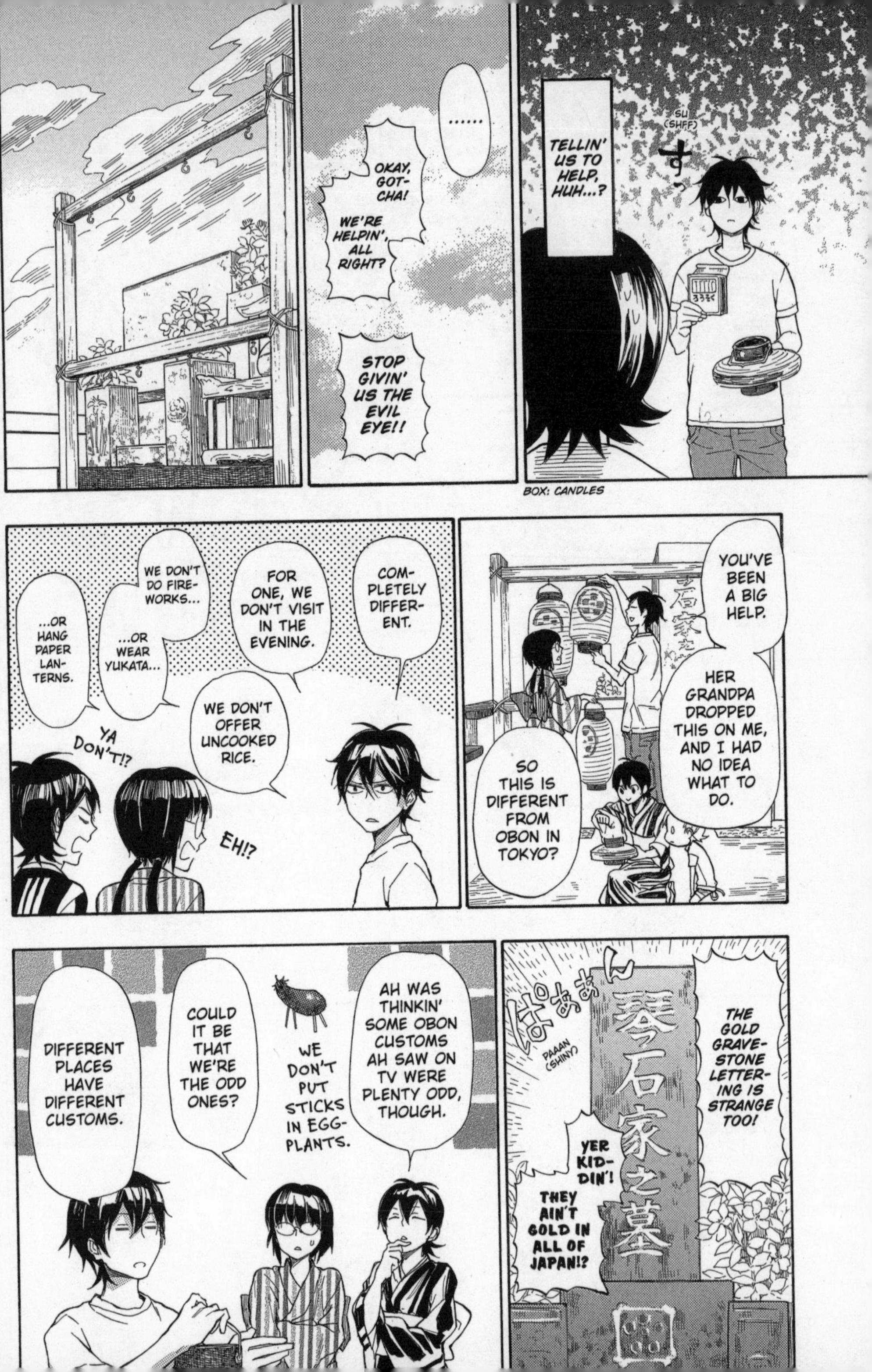
SU (SHFF)
すっ
TELLIN' US TO HELP, HUH...?
......
OKAY, GOT-CHA!
WE'RE HELPIN', ALL RIGHT?
STOP GIVIN' US THE EVIL EYE!!
BOX: CANDLES
YOU'VE BEEN A BIG HELP.
HER GRANDPA DROPPED THIS ON ME, AND I HAD NO IDEA WHAT TO DO.
SO THIS IS DIFFERENT FROM OBON IN TOKYO?
COMPLETELY DIFFERENT.
FOR ONE, WE DON'T VISIT IN THE EVENING.
WE DON'T DO FIREWORKS...
...OR WEAR YUKATA...
...OR HANG PAPER LANTERNS.
WE DON'T OFFER UNCOOKED RICE.
YA DON'T!?
EH!?
THE GOLD GRAVESTONE LETTERING IS STRANGE TOO!
PAAAN (SHINY)
YER KIDDIN'!
THEY AIN'T GOLD IN ALL OF JAPAN!?
AH WAS THINKIN' SOME OBON CUSTOMS AH SAW ON TV WERE PLENTY ODD, THOUGH.
WE DON'T PUT STICKS IN EGG-PLANTS.
COULD IT BE THAT WE'RE THE ODD ONES?
DIFFERENT PLACES HAVE DIFFERENT CUSTOMS.

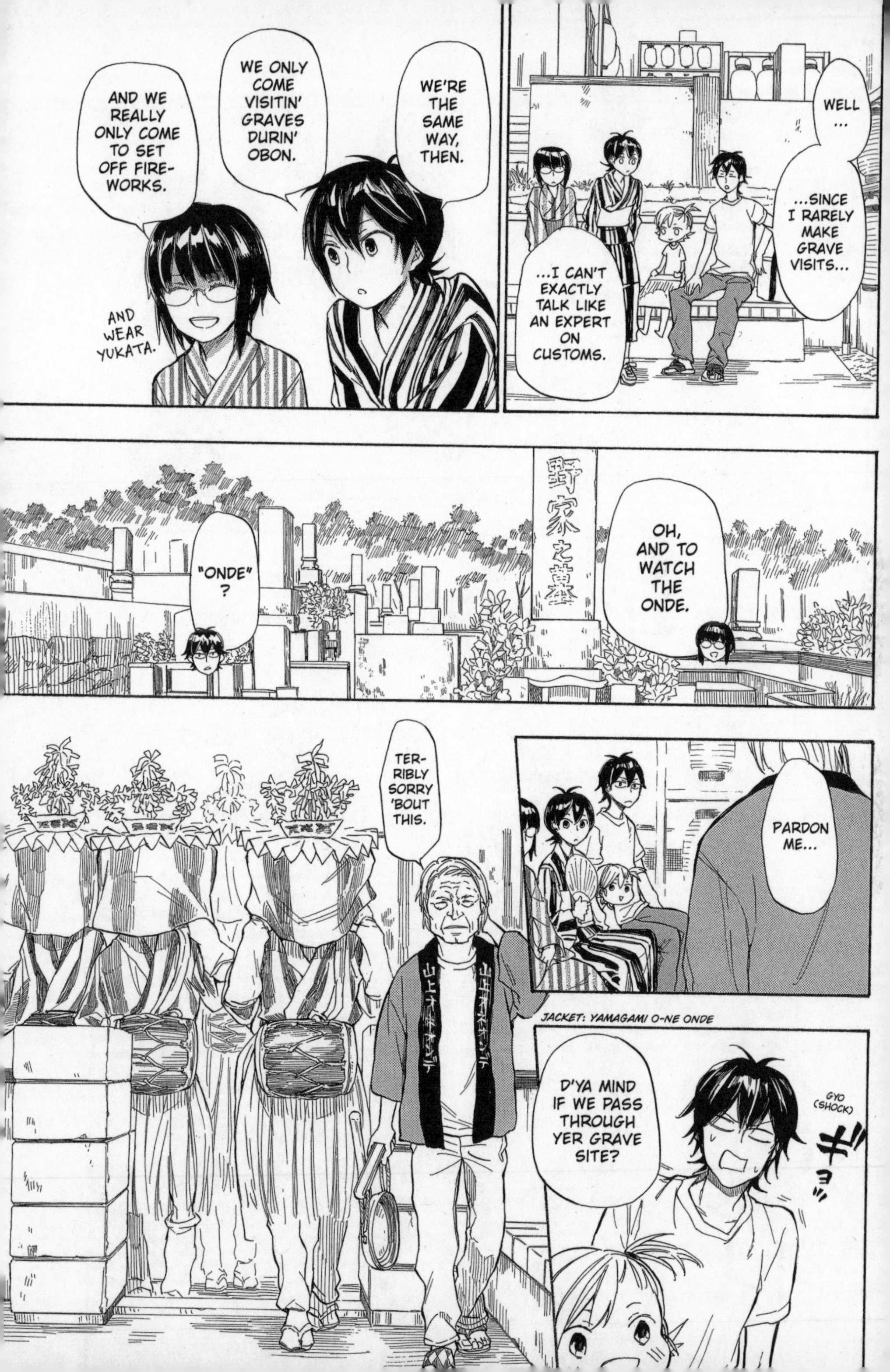
WELL ...
...SINCE I RARELY MAKE GRAVE VISITS...
...I CAN'T EXACTLY TALK LIKE AN EXPERT ON CUSTOMS.
WE'RE THE SAME WAY, THEN.
WE ONLY COME VISITIN' GRAVES DURIN' OBON.
AND WE REALLY ONLY COME TO SET OFF FIRE-WORKS.
AND WEAR YUKATA.
OH, AND TO WATCH THE ONDE.
野家之墓
"ONDE"?
PARDON ME...
D'YA MIND IF WE PASS THROUGH YER GRAVE SITE?
GYO (SHOCK)
ギョ
TER-RIBLY SORRY 'BOUT THIS.
JACKET: YAMAGAMI O-NE ONDE

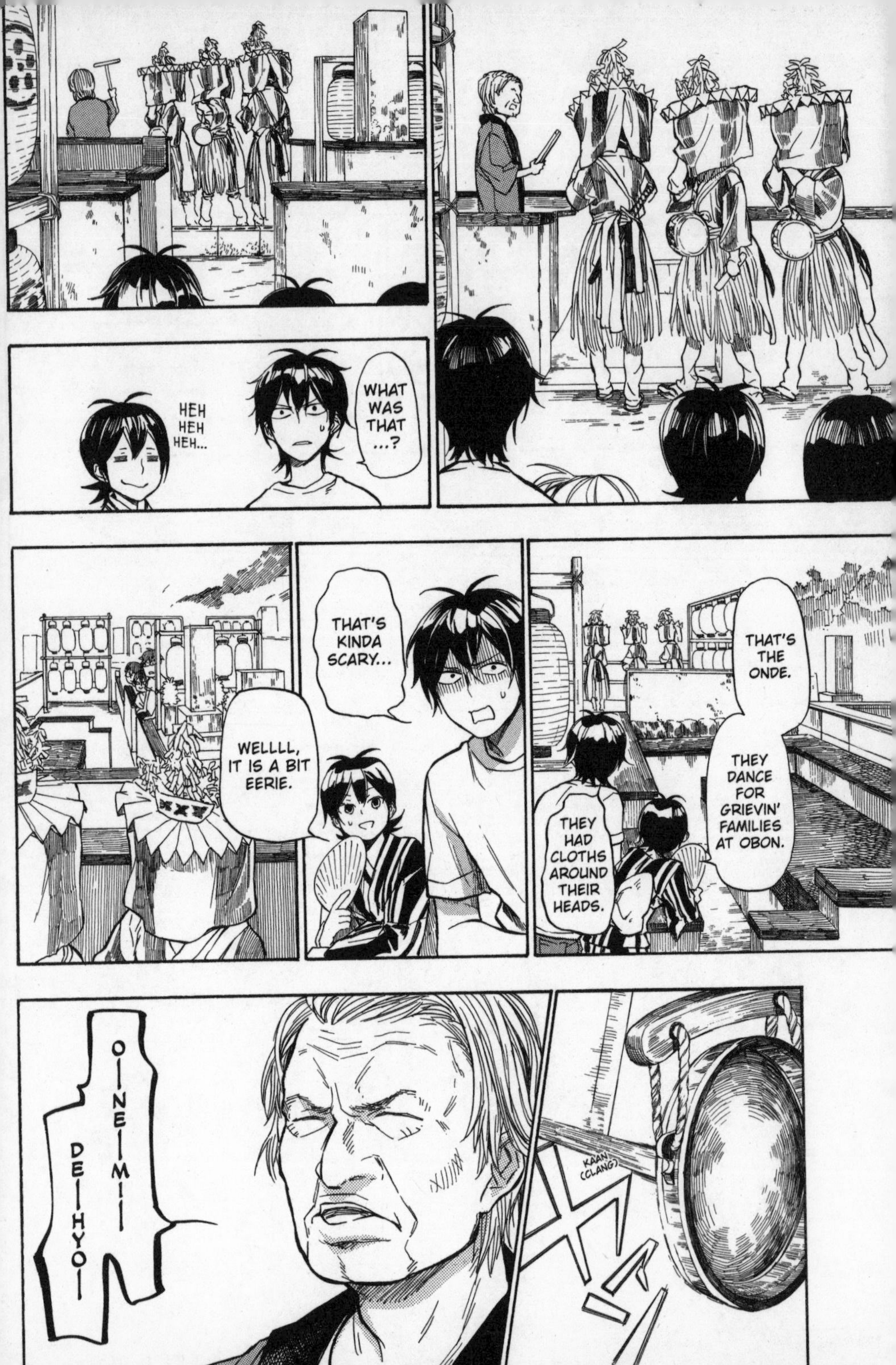
WHAT WAS THAT ...?
HEH HEH HEH...
THAT'S THE ONDE.
THEY DANCE FOR GRIEVIN' FAMILIES AT OBON.
THEY HAD CLOTHS AROUND THEIR HEADS.
THAT'S KINDA SCARY...
WELLLL, IT IS A BIT EERIE.
KAAN (CLANG)
O—NE—MI—
DE—HYO—

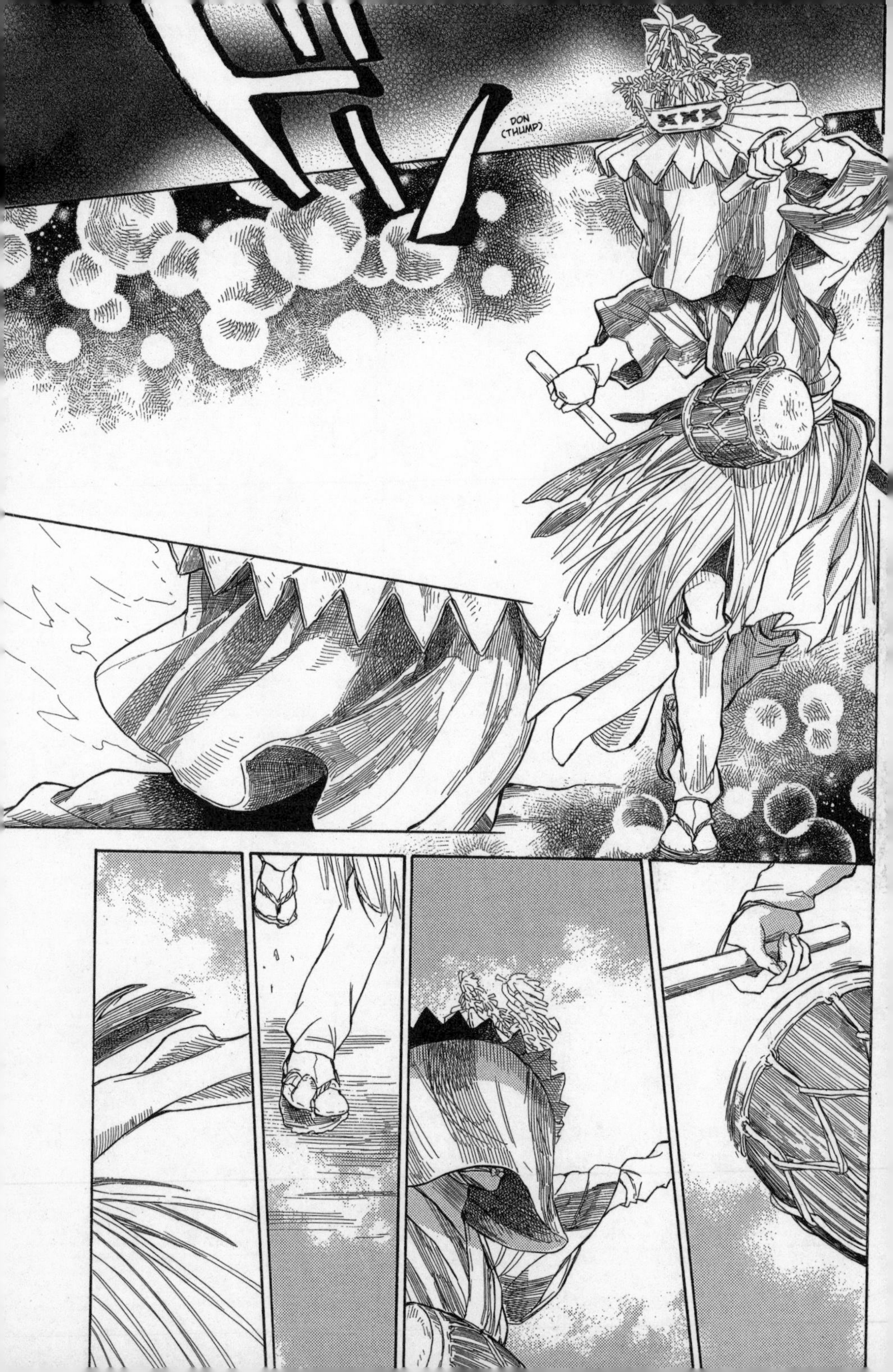
DON
(THUMP)

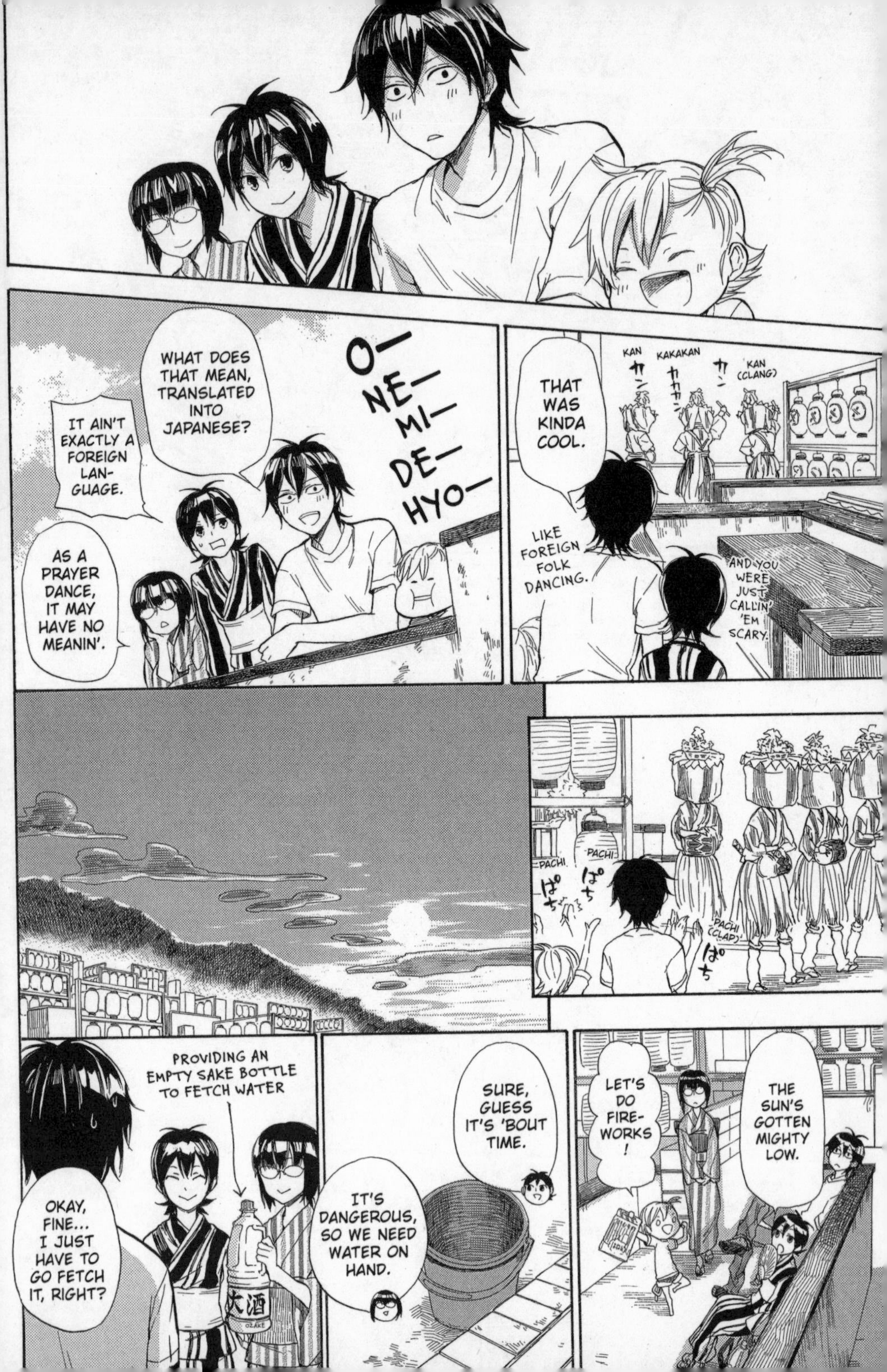
KAN
KAKAKAN
KAN (CLANG)
THAT WAS KINDA COOL.
LIKE FOREIGN FOLK DANCING.
AND YOU WERE JUST CALLIN' 'EM SCARY.
O—NE—MI—DE—HYO—
WHAT DOES THAT MEAN, TRANSLATED INTO JAPANESE?
IT AIN'T EXACTLY A FOREIGN LAN-GUAGE.
AS A PRAYER DANCE, IT MAY HAVE NO MEANIN'.
PACHI
PACHI
PACHI (CLAP)
THE SUN'S GOTTEN MIGHTY LOW.
LET'S DO FIRE-WORKS!
SURE, GUESS IT'S 'BOUT TIME.
IT'S DANGEROUS, SO WE NEED WATER ON HAND.
PROVIDING AN EMPTY SAKE BOTTLE TO FETCH WATER
大酒
OZAKE
OKAY, FINE... I JUST HAVE TO GO FETCH IT, RIGHT?

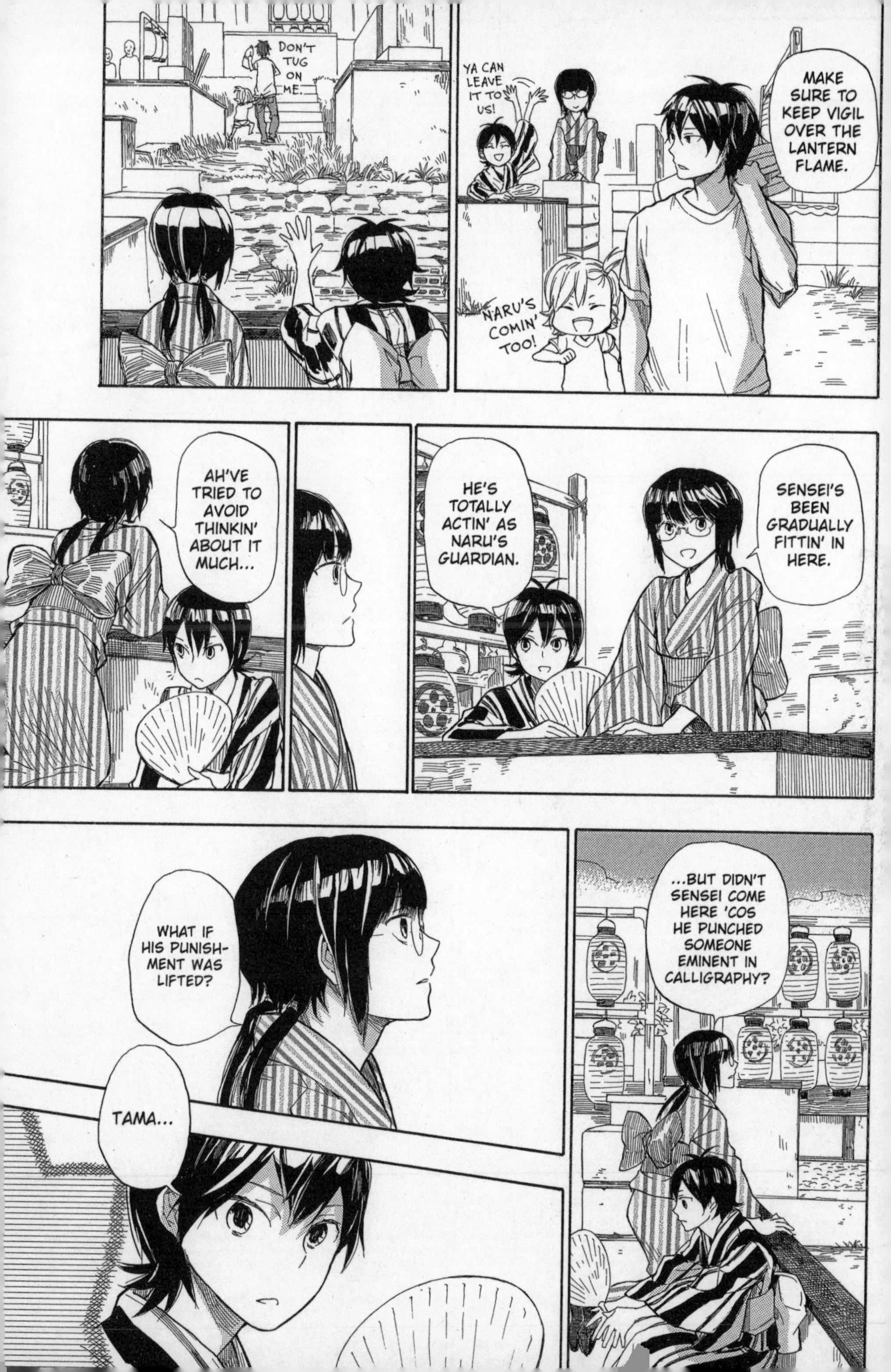
MAKE SURE TO KEEP VIGIL OVER THE LANTERN FLAME.
YA CAN LEAVE IT TO US!
NARU'S COMIN' TOO!
DON'T TUG ON ME.
SENSEI'S BEEN GRADUALLY FITTIN' IN HERE.
HE'S TOTALLY ACTIN' AS NARU'S GUARDIAN.
AH'VE TRIED TO AVOID THINKIN' ABOUT IT MUCH...
...BUT DIDN'T SENSEI COME HERE 'COS HE PUNCHED SOMEONE EMINENT IN CALLIGRAPHY?
WHAT IF HIS PUNISH-MENT WAS LIFTED?
TAMA...

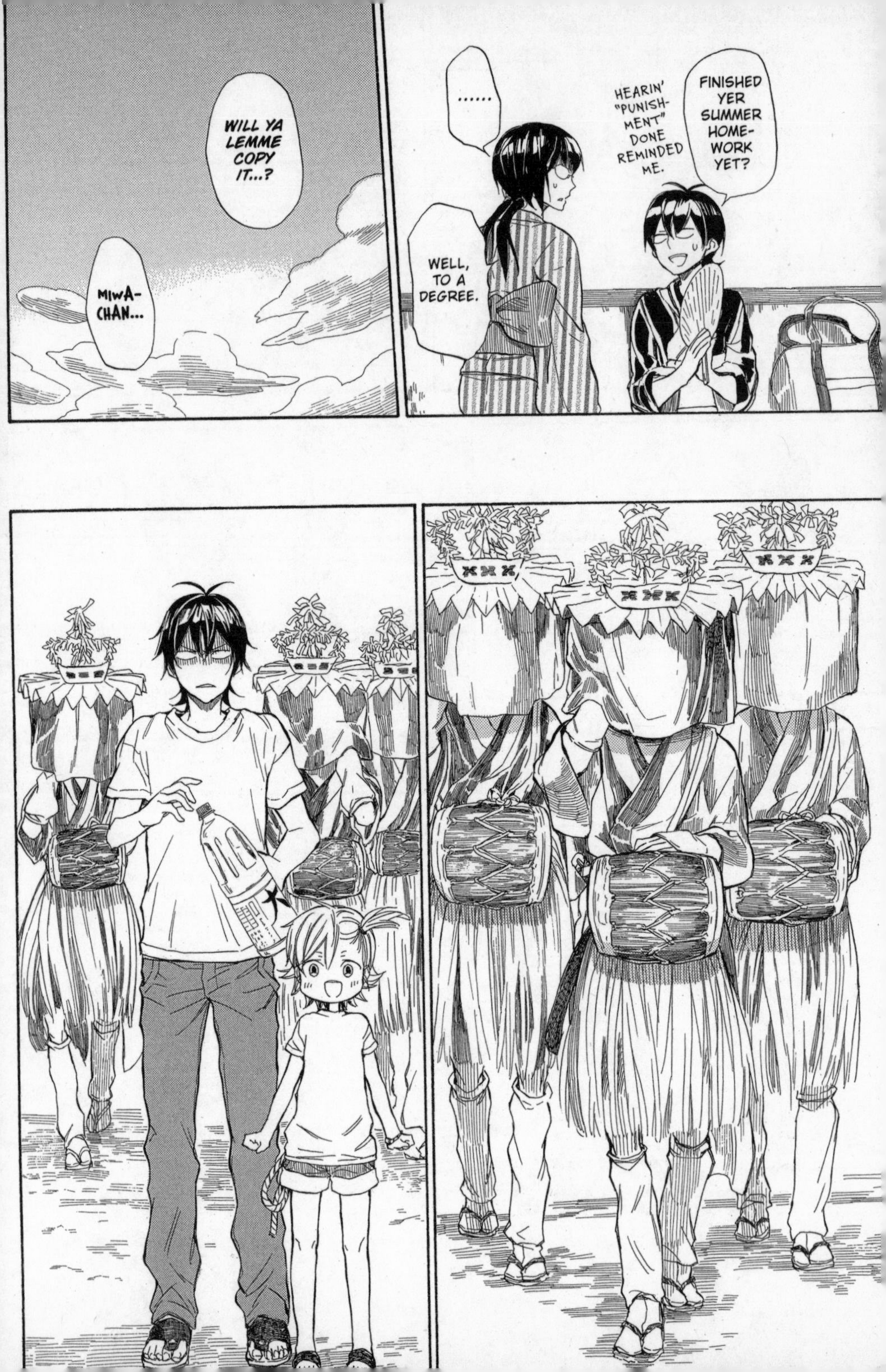
FINISHED YER SUMMER HOME-WORK YET?
HEARIN' "PUNISH-MENT" DONE REMINDED ME.
......
WELL, TO A DEGREE.
WILL YA LEMME COPY IT...?
MIWA-CHAN...

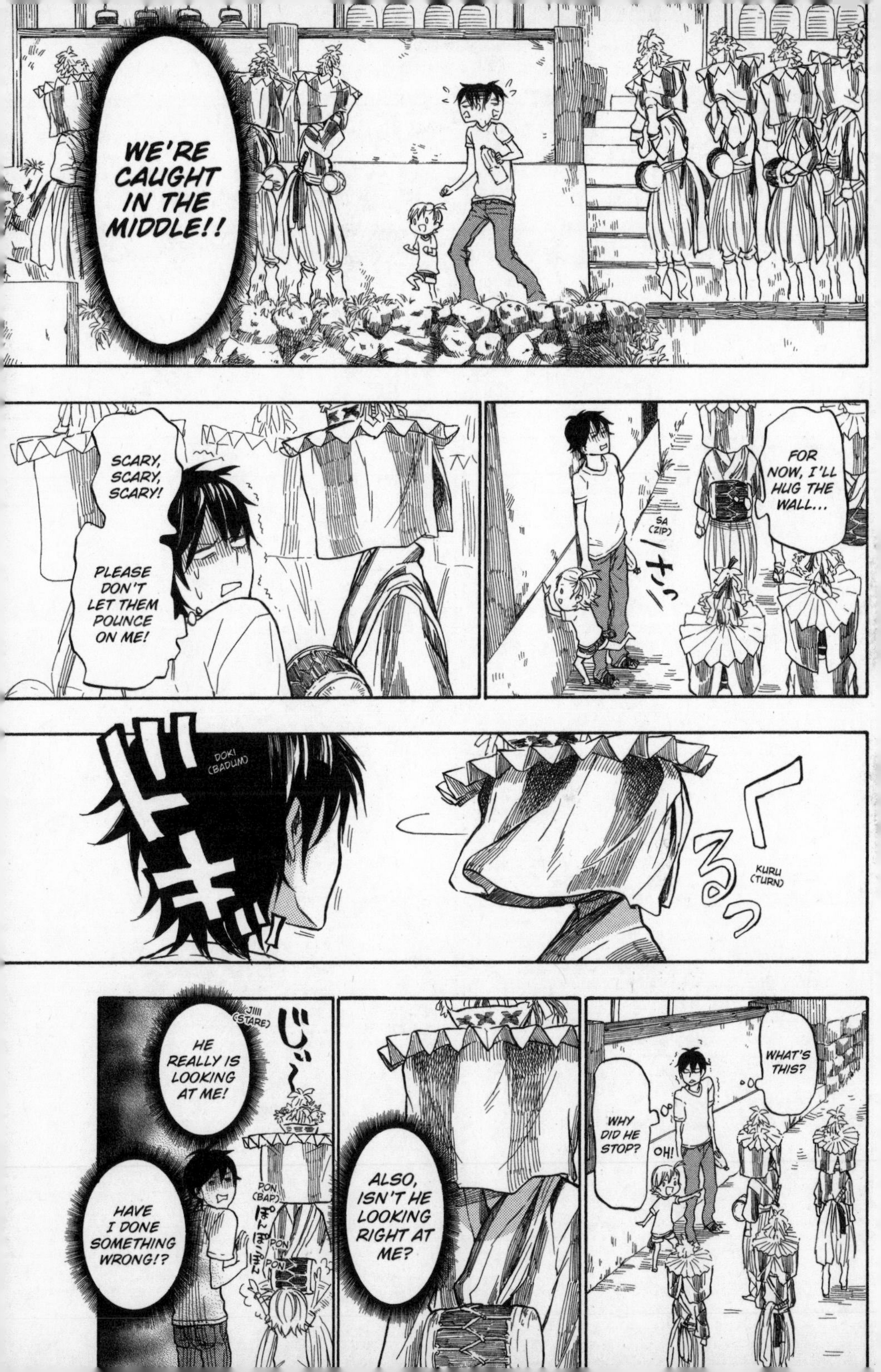
WE'RE CAUGHT IN THE MIDDLE!!
FOR NOW, I'LL HUG THE WALL...
SA (ZIP)
さっ
SCARY, SCARY, SCARY!
PLEASE DON'T LET THEM POUNCE ON ME!
くるっ
KURU (TURN)
ドキッ
DOKI (BADUM)
WHAT'S THIS?
WHY DID HE STOP?
OH!
ALSO, ISN'T HE LOOKING RIGHT AT ME?
JIIII (STARE)
じ～
HE REALLY IS LOOKING AT ME!
PON (BAP)
PON
PON
HAVE I DONE SOMETHING WRONG!?

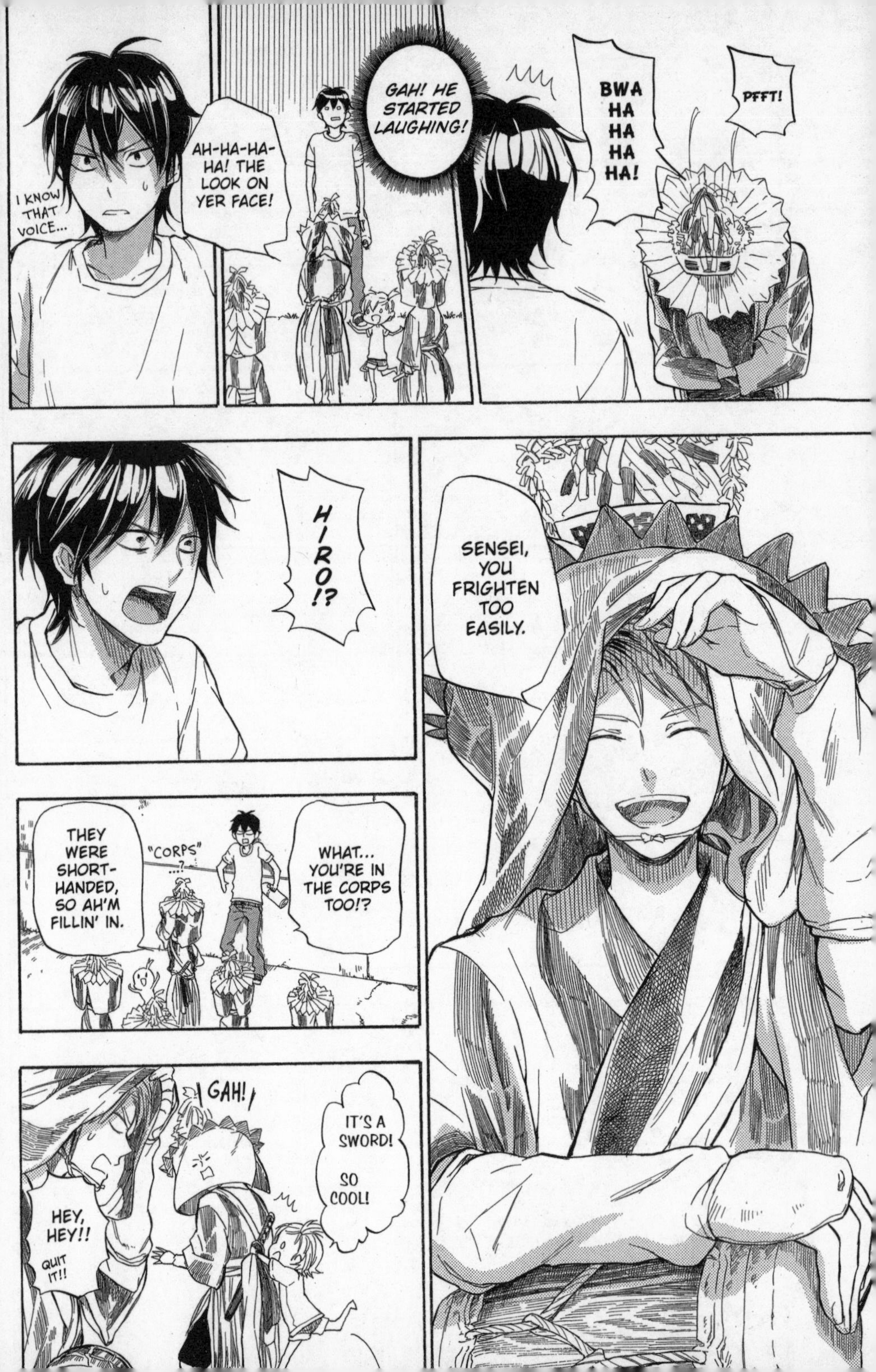
PFFT!
BWA HA HA HA HA!
GAH! HE STARTED LAUGHING!
AH-HA-HA-HA! THE LOOK ON YER FACE!
I KNOW THAT VOICE...
SENSEI, YOU FRIGHTEN TOO EASILY.
HIRO!?
WHAT... YOU'RE IN THE CORPS TOO!?
"CORPS" ...?
THEY WERE SHORT-HANDED, SO AH'M FILLIN' IN.
IT'S A SWORD!
SO COOL!
GAH!
HEY, HEY!!
QUIT IT!!

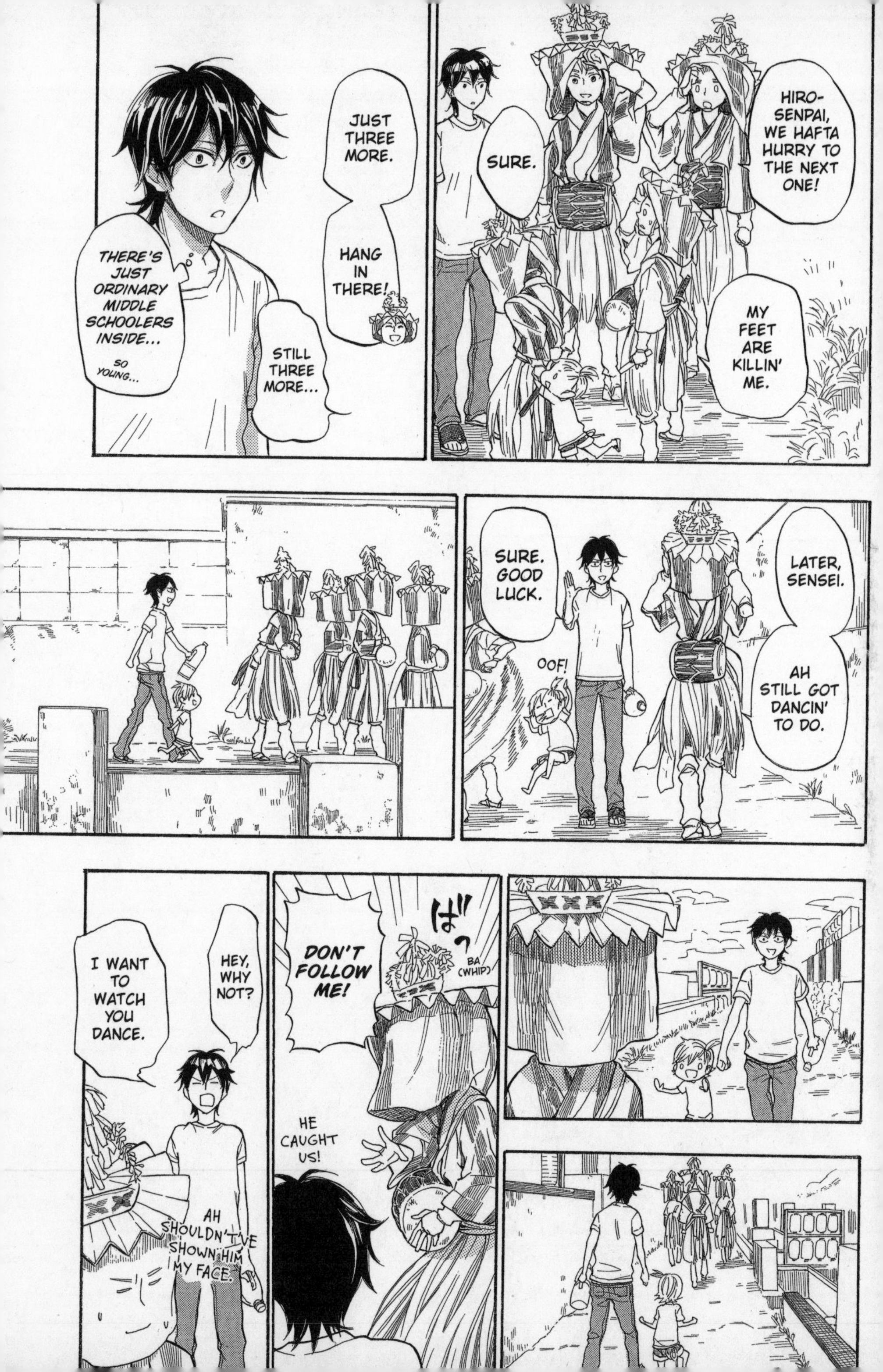
HIRO-SENPAI, WE HAFTA HURRY TO THE NEXT ONE!
SURE.
MY FEET ARE KILLIN' ME.
JUST THREE MORE.
HANG IN THERE!
STILL THREE MORE...
THERE'S JUST ORDINARY MIDDLE SCHOOLERS INSIDE...
SO YOUNG...
LATER, SENSEI.
SURE. GOOD LUCK.
AH STILL GOT DANCIN' TO DO.
OOF!
ばっ
BA (WHIP)
DON'T FOLLOW ME!
HE CAUGHT US!
HEY, WHY NOT?
I WANT TO WATCH YOU DANCE.
AH SHOULDN'T'VE SHOWN HIM MY FACE.

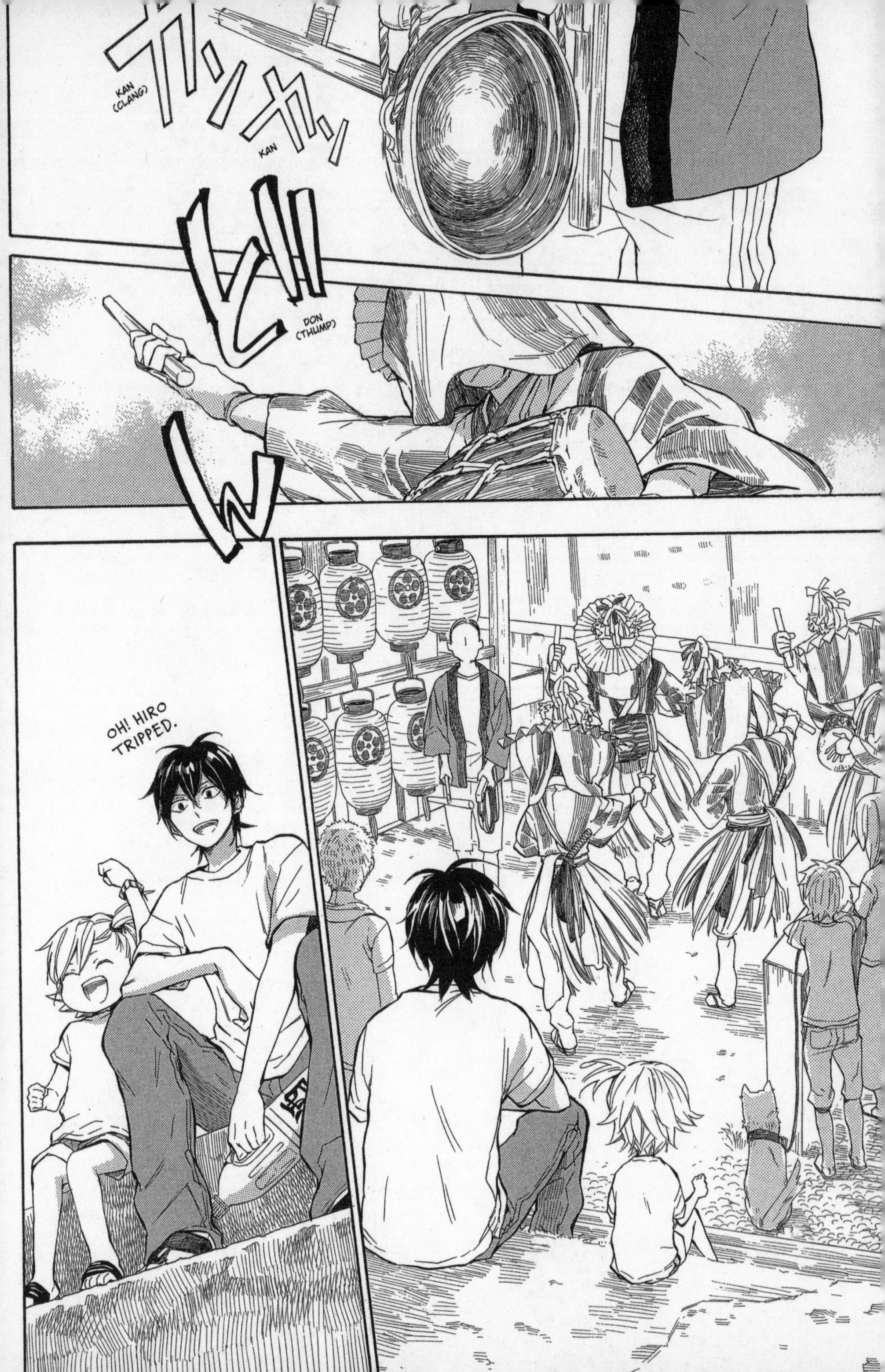
KAN (CLANG)
KAN
DON (THUMP)
OH! HIRO TRIPPED.

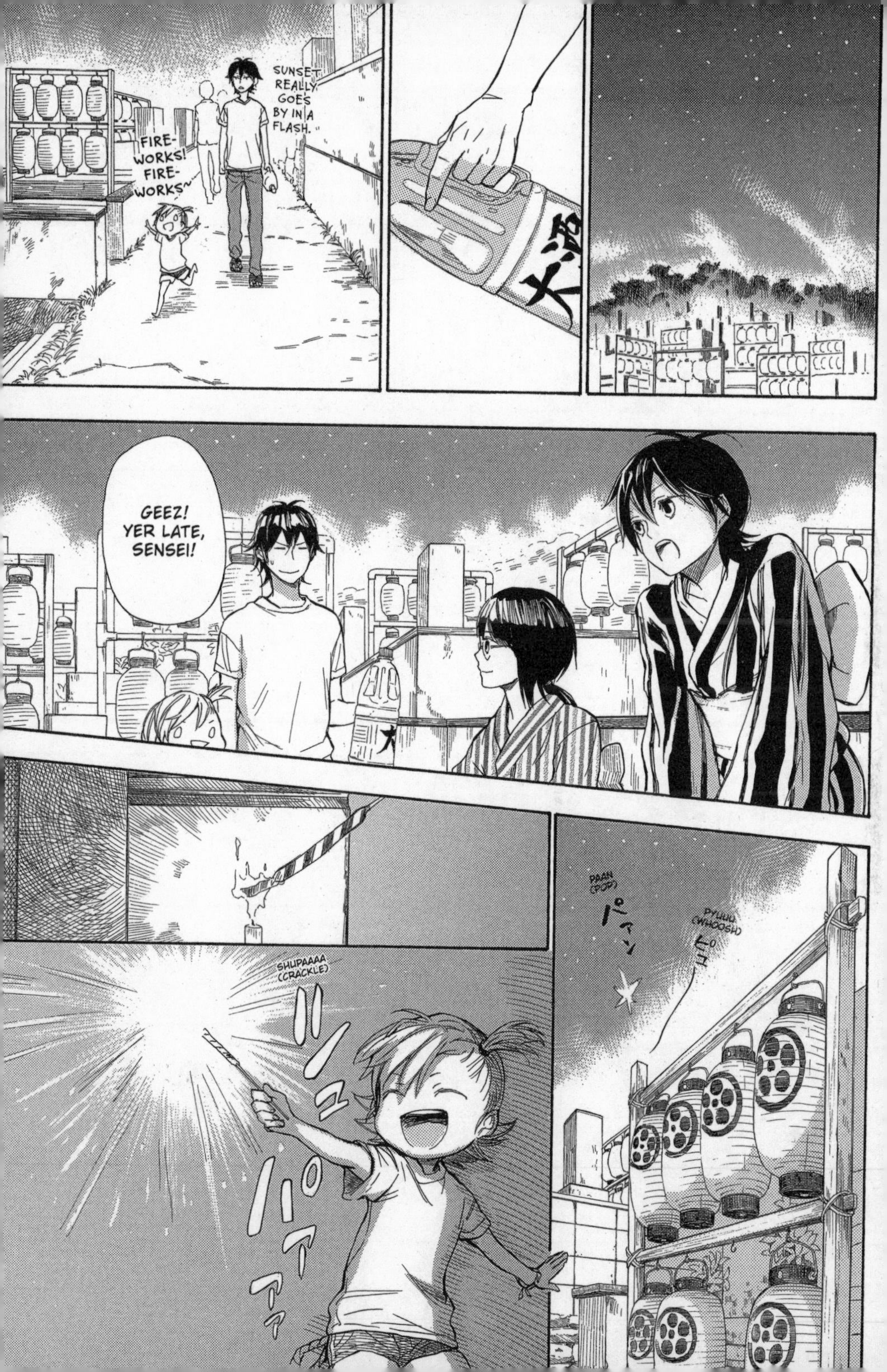
SUNSET REALLY GOES BY IN A FLASH.
FIRE-WORKS! FIRE-WORKS~
GEEZ! YER LATE, SENSEI!
PAAN (POP)
PYUUU (WHOOSH)
SHUPAAAA (CRACKLE)

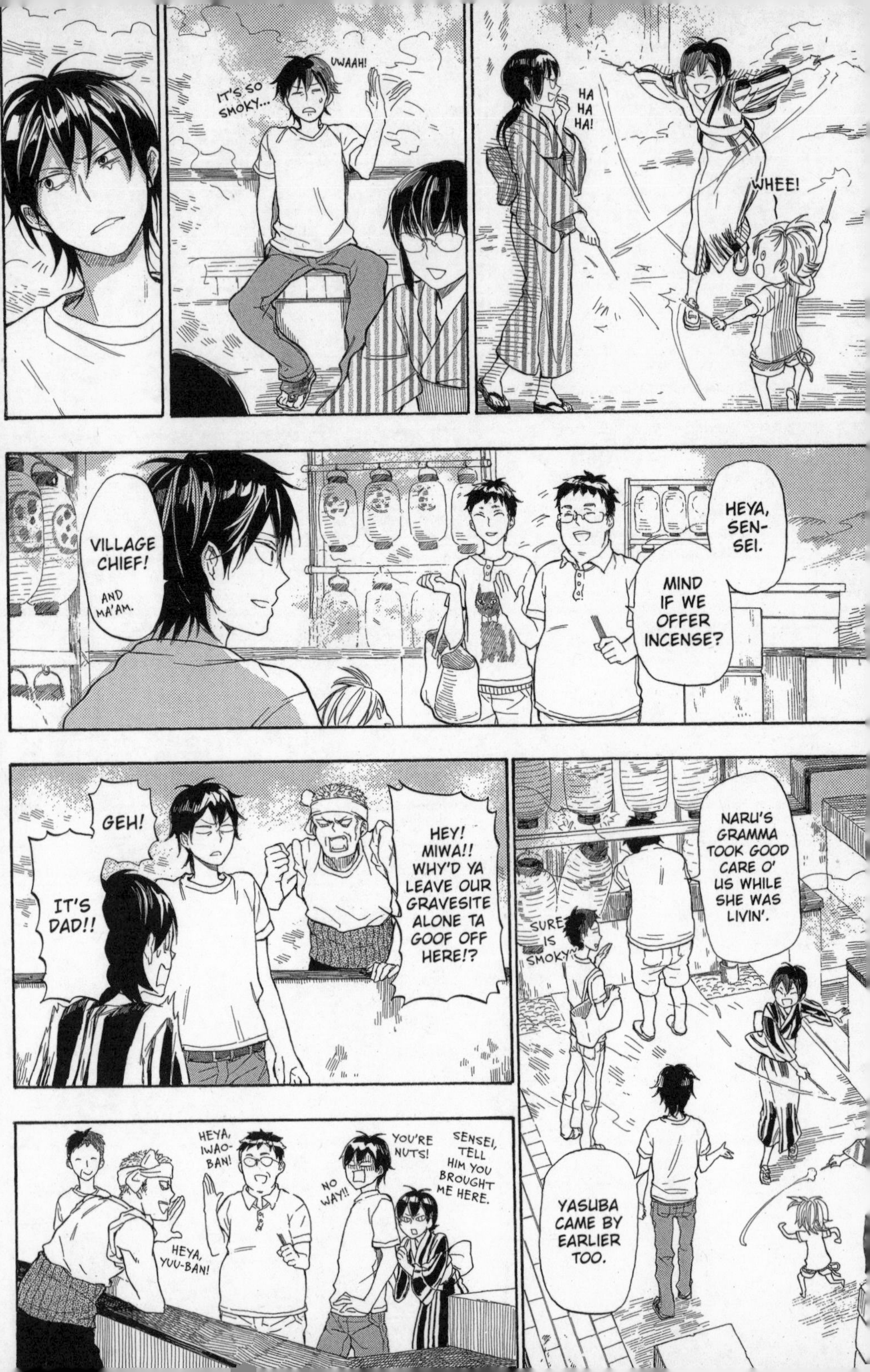
HA HA HA!
WHEE!
UWAAH!
IT'S SO SMOKY...
HEYA, SEN-SEI.
MIND IF WE OFFER INCENSE?
VILLAGE CHIEF!
AND MA'AM.
NARU'S GRAMMA TOOK GOOD CARE O' US WHILE SHE WAS LIVIN'.
SURE IS SMOKY
YASUBA CAME BY EARLIER TOO.
HEY! MIWA!! WHY'D YA LEAVE OUR GRAVESITE ALONE TA GOOF OFF HERE!?
GEH!
IT'S DAD!!
SENSEI, TELL HIM YOU BROUGHT ME HERE.
YOU'RE NUTS!
NO WAY!!
HEYA, IWAO-BAN!
HEYA, YUU-BAN!

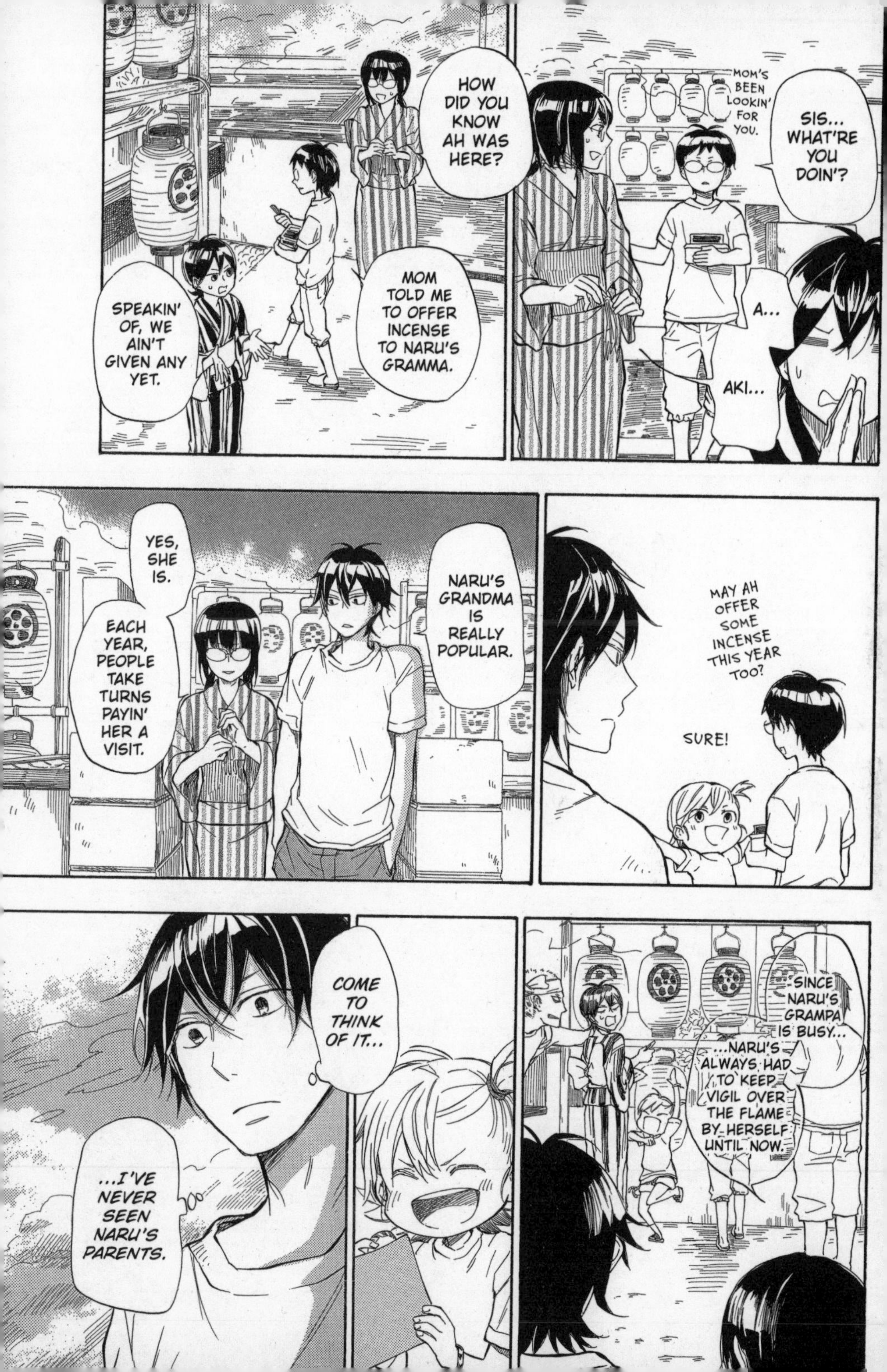
SIS... WHAT'RE YOU DOIN'?
MOM'S BEEN LOOKIN' FOR YOU.
A...
AKI...
HOW DID YOU KNOW AH WAS HERE?
MOM TOLD ME TO OFFER INCENSE TO NARU'S GRAMMA.
SPEAKIN' OF, WE AIN'T GIVEN ANY YET.
MAY AH OFFER SOME INCENSE THIS YEAR TOO?
SURE!
NARU'S GRANDMA IS REALLY POPULAR.
YES, SHE IS.
EACH YEAR, PEOPLE TAKE TURNS PAYIN' HER A VISIT.
SINCE NARU'S GRAMPA IS BUSY...
...NARU'S ALWAYS HAD TO KEEP VIGIL OVER THE FLAME BY HERSELF UNTIL NOW.
COME TO THINK OF IT...
...I'VE NEVER SEEN NARU'S PARENTS.

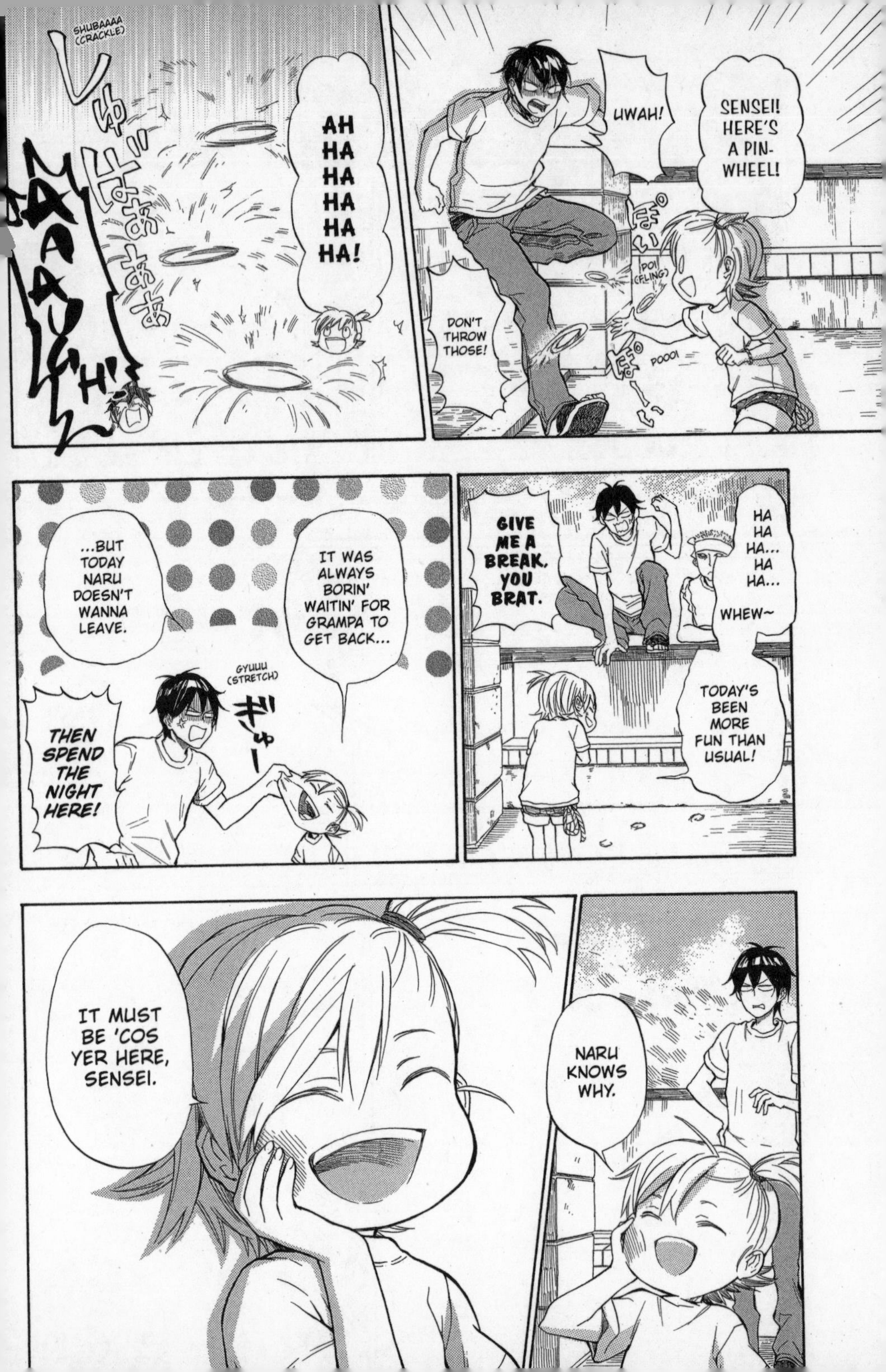
SENSEI! HERE'S A PIN-WHEEL!
UWAH!
POI (FLING)
DON'T THROW THOSE!
POOOI
AH HA HA HA HA HA!
SHUBAAAA (CRACKLE)
GIVE ME A BREAK, YOU BRAT.
HA HA HA... HA HA...
WHEW~
TODAY'S BEEN MORE FUN THAN USUAL!
IT WAS ALWAYS BORIN' WAITIN' FOR GRAMPA TO GET BACK...
...BUT TODAY NARU DOESN'T WANNA LEAVE.
GYUUU (STRETCH)
THEN SPEND THE NIGHT HERE!
NARU KNOWS WHY.
IT MUST BE 'COS YER HERE, SENSEI.

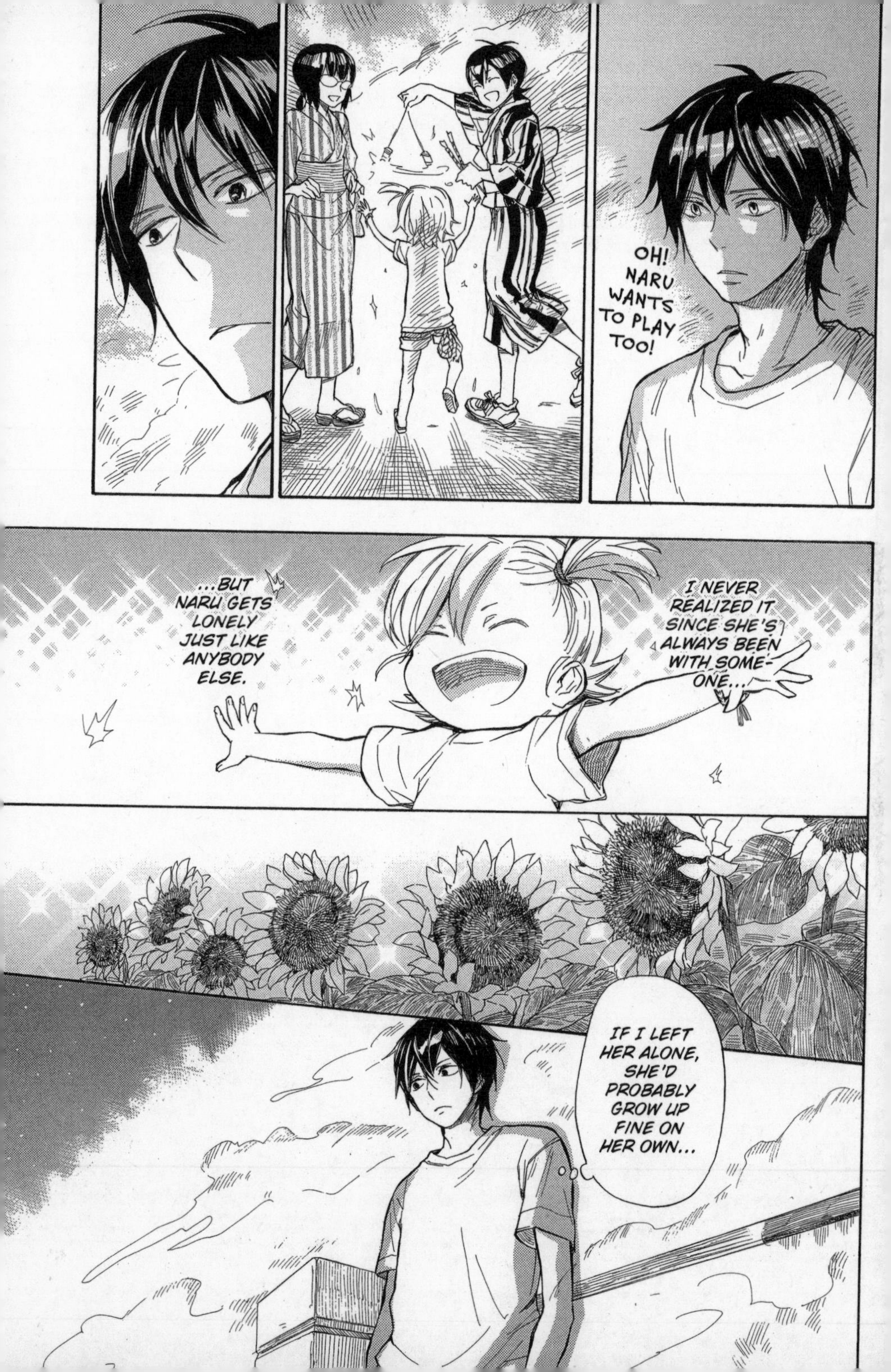
OH! NARU WANTS TO PLAY TOO!
I NEVER REALIZED IT SINCE SHE'S ALWAYS BEEN WITH SOME-ONE...
...BUT NARU GETS LONELY JUST LIKE ANYBODY ELSE.
IF I LEFT HER ALONE, SHE'D PROBABLY GROW UP FINE ON HER OWN...

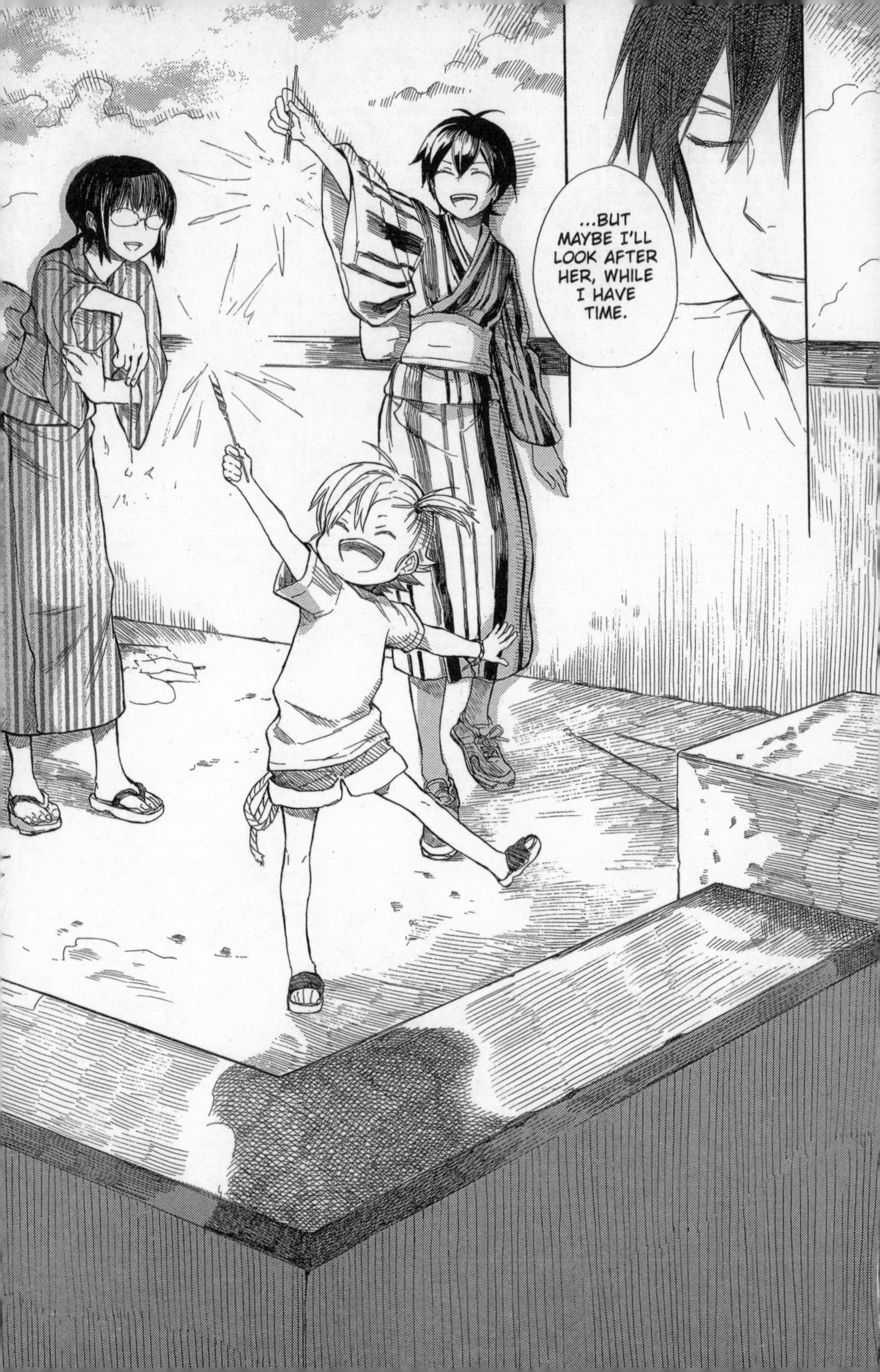
...BUT MAYBE I'LL LOOK AFTER HER, WHILE I HAVE TIME.

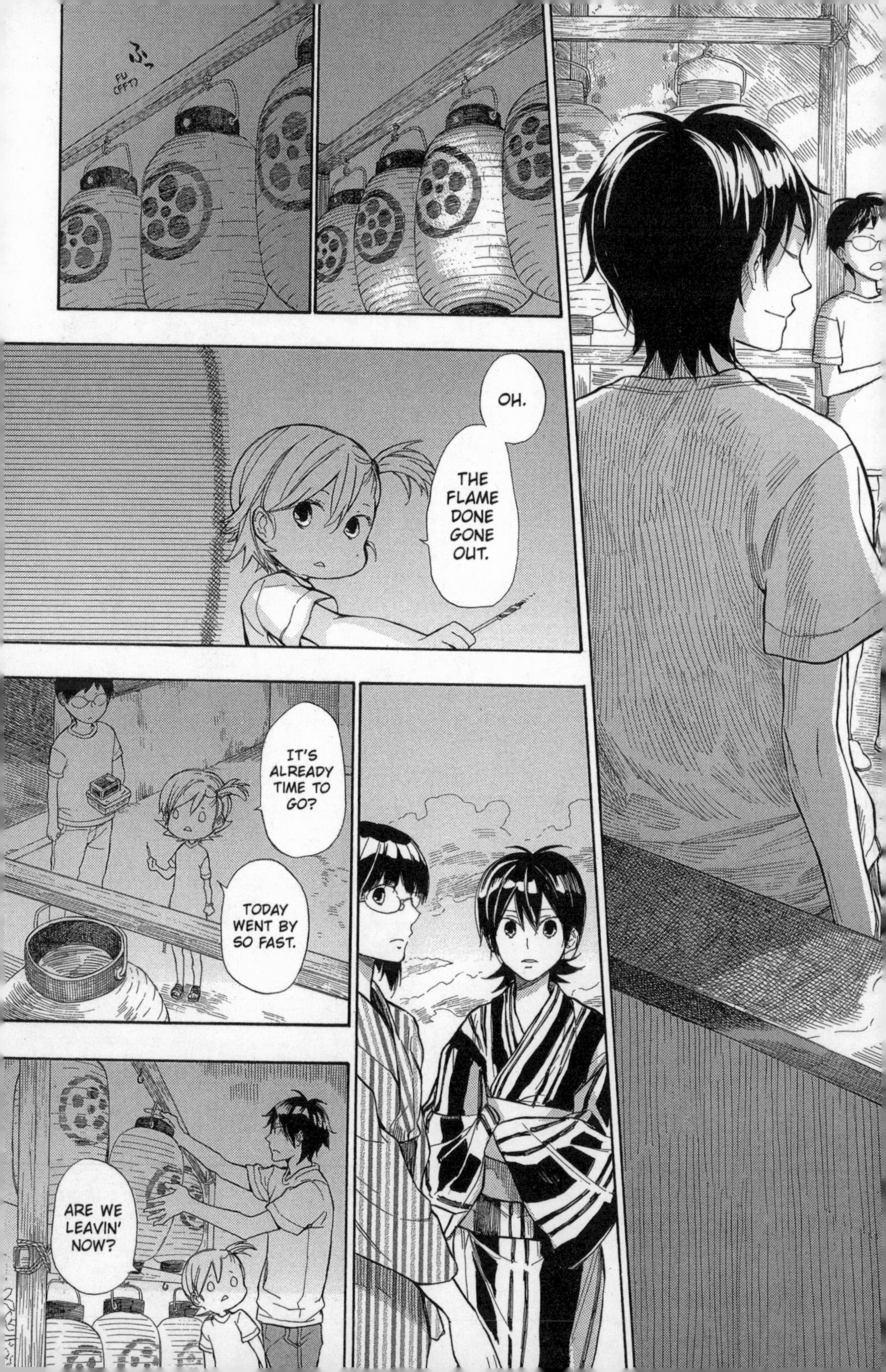
ふっ
FU (FFT)
OH.
THE FLAME DONE GONE OUT.
IT'S ALREADY TIME TO GO?
TODAY WENT BY SO FAST.
ARE WE LEAVIN' NOW?

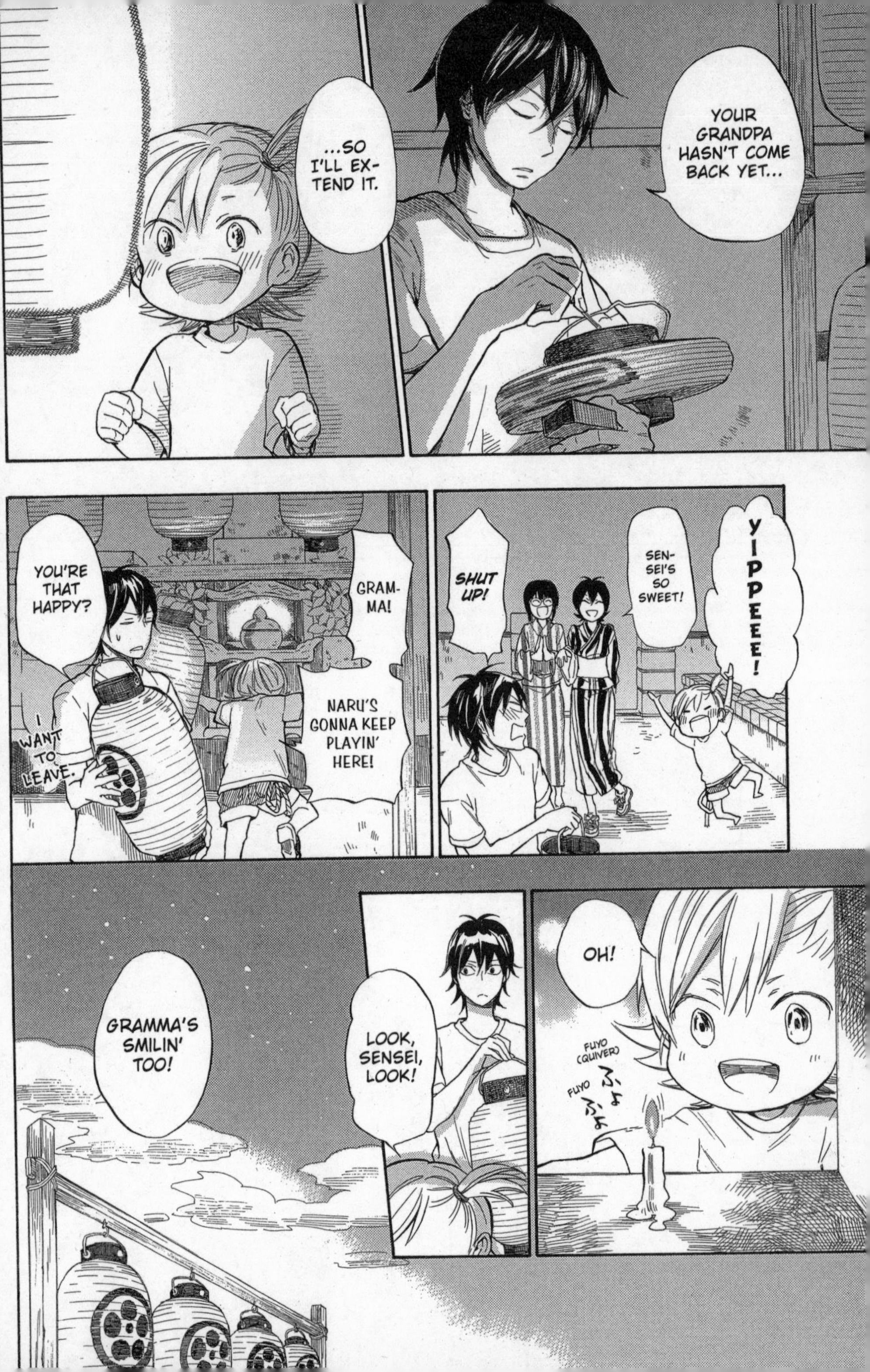
YOUR GRANDPA HASN'T COME BACK YET...
...SO I'LL EX-TEND IT.
YIPPEEE!
SEN-SEI'S SO SWEET!
SHUT UP!
GRAM-MA!
NARU'S GONNA KEEP PLAYIN' HERE!
YOU'RE THAT HAPPY?
I WANT TO LEAVE.
OH!
FUYO (QUIVER)
ふよ
FUYO
ふよ
LOOK, SENSEI, LOOK!
GRAMMA'S SMILIN' TOO!

WHEW...

THIS'S
MIGHTY
ROUGH...

BONUS: DANPO THE 4TH

(Translation: Pond)

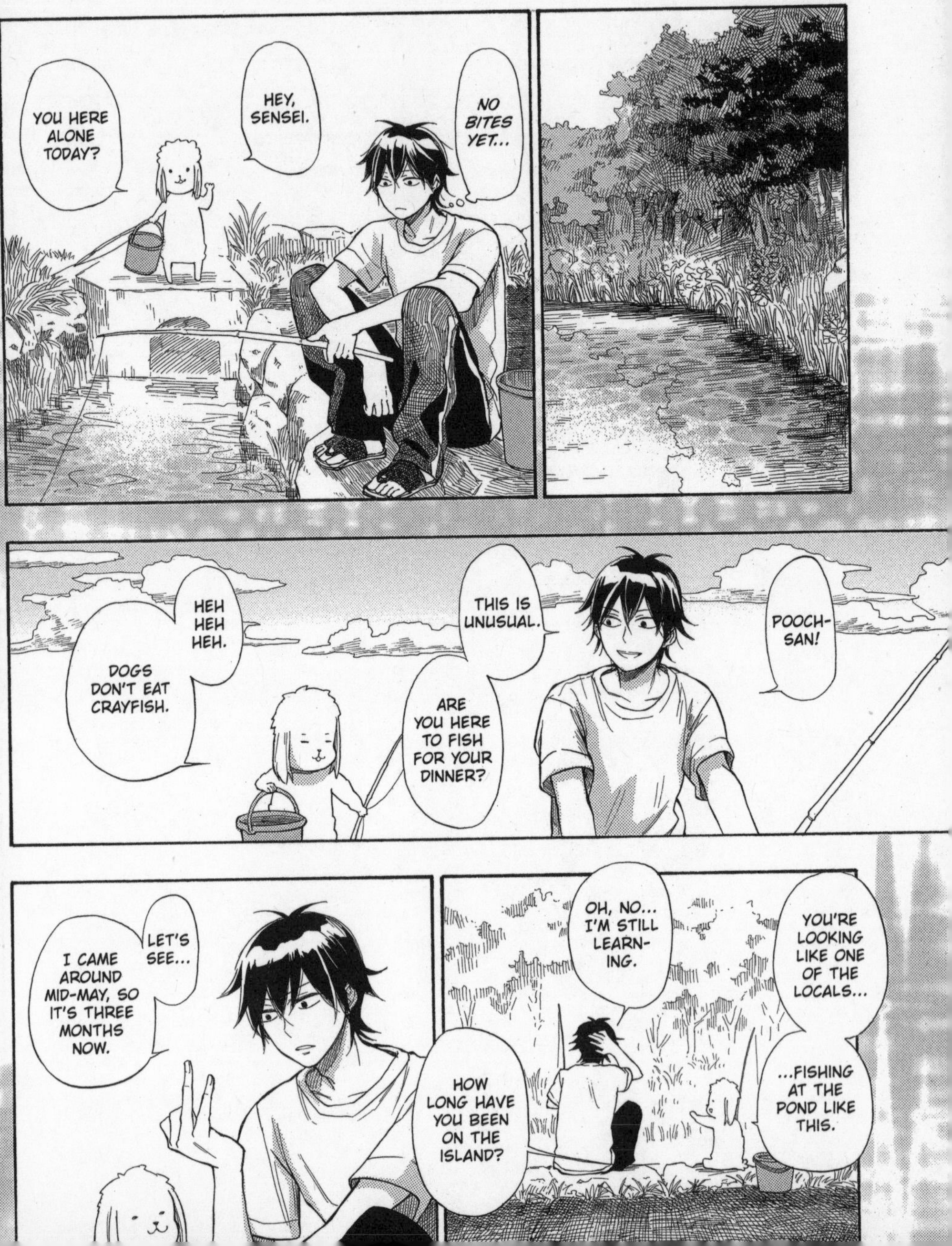
NO BITES YET...
HEY, SENSEI.
YOU HERE ALONE TODAY?
POOCH-SAN!
THIS IS UNUSUAL.
ARE YOU HERE TO FISH FOR YOUR DINNER?
HEH HEH HEH.
DOGS DON'T EAT CRAYFISH.
YOU'RE LOOKING LIKE ONE OF THE LOCALS...
...FISHING AT THE POND LIKE THIS.
OH, NO... I'M STILL LEARNING.
HOW LONG HAVE YOU BEEN ON THE ISLAND?
LET'S SEE...
I CAME AROUND MID-MAY, SO IT'S THREE MONTHS NOW.

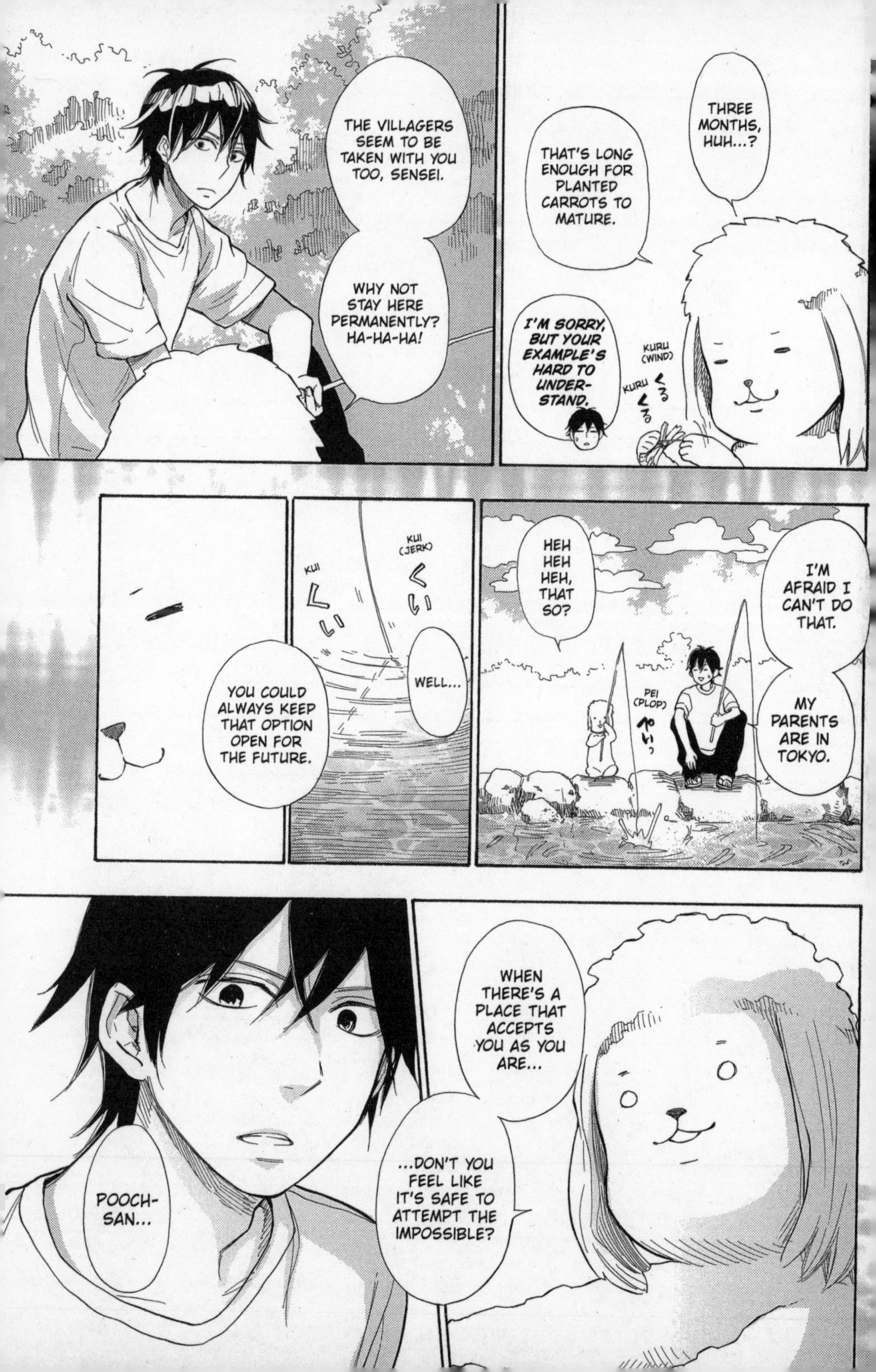
THREE MONTHS, HUH...?
THAT'S LONG ENOUGH FOR PLANTED CARROTS TO MATURE.
KURU (WIND)
KURU
I'M SORRY, BUT YOUR EXAMPLE'S HARD TO UNDER-STAND.
THE VILLAGERS SEEM TO BE TAKEN WITH YOU TOO, SENSEI.
WHY NOT STAY HERE PERMANENTLY? HA-HA-HA!
I'M AFRAID I CAN'T DO THAT.
MY PARENTS ARE IN TOKYO.
HEH HEH HEH, THAT SO?
PEI (PLOP)
KUI (JERK)
KUI
WELL...
YOU COULD ALWAYS KEEP THAT OPTION OPEN FOR THE FUTURE.
WHEN THERE'S A PLACE THAT ACCEPTS YOU AS YOU ARE...
...DON'T YOU FEEL LIKE IT'S SAFE TO ATTEMPT THE IMPOSSIBLE?
POOCH-SAN...

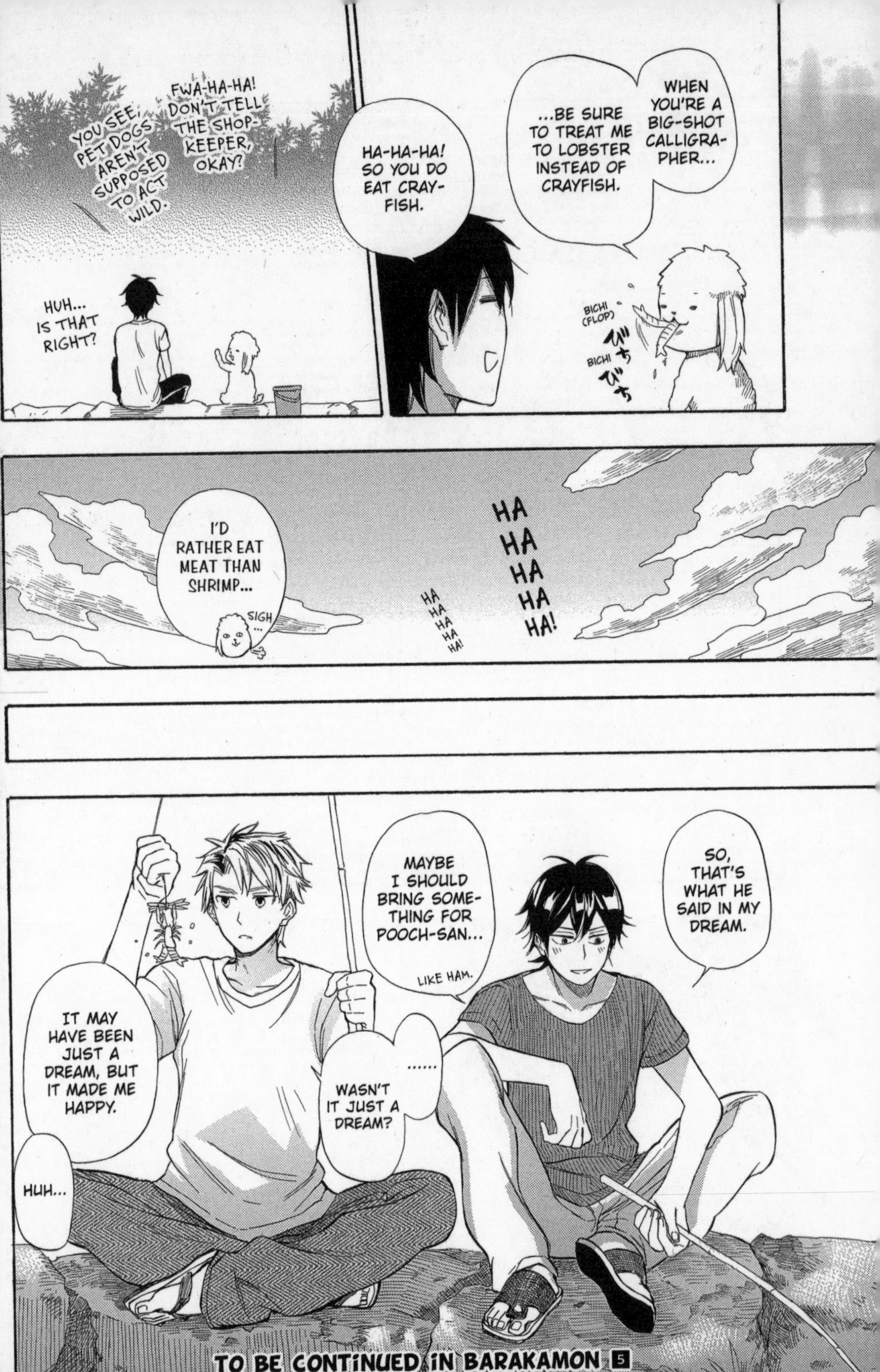
WHEN YOU'RE A BIG-SHOT CALLIGRAPHER...
...BE SURE TO TREAT ME TO LOBSTER INSTEAD OF CRAYFISH.
BICHI (FLOP) びち
BICHI びち
HA-HA-HA! SO YOU DO EAT CRAYFISH.
FWA-HA-HA! DON'T TELL THE SHOPKEEPER, OKAY?
YOU SEE, PET DOGS AREN'T SUPPOSED TO ACT WILD.
HUH... IS THAT RIGHT?
HA HA HA HA HA!
HA HA HA HA HA!
I'D RATHER EAT MEAT THAN SHRIMP...
SIGH...
SO, THAT'S WHAT HE SAID IN MY DREAM.
MAYBE I SHOULD BRING SOMETHING FOR POOCH-SAN...
LIKE HAM.
......
WASN'T IT JUST A DREAM?
IT MAY HAVE BEEN JUST A DREAM, BUT IT MADE ME HAPPY.
HUH...
TO BE CONTINUED IN BARAKAMON 5

TRANSLATION NOTES

COMMON HONORIFICS

no honorific: Indicates familiarity or closeness; if used without permission or reason, addressing someone in this manner would constitute an insult.

-san: The Japanese equivalent of Mr./Mrs./Miss. If a situation calls for politeness, this is the fail-safe honorific.

-sama: Conveys great respect; may also indicate that the social status of the speaker is lower than that of the addressee.

-kun: Used most often when referring to boys, this indicates affection or familiarity. Occasionally used by older men among their peers, but it may also be used by anyone referring to a person of lower standing.

-chan: An affectionate honorific indicating familiarity used mostly in reference to girls; also used in reference to cute persons or animals of either gender.

-sensei: A Japanese term of respect commonly used for teachers, but can also refer to doctors, writers, and artists. Hence, Village Chief is not implying that Handa is a teacher when he calls him "sensei."

Calligraphy: Japanese calligraphy has a long history and tradition, with roots stemming from ancient China. One of the traditions carried over was the Chinese expression of the "Four Treasures," which refers to the brush, ink, paper, and inkstone used in calligraphy. Traditionally, an inkstick—solidified ink—is ground against an inkstone filled with water in order to produce ink with which to write. This time-consuming process helped to teach patience, which is important in the art of calligraphy. However, modern advances have developed a bottled liquid ink, commonly used by beginners and within the Japanese school system.

Gotou Dialect: Many of the villagers, especially the elderly ones, are actually speaking the local Gotou dialect in the original Japanese. This dialect is reflected in the English translation with some of the grammar elements of older Southern American English to give it a more rustic, rural coastal feel without making it too hard to read (it's not meant to replicate any particular American accent exactly). This approach is similar to how dialect is made accessible in Japanese media, including *Barakamon*, because a complete dialect with all of its different vocabulary would be practically incomprehensible to most Tokyo residents.

PAGE 5
Master Takahashi: Takahashi Meijin (real Toshiyuki Takahashi), a longtime executive at Hudson Soft and figure in Japanese video game culture, gained fame in 1985 for his ability to fire sixteen shots per second in the video game *Star Force*.

PAGE 7
black rotary phone: *Kurodenwa* (black phone) specifically refers to the standard phone models first provided by the Japanese Communications Ministry during the expansion of telephone access in the 1950s but is often used to refer to rotary-dial phones in general.

PAGE 9
"If you pity me, give me money…": "Doujou nara kane o kure" was a particularly famous line from the 1994 Japanese TV drama series *Ie naki Ko* (*Nobody's Girl*). The series was partially an homage to the 1878 French novel *Sans Famille* (*Nobody's Boy*) by Hector Malot, but the story is fairly different aside from also being about a young child having a horribly difficult life.

PAGE 14
kaei: The calligraphy institute from which Handa won grand prize at the start of the series.

kobaien: A longtime Japanese maker of inksticks, founded in 1577.

PAGE 31
Hol' on there now, Pops!: In Japanese, Naru uses the word "otottsuan," which is an old-style or dialect version of "otou-san" or "oyaji," meaning "father" or "older man" (i.e., someone around a father's age).

PAGE 38
gaze: The word Naru used, pronounced "gah-zeh," is an old/regional term for *uni* (sea urchin).

PAGE 42
Kamen Rider: A Japanese superhero TV and manga series created by Shotaro Ishinomori in 1971, which was very popular and spurred a long-running franchise. The hero's helmet really does look like a grasshopper's head!

PAGE 43
oniyanma: The largest species of dragonfly in Japan, *Anotogaster sieboldii*.

PAGE 51
champon: A Nagasaki regional dish of ramen noodles and various ingredients, such as seafood and vegetables, cooked together in broth.

PAGE 52
Surprise!: The girls' joke setup, including fanfare, is mimicking the Japanese hidden-camera TV series *Dokkiri Camera*, which was similar to the American series *Candid Camera* and *Punk'd*.

PAGE 72
big girl/sister: Naru's misunderstanding in Japanese comes from *oneesan* being used to mean both "older sister" and "young woman." The actual "older sister" meaning was persevered because it's crucial for Naru's later interaction with Aiko, but fortunately Tama is actually Aki's older sister, so it's a somewhat plausible misunderstanding in English.

PAGE 76
miso soups: Naru's singing about miso soup with a bunch of different seafood and using the dialect words for them. You may remember *mina* (snail) from the start of Volume 3, and *gaze* (sea urchin) from page 38. *Kaddoppo* is most likely the dialect word for "boxfish," a type of puffer fish; she's possibly altered from the usual dialect word pronunciation in the singing.

PAGE 78
Ariko(?): Naru's misreading of the middle hiragana "い(i)" as "り(ri)" in Aiko's name is a pretty common error, since the differences between the two can be fairly subtle when handwritten.

PAGE 82
My!! What a pickle!: The original dialect phrase the shopkeeper used was "Na ne!! Shiyanaka yo," which got a note explaining it as meaning "Sore wa taihen da" (That's terrible). It shows up again in the *Barakamon News* at the end, so keep an eye out for it!

home run bar: A type of ice cream bar.

PAGE 93
Bokuteki Ink: An actual brand of liquid ink, which comes in that shape of bottle.

PAGE 94
Tama's favorite: Tama wrote "Taito," a surname kanji character, which is the kanji with the highest stroke count (84!). It consists of three copies of the kanji for "cloud" and three copies of the kanji for "dragon."

PAGE 96
deeper meaning of "cat": *Neko* (cat) is slang in the BL genre for the submissive partner in a homosexual relationship, derived from a soundalike slang term for "girl lying down." This makes the next kanji Tama proposes writing even funnier...

PAGE 100
Kobo: Kobo Daishi, known during his life as Kukai, was a Japanese Buddhist monk who founded the Shingon school of Buddhism. He was also a very famous scholar and calligrapher.

PAGE 105
Master Craftsman Chiyogiku: A made-up name, possibly a reference to Toshiro Mifune's character Kikuchiyo from the movie The Seven Samurai.

wakame seaweed: An edible seaweed very commonly used in Japanese cuisine, especially in miso soup.

PAGE 112
Yuigadokuson: According to a sutra about Gautama Buddha's birth, he was born from his mother's right side, took seven steps in the four directions, and then said "In the Heavens and on Earth, only I am the venerable one." The Japanese translation of that line is "Tenjou tenge yuigadokuson," and is often used to parody conceitedness; of course, Miwa's dad uses it sincerely.

PAGE 141
not-pretty peppers: In Japan, stores dealing with individual fruits and vegetables tend to sell only perfect-looking ones, with higher prices to match.

PAGE 148
Soruga: Interestingly, the dialect word for the grain/fodder plant *Sorghum bicolor* is closer to the English word, "sorghum," than the standard Japanese word, "morokoshi."

PAGE 149
Straw Millionaire: Reference to the Japanese folktale *Warashibe Chouja*, about a man who starts with a single piece of straw and goes on to become very wealthy through a series of trades, in which people give him something more valuable in exchange for the item he currently has because they especially needed it at the time.

PAGE 157
Squex Manga Prize: Reference to *Barakamon* publisher Square Enix's yearly competition for aspiring manga creators.

PAGE 172
Japanese grave sites: Instead of having individual burial plots and gravestones, Japanese grave sites (*haka*) tend to be family ones, with a single stone listing the family name and having places in front of the stone to put offerings and flowers and space for cremation ashes underneath.

Obon: Japanese Buddhist celebration of welcoming the spirits of the deceased back to visit their families. It generally takes place in mid-August, or mid-July if following the lunar calendar, and is a very busy travel season, as people return home to visit their family grave sites.

PAGE 176
Lan'ern: In Japanese, Naru calls the paper lanterns "toro," but the standard Japanese word for them that Handa uses is "chouchin."

PAGE 180
Fallin' umbrellas: The original word *rakkasan* is actually a literal Japanese translation of the French word "parachute," but generally the Western term is used instead.

PAGE 181
yukata: Cotton kimonos, which are generally worn for summer festivals and can range from simple and elegant to cute and colorful.

PAGE 182
don't do that in Tokyo: Hanging *chouchin* paper lanterns is actually a common feature of Obon celebrations throughout Japan, and most places treat it as a joyous summer festival at which to wear yukata and dance, rather than the somber affair Handa seems to be assuming—though like he says later, he really doesn't have the personal experience to talk about customs. The fireworks are definitely unique to Nagasaki, though.

eggplants with sticks: *Shoryoma* is an Obon tradition in northern Japan, where matchstick "legs" are stuck into cucumbers or eggplants to form "horses" or "cows," meant to act as rides for the spirits of the deceased.

PAGE 186
Ozake: The bottle has 大酒 (*ohzake*) on it, which means "heavy drinking"; it's likely a parody of the sake brand Ozeki (大関).

PAGE 206
Oidon & Otoko: The use of "oidon" as a singular first-person pronoun is already somewhat known in Japan from the 1970s manga series *Otoko-Oidon*, which had a protagonist that used the word that way.

BARAKAMON NEWS

Vol.510

A column that asks, "Eh!? Where's the followup explanation!?"

ınd
ɔ, I'll
ıote
few
ɔther
its of
lialect
hat
ıave
veighed
ɔn my
nind.

TSURAPPONEN NIKKAA

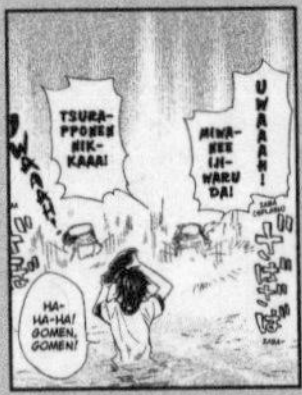
UWAAAN!
MINIKKEE IJI-WARU DA!
TSURAPPONEN NIKKAAA!
HA-HA-HA! GOMEN, GOMEN!

⬆This literally translates as, "I despise the bones of your face" (ha!). It seems to mean, "I don't want to see even your face!!"

Everyone, thank you very much for buying volume four of *BARAKAMON*!!

All thanks to your warm support, would you believe it!? We've broken seven hundred thousand units total (as of volume four's release date)!! Wow!! Thank you so very much!!

Now then, *BARAKAMON* takes place on an island at the western edge of Kyushu. Dialect is mixed in here and there and occasionally ends up passing by without any explanation.

Apparently, he "oidon" here maps to 'oretachi" ("we guys"). In other words, "oi"="ore" ("I" [masculine]), 'don"="tachi" (plural), so "oi" and "oidon" have separate meanings. Huh...!!

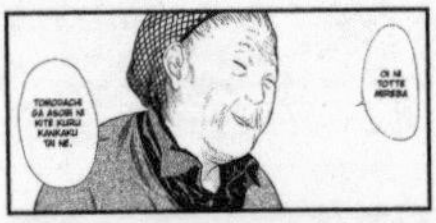
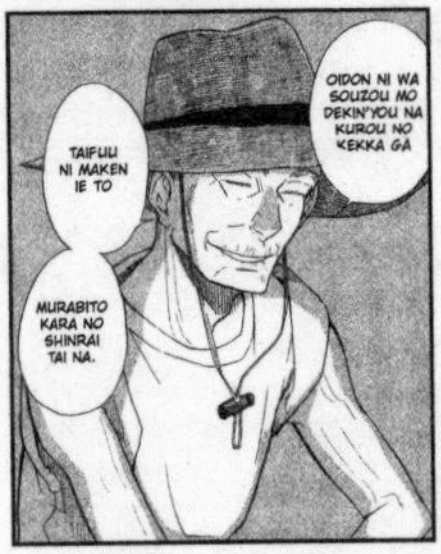
OIDON NI WA SOUZOU MO DEKIN'YOU NA KUROU NO KEKKA GA
TAIFUU NI MAKEN IE TO
MURABITO KARA NO SHINRAI TAI NA.

One is a first-person pronoun. Naru's grampa uses the pronoun "oi." I was so sure it mapped to the masculine first-person pronoun "ore," but then the shopkeeper at Kinoshita General Store said "oi"!! A woman, saying "oi"!!

And occasionally the word "oidon" is used, but I've been told it has a different meaning from in the phrase, "Oidon wa otoko tai!" ("Ah'm a man!").

LOVELY GOTOU GALLERY

This time, we snapped pics of the Buddhist prayer dance (a.k.a., *chankoko*) that appeared in Act. 36 On*de*.

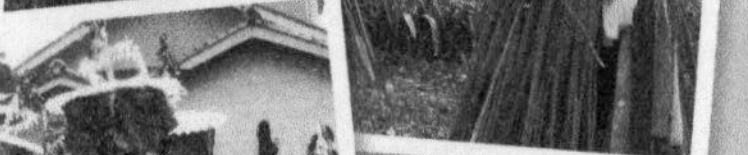

➡The dancers were mostly middle school boys. I'm told that chankoko training begins when summer break starts, in preparation for Obon.

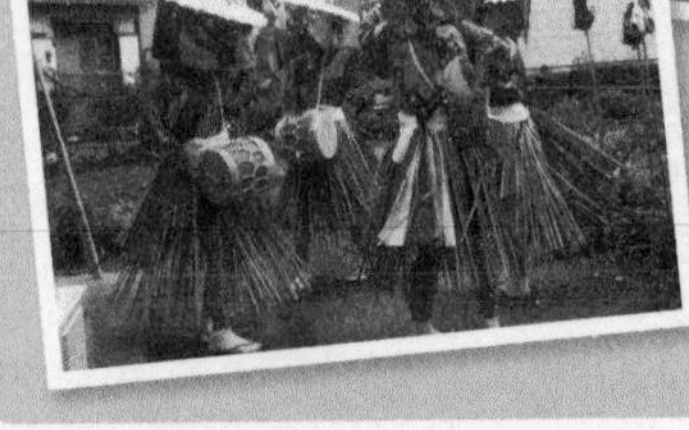

⬅Dancing in those outfits in midsummer... if you were to faint: "My!! What a pickle!!" Be careful not to get dehydrated!!
Photo: Satsuki Yoshino

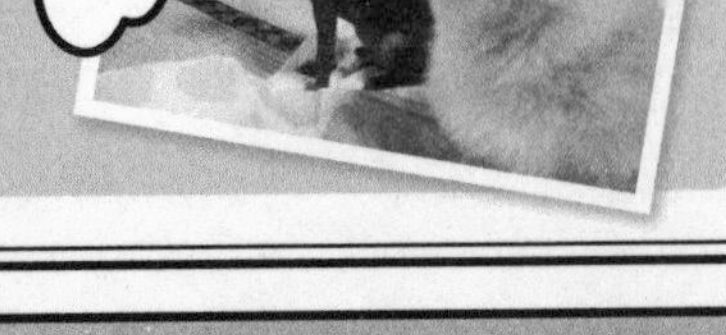
I LOOK MIGHTY COOL...

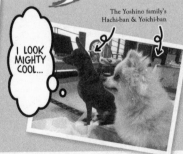

The Yoshino family's Hachi-ban & Yoichi-ban

I'm told this is a word used in a similar spirit as the "don" ("Br'er") from "Usagi-don" ("Br'er Rabbit"). Converted to standard Japanese, "-ban"="-san"; so their "Yuu-ban"="Yuu-chan" and "Iwao-ban"="Iwao-san," or something like that.

That said, while this has turned out to be a rather rustic column (ha!), there are many dialects that are difficult to map directly into standard Japanese. But somehow, it feels nice to listen to them. Even though you may sometimes go "?" just like our city-boy, Sensei, from Tokyo, I sure hope you're enjoying it along with us.

Well then, I sincerely hope to see you all again in Volume 5!!

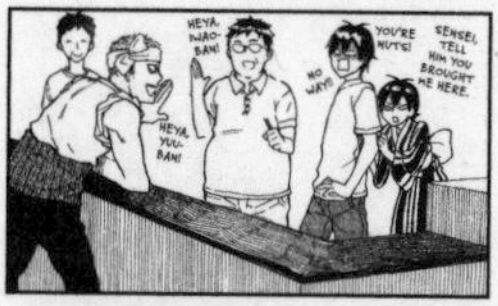
SENSEI, TELL HIM YOU BROUGHT ME HERE.
YOU'RE NUTS!
NO WAY!
HEYA, IWAO-BAN!
HEYA, YUU-BAN!

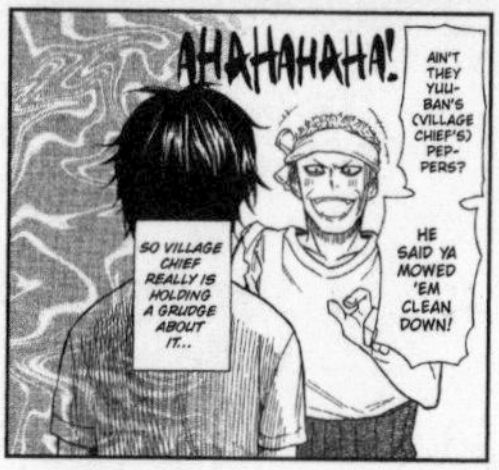
AIN'T THEY YUU-BAN'S (VILLAGE CHIEF'S) PEPPERS?
AHAHAHAHA!
HE SAID YA MOWED 'EM CLEAN DOWN!
SO VILLAGE CHIEF REALLY IS HOLDING A GRUDGE ABOUT IT...

There's also the suffix that the island dads use when calling out to each other—"-ban."

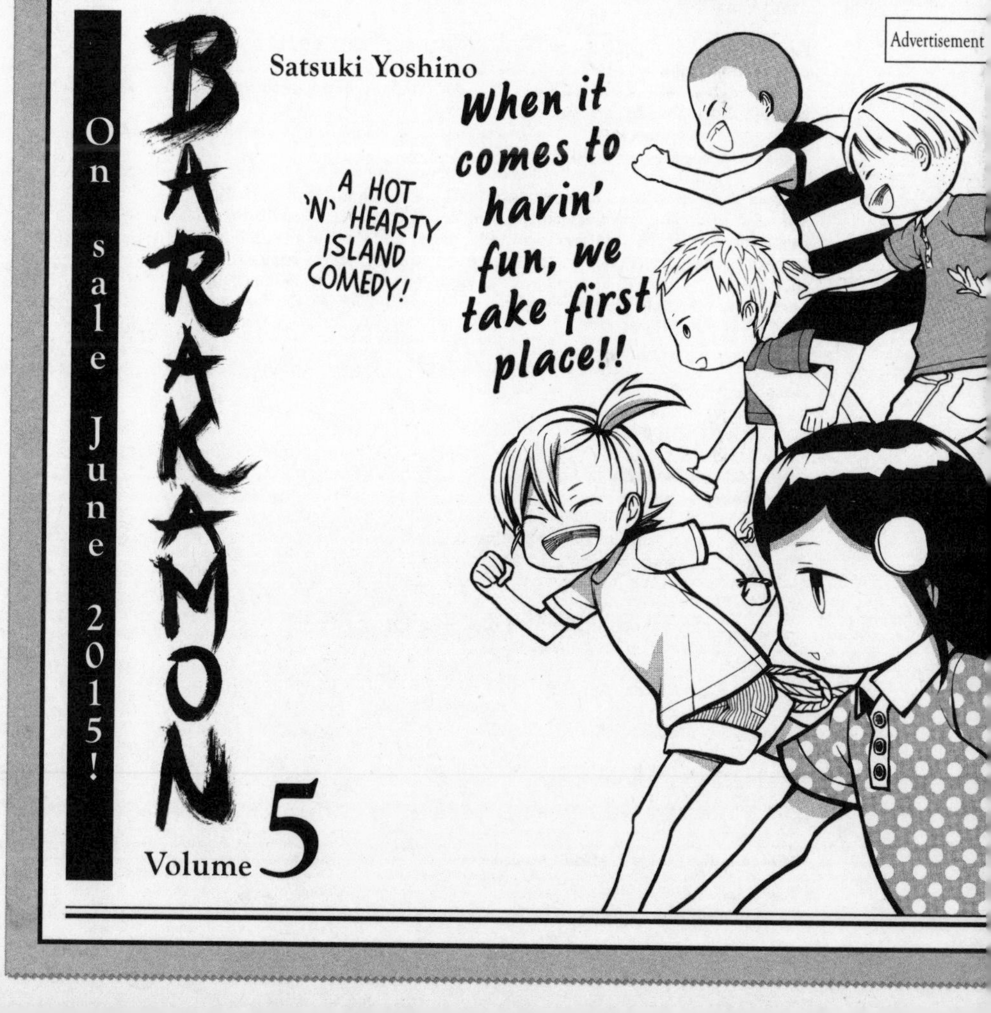

BARAKAMON 4

SATSUKI YOSHINO

Translation/Adaptation: Krista Shipley, Karie Shipley
Lettering: Lys Blakeslee

This book is a work of fiction. Names, characters, places, and incidents are the product of the author's imagination or are used fictitiously. Any resemblance to actual events, locales, or persons, living or dead, is coincidental.

Barakamon vol. 4 © 2010 Satsuki Yoshino / SQUARE ENIX CO., LTD. First published in Japan in 2010 by SQUARE ENIX CO., LTD. English translation rights arranged with SQUARE ENIX CO., LTD. and Hachette Book Group through Tuttle-Mori Agency, Inc.

Translation © 2015 by SQUARE ENIX CO., LTD.

Yen Press
Hachette Book Group
1290 Avenue of the Americas
New York, NY 10104

www.HachetteBookGroup.com
www.YenPress.com

Yen Press is an imprint of Hachette Book Group, Inc. The Yen Press name and logo are trademarks of Hachette Book Group, Inc.

The publisher is not responsible for websites (or their content) that are not owned by the publisher.

First Yen Press Edition: April 2015

ISBN: 978-0-316-34029-8

10 9 8 7 6 5 4 3 2 1

BVG

Printed in the United States of America

POOCH IS FEMALE.

EH !?